The World of t...

D0753104

N

Bukhara

Tianjin

Yokohama

Nagasaki   Kobe

Shanghai

Ningbo

Fuzhou

Bengal

Karachi

Calcutta

Canton   Xiamen

Gulf of
Bombay

Ahmedabad

Surat

Bixar

Hong Kong

Bombay   Pune

Bay
of
Bengal

Mahabaleshwar

Rangoon

Goa

Malabar
Coast

Western
Ghats

Ceylon

Penang

Singapore

Java

INDIAN OCEAN

THE
SASSOONS

THE
SASSOONS

THE GREAT GLOBAL MERCHANTS
AND THE
MAKING OF AN EMPIRE

JOSEPH SASSOON

Pantheon Books, New York

All rights reserved. Published in the United States by Pantheon Books,
a division of Penguin Random House LLC, New York. Originally published
in hardcover, in slightly different form, in Great Britain by Allen Lane, an imprint
of Penguin Books Ltd., a division of Penguin Random House Ltd.,
London, in 2022.

Pantheon Books and colophon are registered trademarks of
Penguin Random House LLC.

Library of Congress Cataloging-in-Publication Data
Name: Sassoon, Joseph, author.
Title: The Sassoons: the great global merchants and the making of an empire /
Joseph Sassoon.
Description: New York: Pantheon Books, 2022.
Includes bibliographical references and index.
Identifiers: LCCN 2021059644 (print) | LCCN 2021059645 (ebook) |
ISBN 9780593316597 (hardcover) | ISBN 9780593316603 (ebook)
Subjects: LCSH: Sassoon, David, 1792–1864—Family. Sassoon family.
Great Britain—Social life and customs—20th century. Jewish families—Great Britain.
Jewish businesspeople—England—London—Biography. Jewish businesspeople—
China—Shanghai—Biography. Jewish businesspeople—India—Mumbai—Biography.
Opium trade—India—History—19th century. David Sassoon & Co.—History.
Jews—Iraq—Baghdad—Biography.
Classification: LCC CS439 .S22 2022 (print) | LCC CS439 (ebook) |
DDC 929.20941—dc23/eng/20211207
LC record available at https://lccn.loc.gov/2021059644
LC ebook record available at https://lccn.loc.gov/2021059645

www.pantheonbooks.com

Front-of-jacket images: (ship) by Jacques Callot. Artokoloro / Alamy;
(opium poppy) Chronicle / Alamy; (Bombay) by William Daniell, 1836.
Historic Illustrations / Alamy
Back-of-jacket image: (Bombay) Historic Illustrations / Alamy
Jacket design by Madeline Partner

Printed in the United States of America
First United States Edition
2 4 6 8 9 7 5 3 1

For Aya

CONTENTS

CONTENTS

A NOTE ON NAMES AND CURRENCIES

NAMES

Cities and countries in this book are referred to by the name used in the historical context, so Bombay rather than Mumbai, Ceylon rather than Sri Lanka, etc. Similarly, names in China are what the family used in its correspondence.

With regard to members of the Sassoon family, one point is worth mentioning: Most Anglicized their names, and so Abdallah became Albert and Farha became Flora. Arabic names are used in the book until officially changed, so it is Abdallah until he settled in London, when he adopted the English name Albert.

Some family members used the term *ha-tsa-'ir* (the young) to distinguish them from older members who were still alive. Thus Sassoon David Sassoon sometimes signed his letters as "the young Sassoon" in order not to be confused with his father, who was still alive.

CURRENCIES

Obviously the pound sterling and the U.S. dollar have undergone dramatic changes since the nineteenth century, and both are worth considerably less than they were 150 years ago due to inflation. The website Measuring Worth (www.MeasuringWorth.com) was used to bring a sense of values today, although this is far from being accurate as there are multiple ways to measure the value of currencies.

As most of the story takes place in India, the Indian currency, the rupee, is mentioned regularly. The appendix compares the value of the rupee in pounds sterling and U.S. dollars from 1850 to 1910.

THE SASSOONS

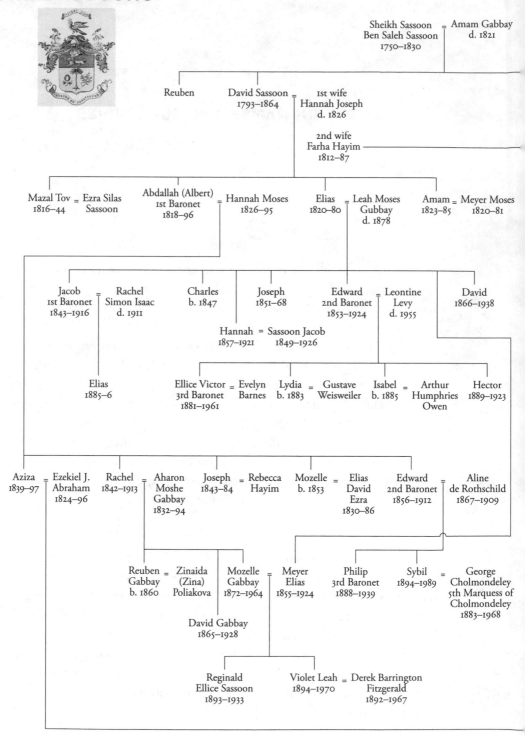

Sheikh Sassoon Ben Saleh Sassoon 1750–1830 = Amam Gabbay d. 1821

Reuben | David Sassoon 1793–1864 = 1st wife Hannah Joseph d. 1826

2nd wife Farha Hayim 1812–87

Mazal Tov 1816–44 = Ezra Silas Sassoon | Abdallah (Albert) 1st Baronet 1818–96 = Hannah Moses 1826–95 | Elias 1820–80 = Leah Moses Gubbay d. 1878 | Amam 1823–85 = Meyer Moses 1820–81

Jacob 1st Baronet 1843–1916 = Rachel Simon Isaac d. 1911 | Charles b. 1847 | Joseph 1851–68 | Edward 2nd Baronet 1853–1924 = Leontine Levy d. 1955 | David 1866–1938

Hannah 1857–1921 = Sassoon Jacob 1849–1926

Elias 1885–6 | Ellice Victor 3rd Baronet 1881–1961 = Evelyn Barnes | Lydia b. 1883 = Gustave Weisweiler | Isabel b. 1885 = Arthur Humphries Owen | Hector 1889–1923

Aziza 1839–97 = Ezekiel J. Abraham 1824–96 | Rachel 1842–1913 | Aharon Moshe Gabbay 1832–94 | Joseph 1843–84 = Rebecca Hayim | Mozelle b. 1853 = Elias David Ezra 1830–86 | Edward 2nd Baronet 1856–1912 = Aline de Rothschild 1867–1909

Reuben Gabbay b. 1860 = Zinaida (Zina) Poliakova | Mozelle Gabbay 1872–1964 = Meyer Elias 1855–1924 | Philip 3rd Baronet 1888–1939 | Sybil 1894–1989 = George Cholmondeley 5th Marquess of Cholmondeley 1883–1968

David Gabbay 1865–1928

Reginald Ellice Sassoon 1893–1933 | Violet Leah 1894–1970 = Derek Barrington Fitzgerald 1892–1967

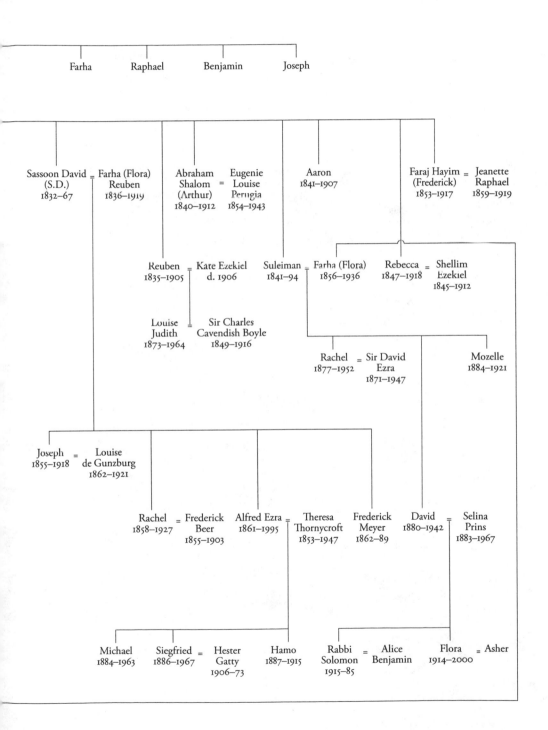

Farha   Raphael   Benjamin   Joseph

Sassoon David = Farha (Flora)   Abraham   Eugenie   Aaron   Faraj Hayim = Jeanette
(S.D.)   Reuben   Shalom = Louise   1841–1907   (Frederick)   Raphael
1832–67   1836–1919   (Arthur)   Perugia   1853–1917   1859–1919
                    1840–1912   1854–1943

Reuben = Kate Ezekiel   Suleiman = Farha (Flora)   Rebecca = Shellim
1835–1905   d. 1906   1841–94   1856–1936   1847–1918   Ezekiel
                                1845–1912

Louise   Sir Charles
Judith   Cavendish Boyle
1873–1964   1849–1916

Rachel = Sir David   Mozelle
1877–1952   Ezra   1884–1921
            1871–1947

Joseph = Louise
1855–1918   de Gunzburg
            1862–1921

Rachel = Frederick   Alfred Ezra = Theresa   Frederick   David = Selina
1858–1927   Beer   1861–1995   Thornycroft   Meyer   1880–1942   Prins
            1855–1903   1853–1947   1862–89   1883–1967

Michael   Siegfried = Hester   Hamo   Rabbi = Alice   Flora = Asher
1884–1963   1886–1967   Gatty   1887–1915   Solomon   Benjamin   1914–2000
                    1906–73   1915–85

PREFACE

It all began with a letter. Returning to my office from lunch one day during a fellowship at All Souls College, Oxford, in early 2012, I was greeted by a handwritten letter addressed to me on my desk, where it had been deposited by the college porter. The return address on the back of the envelope identified the sender as one Joseph Sassoon of Kirkcudbright, Scotland. I had never heard of the town and assumed it was a joke or a mistake of some kind. When I finally opened the letter, however, I found that its author was as described. My namesake had read an article of mine about authoritarian regimes in *Le Monde diplomatique*. He thought it interesting enough, but what prompted him to write was our shared surname. He declared himself a descendant of Sheikh Sassoon ben Saleh Sassoon and believed I might be also, and therefore hoped to hear from me.

I had never been much interested in the history of the Sassoon family. As a child in Baghdad, I had ignored my father whenever he attempted to educate me about my illustrious forebears, going so far as to literally close my ears to annoy him. Later, when I had embarked on this project, there were many occasions when I wanted nothing more than to hear his tales and ask him a few questions for just a few minutes, but sadly the wish came two decades too late. All this is to say that the letter remained unanswered on my desk until my partner Helen heard about it, chastised me for my rudeness, and told me to write back. I did and suggested to this other Joseph Sassoon that we talk on the telephone, only to be mortified two days later when the porter proudly informed me that he had blocked what he thought was a prank phone call for me from a "Joseph Sassoon." When I at last managed to speak to Joseph in Scotland, he told me about his father, the first cousin of the poet Siegfried Sassoon, and his grandfather, the husband of a prominent Gunzburg from Russia. Without his encouragement, I doubt this project would have taken off.

It was a subject with no relation to the book I had just finished, about the archives of Saddam Hussein's Ba'th Party, or the one that had brought me to Oxford, a comparative study of authoritarian systems in the Arab republics, but my appetite was whetted. I visited the National Archives at Kew and the British Library in London to read about the family, and traveled to Scotland to meet Joseph (known as Joey). He shared with me what he knew and the trove of pictures that had been passed down to him. He also referred me to Sybil Sassoon, another family historian and the creator of a comprehensive family tree, stretching back to 1830, that would prove immensely helpful— not least in distinguishing between other namesakes (unhelpfully for the researcher, the family favored just a few forenames, which recur within and across generations) and following individuals as they crossed continents in the age of empire, adapting their names as necessary.

I had no idea where these initial excursions would lead. Unlike Sybil, I was born too late to know any of the cast of this book, even the protagonists of the mid-twentieth century. And although I am descended from Sheikh Sassoon as Joseph hoped, he was the last ancestor we shared. When he fled Baghdad in 1830, fearing the wrath of the authorities, to join his oldest son, his other children remained in Baghdad. Some left Iraq later, but my ancestors stayed put until we too were forced to escape, for reasons similar to those of Sheikh Sassoon. After the Six-Day War in June 1967, life for the country's Jews grew increasingly untenable. The rise of the Ba'th Party a year later exacerbated the situation, and public hangings of Jews followed in 1969. When we finally managed to escape a couple of years later, we left with nothing except for a small bag, closing the door not only on our property but on a land where my family had lived for centuries. This book is thus intended to be not a family history but the history of a family, specifically a branch with which I can claim a connection but of which I am not, in the end, a member.

For me as a historian, what really tipped the balance was the discovery of a trove of untapped archival material. Sometime after reading slipped imperceptibly into research, I went to the National Library in Jerusalem, where most of the family's archives are held. They contain thousands of documents dating from 1855 to 1949: everything from personal letters to account books and menus for dinner parties, seemingly every scrap of paper kept. The letters between family members tended to follow a similar structure: formal at the beginning and end of the letters; in the middle jumping from one subject to another; and often containing stinging criticism if trades had not been profitable or if one member of the family purchased a commodity at a price that another member considered too high. Most of this business correspondence was written in Baghdadi Jewish dialect to prevent outsiders from reading their letters; family members used their Baghdadi Jewish but wrote it in Hebrew characters (some refer to the language as Judeo-Arabic, but this is a relatively new term). The result is indecipherable to all but a few scholars, but fortunately I am fluent in Arabic, Hebrew, and the Baghdadi Jewish dialect. Writing this book, I felt sometimes as if the historian in me, the migrant, and the Baghdadi Jew were all jockeying for position. My hope is that, in the end, they coalesced and did not hinder me from investigating the history in an objective and unemotional manner.

Research in other archives in London, Delhi, Dallas, Shanghai, and Istanbul followed, and with the assistance of some wonderful archivists and researchers, I found much fascinating material produced by and about the family. Some years fell between archives, and for those I relied upon newspapers from China, India, England, the United States, and the Bahamas, and official documents of the relevant councils and chambers of commerce to fill in the gaps. The material grew vast—appropriately, given that the Sassoons straddled three empires: that of their adoptive home, Britain, and those of the two commodities whose trade they came to dominate, cotton and opium. Their legacy lay not only in dusty boxes in darkened storage rooms, however. Following the advice of Robert Caro, the great biographer of Lyndon Johnson, for historians to obtain a "sense of place," I traveled to the Sassoons' former residences in Mumbai, Pune, and the hill station of Mahabaleshwar; the synagogues they built in India and China; their headquarters in Shanghai; their estates in England; even their graves.

The geographical spread is telling. The Sassoons traded with members of seemingly every religion and sect around the globe, traveling extensively not only for business but to explore new horizons, and they felt at home wherever they settled, despite being a tiny minority in terms of both their religion and their migrant status. They were not unique in their time in amassing several fortunes and rising to the upper echelons of society. But unlike their more famous contemporaries, the Rothschilds and Vanderbilts, they bridged East and West. Their story is accordingly not just that of an Arab-Jewish family who settled in India, traded in China, and aspired to be British, but also a vista into the world in which they lived and prospered as well as its major developments—from the American Civil War to the Opium Wars, the opening of the Suez Canal and introduction of the telegraph as well as the mechanization of textile production. The era they inhabited was driven above all by an encompassing globalization, which they and other merchant families benefited from and influenced, and which shaped our current lives.

Unlike people in our fragmented world today, the Sassoons did not care about the ethnicity or religion of their counterparts; all they really cared about was one thing and one thing only: Could they trust them? This was not because they did not adhere to Judaism's strict rules and traditions but because trust and reputation were the predominant characteristics that differentiated successful traders from others in a world where letters took three to five weeks to reach their destinations and even when the telegraph started, telegrams were expensive and traders were wary that their messages could be read by anyone. The Sassoons had relationships with traders across the world: from India to China to Persia to the Ottoman Empire, to Africa and Britain.

The Sassoons epitomized the way in which migration can influence different regions of the world. With their acumen and hard work, the founder and then the next two generations managed not only to enrich themselves but to contribute to the cities they were living in and to their communities. The Sassoons lived in three main hubs: Bombay, then Shanghai, and finally London. Their landmarks in those cities are still around today, particularly in Bombay (throughout the book, I use the city's old name rather than Mumbai).

I begin in Ottoman Baghdad before the Sheikh's departure and move with his son David Sassoon to Bombay, where he gradually built his business. Family was of immense importance to David, and he was blessed with one that was large by any standard. The book therefore necessarily focuses on the members who played leading roles in taking his business to its mercantile pinnacle, a truly global business distributed around the ports and cities of Asia, Europe, and the Middle East, trading not only cotton and opium but almost every major commodity, from tea and silk to spices and pearls, with a network of contacts and informants that was the envy of traders everywhere. Six personalities successively take center stage: David, the dynasty's founder; his sons Abdallah (later Albert), who would succeed him on his death, Elias, who developed the business in China before setting off to create a rival one, and Suleiman, who managed the business in Asia after Albert's attention was dragged to the West; Suleiman's wife, Farha (later Flora), who took charge after his death and was, I believe, the first woman to run a global business in the nineteenth century; and finally Victor, who presided over the business in its last twenty-five years. They are joined by other Sassoons, not least the war-poet Siegfried, the politician and art collector Philip, and the first woman in Britain to be named editor at a national newspaper, Rachel Beer.

Less attractive to our eyes is the family's involvement with one commodity that played a critical part in their success: opium. I have tried to understand this in its context, in light of the way the drug was perceived in their time, and to avoid passing moral judgment. I show instead how they came to control a large portion of the opium trade between India and China, how they ignored the winds of change around the world as its devastating effects became widely known, and how they used their political clout in Britain to delay prohibition.

This book traces not only the rise of the Sassoons but also their decline: why it happened, how the economic and political world order that had fostered their ascent began to change after the First World

War, and how the realization of their aspiration to join the ranks of the British aristocracy drew their attention away from their business and prevented them from adapting to these new circumstances, leading to the winding up of their companies after the Second World War. In the annals of family histories, there are many such stories of incredible fortunes made and squandered over the course of four generations. None is more famous than *Buddenbrooks*, Thomas Mann's first novel. In it he charts with almost documentary precision the decline of a bourgeois family of German grain merchants over four generations in the middle of the nineteenth century. The Sassoons lacked the Buddenbrooks' deep Hanseatic roots, however. As migrants, they had to establish themselves somewhere and ally themselves with some country. They chose Britain, the dominant world power at this book's beginning but not at its end, and thus needed and wanted, probably more than anything else, to be accepted as English. They found success—Sassoons who had been born in Baghdad joined the English upper classes, befriending even royalty—but it was a metamorphosis as fatal to their fortunes as any misjudgment in Mann's novel.

THE
SASSOONS

1

BAGHDAD BEGINNINGS

1802–1830

Sassoon ben Saleh Sassoon = Amam Gabbay

Reuben   David

In 1824 a rabbi by the name of David D'Beth Hillel set out from his native Lithuania on an epic journey that took him halfway around the world. He traveled through Palestine, Syria, Arabia, Kurdistan, and Persia, halting his expedition in Madras, India, where he took out an advertisement to announce the book he had written about his encounters, "an account of the manners and customs of the places which he has visited . . . with a vocabulary of words most useful for travellers in five languages, viz., Hebrew, Arabic, Persian, Hindustani, and English." Wherever he went, he attempted to describe the distinctive beliefs and culture of the people he met and to identify the connections of Jews resident in all these countries to the old traditions. He spent a whole year in Baghdad, the principal city in the vast, fertile plains of Mesopotamia, the "Land between the Rivers" Tigris and Euphrates, and vividly depicted life there:

> The modern Baghdad is a very large town. The Tigris passes through the midst of it and on it is a very large bridge built on small boats. The whole town is built of bricks. . . . The nobility,

Baghdad in the early nineteenth century.

the Israelites [a term used for Jews], and the Christians all reside in this [Persian] part. The streets and markets are narrow; the town has a very rude appearance; but the nobles' houses are finely painted inside.

The city the rabbi visited had been founded a thousand years earlier, under the Abbasid Caliphate in the eighth century. For the next five centuries Baghdad prospered, becoming the cultural, commercial, and intellectual center of the Islamic world during its golden age. Its reputation for "genius, enterprise, and learning" remained unsurpassed, as another visitor in the nineteenth century put it; "the burning light of its philosophers shone, when all around elsewhere was dark as any within the history of man."

In 1534, however, the Ottomans captured Mesopotamia, turning it into the *wilaya,* or province, of Baghdad. The incessant conflicts between the Persians and Ottomans that followed, stemming in part from the rivalry between the Ottoman rulers and Persian Safavids, who couldn't accept Sunni control of the city, tipped it into decline. The Ottomans brought with them Mamluks from Georgia as administrators. The word Mamluk means "owned," and they were not Arabs but freed slave soldiers, mostly from the Caucasus, who had converted to Islam after the Ottomans conquered Egypt, Syria, and Hejaz early in the sixteenth century. They proved able custodians and

gradually came to exert more and more power until the middle of
the eighteenth century, when they effectively usurped it. From 1747
until 1831, the majority of Baghdad's governors were Mamluks, ruling
independent of the Ottoman Empire, of which the province technically remained a part. Government during this Mamluk period was
concentrated around the Pasha—equivalent to a regional governor—
and tended to mirror the strength or weakness of the incumbent.
Perhaps the greatest of the Mamluk rulers was Suleiman, who ruled
Baghdad between 1780 and 1802. His death that year saw Baghdad
return to instability and strife: For the next three decades, Pashas came
and went, each subject to the plots and assassination attempts of their
rivals and sometimes their successors. The local population suffered
increasingly from food shortages, and bouts of looting in many parts
of the city were rife.

Jews had been a continuous presence in Mesopotamia for some
twenty-five hundred years, since the forced exile in the sixth century
B.C. following the conquest of Judea by the Babylonians. The community, who came to be known as the Babylonian Jewry, possessed its
own language, called Baghdadi Jewish, a dialect of Arabic written in
Hebrew letters. There were thriving Jewish communities in all cities
in the province, and there were likely more Jews there than anywhere
else in the Arab East. According to Rabbi Hillel, there were about six
thousand Jewish families and five large synagogues in Baghdad at the
time of his visit. A later traveler estimated seven thousand out of a
total of fifty thousand and noted the prominent role Jews played in
the province: "The commerce and even the government, fall into the
hands of a few Jews and Armenians." Jews typically were, with Armenians and Persians, the major merchants and bankers of the Islamic
territories. The most important of these were not only in their (various) home provinces but in the Ottoman capital: One Ezekiel Gabbay, an important Baghdadi banker, was even appointed *sarraf bashi*
(chief treasurer) at the court in Constantinople, where he became one
of Sultan Mahmud II's favorite advisers as a reward for helping the
Sultan deal with an especially troublesome Pasha in 1811. He went
on to develop a lucrative business selling senior administrators' posts
around the empire, and there were tales of occasions when "as many
as fifty or sixty Pashas crowded the antechamber of this standing Jew"

to appeal for his support for their appointment or reconfirmation. Many honors were bestowed on him, and his brother was appointed *sarraf bashi* in Baghdad.

Ezekiel and his brother both came from a class of wealthy Jews who handled the finances of, and lent money to, local rulers in provinces across the Ottoman Empire. Such Jews were of particular interest to Rabbi Hillel:

> The treasurer of the pasha is an Israelite who rules over [the Jewish community]. The common Jews call him the "King of Israel," and he has great power to punish them by money or stripes, according to his wish, even when not lawful. In ancient times it was required here that the treasurer of the pasha should be [of] the seed of David, and it was in inheritance from the father to son.

During the Mamluk period, the chief treasurer was chosen from the Jewish community by the Pasha, as most of the mercantile class was Jewish. He was known as the *nasi* (Hebrew for "president") and was the community's representative to both the local and the imperial administrations. It was a position at least equal to the religious head of the communities, known as the chief rabbi, and the holder's influence extended to other Jewish communities outside the province of Baghdad, to those in Persia or Yemen. This system of two heads, lay and spiritual, lasted until 1864, when the Ottomans appointed a single leader known as the *hakham bashi* (chief rabbi) to be responsible for the community's affairs. Such privileges came with responsibilities: The chief treasurer was expected to donate generously to charitable causes, including religious ones, and to support his co-religionists. One gentile traveler to Baghdad claimed that there were no Jewish beggars: "If one of their class fall into distress, another wealthier relieves him." The relationship between the *wali* (governor) or the Pasha and their treasurer was necessarily close but also potentially volatile, and if it soured, treasurers were liable to be imprisoned or even killed. The political backbiting between Constantinople and the provincial administration was unrelenting; each center of power schemed endlessly to extend its influence over the other and ensure that key appointments in both courts were held by people they trusted. The treasurer needed strong connections with the Sultan's court in Constantinople, but not so strong as to make the *wali* feel threatened. This delicate balancing act was, as Rabbi Hillel reported, passed from father to son for more than a hundred years, but by the nineteenth century it was increasingly "won in competition with other Jews and this resulted in money being paid for this honour and even in Jews having their competitors killed or discredited." Realpolitik had in fact long played a role in appointments, but turnover certainly increased after the eighteenth century and political instability invited a new ruthlessness: During the year the rabbi spent in Baghdad, two holders of the office were murdered by competitors, who then succeeded their victims.

Even before Sheikh Sassoon ben Saleh was appointed by the Sultan's *firman* (decree) chief treasurer, and thus lay head of the Baghdad Jewish community, in 1781, soon after Suleiman the Great acquired the pashalik, there were reports that individuals in Baghdad's administration intended him harm. Born in 1750, Sassoon made his name by marrying into one of Baghdad's most prominent Jewish families. The union produced six sons and one daughter, and in accordance with the Arab custom of renaming the parents after their oldest son, Sassoon was known as Abu Reuben ("father of Reuben"; his wife would have been Um Reuben). Little is known about Reuben except that he died of a disease in 1802, but the name remained, and for generations to come the family would be called Beit Abu Reuben ("the house of Abu Reuben"). David, Sassoon's second son, who had been born in 1793, assumed the role of heir to the business and, potentially, his father's office. He grew up in the shadow of the most eminent Jew in Baghdad, the "head of [the] community and president of a generation." Sassoon was known for his close relations with the Pasha and, indirectly, the Sultan, extolled by one poet as "one of the most honest and just presidents who worked hard for his people and community." In 1808, he arranged for David, aged fifteen, to marry the fourteen-year-old Hannah, from an affluent Jewish family from Basra, in the south of the province. (The union would grant him his first grandson, Abdallah, in 1818, and then another, Elias, as well as two granddaughters, Mazal Tov and Amam.) Sassoon was by this time one of the longest-serving *sarraf bashi* in the city's history, having remained in his post not only through Suleiman Pasha's reign, the last two decades of the eighteenth century "the golden era of the Mamluk Dynasty in Baghdad," but also for the tenure of his successor, and his successor's successor. But by late 1816, thirty-five years after his appointment, clouds were gathering.

The Ottomans under Sultan Mahmud II (who reigned from 1808 to 1839) made their first attempt to expel the Mamluks from Baghdad in 1810. Ottoman troops managed to kill Suleiman Pasha (son of Suleiman the Great) but ultimately failed to wrest back control of Baghdad Province. In the ensuing chaos a number of Pashas tried to exert themselves over the city in quick succession, each ousted by the next. The sheer pace of events meant that some pashas effectively ruled before their formal appointment arrived in Baghdad, while for others the opposite was the case. Sa'id Pasha was in control during the years 1813–16, but lurking in the background was an ambitious Mamluk named Dawud. Born into slavery in Tiflis, Georgia, he was brought to Baghdad, was sold and resold, converted to Islam, and served in Suleiman the Great's household. The Ottoman archives paint a striking picture. A talented writer and warrior, he could be generous, enlightened, and fair, but also cruel, corrupt, and avaricious. Dawud began to plot his rise early in Sa'id's reign, assisted by a Baghdadi Jew who aspired to replace Sheikh Sassoon as chief treasurer, Ezra ben Nissim Gabbay. Ezra in turn had a powerful ally in his brother Ezekiel, since 1811 the *sarraf bashi* to the Sultan in Constantinople and an influential figure throughout the Ottoman Empire—one report indicated that the Dutch vice consul turned to him to settle a quarrel with a local governor of a district somewhere in the empire.

After a number of skirmishes in the winter of 1816–17, Dawud finally captured Sa'id and had him executed. Shortly after Dawud came to power, a decree was duly carried to Baghdad announcing the end of Sheikh Sassoon's term and the appointment of Ezra Gabbay as the new chief treasurer. It was a neat echo of Dawud's own confirmation and the decree announcing it, which had been carried from Constantinople by the son of the Sultan's Jewish *sarraf bashi*.

British traders were by this time well established in Baghdad, and the East India Company had been given permission to establish residency there two decades prior. Their hopes for Dawud were initially high, but they quickly realized that his character meant Baghdad was unlikely to return to the stability of the final decades of the last century. A British political agent described him in the most villainous terms:

> His dissimulation is most profound, and frequently, like his cruelty without the least apparent motive. The most solemn oaths and engagements have not the least weight with him; his most faithful servants are by no means sure of his favour and those on whom he smiles the most, are frequently the unsuspecting subjects of his aversion. His administration has become a continued scene of rapacity, persecution and treachery.

The British had other reasons to dislike Dawud, whose policies emulated those of Muhammad 'Ali in aiming at reducing European (and Iranian) influence over his country, but he was certainly capable of great capriciousness. Even Dawud's closest ally, the *sarraf* Ezra, wasn't immune to it: In 1818 a disagreement over loans raised to support Dawud's regime led the Pasha "in a fit of passion" to order that Ezra "be put in irons and thrown into a Dungeon, whence he was next day liberated at the intercession" of a senior representative of the Ottomans.

Indeed, once Dawud had consolidated power and popular support, he showed his real intentions and declared his decision to refrain from paying duties to the Ottoman Sultan in Constantinople. That crisis was overtaken by another, the resumption of hostilities with Persia. Troubles also flared up with Kurdish tribes after a period of relative quiet. Dawud was supported by the Sultan in his battles against the Persians and Kurds but was unable to defeat either, and the years 1819–23 witnessed large-scale demographic dislocations in the province as his subjects fled the "scorched-earth tactics of the Persians" and resulting famine. In late 1823 Dawud negotiated a truce, but this raised suspicions in Constantinople and the Ottoman regime again began to ponder ending the autonomous state of the Mamluks.

Once Dawud Pasha became governor, the problems confronting Sheikh Sassoon became insurmountable. Dawud did not see Sheikh Sassoon as an ally and was worried about his strong relationship with Constantinople. The thirteen years between the resignation of Sheikh

Sassoon from his job and his family fleeing Baghdad are important in understanding the context of their departure from their beloved homeland. Dawud's relationship with the Jewish community in Baghdad was somewhat complicated. On the one hand, he had gained his position with the help of Jewish influence with the Sultan; on the other hand, he soon developed a reputation for oppressing the Jews. In reality, greed was his main motive as he attempted to amass as much wealth as possible.

Under pressure to send money to Constantinople, Dawud turned to the Jews for loans. When some of Baghdad's wealthiest merchants refused, he had them arrested and demanded payment from their families on pain of death. He was aided in this scheme by his teacher, a man nicknamed "the informer" by the Jewish community, and an "apostate Jew" who had converted to Islam after becoming infatuated with a Muslim dancer and who provided Dawud with the information he needed to extort large sums of money. Between them, "this wicked triumvirate thus brought great misfortune and many hardships on the Baghdad Jews," who, as a result, began to emigrate to "distant parts where the hands of Dawud could not reach them." It was the beginning of the dissipation of Baghdad's Jewish community as families set out across Asia, to Aleppo, Damascus, and Alexandria, and as far away as Australia.

The tensions that provoked this centrifugal movement grew more acute in 1826, when the Sultan, concluding that the Mamluks were a reactionary force blocking his reforms, announced the abolition of their army, forcing Dawud to raise even more money to pay his troops while still accommodating Constantinople. He turned on his most loyal supporter, imprisoning Ezra as he had eight years earlier, in the hope of extracting more assets from his family. This time, however, intercession from Constantinople was either not forthcoming or went unheeded. Unable to face life in prison, Ezra promptly died, paying "with his life for all the goodness he has shown to the Pasha."

Our main source for information regarding Ezra's downfall is in fact another of Sheikh Sassoon's descendants, an archivist and historian named David Solomon Sassoon who in the 1940s wrote the first reliable history of Baghdad's Jews. According to him, after Ezra's imprisonment late in the 1820s, Dawud had David Sassoon arrested in an attempt to force a ransom from his father, Sheikh Sassoon. David was in serious danger but "escaped in a miraculous way," though details are scant. Whether David literally escaped or his freedom was bought by his father is unclear, but either as a condition of his liberation or out of a reasonable fear that he might be subject to the same ordeal again, he was to leave Baghdad immediately. After making inquiries with Major R. Taylor, a British political agent in Baghdad who reported to India and was a reliable source of information about both the Gulf and the subcontinent, Sheikh Sassoon specially chartered a boat to take David to Basra, where, on his father's advice, he did not linger but continued on to Bushir, about five hundred miles southeast on the coast of Iran. It was sage advice, for it seems Dawud Pasha did indeed change his mind and ordered the prisoner's recapture, but by then David was out of reach. In a matter of months, Sassoon had joined him in Bushir. The Sheikh was in his seventies and his health was deteriorating; from now on David would take charge of his own future, as well as those of his four children and their stepmother, whom he had married after Hannah's death in 1826. The family had no choice but to leave—refugees rarely do—but the timing was fortunate. Violence in the province grew increasingly prevalent toward the end of the decade and its use by the regime almost systemic. The attention of Sultan Mahmud II, which had been diverted by the war in Greece (the first independent country to be carved out of the sprawling Ottoman Empire) and several with Russia, turned to Baghdad and the intolerable independence of the Mamluks. In the aftermath of a humiliating defeat at Russian hands in 1829, the Sultan dispatched an envoy, Sadiq Effendi, to relieve Dawud of his position and replace him with a new, non-Mamluk governor. The Pasha cordially received the envoy before learning of his dismissal, and when his pleas for time to make entreaties to the Sultan were rejected, "danger was balanced against danger, fear with fear: without haste or panic the formal ambassador of the Sultan was sentenced to death by murder." The assassination was meticulously organized: Dawud waited outside the chamber while it took place and entered after the deed to verify Sadiq's death. He initially sought to conceal the crime from the public and pretended that the envoy was only sick, but word was out by nightfall. News spread swiftly, and food prices rose the next day in anticipation of the

Bushir in the 1830s.

Sultan's response to this insult. The city went into lockdown: Major Taylor reported, "Nothing enters or leaves the City but by stealth, vegetables of any kind are not to be obtained for money."

In the midst of this crisis, as the Sultan prepared to dispatch an army to expel the Mamluks from Baghdad once and for all, the city was devastated by other means. The plague struck in March 1831, spreading outward from the Jewish quarter across the city. Dawud's tenuous control of the situation meant that no quarantines were imposed and caravans continued to travel to and from plague-infested areas, distributing the disease around the province. Normal life in the city came to a halt. Food supplies ran short, corpses piled up in the streets, law and order crumbled. At the height of the plague another disaster hit: After torrential rain that exceeded anything in living memory, the Tigris River flooded. One English traveler, who "was sleeping at the top of the house" when the river burst its banks, vividly described being "awakened by the uproar of the waters rushing past the hall" and said, "No outcry accompanied the convulsions; I heard no shriek nor wail; but as I seated myself on the upper part of the wall, I could perceive . . . the turbid waters, silently sweeping by."

One local depicted the ensuing destruction as "God's wrath on the city which was flooded on all sides while plague and death spread. No one had ever heard of such a calamity in the region." Another reported that "only a few of the Baghdad people were left at the city in the midst of death, flood, and plague." It was estimated that more than 15,000 lives were lost, and the population of Baghdad and its afflicted districts plunged from about 150,000 to 80,000.

The flood and epidemic signaled the end for Dawud. Many Baghdadis wanted to flee the city but all exits were fraught with danger. Tribesmen controlled the roads, and the boats were crowded and plague-ridden. The Pasha and his entourage longed to escape, though not at the cost of their "hoarded wealth." The British Resident and his party managed to depart by boat for Basra; those who remained barricaded themselves in their houses, refusing entry to any outsider for fear of infection. According to one report in the Ottoman archives, Dawud quit Baghdad when the flooding abated, only to find that his support in the *vilayets* (provinces) had evaporated: "His armies and supporters have been made extinct by the plague while his treasurer, family, wives, children, bankers" had been removed. Another informed the court in Constantinople that the new governor, Ali Pasha, had made peace with the residents of Baghdad as well as with the tribes in the south:

> The inside of Baghdad has been cleansed from the dirty existence of people like the former Pasha and those who supported him. And with the re-establishment of the Sultan's rule, all the destruction and atrocities committed by the rebels is now replaced by the Sultan's tranquillity.

The schism between Constantinople and unruly Baghdad was ended, with the latter serving as an imperial province until the First World War. Dawud was banished and the hunt for the assets he had looted during his reign began. Constantinople sought to estimate how much he had embezzled "by force from the people of Baghdad, Basra, and Kirkuk," and plans were drawn up to search all his palaces, harems, and properties, and to capture and interrogate Ishaq, Ezra's successor as chief treasurer, about the location and scale of the hidden money. The investigation generated a list of Dawud's victims, spanning all the province's religions, sects, and cities, and indicating that some were killed after he had embezzled money from them. Yet Dawud, with his gifts of "tongue and mien" and an enormous personal fortune, was spared execution. In an extraordinary turn of events, by 1845 he had even found favor with the new Sultan, Abdul Majid, and even collected a few posts before his death in 1851.

At the time of his flight from Baghdad, Sheikh Sassoon was still one of the most prominent Jews in the city, and there was much speculation about his motives for fleeing. One theory held that he fled for fear of the plague and floods, despite the fact that Sassoon left his other sons and daughters behind in Baghdad and neither he nor David returned after the plague had waned and floods receded. In a sense, such stories have continued unabated in the form of family lore. Eight decades after David's escape, his grandson Edward Sassoon, MP, in a lecture given in late 1907 on the subject of "the Orient," told one such tale, erroneously supposing that his grandfather was the chief treasurer:

> My own grandfather happened to hold the position of State Treasurer at Bagded [sic]. Whether he was a trifle too honest in his dealings with the Pashas or whether he was suspected of amassing wealth, certain it is that the place got too hot for him. It was bruited that energetic measures were being hatched against him, and, I suppose, arguing that discretion was the better part of valour, he left the scene of his activities with his family, and by easy stages—travelling, as you may imagine, 100 years [ago] was not like travelling in the Pullman car . . . a good many other Jewish families followed on and it is this that formed the nucleus of the prosperous communities you see in India.

A decade later another member of the family again referred to David as the chief treasurer. In a letter to one of the Rothschilds explaining the reasons behind the departure from Baghdad, he wrote:

He was the head of the Jewish Community and as such he was responsible to the Pashas for the conduct of the Jews. In those days the Turks would not take Jews or Christians for the army but they were made to pay so much per head in lieu of military service. David Sassoon was made responsible for the money to be collected from the Jews and as in many cases they were too poor to pay, he had to make good. Whenever the Pasha was in want of funds he used to make fresh levies on the Jews with threats to David Sassoon that if he did not pay up, he would be put in prison and executed. These demands for money became so numerous that David Sassoon could not meet them so one night he bolted from Baghdad and went to India. I think this is the true version.

Such stories endure in part because of a lack of information. David Solomon Sassoon's history didn't settle the matter because we simply don't know when David escaped to Bushir or when his father joined him. David must have left after his marriage to his second wife, Farha, which took place in Baghdad in 1828, and likely before the demise in 1830 of the Sultan's envoy, while Sassoon probably quit Baghdad before the natural disasters. What we do know is that the Sheikh died in exile in Bushir in 1830, prompting his son to seek a new life in Bombay.

The father's fall from grace was finally complete. Having suffered the indignity of fleeing his homeland like a fugitive, however, the son had with his immediate family escaped the tyranny of Dawud to begin a new chapter in foreign lands. Sassoons continued to live in Baghdad, and in time the family reclaimed its position among the city's economic elite. Sheikh Sassoon's eldest son would follow a similar trajectory but on a truly global scale, and his descendants—unlike those of his siblings—would reach mercantile preeminence not in one province of one empire, but throughout the world.

2

EXILE AND A NEW LIFE

1831–1839

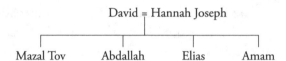

Bushir lay on the coast of southwestern Iran and in previous centuries had been the primary port in Persia. By the time of David's arrival, it was slowly reestablishing itself as an important commercial hub for the East India Company in Persia. The harbor bustled with Indian merchants and wares carried on ships flying the British ensign. David mingled in the bazaar, listening to stories from sailors and traders returning from India about the subcontinent, and building relationships that in years to come would serve him and his business. Though he was in a foreign land without his family's support, David had two substantial assets: extensive contacts in the Gulf and Persia, developed over his father's many years collecting taxes for the Ottoman Sultan, and the good reputation of the Sassoons among merchant families operating in the Ottoman Empire and Iran. He was quick to contact leaders of the Jewish communities in Shiraz and Aleppo, he visited Persian merchants and paid his respects, and whenever a British official visited Bushir, he made a point of being there to greet him, even though he did not speak English.

All this allowed David to learn about India in general and the city on its western coast that was the source or destination of so much of the trade passing through Bushir in particular. He could have opted for Isfahan, Persia's largest trading center, or followed other Baghdadi Jews to Bahrain to take advantage of the burgeoning flow of goods between the Gulf and India. But memories of the family's suffering at the hands of Dawud were fresh and the relative security offered by British rule accordingly attractive, so the decision was made: The Sassoons would cross the Arabian Sea and begin a new life in India. Shortly after the ailing Sassoon died late in 1830, David and his young family began to prepare for the hazardous journey to Bombay.

A NEW HOME

The city had been in British hands since 1661, when King Charles II received the archipelago of seven islands from the Portuguese crown (which had acquired them from the Muslim Rajputs in 1534) as part of the dowry of his wife, Princess Catherine of Braganza. The King in 1668 leased Bombay to the East India Company (EIC) for an annual rent of £10. Within a couple of decades, the EIC had initiated a program of land reclamation that continued until the late eighteenth century and fused the islands into contiguous land. Bombay's large, deep harbor made it one of the most suitable moorings for ships on the west coast of the subcontinent, and it became the commercial heart of western India, with Calcutta and Madras, one of the jewels of the British colonial order. Unlike Calcutta, which was founded as an East India Company trading post, Bombay's past was not purely colonial. It owed its emergence not to British traders but to the Indian merchants who had migrated there from Surat to the north as well as to immigrants from overseas. Rabbi Hillel described the city as a "small island in the ocean," dependent on the sea even for its basic needs, with the fort, a district "enclosed with two strong walls" that were separated by a trench, at its center. The fort was the seat of local government and locus of business, home to British officials and merchants hailing from the breadth of Eurasia. Inside were "many fine streets and houses in which gentlemen reside" and "also fine shops, the owners of which are chiefly Parsis." As the rabbi reported, other districts were altogether more squalid and congested, and "the streets

Bombay in 1826.

where the natives reside are very narrow." The fort was built in the early eighteenth century to protect the city from outside threats and evolved a commercial, civic, and social core. "On the southwest side of the Fort," Rabbi Hillel wrote, "is a little island called *Colaba;* it is in a good situation with nice houses and gardens in the ebbing of the sea." Already by 1794, official estimates put the number of houses at one thousand within the walled town and over six thousand five hundred outside the walls. The city already had all the contrasts between slums with open sewers and an array of Gothic buildings lining the city.

Unlike Baghdad, Bombay was ruled not by a distant emperor but by a joint stock company owned by stockholders reporting to a board of directors in London. Originally founded as a trade monopoly in 1600, the East India Company had at first operated primarily in Bengal, in the east of the country. It was there, against the back-drop of Mughal decline and in the face of fierce competition from its French counterpart, that the shift in the Company's aspirations from trade to territory became appreciable. Triumphs over the French and the Bengali rulers in the 1740s and 1750s, climaxing at the Battle of Plassey in 1757, resulted in the establishment of Company Raj, the direct rule of the EIC over Bengal and Bixar. It acquired the right to collect revenue and within two decades had established a capital in Calcutta and appointed its first Governor-General, Warren Hastings.

The Company asserted its interests over more and more of India, and increasingly took on governmental powers with its own armies and judiciary, though it seldom turned a profit, not least because its employees diverted funds into their own pockets at an astonishing rate. Within a few years of the appointment of Lord Wellesley as Governor-General in 1798, the last vestiges of resistance were overcome and the Company was confirmed as the absolute master of the country. As the historian William Dalrymple underlined in his in-depth research on the EIC, the unique situation meant that "India's transition to colonialism took place through the mechanism of a for-profit corporation." For David, upon arriving in Bombay, it must have felt bizarre, coming from the Ottoman Empire, that a company rather than a country was in charge of India's destiny. Already in the early seventeenth century, India's population was about 150 million (to England's 8 million), produced about "a quarter of global manufacturing," and was the source of many luxuries such as fine cotton, textiles, and indigo.

In Britain, the Industrial Revolution was in full swing, and the search for markets for British manufactured goods consequently ceaseless. India's potential to be that outlet, coupled with a vogue for laissez-faire economics and increasing calls by politicians, religious leaders, and other public figures for Britain to improve standards of living in its greatest imperial possession, to invest in infrastructure and ameliorate the conditions of the impoverished masses there, paved the way for the Government of India Act of 1833. The East India Company's last monopolies were rescinded, though its political and administrative authority was renewed for another twenty years, opening up new horizons for other trading firms at the moment when India began to assume a pivotal economic position within the British Empire, becoming the focal point in the triangular trade between Britain and China.

While Bombay boomed, and between 1824 and 1833 exports of cotton rose 20 percent and opium more than 100 percent, India as a whole was experiencing an economic depression. British monetary policy was exploitative: India had been accustomed to using gold for its currency, but in 1835 the British, keen to extract gold from the country, declared the silver rupee the sole legal tender, only for a contraction in the supply of silver to make the value of the rupee plummet. Nonetheless, there was a marked revival in India's economic fortunes after 1834, and Bombay was a major beneficiary. As India lacked a local banking system, the EIC introduced agency houses, which performed banking functions to facilitate trading. These agency houses later became "a prevalent feature of British mercantile enterprise in India" and were needed to handle the new business, and were instrumental in bringing modern capitalism to India at large. Agency houses were responsible for selling consignments, but in the case of many commodities, including cotton and opium, the agent would not receive his fee until after he had made the sale. This occasionally created a conflict of interest and attempts to deceive the trader. Negotiations over agents' fees differed from one agent to another but varied from 1.5 to 2.5 percent, often with added incentives if the agent managed to sell a shipment at a higher price than expected. Sometimes there were written agreements with agents but in many cases the arrangements were simply verbal, and ensuring that they were properly fulfilled took time and energy on the part of the family, as agents constantly demanded higher fees and some payments in advance. Any delay by agents led to losses, and disagreements inevitably erupted that required legal recourse.

Economic growth drew people to the city, and its population would more than double over the course of a decade to almost 500,000 by the mid-1840s. Opium and cotton were the two commodities above all others that transformed the city's finances and benefited the new global merchants. The trading scene included many entrepreneurs and firms, both local and foreign, but two loomed especially large. Chief among the British contingent was a trading firm named Jardine Matheson. Established in 1832 as a partnership between the Calcutta-based merchant James Matheson and surgeon-turned-merchant William Jardine, it was headquartered in Hong Kong and focused on trade with China, which it dominated until the middle of the century. Jardine had since the early 1800s owned a fleet of vessels for trade in China and dealt in opium, and began to encourage dealers to ship their opium directly from Bombay without EIC oversight, with such success that—having failed to monopolize the trade in the east of the country—the EIC decided instead to levy a tax on exports. Foremost

among the locals was Jamsetjee
Jejeebhoy, a merchant and member of the Parsi community—
Zoroastrians whose ancestors had
fled Persia in the eighth century
and who had played a significant
role in Bombay's development in
the previous century. Jejeebhoy
was famous for his profitable
undertakings with British trading
partners, his coziness with colonial
officials, and his foresight: At the
beginning of the century, before
opium had become big business in
Bombay, he personally traveled to
China to establish a distribution
network there. For the most part,
the Company looked benevolently

Jamsetjee Jejeebhoy, a most
successful Parsi entrepreneur in
Bombay.

upon such entrepreneurs: The more opium Jejeebhoy exported, the
more taxes they would collect. For these global merchants (and David
would become one of them), fighting British colonialism or the EIC
was not on their agenda; they simply wanted to prosper in the shadow
of the ruler. Once the EIC's monopoly was over, in a way, it became
easier to build relationships that would last for decades with senior
British officials who would return to London and still be allies to
these merchants.

David strived to familiarize himself with these merchants and the
commodities they traded. He began learning Hindustani as soon
as he arrived, adding it to his fluency in Arabic, Hebrew, Turkish,
and Persian, and spent his days by the cotton exchange talking to
traders and agents, scrutinizing the international news for anything
that might send prices up or down, and making contact with his old
acquaintances in Baghdad and the Persian Gulf. Not long after his
arrival, he started exporting textiles, on a small scale, to merchants
in the Ottoman Empire. He was then a small player, of a different
order of magnitude than Jardine Matheson and Jejeebhoy, and his
name is notable by its absence in the newspapers and archives of

the time. He started as a small player and his elevation into the first rank of businessmen in Bombay was gradual. There was no single event or trade that dramatically changed this state of affairs; he just continued developing his network of traders and exploiting opportunities when they arose. When, after much debate, the city council issued in 1840 a list of members of the "native community" allowed to use the venerable title of Esquire, David's name was not on it. Only in 1841 was he recognized as one of the principal members of the Arab-Jewish trading community in the city. The first mention of his name in the local newspapers came two years later when, seeking to gain a foothold in the agency business, David partnered with a French family to form Altaras, Sassoon, Sons & Co. He had watched the agency business developing as trade in Bombay boomed in the second half of the 1830s and realized that, in addition to profits, it offered opportunities to build relationships with merchants across the world. These agencies constituted the bridge between merchants. The Altaras were themselves a case in point: The family had originated in Aleppo but had migrated to Marseilles and grown prominent in the business community both there and in India. One member of the family was technically the French Vice-Consul in Bombay, though this was almost certainly an honorary title rather than an active diplomatic role. The partnership was short-lived, however, and less than a year later a public notice declared that Altaras, Sassoon, Sons & Co. was dissolved by mutual consent. We do not know why. Perhaps the compromises such an enterprise inevitably involved were too great for David—certainly he had a domineering streak. Perhaps the collaboration had served its purpose, for David Sassoon would never again feel it necessary to bring in outside partners. He and his sons were capable of being merchants and agents on their own.

RAISING A FAMILY

When David arrived, Bombay was not yet the trading titan it would become in the middle of the century. Its inhabitants numbered just two hundred thousand, though they were very diverse: Hindus, Muslims, Parsis, Armenians, Portuguese, and a small number of Jews. This mix made for "a much more complicated colonial geography" than elsewhere in India, though of course "a racial divide overlaid the city, and West remained distinct from East." A Jewish presence had been established in the sixteenth century by an eminent Portuguese trader, but it wasn't until the second half of the eighteenth century, when four distinct waves of migrants came to the city, that a genuine community gained a foothold. The first of these, labeled the "Native Jew Caste" by the British and the Bene Israel by other Jews, was drawn from the belt between the Gulf of Cambay and Goa on India's western coast; the second comprised Arab Jews from the Ottoman provinces of Baghdad, Basra, and Aleppo; the third, Cochin Jews from the Malabar Coast; and the fourth, Persian-speaking Jews from Afghanistan, Bukhara, and Mashhad. The migration of the Arab Jews during the last couple of decades of the eighteenth century was motivated by economic reasons, and the first Baghdadis to come to India settled in Surat—though they maintained a spiritual and religious connection to their old home, according to our itinerant rabbi. When he visited Bombay in 1828, he found a few Arab Jews presided over by a particularly wealthy merchant by the name of Solomon Jacob; he had settled there in 1795 and until his death in 1834 remained a prominent figure in the public life of the city. By the early 1830s, a group of twenty to thirty families—out of a total Jewish population of 2,246—called themselves "Jewish Merchants of Arabia, Inhabitants and Residents in Bombay." Although Baghdadis made up a minority of this group (one traveler to the city in 1837 estimated the number of Baghdadi Jews in Bombay at 350), their successes evidently outshone those of Jews from elsewhere in Arabia, and in time all their Arab co-religionists would come to be referred to as Baghdadi Jews no matter where they came from. It was an auspicious time for the Jewish community in the city: In 1834, a new British Governor of Bombay, Sir Robert Grant, arrived. As an MP in Britain, he had lobbied for the repeal of "civil disabilities affecting British-born subjects," and he continued in his liberal policy as Governor, which meant that under his tenure the British were more welcoming to the city's Jews than at any time previously.

David was himself profoundly attached to Judaism. He was pious and a devoted student of the Talmud, despite the demands his business made of him—traits he managed to instill in only one or two of his sons, though he insisted that all of them have a comprehensive Jewish education, and appearances were at least maintained while he was in charge of the family. He was quick to find an appropriate synagogue when he arrived in Bombay and regularly attended public worship there.

Even when his attention was focused on entering the textile trade and creating a network of agents and traders in India and abroad, he refused to work on the prescribed day of rest. Later, the Sassoons' offices would close both on Sundays, the usual day of rest in Bombay, and Saturdays, the Jewish Sabbath. In time, as David grew more affluent and more embedded in Bombay's Jewish community, its more learned and influential members could be found at his house on Saturday afternoons, discussing biblical passages, listening to a visiting scholar, or studying religious texts together. In the 1850s, this group would be organized as "Hebrath Beth David" (Brotherhood of the House of David), a club for discussing matters of shared interest and strengthening the bonds of friendship, modeled on groups from old Baghdad. David's social circle was by no means restricted to those who shared his faith, however. One of his closest friends in Bombay was John Wilson, a Scottish Christian missionary and an orientalist scholar who later founded the Wilson College in the city. Wilson was fascinated by non-Christian religions, and one of his many books was a treatise about Zoroastrianism, the faith of the city's Parsi community. The two met soon after David's arrival and became firm friends, often spending "their evenings together studying the Old Testament in the original, through the medium of Hindustani eked out by snatches of Arabic."

But David's strongest ties were always within his own family. To the four children Hannah bore him in Baghdad, Farha added six sons and four daughters in Bombay. Together they formed a little army of eight sons and six daughters—enough to build an empire. David did not distinguish between children from his first and second marriages and successfully banished the idea of half brothers or sisters among his fourteen children: They were one family with one name and the shared aim of protecting it. There were nonetheless significant differences between these siblings, as we shall see, and the age span between them was substantial. The first of his children, Mazal Tov, was born thirty-nine years before the last, Mozelle. In fact, by the time of Mozelle's birth, Mazal Tov had died and Abdallah already had four of his five children.

David paid considerable attention to his children's education and intellectual development, overseeing it personally as well as involving his sons in the business from an early age. Education was assuming more importance in India; when the EIC's charter was renewed in 1813, it agreed to allocate more to education in its budget. Needless to say, the English regime fundamentally changed the traditional ways of education and old practices. The Bombay Education Society was formed in 1815 to educate poor Anglo-Indian children, but there was "neither a central body which oversaw the education process, nor were there any text-books." Christian missionaries were arriving in India in the early nineteenth century and starting new schools. By the 1830s, several thousand Indians were studying English in Calcutta alone. This stemmed from a decision by Thomas Macaulay, a senior British civil servant, that Arabic and Sanskrit would not benefit India in the

David and three of his sons, Elias, Abdallah, and
Sassoon David (S.D.), who is in Western clothes,
late 1850s.

long run, as a result of which he shifted education to English. Britain imposed English as a new official language, spoken by increasingly large numbers of Indians who could communicate with their rulers, but "it also helped to widen the gulf between them and the mass of their countrymen."

David's goal was above all to train his sons for success in business, and the weight of expectation and burden of scrutiny fell heaviest on Abdallah and Elias, his two eldest. As teenagers, both were brought by David to the market, to familiarize them with the world of trade and introduce them to his contacts. Abdallah was sent to Baghdad at least twice to perfect his Arabic, meet his uncles and cousins, and learn the fundamentals of trade in the city's bazaar. It was a long apprentice-ship: From adolescence on, David encouraged Abdallah to hone his negotiating skills, to meet new traders and build relationships that could be relied upon in the future. The study of Hebrew and Jewish manuscripts aside, education for most of David's children followed the English curriculum, taught by English tutors living in India. Younger ones would be sent to England to finish their schooling, where the fifteen-year-old Abraham Shalom could be found penning an essay on the Crimean War (1853–56) as it unfolded. He explained, with char-acteristic loyalty to the British imperial project, that the "causes of the present war are, that Russia wishes to extend her dominion into lands to which she has not the least right," and concluded that Britain had an obligation to defend its empire and its allies and therefore "the present war is just and right."

David encouraged his sons to travel, usually around age fifteen, to teach them independence and prepare them to take responsibility for different bits of the family businesses. These expeditions weren't in-tended to supplant formal education or signal its conclusion but to complement it. A letter from David to the fifteen-year-old Suleiman in Hong Kong reveals the son's simultaneous engagement in study and business, as well as his father's close management of both, even from afar. After the usual opening, "My dear son Suleiman David Sassoon, may God protect you and prolong your life," Suleiman was rebuked for not writing more frequently, and his application to his studies was called into question. "I did not receive your letter last week. Let me know in your next letter whether you have gone to Mr Graham to be tutored; if not then apprise me for the reason." Only then did David proceed to the business. Suleiman had written to his father asking for money and the allocation of half a chest of opium for sale. "Oh, my son, have you forgotten I set up a special fund for you with five thousand rupees, so you do not need my assistance. Why are you looking for partial investment of half a chest? With the help of God, by the end of the year we will inform you with your full allocation and hope you can use your fund to make money." One month later, David informed Suleiman that he would send reports on how the funds were doing (he had set up one for each son) and that he had taken the liberty of withdrawing money from Suleiman's fund to purchase opium on his behalf, ordering him to "strive to sell it profitably." From another young Sassoon, we learn more about the sons' training: "Regarding my learning the official business, I am going on very well in improving my writing and education by copying letters and I intend to learn bookkeeping . . . every day one hour."

David's letters to his sons reveal him to have been a demanding and strict father, though his care for their well-being runs through them. His next concern was always the family's good name—an intangible but priceless asset—and this was hammered into his sons ceaselessly. He was punctual and responded to all correspondence the same day and expected all his sons to adhere to the same standard. He abhorred mistakes, especially ones that were expensive or public, and reprimanded his offspring whenever they fell short of the principles he imposed upon them. (It's easy to imagine his mortification and fury at the sight of an advertisement taken out in one of Bombay's newspapers by one of his sons offering a reward to whoever found and returned a large sum of cash misplaced somewhere between Bombay and Pune.) His methods worked: Throughout their careers, outsiders observed his sons' calm appearance, their ability to inspire confidence in their interlocutors and subordinates, and their adeptness at playing their cards close to their chests. No wonder Jejeebhoy declared that "the chief cause of David Sassoon's success was the use he made of his sons." David commanded the reverence of his children. Whether they agreed or disagreed with him on business or personal matters, their deference was assumed. Wherever he sent them, they went.

A meticulous travel log by Abraham Shalom describes a trip from

Canton to London in 1855, when he was just fifteen, accompanied only by boys of the same age. He first traveled to Hong Kong; from there on a ship of the Peninsular & Oriental Steam Navigation Company (P & O) to Singapore, then to Penang; crossed the Bay of Bengal in an eight-day voyage to Ceylon; and continued on to Aden in twelve days. At each port he described the city and its geography, its products and residents. From Aden another steamship took him to Suez, from where they traveled overland to Alexandria. He was supposed to make a detour to visit Cairo but was deterred by a cholera epidemic raging there. Describing the journey across the desert to Shoubra, north of Cairo, he wrote:

> Each van is something like a small omnibus in shape but hung only upon two wheels, the door is behind and the six passengers sit three on each side, whilst the driver sits upon a box in front. Each van is drawn by two mules and two horses, two abreast, the horses being in front. With each detachment of 5 or 6 vans, rides a sort of courier whose duty is to provide, as far as possible, that every carriage and every passenger shall cross the desert in safety.
>
> My Arabic knowledge was now of great use to me, as far as pleasure is concerned. I offered a present or as it is called by the East baksheesh to the courier and had the pleasure of riding his horse during the greater part of the journey until the sun became too powerful. I must say that I extremely enjoyed the ride and particularly at dawn when the weather was cool and refreshing, and you can fancy that galloping through the wide-open desert at that fine hour on a swift Arabian steed was of no little value.

From Cairo, he took a train to Alexandria, and after a short stay boarded a steamer to Marseilles via Malta. From Marseilles he took a train to Paris, where he remained for ten days and seems to have enjoyed himself enormously. The final leg of his journey, to "the seat of imperial power and mother country," appears to have been a comparative low point: "I never felt so sick in my 50-day voyage while crossing oceans and seas as I did while crossing the Straits of Dover."

Abraham Shalom's journey fused together travel, education, and business. The family traded in most of the countries he visited and there were always useful contacts to be cultivated, even by a fifteen-year-old. The travel journal of Aharon, Abraham Shalom's elder by one year and Suleiman's twin, reveals an altogether more adventurous spirit. Aharon, the only of David's sons never to engage in the business, wrote to his sister-in-law Flora after visiting Oslo in Norway, "from a land where the sun never sets for 3 months in a year." On the island of Magerøya, one of the most "extreme northern habitation on the globe," he climbed the North Cape with a guide, reaching the summit just before midnight to witness the Arctic sun at its zenith.

The relative austerity of Abdallah's expeditions compared to those of his younger brothers is a sign that David was beginning to work his way up the ranks of businessmen in Bombay, having created slowly but surely a network of agents and traders both in India and beyond that would elevate him farther still. His two eldest sons were by his side, aiding him and learning the business. It was also an early indicator of the global nature of his ambitions. The independence and openness to new cultures, people, and environments that these trips instilled in his children equipped them for life overseas. These were qualities David prized and ones that would in short order be needed. News was circulating in India of fresh opportunities in China, and David had seen the growing profits of his Parsi peers and rivals at Jardine Matheson, the established traders of one of the nineteenth century's most lucrative commodities: opium.

3

WARS AND OPPORTUNITIES

1839–1857

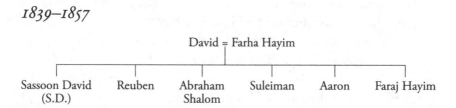

An important event that changed the trajectory of the Sassoons took place in 1839: the First Opium War. To understand its significance, it is important to look at this commodity and how it assumed such a critical role in the Sassoon business. The controversial story of opium is woven throughout more than eighty years of the Sassoon dynasty, whose control of the opium trade in India and China by the late nineteenth century was inextricably linked to their wealth and influence.

The powerful narcotic on which so many fortunes in the East were founded is derived from the *Papaver somniferum* plant, or opium poppy. The earliest evidence of its use by humans dates back roughly seven thousand years to sites scattered around the Mediterranean. The poppy seed's intoxicating properties were well-known in ancient Greece and Rome, referred to by everyone from Homer to Virgil. Arab physicians learned about it from the Greeks and called it *afyun,* after the Greek *opion.* Arab traders are said to have introduced the plant from Persia to western India in the eighth century.

The region's mild climate, rich soil, and plentiful irrigation suited the plant, and in time opium came to be one of the subcontinent's staple crops. It was at first grown primarily for local consumption; there are stories of Indian mothers using poppy powder to soothe the gums of their teething babies, for example. But it was outsiders—Dutch merchants— who first created a trade link from western India to Canton in China in the late seventeenth century. The Portuguese, who had established themselves in western India during the sixteenth century, were quick to follow and soon wrested control of the opium trade with China from their Arab and Indian rivals.

Opium flower, c. 1850.

Opium production was concentrated in three regions in India, Benares and Patna in Bengal, and Malwa in the west, and every chest shipped from India bore one of their names. Malwa opium was known for its quality and commanded a premium in China. Opium was priced and sold for export by the chest, carefully packed in two layers and weighing 160 pounds or, for a Malwa chest, 140. The EIC entered the trade in 1708, and production grew with its territory over the course of the eighteenth century. By 1793 it was the largest exporter of opium to China and its trade was a catalyst for British expansion in the country more generally. This growth had in part been facilitated by the Company's monopoly in Bengal, which gave British contractors the power to dictate prices, forcing farmers to sell their crops at low prices, and sometimes even at a loss. This practice came to a halt in 1799, after the EIC decided to abolish the contract system and administer its monopoly directly.

Over the first three decades of the nineteenth century, the land dedicated to opium cultivation in Bengal ballooned from twenty-five thousand acres to almost eighty thousand as the Company sought to grow its revenues, and by 1840 Bengal was exporting to China around fifteen thousand chests each year. The opium trade became a rich source of revenue for the EIC, averaging about 6 percent of national income, and became a significant element in the British mercantile system of exports and imports from China. Opium constituted an integral part of a triangular trade: British people had become addicted to tea (and developed a taste for Chinese silk) but had nothing to export to China in return, and opium filled this trade gap. In eastern India, where the Company controlled the cultivation and purchasing of opium, it made sure that Patna and Benares were the only regions that could produce and export to China. In the east, however, Parsi traders—chief among them Jamsetjee Jejeebhoy—began competing with the Company, buying opium from Malwa and exporting it to China via Bombay. Another source of competition at that time was opium from Turkey heading to China. To fend off these challenges, the Company increased production and slashed prices, with Patna and Benares chests falling from a high of $2,000 in 1822 to just over $600 by the early 1830s. Late in the following decade, an American doctor observed that the poppy was grown everywhere in India and opium was manufactured as freely as rice. For the farmers, it was simply a question of profit, depending on the season, whether they cultivated poppy, wheat, or rice.

OPENING CHINA

Although it was not the staple that it was in India, opium had been part of China's history long before the nineteenth century. It had been introduced by Muslim traders in the eighth century and began to be consumed recreationally on a large scale by the seventeenth century. After the Charter Act of 1813 loosened the EIC's monopoly on trade in India, the floodgates opened. The number of merchants increased significantly, and with it the volume of opium shipped. Transport of opium continued to be crucial to the trade, and many traders, such as the Sassoons, were investing in shipping. In the late 1850s the family acquired a couple of ships in order to control the cargo and to ensure the loyalty of the captains, because of their critical contribution to making trades profitable. As the trade expanded, merchants began using clippers—fast, narrow-hulled ships, constructed mostly in British or American shipyards. With their expansive sails they were known for their speed and were ideal for carrying large consignments of opium and tea, and were capable of making two or three voyages per year before the arrival of monsoon season. Even the fastest clippers could make no more than this, for none could withstand the adverse northeasterly monsoon. Crewed by "seamen and gunners who were ready to face death-or-glory adventures in return for high profits," these ships ferried their cargo from India to ports on China's coast for distribution inland. By the late 1850s, this "opium fleet" comprised more than one hundred vessels.

As the number of addicts in China soared and its trade surplus was reversed, draining the country of silver—the basis of its currency—the Chinese attempted to stem the flow of opium. Their efforts were fiercely opposed by Britain, whose subjects' interests in China were so meshed with opium trading that its government was determined not only to preserve the trade but to expand it. Some estimates put the combined direct and indirect annual transfer to London at £2 million per year by the end of the 1830s—sufficient to make Chinese attempts to suppress opium traffic reason to go to war. The final straw came in

From the First Opium War, 1842.

1839, when a new tough maritime commissioner named Lin Zexu was appointed by the Chinese emperor. When his troops began confiscating opium in Canton and blockaded British ships on the Pearl River, hostilities broke out. (One source, writing two decades later, mentions that the war was provoked by the seizure of opium chests belonging to David Sassoon, though this story is unconfirmed, and given that Sassoon's share of the trade was dwarfed by that of Jardine Matheson and others, the story seems doubtful.) In London, Jardine lobbied the government to force China to change its policies. As this was beyond the capabilities of the East India Company, Jardine called "for action by the British government to achieve the desired result."

The First Opium War of 1839–42 dramatically changed the picture for China, India, and Britain and, indirectly, for the global merchants. Early in 1841, the British sent an expeditionary force to China and occupied Hong Kong. Subsequent campaigns against the weak Chinese were likewise successful, and in spite of a counteroffensive, the British managed to capture Nanking in late August 1842, bringing an end to the First Opium War. China signed the Nanking Treaty, which saw them cede Hong Kong to Britain and open five other ports (Shanghai, Canton, Ningbo, Fuzhou, and Amoy) along the southeast coast to foreign merchants. Furthermore, the Chinese had to abolish the trade monopoly imposed on foreign traders in Canton, allowing foreign merchants into China and permitting them to trade with whomever they wished. Another treaty the next year awarded most-favored-nation status to Britain and added provisions to its extraterritoriality.

It was the opening of China. Once the war ended and the dust had settled, foreign firms rushed to enter this market and capitalize on its opportunities. William Jardine, the brain behind developing the opium trade in Malwa, was also a pioneer in its distribution. In 1847, he formed a syndicate with three other Bombay firms—R. F. Remington; Colvin, Ainslie, Cowie & Co.; and Jamsetjee Jejeebhoy—to pool resources and share clippers (the Sassoons were not included as they were insignificant in their share of trade). The same year, a revolutionary change in the opium trade took place: The Peninsular & Oriental Steam Navigation Company (P & O) began to ferry opium from Bombay to China. P & O had its origins delivering mail to the

Iberian Peninsula and carrying passengers to the Mediterranean and had only recently stretched farther east. In the face of stiff competition from the incumbent carriers, Jardine Matheson & Co. and the Apcars (a family of Armenian migrants to India), P & O managed to capture a large amount of the opium trade. It was the only steam company in the region at the time and had already reduced the travel time from Southampton to Calcutta from forty-two days to thirty-seven, though its success was in part due to a convergence of private and imperial interests. The British had achieved naval dominance of the Indian Ocean by 1815 and supported steam as a means to complement its military power. P & O was given "large subsidies to carry mail from one British colonial port to another. This in turn ensured the existence of a large merchant marine." The new steam carriers reduced costs and risk, "the low volume and high value of opium made it the ideal cargo," and the opium trade blossomed. The EIC held monthly auctions, up from nine times a year, and the number of chests exported increased from just 4,000 chests in 1839 to 68,000 chests by 1857, with a total value of £8.25 million (more than £750 million today).

If the big traders had a disadvantage, it lay inside China. The system of agents there was even more complicated than in India and currency trading even less straightforward. Foreign merchants, ignorant of the language and local customs, were forced to rely on Chinese agents, known as compradors. Because their role as intermediaries was unassailable, compradors could engage in their own private business without the knowledge of the merchants. "As long as their business activities went well, there was no problem; however, once they fell into bankruptcy for some reason or another, such a system of trade gave rise to great problems between the Western mercantile houses and the Chinese merchants." David, who had been quick to realize that China would be a substantial market not only for opium but for other commodities too, was also quick to see the advantages of establishing a more reliable bridge to the country. In the mid-1840s, just a year or two after the end of the war, he decided to send Elias, his second son, at the age of twenty-four, to explore the family's options.

Elias, after scouring the ports and main cities in China accessible to foreigners, settled briefly in Hong Kong before moving on to Shanghai, all the while sending regular reports to his father in Bombay.

Why David dispatched Elias rather than his older brother Abdallah is unclear; Elias was certainly the more energetic and tenacious of the two, and it seems he was the first in the family to recognize the potential in China, but perhaps David was also motivated by a desire to keep his heir close. Over the next couple of years, Elias traveled from one port to another, establishing contacts, learning about the opium trade, building relationships with Chinese agents, and studying the market. By 1845, he was registered as a foreign resident in China, and within a few years David had either opened an agency in or sent representatives to each of the five treaty ports. One of these, Shanghai, would become a hub for the family business second in importance only to Bombay, and the majority of trade to and from China was conducted from there. It was a sign of Elias's contribution as well as the importance of China to the family business that, when David Sassoon & Co. formally began operating in China in 1852, Elias and Abdallah were named its two partners.

It was a small operation at first, in a different league from the big traders. In a manifest of exports from Bombay for mid-November 1854, the Sassoon name appeared near the bottom, with five chests of Malwa opium, compared to Jardine Matheson's two hundred and twenty, below dozens of local traders, from Cooverjee Hormusjee to Gunnessdass Crustnajee. (On the list of imports, we can see David importing silk, sugar, copper, pearls, and nutmeg.) It was around this time that David seized the initiative, undertaking a series of innovative measures to compete with the well-established firms and gain a bigger share of this lucrative market. At his instruction, overtures were made to suppliers in India; they were offered higher advances and even connected with traders outside China, mostly in Persia, to ensure that the Sassoons, rather than their competitors, were always their primary customer. Meanwhile, Elias was roaming China in search of new customers and negotiating directly with the compradors. The trade boomed, and from then until the First World War, opium was prominent in the Sassoons' global trade portfolio and contributed substantially to their profits, especially during the three decades from 1860 to 1890, as attested by its prominence in the family's letters and in the few remaining account books preserved in the archives.

The expansion of the opium trade both enabled and motivated

the Sassoons to grow into new areas of business, and sometime after P & O's steamers entered the scene, they sought to follow. Cargo traveling by sea during this era was often lost to storm or shipwreck, eating into merchants' profits, but David and his sons felt that inadequate or irresponsible management on board the vessels was also to blame, and the haphazard way goods were stored exacerbated fire or water damage. As the business extended geographically and the number of commodities they traded increased, they began investing in steamships, either as owners or as direct shareholders, in order to exercise more control over their direction. *The North-China Herald,* published in Shanghai, gives a good indication of the extent to which the Sassoon enterprise became tied to shipping in later decades: Every day, ships entered and left Asian harbors carrying goods belonging to the Sassoons' business empire. Steamships were not just the means of trade but also assets that could be sold if business waned or a ship suffered from operating problems, and the family's correspondence is littered with examples of the challenges and dilemmas ship owners faced. In one such instance, they can be seen weighing whether to repair a damaged steamship or sell it: The cost of labor and replacement parts was substantial, and the decision had to consider the amount of time the ship would be unseaworthy, but the ship's shaft and pistons were in good condition and once repaired it would run on less coal, according to an inspection by an expert.

The different Sassoon offices made a point of cultivating the steamship captains they hired, getting to know them well and offering financial incentives for good work. One letter records a gift to a Captain Brown of five boxes of Patna opium as a reward for the profits made from a shipment of opium. Another, from a different captain to Sassoon David (S.D.), states, "There is no man in the world, with whom I would rather be associated in any speculation than yourself. Firstly, because I am under a deep debt of obligation to Mrs. Sassoon and yourself for your very great kindness when we arrived in Shanghai as houseless wanderers. Secondly, whatever you touch turns to gold."

WHITE GOLD

As tensions between foreign merchants and the imperial authorities in China reached a pitch toward the end of the 1830s, business in Bombay was picking up. These years saw the establishment of modern capitalism in India, as traders and agents began to offer "advances to encourage cultivation and secure supply of commodities," especially cotton and opium, for export. India was gaining a foothold in the English cotton market, which had been accustomed to American fare, and the lion's share of the goods flowing from India to Liverpool passed through Bombay. International trade was blossoming, and the number of European and foreign firms in India proliferated as a result. By pooling their resources, these firms managed to increase their share of the export profits over the heads of local companies. Joint stock enterprises were created and company registration commenced in 1851; within a decade, sixty companies in fields from banking to insurance, cotton mills to navigation, were headquartered in Bombay. The banking and agency systems flourished in parallel, encouraging more investment and stimulating brisk trade. In some parts of the country, trade expanded by more than 50 percent, and in regions like Sind (now part of Pakistan) traders invested heavily to meet the increase in demand for commodities such as indigo, wool, salt, cotton, and opium. The European and foreign houses in Bombay were the prime movers in setting the direction of trade.

David began this period exporting textiles, mostly manufactured in Britain, to Persia, Iraq, and other Persian Gulf countries, and importing local products from the Gulf for sale in India. His strategy was initially distinguished by its caution: starting small, gathering as much information as possible, and entering new markets or trading new commodities only slowly. At that time Indian cotton was not known for its quality, and he took his time entering the business. He was convinced by witnessing the surge in demand for Indian cotton that followed a weak harvest in the United States. Powerful trade circles, such as the Manchester Chamber of Commerce, had already recognized that India could displace America as the most important source for this "white gold," but until the steam age, high transportation costs made Indian cotton less attractive. In the 1850s, the Sassoons were able to add Chinese (and even Japanese) cotton to their business, although they believed the Chinese fare, particularly from Shanghai, could not compete with the quality of its Indian counterpart and they correctly anticipated a dramatic decline in its price. There were profits to be made, though David had to contend with the vicissitudes of dealing with brokers and agents around India and in other parts of the world, deceit and discrepancies in weighing cargoes of cotton, and the inchoate state of cotton manufacturing in India. And despite their investment in steam, shipping proved an unrelenting challenge throughout the century: Sunk or damaged ships frequently led to severe losses and increased the cost of maritime insurance.

Perhaps the greatest question facing India's cotton merchants was whether to import machinery to India to avoid sending the raw material to Britain and then reimporting finished products for sale. It was an issue tied closely to British colonial policy, which had tended to see India as the handmaid of Britain's economy: a source of raw materials for British manufacturers and a huge market for British products. Textile manufacturers in cities such as Liverpool lobbied against permitting exports of machinery to India as this would negatively impact their exports; opposing them was the machinery manufacturers' lobby. The latter would eventually win the day as free trade increasingly took hold of the British political imagination. The Prime Minister, Robert Peel, argued against export restrictions on the grounds that they violated the principle of free trade, and after some years of discussion in Parliament, in 1843 India was allowed to import machinery. By the following decade, as major improvements in transport were made and the institutions that enable industry—from banking and insurance facilities to the introduction of the legal concept of limited liability—developed, India had the infrastructure to support manufacturing. The Sassoons, still cautious, were not the first to import machinery but they were by no means the last either, and by the 1880s the family would own more cotton mills than any other in Bombay, and when the industrialization of the cotton textile industry was initiated by Parsi entrepreneurs in the mid-1850s, Elias Sassoon was appointed to the board of one of the first mills.

The business was growing. By then David had already added tea and silk, the two commodities that China was exporting, to his portfolio of commodities (albeit on a smaller scale than with opium and cotton) and he now branched out into rice and insurance. He had seen the sizable commissions agents could earn facilitating trades, and that too was added to his repertoire. The appeal was obvious: Agents paid the shipper between half and two-thirds of the estimated value of the goods, which were considered the property of the shipper until they were sold. If the goods were sold at a loss, the shipper needed to reimburse the agent for some of the cost. In other words, most of the risk in the transaction was borne by the shipper, not the agent.

David was at this point no longer a lone trader. His third son, Sassoon David (S.D.), who was the first Sassoon to be born in Bombay, in 1832, joined his two older brothers in the business. Branches, called houses, such as the House of Bombay or the House of Shanghai, were opening along the Chinese coast, and another was planned for Calcutta, and David's fourth son, Reuben, was being trained to run one of them. The diverse locations in which the family did business and the range of the commodities they bought and sold inevitably made for a complicated trading system, the efficiency of which rested on one fundamental principle: confidence in those with whom they traded. From his family's experience in Baghdad, David knew the necessity of building strong and durable relations with traders along multiple routes and of gathering accurate information. Without trustworthy traders, the supply of commodities could be thin and unreliable. David assisted such traders where he could but drew the line at offering loans—the Sassoons were never bankers. When informing one of his sons that a trader they both dealt with had requested a loan for eight months, he was blunt: "I have not answered him as I have no interest in getting involved in such obligations, as they mostly end in frictions." The family's accounting books from this era are a testament to all of this. The family archives at the National Library in Jerusalem contain many of these ledgers, each filled with countless trades, increasing in volume and variety and directed from branches across ever-greater swaths of the East, as David's company began to emerge as one of Bombay's leading merchant houses.

The ledgers also reveal another signature Sassoon endeavor: philanthropy. One-quarter percent of each trade was charged as a cost, in the same way that maritime taxes, office charges (for clerks), and accounting fees would be set against a chest of opium, say. Each office was charged with these costs and the net figure was recorded. The charity (the ledgers used the Hebrew *tzedakah* or *mitzvah*) surcharge was added regardless of whether the trade was profitable. But this generosity was not without its benefits. As well as the prestige accrued through the public acts of benevolence this surcharge funded, a school David set up in Bombay for boys to study both secular and religious topics, for example, also functioned as a pool from which educated, talented young men could be recruited to the firm. Some would go on to work for other companies or start their own, but the connection to their benefactor would never be forgotten. A similar school was founded for girls, and a third, known as the David Sassoon Industrial and Reformatory Institution, was established for underprivileged juveniles, including former prisoners, to learn a trade such as carpentry or metalwork. The board of each institution consisted of one or two of his sons, together with two or three British men living in India, and at least one or two Indians from the mercantile circle. In keeping with his faith, David sought to close the reformatory on Saturdays as well as Sundays, but the government of Bombay denied his request as "it would be manifestly disadvantageous to the inmates of the institution as well as unfavourable to discipline." To varying extents, and with different emphases, all the great merchant families of Bombay engaged in philanthropic projects of this kind, and the Sassoons can be seen mingling, and on occasion cooperating, with a dynasty whose star would in time eclipse their own. Jamsetjee Tata, a pioneer industrialist, was in the cotton and opium businesses, and he too gave generously to educational causes, particularly for girls, as well as health projects. Years later, realizing the importance of memorials for dynasties, the Sassoons would even contribute to the erection of a memorial in Bombay for Jamsetjee Tata called the J. N. Tata Memorial. The family's philanthropic activities spanned different areas; David and two of his sons were among the subscribers to the Agri-Horticultural Society of Western India, and he donated to the general improvements of the Victoria Gardens in Bombay.

BECOMING BRITISH

David's stature in Bombay and beyond likewise grew with his business and philanthropy. As a merchant, he exemplified the spirit of the Industrial Revolution and free trade, and in the public role he played in Bombay, he embodied the diffusion of British beliefs and ideas throughout the empire's colonial possessions. His interests aligned perfectly with British imperial ones, especially in China, and there can be few more perfect illustrations of this dynamic than the financial contribution he made to a large ornamental tablet presented to Captain John Dalrymple Hay in 1850 for his services to commerce in China during the Opium War. Three years later, David was granted citizenship in recognition of his services to the British Empire and swore an oath of allegiance to the Queen:

> I David Sassoon of Bombay, Jew merchant, do swear that I will be faithful and bear true allegiance to the Sovereign of the United Kingdom of Great Britain and Ireland and the Territories as dependent thereon and that I will be true and faithful to the East India Company.
> Thirty th [sic] day of September 1853.

Twenty years after his arrival in Bombay, he still had not learned enough English to sign his own name. It was signed in Hebrew. Despite his identification with the British and loyalty to their empire, even when he began to attend ceremonies where British officials lauded his generosity, he invariably replied in his native Arabic.

It is striking how rapidly his star rose once he became a successful merchant and how quick he was to immerse himself in public affairs. By the 1850s, the ceremonies came thick and fast. The *Bombay Almanac* in 1853 named him one of six "Jew Merchants" in the city; two years later, he was listed as one of "Her Majesty's Justices resident in Bombay qualified to act as Justices for the town of Bombay and Islands of Bombay and Colaba." A traveler to Bombay described him as an impressive presence, taller than most in the city, invariably wearing immaculate Arab garments and exuding dignity and confidence in his speech. One British official who over the course of a long career held many senior positions in the administration of India and befriended David recalled:

> Prominent among those possessing original character was David Sassoon, a Jew. . . . He amassed a large fortune in trade, and his firm became one of the wealthiest in British India. When laying the foundation stone [of the Sassoon Hospital in Pune, Chief Commissioner] Sir Bartle Frere addressed him in suitable terms, to which he replied by reading a short address in Arabic. He was then advanced in years, and his grave countenance, commanding figure, rich turban and flowing robes, made up a picture worth beholding.

It would be wrong to assume that David's reputation entirely shielded him from the oldest prejudice. Anti-Semitism was by no means uncommon in British society, and respected Jewish business-men could experience it even as they were lauded for their achieve-ments. When he purchased a new home in 1851, *Allen's Indian Mail* reported: "The Red House of Bombay, the princely mansion of Sir Charles Forbes, and subsequently inhabited by several partners of his firm has been brought to the hammer. It was purchased by Mr. [David] Sassoon the Jew banker." It was an infelicitous slip—as men-tioned, David was no banker—and one indicative of the scrutiny he and his family experienced in Bombay. They were, as both Jews and migrants from the Arab world, almost inevitably a curiosity to the British there. One newspaper, describing the admission of five "Hebrew girls" to an English school in Bombay, noted, "They have laid aside the costume of their own country; all appeared unveiled and some of them wore attire like English girls." Three of the girls were relatives of David, described as an "enlightened man, who has for some time past been exerting himself to the uttermost to extend intel-lectual improvement and general education among his race." Another newspaper commented on what it termed a "movement" among the Jews in Bombay, led by David, to break the "Oriental customs of secluding their females and allowing them to remain without even the rudiments of education." Overall, however, the city welcomed the Sassoons and Jews in general, and this tolerance was still evident

No 25391
BOMBAY MUNICIPALITY
The B. E. S. & T. Undertaking.
ONE ANNA COUPON.
FOR JEWS ONLY
AVAILABLE ON TRAM SERVICES.
(For use only on Saturdays
& Jewish holidays.)
To be handed over to the Tram
Conductor who will issue a
ticket in lieu hereof
J/R. TALEYARKHAN,
Traffic Manager.
Issued by
C. 32 (52-100/100 L) 6-49.

Tram ticket for a Jewish passenger, issued by
the Bombay tramways from the 1870s onward.

in the 1870s when a tram service began operating in Bombay and special concessions were made to accommodate Jews on the Sabbath so that they could avoid using money. Observant Jews could purchase in advance a coupon that stated: "For Jews Only Available on Tram Services (For use only on Saturdays & Jewish Holidays) to be handed over to the Tram Conductor who will issue a ticket in lieu hereof."

A little more than a decade after the conclusion of the First Opium War, that conflict found its echo in another isolationist kingdom: Japan. By the 1840s, the United States harbored expansionist ambitions, particularly in the Pacific, fueled by the need for new economic opportunities. American imperialism in the 1840s and 1850s took the form of maritime expansion in the Pacific. In July 1853, a fleet of American warships under the command of Commodore Perry sailed into Tokyo Bay and demanded that the Japanese open their ports to foreigners. The following March, Japan signed the Treaty of Kanagawa (located in Yokohama), ending two centuries of seclusion. David moved quickly: His firm was among the first to enter Japan, and they swiftly concentrated their business in the ports of Nagasaki and Kobe, and later Yokohama. The endeavor was in keeping with one of his cardinal rules—diversify sources of imports and increase trade routes, a model established during the expansion that followed the First Opium War.

After a period of stability, the situation in China was once again growing tense. Even as China's sovereignty was undermined by outside interference, civil wars raged in a dozen of its provinces, further reducing its military capabilities. The Chinese were not buying enough British goods or, more accurately, were too poor to acquire them, swinging the trade balance back in China's favor. The British sought to extend their trading rights in China, and to legalize the consumption of opium there, as the government wanted to escape the perception that it was encouraging the large-scale trade of a banned substance. An opportunity presented itself late in 1856 when Chinese officials boarded the *Arrow,* a British-registered ship docked in Canton, and arrested several of its crew. It has been argued that it was actually a Chinese-owned pirate ship, but in any case, its requisitioning was deemed by the British a gross infringement of a binding agreement and sufficient reason to commence hostilities. The Second Opium War, also called the *Arrow* War, began. France, hoping to gain some rights of its own in China, joined Britain, compounding the military imbalance. In June 1858, the Treaty of Tientsin (Tianjin) was signed, opening several new ports to Western trade, and guaranteeing the right of foreigners to reside in these ports and to travel in the interior of China, as well as the freedom of movement for missionaries. Despite this, the Second Opium War rumbled on until the Peking Treaty of 1860, but Tientsin saw China legalize the consumption of opium, opening the door to a surge in production and imports. Whether legalization actually led to "a perceptible increase in opium consumption" is debated, but the intent behind the treaty is not. The British Ambassador to Peking later admitted to Parliament: "We forced the Chinese Government to enter into a Treaty to allow their subjects to take opium." The opium business accordingly boomed from 1858, and British tax revenues, as well as those of merchants in India, increased substantially, making Bombay one of the great commercial and industrial centers not only on the subcontinent but on the globe. Opium became the world's most valuable traded commodity in 1860 and remained so for a quarter of a century. Whether or not opium was, as it is often seen today, a tool used ruthlessly by the British to drug and weaken a nation, it is important to remember that it was legal in the United States and Europe—included in *The Economist*'s weekly list of commodities—until 1916, after which a doctor's prescription was required to purchase it in Britain. One senior British official summed up the thinking of this era: "I can see no reason why the revenue derived by India from opium should be considered more precarious than that derived by England from gin and tobacco."

The triumph of British imperial muscle in China coincided with a moment of profound weakness in India: the Rebellion of 1857. Festering grievances among Bengali troops, resentment at the usurpation of Hindu princely states, and the activities of missionaries fueled a series of mutinies and protests against foreign influence in Bengal. These spread across the east of the country, and for a time British control of its most prized possession seemed uncertain. To quell the revolt, British troops "unleashed indiscriminate terror, ravaging the countryside and killing randomly," and between rebellion and reprisal both Delhi and Lucknow were sacked. The uprising was suppressed but it marked the end of Company Raj. The Government of India Act of 1858 transferred all the territories and powers of the East India Company to the Crown, appointed a Secretary of State for India to the British cabinet to oversee India's affairs, and established the Indian

The weighing of cotton, 1862.

Civil Service to administer them. At the apex of this new system was the Governor-General or Viceroy, appointed by the British sovereign to rule, autocratically, spurning any recourse for representative government in India.

Bombay was far from the epicenter of the rebellion and somewhat shielded from it, so David and his family remained for the most part bystanders in one of the most tumultuous episodes in the three centuries of Britain's involvement in India. According to a journalist's report, David, as head of the Jewish community in Bombay, contacted its Governor "proffering the services of the whole Hebrew community," and thereby induced other communities in the city to show their solidarity with the British. After the uprising, he contributed to a fund to provide assistance to the widows and orphans it had created. David had sworn allegiance to a country in which he had never set foot and whose language he couldn't speak, but it had provided him and his family with refuge, and his fortunes were utterly tied up with it. If anything, it seems that the events of 1857–58 strengthened that commitment. The Sassoons' ascent as serious global traders coincided with the elevation of "free trade" to a fundamental principle and a central plank of policy in Britain. The Sassoons' interests and those of the British Empire converged during this period, and this fortuitous concurrence of ideology and Sassoon business activities would serve both well for more than half a century.

4

BRANCHING OUT

1858–1864

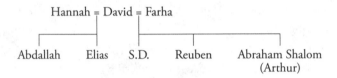

Hannah = David = Farha

Abdallah   Elias   S.D.   Reuben   Abraham Shalom
(Arthur)

The climax of the celebrations in Bombay marking the transfer of power from the East India Company to the British Crown occurred not at the residence of the outgoing Governor, Lord Elphinstone, but instead at that of "one of the merchant princes of Bombay." The *Illustrated London News* extolled the magnificence of the party: "Monday, the 28th of February, 1859, will long be remembered by the *élite* of Bombay for the grand entertainment given by Mr. David Sassoon, the well-known wealthy Jew merchant of Bombay and China, in honour of the assumption of the Government of India by her Gracious Majesty Queen Victoria." The party was held at David's new home and attended by five hundred guests. By late 1858, David Sassoon felt secure enough to start flaunting his wealth and purchased a grand house in Byculla, one of the most affluent neighborhoods in Bombay, and called it Sans Souci (in French: "No Worries") after the summer palace built by Frederick the Great in Potsdam around 1745. Frederick's palace was "modelled on an Italian *palazzo* of the Renaissance" and it was intended as a refuge for the King from the demands

David Sassoon's house in Bombay, Sans Souci,
decorated for the "grand entertainment" of 1859.

of the court in Berlin. In fact, the house in Bombay "owed rather more
to Persian fantasy than Potsdam," and its "tinkling fountains blended
with the chatter of green parrots in the banyan trees." Its purpose was
not purely relaxation either, but rather to entertain and impress the
senior British officials and the elites of the city. Given his adherence to
Judaism, he built a special room that was filled with sacks of victuals
and utensils. "It would be used on the eve of Passover to bake the
matzos or unleavened bread eaten during the eight days of the festival."

The gateway to the mansion was decorated with the crown of England surrounded by flags and banners for the party, and its gardens
were brilliantly illuminated. The symbolism did not pass unnoticed.
"After complimenting Mr. Sassoon on the magnificence of the entertainment, his Lordship, adverting to the time when fears were entertained of the loyalty of a portion of the inhabitants of Bombay, said
that he had then the gratification to find the Jewish community foremost in the ranks of loyalty." Three decades after his humbling escape
from Baghdad, David found himself one of his new home's grandees,
fêted for his loyalty and wealth rather than persecuted. A rabbi from
Palestine visiting Bombay the same year echoed *The Illustrated London
News*'s description:

> The whole [Jewish] community of Bombay has a single Prince, who is the head over them all. He is the aristocrat, the most upright among men, both wealthy and righteous, old and revered presence, generous and philanthropic . . . namely Sheikh David Sassoon Saleh.
>
> His robes are long and wide, and he has a great turban on his head, exactly as he dressed in the city of Baghdad, and purity and glory hover over him.

The house in Bombay still stands today, repurposed as Masina Hospital, a large medical center. Obvious traces of the Sassoons are now few, but an observant visitor might spot the family coat of arms, with its Hebrew and Latin mottoes (more on that later), in the middle of the elaborate staircase, sculpted from oak specially imported from England, that connects the building's two floors. In the garden, new buildings were added, but the house still stands, and one can look out from the balcony and imagine the large garden where numerous parties were held during that time.

More easily found is the marvelous blue exterior of the synagogue David built nearby. An inscription inside Byculla's Magen David Synagogue declares "that this house of prayer was erected at the sole expense of David Sassoon and completed in 1861." The building was renovated and enlarged by a grandson, Jacob Sassoon, in 1910, and restored by the Indian government to its former glory in 2019. Today the synagogue still serves the small Jewish community that resides in Mumbai. The synagogue, the grand home, and the parties hosted there served a purpose larger than mere pomp. Well aware of the fundamental interconnectivity between politics and business, David used the status they reflected and afforded to lobby the British authorities (and key decision makers in other regions) to defend his firm's interests. When, six weeks after the party, a tariff on imports was suddenly increased to raise the Indian government's revenue, David was one of six lobbyists who represented Bombay's mercantile community to the city's new Governor in calling for a return to the old rates, or at least an exemption for goods already in transit or arrived at port. In this instance, David's influence was rebuffed—the merchants' entreaties were rejected—but the role he assumed, intertwining politics and economics in defense of interests that were both specific to his firm and general to the merchants of his city, was one he would play again and again. Tariffs, with currency fluctuations and shipping, grew only more important to David's bottom line as the family firm expanded, in terms of both opening new branches and trading new commodities. So too did the deployment of his sons. Abdallah was by his father's side in Bombay, orchestrating the expansion and building relationships with traders and agents through endless correspondence. Elias remained in China, extending the network of opium suppliers and retailers that had transformed the family from upstarts to major players in the trade in less than two decades. No less effective was David's placement of Sassoon David (S.D.), his third son and the first from his second marriage. S.D. was an interesting character. As with all David's sons, he was dispatched abroad for an apprenticeship—in his case, Baghdad, where he was introduced to the woman he would marry, and then Shanghai. In 1858, aged twenty-six, he was the first member of the Sassoons to move to London, creating the third hub in the company's network. London was not only the capital of the British Empire but had also become the financial center of the world, and the family needed a presence there.

Unlike his brothers, S.D. loved nature, collected books, and immersed himself in Talmudic study. Observers saw him as the "pioneer of the House of Sassoon in England" and the one who built the foundation for his siblings' later success there. Tall and thin, he did not enjoy the robust health of his brothers. He was seen as a dreamer and introvert—the opposite of his brother Reuben—though hardworking. He loved writing and edited the first periodical in Bombay in Baghdadi Jewish dialect, demonstrating a journalistic inclination that would one day be inherited by his daughter. In London he established smooth relations with Lancastrian industrialists, hungry to buy raw cotton and sell textiles in return, and companies based in the City of London, the financial district, interested in shipments of tea, silk, and metals, and bonded with British politicians and members of the aristocracy. Recalling S.D. from Shanghai and sending him to London proved to be a masterly move on David's part. Over the next decade, the business in London would expand to such an extent that Reuben, then an apprentice in China, would be dispatched to

Ashley Park, an estate in Surrey purchased in 1867
by David Sassoon for his son Sassoon David Sassoon (S.D.).

help deal with the sheer volume of transactions. Intuition, as well as
the need to gather information, was what drove him to send Elias to
China, and then to send S.D. to England. Reuben's younger brother
Suleiman would follow his siblings to Hong Kong and Shanghai but
never made the westward migration. In this he was unusual.

The historian Sugata Bose posits: "With the solitary exception of
the Sassoons, none of the Asian intermediary capitalists was able to
break into the arena of high finance in the colonial era." He argues
that unlike most of the Indian, Chinese, and Baghdadi Jewish capitalists who sought mostly to control the bazaar economies of the Indian
Ocean, only the Sassoons "were able to penetrate the echelons of higher
finance in London from the mid-1850s onward." David also was wise
in shuffling his sons, thus making the brothers interchangeable, which
allowed all of them as a family to respond in full strength during times
of crisis. Over the next three decades most of David's sons and their
families would gravitate to England. His grandchildren would have
little interest in living in India or China, and the direct connection
to his Baghdadi roots and language would be severed. David couldn't
have predicted this, though he set the process in motion. In 1861, he

financed for S.D. the acquisition of an estate in Surrey, about seventeen miles from London, at a cost of £48,500 (about £5 million today). Ashley Park, as the grand manor was known, would become one of the most prominent symbols of both the family's wealth and their changing aspirations for decades to come.

TRADING OPPORTUNITIES

The first half of the 1860s was a period of intensive expansion for David's business. Following the legalization of opium consumption in China, the British strived to generate as much revenue from the drug as possible. The government of India decided how much opium to bring to the market and how much land was dedicated to its cultivation. Whenever the government detected a decline in production, it increased the price paid for raw opium to stimulate it. Opium was by far the most valuable import to Shanghai in the latter half of the nineteenth century, worth about 16.4 million taels (about £1.7 million or $8.5 million at the time) in 1865. As opium became more widespread in China, it came to be used as a form of currency and means of payment by Chinese shopkeepers.

It has been argued that "without the drug, there probably would have been no British Empire." Certainly, the number of imperial subjects involved in the trade grew and grew. As traders in Bombay and Calcutta strived to capture a greater share of the profits, more and more firms followed the Sassoons in offering annual cash advances to farmers to ensure a steady supply. By the 1860s, an estimated 1.5 million small peasant households cultivated the poppy plant nationwide, delivering the raw crop to the nearest government office. The work was arduous, and the security the advances offered didn't mean the peasants weren't vulnerable to exploitation. A recent empirical study suggests that many "peasants produced opium at a loss" and persisted in this "unremunerative venture" because of a lack of alternatives. Once they accepted the advances offered by traders and the government, they were "caught in a web of contractual obligations from which it was difficult to escape." Some authors emphasized the importance of opium for the Indian peasant and its contribution to agriculture.

"The true advantages of poppy cultivation were not excessive cash profits, but security and mitigation of risk in exchange for a four- to five-month commitment to demanding, arduous work."

As demand and competition for Indian opium soared, the Sassoons even looked abroad to diversify their supply chain, complementing their trade in Malwa and Patna opium with their Persian and Turkish equivalents. In a letter from Pune to Bushir (the city to which the family escaped from Baghdad and lived in for a year before moving to Bombay), Abdallah complained to an employee that the prices of Persian opium were low and that the Chinese preferred the Indian fare. An annual report by the Bombay Chamber of Commerce confirmed that only one significant shipment of Persian opium had arrived in the port, and it came via Singapore. The report indicated that "Messrs. D. Sassoon, Sons, and Co., have hitherto been the chief consigners." In later decades as demand increased still further, Persian opium would be sold throughout China.

Selling opium to China required a keen knowledge of the risks involved in currency trading, especially the peculiarities of silver. The Chinese insisted on getting paid in silver, and the country's prosperity in the seventeenth century had been due in part to its influx. For foreign traders, the complication was China's so-called bimetallic monetary system, which used both silver (in the form of bullion called *sycee*) and copper (round coins with square holes). This meant the value of a single currency was linked to two different metals, whose prices fluctuated—sometimes dramatically—and monetary volume depended on their availability. Although there was in theory a fixed exchange rate between silver and copper, in practice the market dictated the rate, making it harder for traders to gauge their risk. Competition from silver dollars, which had been introduced into China in the seventeenth century and had become widely accepted, and the revival of paper money in the nineteenth century further complicated the monetary system. Pitfalls were everywhere, and we can see from one report from 1859 that David Sassoon & Co. used paper notes to purchase gold after a legal disagreement erupted with a Chinese agent which ended up in court.

The legal system in China was not easily navigated, and conflicts with local traders and agents that ended up in the courts were not infrequent. In one case in Shanghai in 1858, the Sassoons bought gold and settled the trade with bank orders that were guaranteed exclusively on the date of the payments. The local trader came to the Sassoons a day after the bank order matured, which meant it was worthless, but a series of misunderstandings and unfamiliarity with the workings of the system meant that the ensuing case was settled only a year later. The judge ruled against the defendant (the Sassoons) and forced them to pay the full amount claimed by the Chinese plaintiff, with interest. When such disagreements occurred, there tended to be little common ground between foreigners and locals; each side thought and operated within its own cultural and legal frame of reference. Foreign firms struggled to reclaim their money from compradors even in cases of misappropriation, and when the British did intervene, the losses incurred by trading houses were permanent. The three-tiered distribution system operating in China during the nineteenth century formed a hierarchy of big wholesale dealers, large-scale retailers, and local distributors. The first of these had a lot of clout and tended to receive favorable treatment at the hands of Chinese officials. Furthermore, foreign traders also faced harassment by officials who impeded their efforts to purchase tea and silk by refusing to honor their transit passes, which exempted them from paying transit fees.

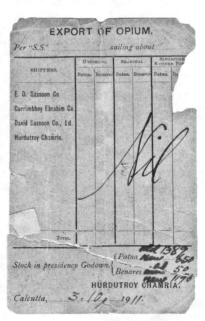

Opium export ticket from Calcutta, 1911.

Even without officials, trading in China could be a fraught business. In a bizarre episode, a boycott was declared by a group of Chinese opium traders when a Sassoon employee refused to sell to one of them. The group insisted that the employee's patron, Suleiman, personally involve himself and find a resolution before they purchased any more opium from the firm. In a memo to Suleiman, the wife of Mordechai, a senior

employee who was away traveling, complained about the state of
affairs in China ("What kind of a place is this where one has to trade
with someone if he incurs losses? Aren't there laws that prevent this?")
and implored him to visit Shanghai for a few days from Hong Kong
to deal with the matter. The Chinese traders had 474 chests of opium,
enough supply for at least 15 days, but had failed to pay for them.
Suleiman advised Shanghai to refrain from selling any more opium
to this guild of traders until payment was received. Shanghai was sitting on about 1,800 chests from Calcutta and worried about the cost
of a prolonged strike, especially as any disruption to trade made the
Chinese banks reluctant to deal with them, as well as the prospect
of losing ground to the native Chinese producers, who were gaining
momentum. A few days after the strike began, Shanghai pleaded with
Suleiman to write a conciliatory letter to the guild to end the strike. It
became increasingly clear during negotiations that striking merchants
wanted to reduce the Sassoons' share of the supply to northern China
so that they could fill the vacuum with Chinese opium. One month
and an appeasing letter from Suleiman later, a meeting was called to
end the strike. Despite Mordechai's misgivings, fear that other merchants would "jump at the opportunity" to replace the Sassoons won
the day; the strike was officially over and "the market was expected to
stabilize in a week or two."

Opium trading was a complicated business, then, and with the cost
of shipping, insurance, and taxation, an expensive one too. The trade
was also impacted by the transport system. When P & O arrived on
the scene in 1847, David was getting established, and in the 1850s was
described as a "considerable shipper," though, like Jardine, he was still
mostly exporting in his own vessels. One method of gaining a foothold in shipping was investing in a shipping company, and in early
1864 *The London and China Telegraph* reported that Reuben Sassoon
had been appointed deputy chairman of the board of the China Steam
Ship and Labuan Coal Company.

But there were ways for merchants to boost their profits. One was
to abstain from buying any opium for a week, allow the prices to drop,
and then purchase new stock. Another was to wait patiently when
prices in China declined and hold on to stock until they revived. The
financial strength of David's firm allowed this luxury; other merchants

borrowed to buy and were obliged to sell immediately, at whatever rate the market could bear. Similarly, when their competitors were buying and paying over the odds, the Sassoons tended to have enough stock in hand to protect them from panic buying or selling. They also had sufficient reserves of cash to allow trusted merchants to make partial payments for shipments rather than the whole amount, as many lacked the financial capability to pay in full. The flexibility afforded by the firm's different branches also worked in their favor: They could quickly raise prices if an opportunity presented itself in one location, or reduce them swiftly to facilitate a trade in another. Despite the quantities the Sassoons dealt in, they managed to be surprisingly agile. Especially once they had proved themselves and been appointed partners, David's sons were afforded a reasonable degree of autonomy, with their own accounts and license to make decisions on the spot rather than constantly refer back to the head office in Bombay. All of these strengths were undergirded by an axiom: Quality prevails. In the long run, there would always be buyers for quality goods. Hence the firm's emphasis on Malwa opium. Abdallah, David's second-in-command in Bombay, in particular was tough on anyone who bought low-quality opium, fearing the firm might get stuck with it.

DIVERSIFYING RISK

In the complex, densely interconnected world of the global merchants, the management of risk was paramount. David, risk-averse by nature, was a fervent supporter of diversification. Like the Parsis before him, David made property an integral part of his firm's portfolio. Each partner owned not only their personal homes but also properties to rent for the firm and for their own accounts to increase the yield on their investments. Diversification also meant expanding into finance and banking. Although David did not enter the banking world, his business relied upon stable and supple banking in India and China, so he ensured that his progeny were appointed to the boards of banks in both these countries. One of his sons always occupied a seat on the board of the Bank of Bombay, the main financier of trade in the city, while another replaced the late Sir Jamsetjee Jejeebhoy on the management committee of the Government Savings Bank.

Such appointments certainly didn't hinder the financing of the family firm, but no less valuable was the information about the activities and health of their competitors as well as the general economic outlook in the region that they provided.

Maritime insurance was another tool to manage risk. It was expensive, ranging anywhere from 2 to 5 percent of the value of the cargo, but vital given the high frequency of ships sinking or being damaged by the treacherous weather prevailing on many of the shipping routes in Asia and to Britain. Even before entering the business directly, the Sassoons invested in insurance companies; according to *The London and China Telegraph,* Suleiman David Sassoon was one of the five directors representing David Sassoon & Sons on the board of North China Insurance. Later, the Sassoons entered maritime insurance, albeit on a small scale. This kind of vertical integration was atypical for traders at the time, and speaks volumes about the understanding and ambition of what was becoming one of the great dynasties of the nineteenth century.

Not all these new endeavors were successful, however. In China, the firm's second fulcrum, when the introduction of railways was mooted by the British, the Sassoons saw the potential for a lucrative investment, and one that would further their interests in the country. In a letter to Sir MacDonald Stephenson, who was responsible for conducting a feasibility study, Messrs. Sassoon declared an interest in the welfare of China's citizens that had not previously been on display: "It is our conviction that the completion of the various lines . . . will confer a great benefit to the country, both socially and commercially. As an experimental line we think that connecting Shanghai with Soochow would be most suitable, as likely to pay best." In the end, the scheme came to nothing.

More reliable were the commodities that flowed in the opposite direction. Tea was one pillar of the triangular trade between Britain, India, and China, and like opium, it formed part of the foundation of the empire. Tea drinking, which became a national custom of the British from the eighteenth century, had partly fueled the growth of shipbuilding in Britain in the nineteenth century, as the merchant fleet responded to the demand for tea and sugar. The average British worker by the late eighteenth century spent 10 percent of total food expenditure on tea and sugar, compared to 12 percent on meat and 2.5 percent on beer. It was argued that tea was a driving force behind industry and had become essential in the diet of the British worker. When David realized the strong demand for Chinese tea and to a lesser extent for silk, he aspired to become an important cornerstone of the triangular trade between India, China, and Britain. Tea prices fluctuated depending on the harvest, quality of tea, and demand. As tea is perishable, storing it when demand was weak added to the cost. The House of London reported in 1864, "[The] tea market has come to a standstill, and those who bought tea in haste and paid taxes on it, are losing money. Furthermore, news that green tea is being shipped from America and that will reduce prices further." As more varieties of tea became available on the market, the Sassoons recruited professional "tea tasters" to advise them on the quality of different categories: "Dr Juna came for dinner at our house, he seems to be a nice man but not very smart. Hopefully, employing him in Shanghai will help us and we will be pleased with his services." It seems that Dr. Juna was not hired, but a Mr. Bernard received a four-year contract to become the company's tea expert. Sometimes, when tea prices dropped, the Sassoons stored the tea in the hope of better days, but that was clearly risky. As with every commodity, calculating maritime taxes on a shipment of tea was key. A letter from Shanghai to Hong Kong asked for guidance: "Inform me definitely how much tea we need to buy and what will be our exact investment so we would be ready for this season. Tea crop this year will be premature, so inform me if *Agamemnon* or other steamships are sailing in the appropriate maritime taxation, so we will mobilize in order to have these steamships arrive in London and sell as quickly as the English houses are doing."

Although silk never equaled the tea trade in prominence or scale, it provided decent profits in good times, when demand—particularly for silk of excellent quality—was high. A report by an English employee in Shanghai to Abraham Shalom in Bombay captures the contingencies weighed by traders of this luxury, as well as the sheer reach of the family's network:

We have had a very active market since my last [report] and about 2000 bales have been settled, 450 of which went forward by the French market . . . and 900 bales go by bearer [sold to miscellaneous traders]. The value of all classes is enhanced, but the sterling cost is very little higher, as exchange has continued to decline. . . . [We] have also been good in enquiring for the finer kinds for the London market. Shipments that are pretty clean and good thread, I think it is likely to pay well.

Such awareness of events around the globe served the Sassoons well; when reports of a disastrous silk harvest in France and Italy reached the House of London, they knew this would inflate prices in Europe and immediately arranged for more imports from the Far East.

As with tea, innovation gave the Sassoons an edge over their rivals. They hired a silk expert to enhance their understanding of the nuances of each type, though the advice was expensive and, on occasion, misleading. In later decades, as we shall see, this competitive streak and drive to develop the business diminished. In 1865, an English expert, described by S.D. as "a very sharp and smart young man who knows the silk market well and had good recommendations," was hired. It may be thanks to him that the House of London recognized the potential of Japanese silk and, noting the weak exchange rate of the Japanese currency, instructed Shanghai to purchase it for sale in Britain and Europe.

Rice followed the same pattern: Due diligence was exercised and the firm was poised to enter the market when conditions were ripe for profits. As with opium, the family was dexterous in diversifying its suppliers of the crop and in its ability to take advantage of price differentials between different locations: "I am surprised how the rice market in Shanghai is at standstill, while in Calcutta, it is still high. If you find that the harvest in China this year is not of high quality and given that prices in Manila are low while in Ningbo are high, I hope you will buy the [Philippine] rice." Whether the commodity in question was silk or rice, the Sassoons grasped at an early stage in their trading history that in most cases, there would be demand for high quality. Many years later, in the twentieth century, the trustees of the Sir Sassoon David Trust Fund in Bombay granted a modest sum of four thousand rupees for work on pathological research on rice crop diseases in North Sind.

Although its focus had turned to other, more lucrative commodities, David's firm maintained its original core business trading textiles: shirting, wool, indigo, and other fabrics sold in Cairo, Beirut, Aleppo, and Baghdad. The same principles applied: diversifying suppliers; avoiding speculation, but when speculation prevailed, offering merchandise at high prices; being as cognizant as possible of price movements in all locations; and finally, endeavoring to prevent embezzlement. One of the difficulties that cotton merchants faced was the attempt by brokers and agents to cheat on the weight of shipments. Unscrupulous agents would remove some cotton and dampen any bales that had dried out in transit to compensate, with the result that, at the final destination, recipients would complain that 4 to 5 percent of the weight was missing. Agents of shirting likewise dampened shipments to increase their weight. When one such shipment arrived in Manchester, the firm absorbed the loss rather than pass it to their customers. Their reputation was safeguarded, though it led to recriminations among the brothers and a flurry of messages about the importance of having agents and brokers who could be trusted.

When the family found reliable partners, they did everything they could to keep them happy. "I want us to be absolutely perfect in our dealings with Agha Muhammad," wrote Abdallah to Reuben. Agha Muhammad Ali was their main supplier of opium in Persia and had declared a few months earlier that he would do business only with the Sassoons. Abdallah encouraged Reuben to write to the traders in the Gulf and Persia to build stronger relationships, and when he complained of struggling with the Persian language, Abdallah advised him to avoid complicated words and assured him that the more he wrote, the better his Persian would be. This ability to trade in different locations and take advantage of any disparity in prices gave the family a substantial market advantage. An instruction from Hong Kong to Shanghai for shirting could apply for almost any commodity:

Shirting prices on your side [Shanghai] are very good, and
the hope is that you will be able to sell what was delivered to
you, and given our cost we will be able to make good profit.
Sell in Tientsin [Tianjin] even though we will not be able to
cover agency fees. . . . In Ningbo, prices are high and possibly

we can make 8% on sales. In other words, when you see that your market prices are lower than Ningbo, do not sell, wait, and do not send shipment there, so we do not incur double transport costs, and sell whenever you see profit.

When prices dropped across the board these principles couldn't turn loss into profit, but they did at least help mitigate it. Time and again, the question that arose in the correspondence was the reliability of the information gathered by the brothers from their trading sources. We find one of David's sons advising another not to trust the information emanating from the English trading houses, on the grounds that they were trying to promote their own trade and thus could not be relied upon. When agents were able to confirm a source or the price of a commodity, it was quickly taken to one of the Sassoon houses. Each branch was supposed to write instantly to the others to update them. Almost daily, letters were transferred on ships sailing from one port to another, and as soon as a ship docked, a messenger would rush the pouch containing the letter to the addressee. In later decades, the telegraph was used to send updates on prices, but rarely about the strategy of buying or selling.

One of David's dictates to his sons was repeated in almost every letter: Strive to make a profit. He ordered his sons to prioritize quality as there would always be demand for it, and the potential profits were larger. He was punctilious in transmitting his orders to his sons about trading and righteous in his anger when his instructions were not followed. After Suleiman purchased the wrong type of silk, David wrote furiously to tell him, "None of this material is suitable for sale. Maybe you did this so I do not ask you again for anything. You are going to have to accept any price offered." His micromanagement centered mostly on trades and appointments in the family's branches. In one memo, he directed Suleiman, "Sell Patna opium at 758–760 Rupee per chest, if you hear however that prices in Shanghai have risen, request a higher price per chest," and proceeded to list exactly what he should buy, in what quantities and at what price, as well as from which city. Only in regard to opium did he allow his son some latitude: "If you purchased more opium, do not worry."

Conflicts between members of the family were inevitable, and as commander in chief, it fell to David to adjudicate and heal the wounds. In this he was largely successful, but by the late 1850s, he sensed growing enmity among his sons, not least between those working in tough locations such as Shanghai and those enjoying a softer life in London. One such rift had opened between his eldest, Abdallah, and his fourth son, Reuben, over conflicting trade strategies and Abdallah's claim that Reuben was not pulling his weight, costing the firm money. Each of David's sons, while committed to the firm and their father's authority, increasingly needed allies within the family, especially when they were distant from the decision-making center in Bombay. Suleiman, frustrated at being far from home, developed close relationships with his cousins. One wrote to him from Bombay to thank him for his friendship and assure him, "Whenever you shall need anything from the place I am in, request me in few lines, I shall execute it with the greatest pleasure."

COTTON AND THE AMERICAN CIVIL WAR

Dynasties are built not only on innovation, hard work, and knowing the right people, but also on a measure of good fortune. In 1861, war once again played into David's hands, and S.D.'s perch in London this time proved invaluable. This conflict took place far away, in the United States, but had a profound impact on a major component of the firm's business: cotton. The outbreak of the Civil War that April and the consequent collapse of American cotton sent prices skyrocketing and provoked a frenzy of speculation around the world. "Cotton shipments changed hands many times between speculators before being delivered to factories; with each exchange a small profit could be made." The price of cotton more than quadrupled in the first two years of the war, driving increased production in India. There were even rumors of people tearing apart their mattresses to sell the cotton. In industrial centers such as Lancashire, textile production suffered severe dislocation due to lack of supply, a phenomenon that became known as the "Lancashire cotton famine." British politicians and lobbyists, alarmed at the implications for their industries if the slavery system were to collapse in the United States, concluded that Britain should invest in Indian cotton as a replacement for the American crop.

For four years, the production and trade of one of the world's most valuable commodities hinged on the progress of the war. Each time news spread of a possible cease-fire, prices dropped, only to rise more steeply when it did not materialize. Recent advances in communication technology—one of the harbingers of globalization—meant that news was distributed more quickly than ever before. In the 1860s the average time of transit for a telegram from Britain to Karachi via submarine cable was five to six days, roughly the same amount of time it took a letter from Hong Kong to reach Shanghai; it would take until the mid-1870s for the transmission time to be reduced to four or five hours via Tehran. The Sassoons were early adopters of the telegraph and, similar to many global merchants, were agents of globalization. They used the telegraph to transmit information about the progress of the war to one another, all the while cognizant of the opportunities for profit if the right decision were made at the right time. But unlike the letters David and his sons wrote to one another in their Baghdadi Jewish dialect, telegrams for the most part utilized the Latin alphabet and were easily deciphered. The telegraph was very expensive, not confidential, and, due to the need to condense messages to one or two lines, open to mistakes and misinterpretation. Every piece of information, be it political or economic, could affect prices. In one telegram from 1864, one of David's sons in London informed his brother in Hong Kong: "London 13th Sept: Cotton dull penny lower owing to dear money and rumours of peace—don't buy above shilling." Hong Kong, relaying the telegram from London, advised Shanghai to continue buying cotton as long as the price was "reasonable" and could be profitable: "Lowering our purchase price will lower average cost of purchases and bring us profits." The results of presidential elections and battles between the North and South were all critical in deciding whether to hold or sell different cotton shipments. The House of London dutifully gleaned this information from the British newspapers, which closely covered the war, and reported them to the family overseas. Less than a fortnight after the above-mentioned telegram and a month before Hong Kong apprised Shanghai of its contents, London warned that a glut of cotton was accumulating. It predicted that prices would collapse and advised the other houses to keep selling at current market prices to get rid of their stock.

It is an episode revealing of the difficulties merchants faced conducting their business in a market that was globalized but with a communication system that wasn't yet fully reliable. It was essential, then, that each house gather accurate information not only about the market, but also about what competitors and brokers did or intended to do. As Sven Beckert observes, the global cotton trade "rested on credit. Credit rested on trust. Trust, in a global market [that] extended well beyond the kin of any family or tribe, rested on information. Information was accordingly at the core of most merchants' activities." The fraternal trust among the branches, combined with their vantage point in London, gave the Sassoons an edge and allowed them to prosper, though friction and recriminations could and did intrude. Trying to predict the market led to second-guessing, which at times infuriated some branches who were blamed for buying at a high price or for failing to sell when the price was right. Such volatile times demanded nerves of steel, and it is remarkable just how young most of David's brood were to be running the firm's various branches: Abraham Shalom (later Anglicized to Arthur) was in charge of Hong Kong at the age of twenty-four in 1864 while Suleiman was at the helm in Shanghai at just twenty-three. The family was fortunate to be able to rely upon them: David's health had been deteriorating since the beginning of the war and from 1863, though he remained the undisputed commander in chief, his day-to-day responsibilities were increasingly delegated, principally to Abdallah.

Managing risk at a distance, particularly given the endless stream of rumors about a faraway, crucial war, was always challenging, as Abdallah found. At least locally, the Sassoons were determined to be disciplined about purchasing cotton. In November 1864, Hong Kong advised Shanghai that unless there was panic buying there, they should under no circumstances be enticed to buy more cotton. Yet only a week later Abraham Shalom changed his mind. In spite of information from London that cotton prices were depressed due "to large stock and money-tight" conditions, he correctly predicted that the end of the Civil War was not imminent (it lasted another six months, until April 1865) and that once the market realized that war would continue, prices would climb. A few weeks later, he was pleased when writing to his brother to confirm that he had been proven right and that the cotton trade was brisk and cotton prices higher following Abraham Lincoln's reelection and the end of any hope of a negotiated settlement.

From the family's perspective, the American Civil War was in two parts: During the first two years of the war, David was still in control but delegating more to Abdallah; in the second part, as his health began to deteriorate, he took more of a backseat but still received regular updates. The system David created proved itself in those testing days due not only to the trust prevailing among the brothers, but more because each and all shared common objectives.

As the locus of decision-making at the very top of the company started to shift perceptibly away from David toward Abdallah, the makeup farther down the business was also changing. The Sassoons had mostly recruited their staff from their own Jewish community, and from time to time one of David's sons would be sent to Baghdad to encourage young men and their families to move to pastures new. Hiring employees from families the Sassoons knew helped build trust and enabled the company to continue its correspondence in a dialect that was indecipherable to outsiders even as it grew. Pledges by the family to sponsor schools and hospitals in Bombay, together with the prospect of personal riches, convinced many to move to the East, and some graduates of the Sassoon business went on to create their own fortunes. As news of David's success and charitable work spread, young Baghdadi Jews migrated to Bombay hoping to imitate him and make their own fortunes. For them, "to be a co-religionist of David Sassoon was in the middle of the nineteenth century a well-defined career." But hiring these "locals" was not foolproof. Senior employees were often sent to distant locations, outside direct supervision. The family relied heavily on such people and, when problems arose, had to get rid of them without seriously damaging the business. Writing from Pune, India, to his brother Suleiman in Hong Kong, Abdallah complained about one such employee and his repeated demands for a larger cut of the fees for the different trades he conducted in cotton and gold. Abdallah had paid the man higher fees for two trades, but the employee kept badgering him for more. "Since I no longer have

Panoramic view of Pune, 1870.

the strength to hear such claims," he decided to end this relationship, a decision supported by his brothers. In another instance, the family complained that since their new employee had arrived in Ningbo in China, they were "the worst informed" and wondered if he was working behind their backs for his own benefit. They had an equally tough time replacing good employees who wanted to leave their posts. In one case, an employee wanted to leave Ningbo and return to Bombay, and the family was not sure whom to transfer there in his stead and how much to pay him, as business had declined in Ningbo. With the expansion of the family business and the reluctance of Baghdadi Jews to be stationed for long periods in remote areas in Japan and China, a number of English professionals were hired in London and sent to the Far East, as it was felt the business needed their professionalism and sophistication. One son even called on the family to hire only Englishmen on the grounds that they were less greedy and troublesome than the Baghdadi Jews.

By the early 1860s, the incredible success and meteoric rise had taken their toll on David, now in his seventies. He was spending the

David donated to the erection of a hospital in Pune a few years
before his death in 1864. It was completed in 1867.

bulk of his time outside Bombay, maintaining contact with his sons
by letter and returning only infrequently to the city to head off crises,
meet with high officials, or indulge in entertainment. He had built a
summer retreat in Pune, eighty miles inland of Bombay, and called it
Garden Reach. The evenings there were cool and peaceful, while the
beautiful scenery and adjacent lush gardens made for a perfect morning's stroll. Health was on his mind. He contributed to the construction of a nearby hospital, boasting some 150 beds. Though he did not
live to see its completion, the hospital operates to this day and still
carries his name, its 2,500 beds serving Pune's poor, irrespective of
their religion or caste.

David wasn't prone to sentimentality, but if he allowed himself a
moment of reflection, he would surely have recognized the singular
nature of his achievement. The Baghdadi Jewish dialect of his childhood was now spoken in a string of offices, stretching from London
to Yokohama, and inscribed in the voluminous correspondence that
flowed between them. This private language set him, his sons, and
their employees apart. It allowed the different nodes of the information nexus they had developed to communicate with one another
discreetly but also cemented an idea: They were one company, regardless of the territory they operated in and laws they operated under,
with a single name, work ethic, and strategy. Providence had of course
played its part, and the firm was buoyed by the wider growth in inter-

national trade that the industrialization of the world's major economies prompted, but the Sassoons' success exceeded that of all but
a few merchant families. One competitor summed up the period:
"Silver and gold, silks, gums and spices, opium and cotton, wool and
wheat—whatever moves over sea or land feels the hand or bears the
mark of Sassoon & Co."

5

DEATH AND DIVISION

1864–1867

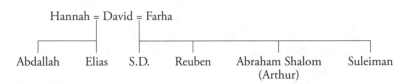

As the American Civil War reached its terminal phase, David's health continued to worsen. He died in Pune on November 7, 1864, at the age of seventy-one. Only his wife was with him at the time, but as soon as the news reached Bombay, Abdallah and the other brothers who were in Bombay rushed to Pune. This "venerable head of the Jewish community of Bombay" was quickly buried in the grounds of Pune's synagogue, the construction of which he had helped set in motion a year before, though it would not be completed until 1867. The synagogue, called Ohel ("Tent of") David, is a strikingly beautiful red-brick building with a tall tower surrounded by a small green park. Today, a mausoleum in its grounds contains David's marble tomb. Each of its four sides is engraved: two with quotes from the Hebrew Bible that speak to his great personality and deeds; another, in English, with the dates of his birth and death according to the Hebrew calendar; and the last with the family crest, a later addition.

David's death, although not sudden, shook the family to its core.

After all, it was he who had in the three decades since his arrival in Bombay started the business from scratch and built it into a global force. He had been the dominant personality, with no relative daring to cross him, demanding respect without qualification and receiving it. It was entirely in keeping with this, then, that the subject of succession was never discussed while he was alive. Deference in this instance would prove detrimental. The very first sentence of David's will, signed in early January 1862, set the parameters of the division of the business that would in short order follow:

> This is the last Will and Testament of me David Sassoon, of Bombay, Jewish Merchant, made in manner and form following that is to say, I appoint my sons, Abdulla [*sic*] David Sassoon and Sassoon David Sassoon to be Executors and Trustees of this my Will.

Elias, his second son, is notable by his absence. Why? Why did he instead name the oldest son from both his marriages? Was it to make it clear that he valued the children of his first and second wives equally? Was David applying the principle of male primogeniture more equitably? Had he fallen out with Elias, or had Abdallah influenced his father's choice? A final question that remains unanswered: Did David even share the contents of his will, which had been drafted three years before his death, with any of his sons? We don't, alas, have the answers. We can say, however, that Abdallah was almost fifty years old when his father died and didn't believe that he needed Elias as an equal partner. But Elias's contribution to the business already far outweighed that of his half brother S.D. After all, he was the one who had built the business in China and created a profitable trade network that took deft advantage of the two Opium Wars.

David gave generously to charitable causes throughout his life, and unsurprisingly that was the subject of the next item in his will. He bequeathed the sum of eighty thousand rupees to one or more of the following:

> The erection at Bombay of a Hospital for sick persons, or the purchase and maintenance at Bombay of a burying-place for

Jews, or the establishment, endowment and maintenance or support of poor and indigent persons of my nation at Jerusalem our Holy and ancient City whose future restoration and Glory are foretold by our Prophets.

In addition to providing money and a monthly stipend to his wife, he ordered his lawyer to take care of all her needs during her lifetime and bequeathed his house in Byculla to her. However, the house on Forbes Street—used both as a residence and as the Sassoons' offices in Bombay—went to his eldest son, Abdallah, with a stipulation that the land would not be sold for fifty-one years after his death so as to maintain "a remembrance of me and of my name in Bombay." Money was left to each of his daughters irrespective of their marital status and he empowered the trustees to pay for the education of all children in the family. One question that arose from the will: As the furniture in all the houses owned by David Sassoon was bequeathed to his wife, it was not clear who should inherit the horses and carriages. Abdallah wrote to his brothers that from his point of view, he was willing "to give up these carriages to the widow [his stepmother, Farha] if the others consented."

Having settled the personal issues, David turned his attention to the business:

I declare that from and after my decease my said eldest son Abdulla [*sic*] David Sassoon will be the head of the co-partnership business which I and he now carry on in conjunction with my son Elias David Sassoon and other persons as Merchants under the style or Firm of David Sassoon and Company. And I desire the partners in the said business to continue to use the name or style of [David Sassoon & Co.] . . . and to respect and defer to my said son Abdulla David Sassoon as the senior Partner and head of the said business.

Thus, without any ambiguity, David crowned his eldest son head of the firm. Elias was mentioned only once in the will's nine pages, as one of the partners. As if anticipating objections, David underscored the point:

I enjoin upon all my children to respect and obey my said eldest son Abdulla David Sassoon as the head and senior member of the Family and request and advise all my sons to entertain brotherly affection and regard for each other and on no account to allow any quarrel or dissension to arise amongst them, but to live in peace and harmony with each other that they may enjoy together the bountiful wealth which the Almighty God has bestowed upon us.

This final wish would be in vain. The business would remain united for three painful years before it was formally divided. It is not known when Elias announced to the family members his intention to branch out on his own. It seems that he and Abdallah attempted to reconcile at first. There is in the family archives a draft of an agreement between the two dated September 25, 1865, almost a year after their father's death. It stated that a joint fund was to be set up by the end of that year and that all proceeds in China, England, and Japan (but not in India), including income or profits from investments, would be divided between the two in accordance with their share of investments.

More important was the section in the draft agreement dealing with all agency fees from opium trading, which, after deducting salaries and rental expenses, were to be divided 60/40 between Abdallah and Elias respectively. Another section aimed to prevent nepotism within the family: "Children of partners that work in [the company's] offices to be trained, would have no entitlement [to any profit] unless there is a consensus that they are essential. Master Abdallah will decide their salaries as he deems right." The agreement also called for the charity contribution of 0.25 percent per transaction initiated by David Sassoon to be continued. Here again, Abdallah would decide where these contributions would be directed, but he could consult his partner Elias if needed. The document has a few unclear edits in pencil and it states that it was handed to a legal expert to finalize. Only Abdallah's name appears on the draft; the agreement was never formalized. We don't know who pulled out of the deal. Perhaps it was opposed by the pair's other siblings, as it clearly demoted them, reducing their share of the company profits and authority in decision-making. Suleiman, who had toiled for years in Hong Kong and Shanghai, as well as Arthur and

S.D. in London, with their critical connections to the great and the good in Britain, undoubtedly would have had reservations. Perhaps Elias, ambitious as ever, simply determined that his brightest future lay outside the family business.

There is no mention in the archives of any rift between Abdallah and Elias in the first two years after David's death, but it seems that immediately after the details of the will became known, another old dispute resurfaced. It centered on Abdallah's frustration with what he perceived as his brother Reuben's inattention to the business and unwillingness to heed his advice. In late January 1865, a couple of months after David's death, Abraham Shalom (Arthur) wrote to Suleiman that he was happy to see that good relations between Abdallah and Reuben had been restored: "It is time for all the brothers to unite to crown Abdallah, and with God's help. May we love each other and work in solidarity to maintain the great reputation of our family that our father, may his soul be blessed, built." Abraham Shalom attributed the improvement in relations and decrease in tension to the departure of his widowed mother to London.

There is no doubt that the family felt the void left by their father keenly. Consoling Suleiman, S.D. wrote:

> Oh, my brother, do not grieve, and we must accept this thing with love from God. We cannot forget our father and his kindness, not even for one minute. Let us hope that we will continue in the path of our father. Amen.

Yet, the wheels kept turning. In spite of the Jewish tradition of observing seven days of mourning after the death of a family member, only four days after David's passing, business correspondence started to be sent from Hong Kong to Shanghai.

Abdallah rallied his brothers and emphasized the need for unity to continue what their father had begun: "We are all transient on this earth, but what our compassionate father left us, we must continue. We must be loving and supportive to each other, so that we raise our name in this world." With the support of his brothers, Abdallah laid out his plans to build a statue of his father in Bombay, enshrining his memory in the city David had made his home. In the same letter that announced his leadership of the family, he told his brother Suleiman that he was hosting an "evening party" for the Governor and 150 guests, contrary to Jewish tradition, which dictated that grieving families did not hold large celebrations until a year had passed after the death of a loved one.

All members of the family were instructed to collect donations from the business communities in India and China for the memorial. Abraham Shalom, in charge of the House of Hong Kong, complained that few were replying and offering only small amounts, and a few months later, Abdallah grumbled that the only thing to reach him from Hong Kong had been empty promises. If they were disappointed by the response, the family would have been reassured that the statue's unveiling, which was marked by newspapers around the world, did their father justice. Sculpted by Thomas Woolner (1825–92), the statue was first displayed in the South Kensington Museum, known today as the Victoria and Albert Museum, and then transferred to the entrance of the Mechanics' Institute in Bombay, which the Sassoons founded, when this building was completed. *The Illustrated London News* commented, "The head is well modelled and appears to be a strong likeness, though probably not free from the exaggeration which is Mr. Woolner's besetting fault." David's palms are open, facing upward. "The hands, however, are unexceptionable, and, indeed admirable, both as regards modelling and carving. The attitude is that of Oriental thanksgiving—as though acknowledging the profuse bestowal of the Divine benefits." *The London and China Telegraph* wrote:

> The ease of the attitude and simplicity of the design are as well marked in the draperies which fall from the shoulders backwards in the long, full, and rich folds of woollen cloth, as in the front of the effigy. These seem to have a human form instinct with life within them, and not, as is common, a wooden frame.

Today, the statue adorns the entrance of what is now the David Sassoon Library in Mumbai. Standing before it, one has the impression of a religious figure, a prophet rather than a merchant. More down-to-earth is the marble bust of David, advertised as "Mumbai's most famous Jewish businessman and philanthropist," at the Bhau Daji Lad Museum in Byculla.

CRISIS MANAGEMENT

Just five months after David's death, the company he had founded faced what seemed to be its first existential threat. As the war in America drew to a close, there were signs that the cotton market was losing steam and a great number of traders had too much stock. The sharp rise in cotton output in India during the war had been matched elsewhere, particularly in Egypt and Brazil, and global oversupply was a major concern. By the beginning of April, as General Robert

Statue of David Sassoon by Thomas Woolner, 1869, as it is shown today at the David Sassoon Library in Mumbai.

E. Lee abandoned the Confederate capital to the Union Army, reports circulated that cotton traders were experiencing big losses and that the steep fall in prices was creating havoc as traders did their utmost to unload their stock. The announcement of the peace prompted a flood of bankruptcies. Panic spread around the world from Bombay to Liverpool. In June 1865, the House of Hong Kong informed the House of Shanghai that H. B. Cama, a large merchant house, had filed for bankruptcy, sending shock waves throughout the system. Cama was one of the largest Parsi merchant houses, with offices in London, Calcutta, Singapore, and China. Some reports put the losses left by Cama at more than three million pounds sterling. Its failure rippled outward, each domino knocking down the next, and a number of bankruptcies of other merchant houses followed as a result. By the end of the month, even the Bank of Bombay faced serious financial difficulties. A year later, it was estimated that 80 percent of Bombay's cotton traders were near bankruptcy. Abdallah confessed to his brothers that no one within the family, or for that matter in the financial community of London or Bombay, had expected these difficulties to spread so far, and that all the traders were taken aback by the devastation. S.D. admitted to Suleiman that he could not sleep for worry and opined that every member of the family had to be vigilant in order to avoid large losses, since that would damage the most important element in their business—their reputation.

A new nervousness crept into the family correspondence. Disagreements about trade and more continued, but in tones that were appreciably terser. "I am worried that your House is delaying sending my share of the revenues while you transferred swiftly double that amount to the House of Bombay," wrote Abraham Shalom to Suleiman. Amid all this, the allocation of the inheritance began. Each of David's sons was informed by the firm that the executor had released to them "One Lac [lakh, a unit in Indian currency equal to 100,000 rupees] of Rupees," roughly £10,000, or £1 million today, "as a payment to you out of the residuary estate of your late father." Furthermore, there was a payment of 43,700 rupees in a government bond of 5.5 percent derived from the division of 3.5 lakhs into eight parts—one for each son. The firm was to hold these sums until it received instructions from each son. Needless to say, the sons felt "greatly grieved at the very disastrous state of financial and commercial matters in Bombay which has so largely depreciated the value of the properties/shares appertaining to the estate." The greater part of their inheritance was the company itself.

In the years before David's death, as we have seen, David Sassoon & Co. had turned its attention for the first time to activities beyond trade, such as real estate, insurance, and banking. This was a move that would safeguard the family's interests for decades to come, but the financial crisis that swept India in the mid-1860s decimated and strengthened the banking industry in turn, and for a time it looked to be little compensation for the struggling cotton market. At its nadir, an estimated twenty-four of thirty-one banks in Bombay failed, and many Indian firms that acted as money brokers for small exporting firms were ruined. Some traders, however, managed to survive and even flourish, and those needed well-capitalized and properly managed banks. Even the bankrupt traders stimulated the creation of many banking institutions, because their liquidation required banking oversight, and new corporations emerged from the turmoil: cotton presses, steam navigation companies, marine insurance firms, and shipping agencies.

At the beginning of the decade, the family had invested in the Bank of Hindustan, obtaining a spot on its board of directors a couple of years later. After S.D. conducted a weeklong review with the bank's manager in October 1865, he concluded that the bank's business was healthier than he had feared. A statement by the bank indicated that it had ended the year with a modest profit of £15,000, depressed by "the peculiar and exceptional character" of the events in India, and investors were assured that these unexpected circumstances were over. Fears of another financial crisis prompted a more conservative approach by the family the following year: "No trust remains in the banks. We do not want any shares of any bank whether in London or India." Though the stalwarts of India's banking industry seemed to have stabilized relatively quickly, their recovery was far from assured: From a letter dated 1867 it is clear that the family was once again concerned about the Bank of Hindustan's losses.

The family had also invested heavily in the National Bank of China. It was a serious and prestigious institution, but more important, the bank's profits were solid and its dividends attractive. As merchants realized the potential for banking services given the triangular trade between Britain, India, and China, additional investment was made in the Mercantile Bank of India, established in 1853, after which it filed for a royal charter to be registered in London. Unusually, the Mercantile Bank was a joint Indo-European enterprise rather than a purely British one. Abdallah Sassoon became one of its directors in Bombay. The Sassoons' relationships with Persian traders (and later their relationship with the Shah) were strengthened by the Imperial Bank of Persia, which focused more than the other banks on trade between Iran on one side and the Persian Gulf and Asia on the other, and it facilitated opium and tea trading in the region.

The bank that lay at the heart of the Sassoon enterprise, however, and with which they were associated from its beginning, was the Hongkong and Shanghai Banking Corporation. It was created in

March 1865 "to finance intra-regional trade among the open ports of China, Japan and the Philippines." Although Jardine Matheson was headquartered in Hong Kong and thus a natural partner, it was excluded from the board due to its fierce competition with David Sassoon & Co.—an indication of the depth of the Sassoons' involvement as well as the shifting fortunes of the two mercantile firms. Abraham Shalom was appointed to the bank's provisional committee in August 1864 and later to its board, and for six months in 1867 was its deputy chairman. When he resigned early in 1868, he was replaced by Suleiman. According to the bank's official biographer, the brothers "may well have provided a much-needed stabilizing influence, balancing to some extent the enthusiasm of the entrepreneurs." In return, the bank financed trade between India and China, particularly the opium trade, and the Sassoons' continued association with it gave them a considerable competitive advantage in their trade in the region.

This interweaving of different dimensions of business was characteristic of the Sassoons. As they began to buy and rent property in India and China, they always opted to rent premises to banks they worked with, or even buy land directly from them, as they did with property held by the Commercial Bank in Yokohama. Likewise, renting property to government as offices was profitable (and reliable), but no less important, officials made for useful tenants. Telling Reuben about his recent meeting with the Governor in Bombay, in which he was thanked for aiding the Governor with a bungalow rental and for the family's support in general, Abdallah was pleased to report that the Governor had then invited him to a party at his house. As well as providing an important source of revenue in China, India, and Japan in later decades, investments in banks and real estate fostered stronger ties with Indian traders, particularly the Parsis, such as Jamsetjee Jejeebhoy and the Tatas.

From lard to coal, whenever an opportunity arose and they had the right contact, the Sassoons traded the item. The Sassoons found out that Chinese gold was cheaper than Bombay gold and sold more briskly, and so gold was traded occasionally if one of the branches believed that it could turn a profit. A small branch set up in Singapore began to import sugar from Java to meet the demand in India. Coral was brought from Amoy (Xiamen), and the brother in charge of Hong

Kong at the time, Suleiman, was encouraged to sell the shipment as soon as possible given that the profits from coral were limited; when they realized that high-quality coral would sell in Japan, they began exporting it there.

The decade that saw David's death also saw his firm elevated to the first rank of global traders and laid the foundations for their dominant role in the opium trade during the 1870s and 1880s. Commercial success continued in spite of familial rifts.

SCHISM

Although the panic and bankruptcies of the financial crisis paralyzed most of the cotton trade, opium exports from India to China continued to grow throughout the 1860s and the family was determined to ensure a dominant role for the houses of Sassoon. The Sassoons avoided major losses, but the viability of the agents and brokers with whom they did business was a constant worry. The decline in cotton prices that followed the American Civil War reverberated throughout India, and for shippers and agents operating from Bombay, the risk of financial difficulties increased substantially, compounding persistent problems the family had in their dealings with them. However, the failure of many traders also left a vacuum in the market, which the family used to its advantage. The Sassoons' effective management of risk during the American Civil War and its aftermath allowed them to expand their trading capacity despite the circumstances. By early 1868 calm had returned to the markets, and the various branches were reporting higher prices for cotton and increased demand for all brands of opium. In spite of all this, the chasm between the two eldest brothers, Abdallah and Elias, continued to widen, to the point indeed where it could no longer be bridged.

At the bottom of the rift was the thorny subject of accounting. From the beginning, the company had kept meticulous accounting ledgers recording every trade and transaction. The ledgers for opium exhaustively detail the type, number of chests, and costs—all expenses incurred by each branch are listed, and the usual charitable donation of 0.25 percent allocated per transaction. A snippet from a ledger from 1870 gives a good sense:

28 March: Paid for Hong Kong and Shanghai Bank for the first
    call to purchase shares of Victoria Insurance.
6 March: Paid the money exchangers their expenses.
4 March: Paid for 12 opium chests that were shipped on *Elora*.
5 August: Paid to Oriental bank for purchase of a land plot.
16 October: Purchase of 5 boxes of gold.
21 October: Purchase of silk for Amam [Abdallah's sister].

David had realized early on that his sons would need to learn how
to trade for themselves, to encourage their entrepreneurial instincts
and help them understand the different levels of risk. Thus, in addition to trading on behalf of the family, each of David's sons ran his
own trading business. Time and again, the correspondence prescribes
that a particular loss or gain be attributed to an individual account
rather than that of the family. The potential for conflicts of interest
was substantial, and clashes inevitably erupted whenever the price of
a commodity rose and all the brothers wanted to have it on their own
accounts, and exactly the opposite when the price of a commodity
slid. The boundary between personal and company trading was sufficiently blurred that Abdallah could use it to police Abraham Shalom's
decisions, for example: "I know you are interested in buying lard from
Ja'far Salman. Oh brother, I know you will sell it for half the price. In
fact, we have in our bungalow, Sans Souci, and in other bungalows
enough for you to sell . . . you are independent and can do whatever
you want, but you should know this will be for your account only." If
one brother did not like the price of a commodity, the one proposing
its purchase would have to carry the risk: "Let us stop buying cotton at these prices unless there is a panic in Shanghai. Otherwise the
risk must be for your account." On a different occasion the opposite
took place: When the price of shirting soared in 1865, one brother
complained that Elias had blocked a purchase that could have been
profitable, and this was not fair as it would not be reflected in his
account. The complaints, rebukes, and disapproval for losses or bad
purchases were unrelenting and the system encouraged the personal
attribution of blame at the expense of the collective. While David was
alive, he alone was exempt from this tirade of criticism. It was clear to
all who was in charge.

The budgets of each branch were another long-standing source of friction among the brothers. Demands from the satellite offices to the main one (first Bombay, then Shanghai and later London) for looser budgets and better allocations never ceased. In November 1860, the House of Hong Kong wrote to the House of Shanghai to suggest co-ordinating their demands that headquarters in Bombay double their working budget from one hundred thousand to two hundred thousand rupees. Every member of the family had individual debit and credit records that were prepared and consolidated at the end of the month and later at the end of the year. Each branch had its own team of accountants—all of them Baghdadis writing in the ledgers in their distinctive language. Coordinating their efforts could itself be a source of irritation, as a letter (written in English) from Suleiman in Shanghai to his nephew Joseph in Hong Kong shows:

> I am quite sick for not receiving a/c [account] sales of goods
> at your place as folks in Bombay are extremely anxious about
> it, and by every mail they write to remit to London on a/c
> of these goods. Hoping you will exercise your best efforts in
> making sales as fast as possible.

Branches regularly lambasted one another. Hong Kong can be seen complaining to the head office in Bombay in 1866 about Shanghai's handling of their dealings in opium and demanding that they be reprimanded. The head office likewise received its share of criticism:

> Bombay will send [its] people to Hong Kong soon, and I have
> to hand over the work, fully and neatly to their service. My
> house [in Hong Kong] being subordinate to Bombay House,
> they [Bombay] are not obliged to care for what I or others
> want . . . we have to obey everything they command.

Abdallah's absence is striking. Criticism was seemingly reserved for those in his employ in Bombay. Yet, although he would maintain the respect of the majority of the family, Abdallah would never be able to replicate his father's absolute authority.

Some of the tension between David's sons may have been by design, the father's way of stoking the spirit of competitiveness in his sons to prepare them to best others. Certainly we can see them urging one another on: "Do not let [other merchants] outdo you." And each respected his siblings enough to recognize that their presence in the different trade centers was essential and that no employee, however experienced and reliable, could replace them. As Reuben, seeking to dissuade Suleiman from abandoning his post in China, observed in 1868:

> As far as I understand, at the end of your work period, you
> want to return from China. I ask you to think and let me
> know by whose hand you will finally [trust] the great work of
> our trading house in China? I think it is imperative that one
> of us takes the place as head of the trading houses in China.

Long separation from home and family took its toll on David's sons. It was difficult for everyone, especially during the 1850s, when travel was more physically demanding and hazardous, but it seems this always came second to the imperative to grow and expand the reach of the family business. As David had written to Suleiman eight years prior, opening with the customary paternal salutation:

> To my dear son, the light of my eyes [this was David Sassoon's
> standard line in writing to his sons] . . . you mentioned that
> if you had a permit from me, you would have sailed to India
> and you would have stayed with us for 3–4 months, since it
> has been almost 5 years since our separation and you have
> been in Shanghai 3–4 years, I would have been very happy
> with your arrival, especially as we are in Pune and there is
> nothing to do, because these are times when we have to be far
> from each other.

A year later, we learn that this emotional exchange made no difference. David wrote to Suleiman to say that the search for someone to replace him in Shanghai had been hindered by an argument between Abdallah and Reuben. Saddened by this conflict, David advised Suleiman to focus on core commodities (particularly opium) and not take on any others until another employee arrived to lighten his workload. He reminded his son, once again, that the family's reputation was vital and warned that his being overworked might negatively impact the activities of David Sassoon & Sons. It is unclear whether Suleiman's unhappiness was due to his personal circumstances (he was then a bachelor) or business ones. Born in 1841, he was known to be serious and industrious (and, like his father, possessing a scholarly interest in the Talmud), and he found Bombay's involvement overbearing. He enjoyed exploring and was particularly fascinated by Japan, whose beauty and culture captivated him.

Resentment could and did build when some brothers began traveling extensively for leisure while others remained at the coalface—especially if they expected their share of the winning trades conducted in their absence. By the late 1860s, Arthur (as Abraham Shalom had Anglicized his name) was spending his summers traveling across Europe, all the while writing to Suleiman, then stuck in humid Hong Kong, to describe the beauty and serenity of Bruges and Baden-Baden and ask his brother to sell or buy shipments on his behalf. Adding insult to injury, he also rebuked him for not fulfilling his orders and for being late in transferring money or replying to counterparts.

Tension between the brothers intensified as they sparred about trades and property. Just a few months after the death of their father, S.D. and Reuben clashed over the ownership of Ashley Park, the estate at Walton-on-Thames. According to Arthur, S.D. and Reuben had bought the property in partnership before squabbling about who should control it (in reality, it had been bought by David for S.D.). Arthur, dismayed at the proximity of this conflict to their father's death, was particularly concerned that Abdallah had not intervened to mediate and worried the issue might even end up in court. Although he was not sure who was right or wrong, Arthur was drawn to Reuben, closer in age and the more personable of the two, but ultimately it was S.D. and his family who retained Ashley Park.

David's presence had been sufficient to keep such disagreements in check. After his death, however, they started to bubble to the surface, and the recriminations in the brothers' correspondence grew more acerbic. S.D. wrote to Suleiman, "[I am] sad and upset that you did not reply to my letters and I am extremely disappointed that you refused to transfer the shipment to my account." Abdallah reproached Arthur for not sending him copies of his correspondence with S.D. Meanwhile Arthur complained to Suleiman that the House of Shanghai hadn't credited his account with what was due to him while it hastened to send revenues to headquarters to please Bombay and the new chief, Abdallah. Arthur went so far as to ridicule Abdallah's decision to send "a special ambassador" to help the ailing company of their brother-in-law—"Where does he think he is living that he pretends he could send someone to solve all the problems?"—and criticized offices for interfering in one another's affairs, increasing the company's expenses and restricting its revenues.

Such insubordination—unthinkable in David's lifetime—spilled over to the brothers' employees, who sensed that they could take advantage of arguments between brothers. One London-based employee, writing to Suleiman, suffixed his usual respects and offering of prayers for health and prosperity with a stinging criticism about the way Bombay was handling the sale of some diamonds, crediting itself while London accumulated a debit of £325,000, and expressed his surprise that Bombay had canceled the insurance on opium shipments without even bothering to inform London. Aharon Gabbay, both Abdallah's son-in-law and a senior employee, grumbled to Suleiman that Arthur had not fulfilled his duties when he had visited Calcutta and failed to deal with an issue around maritime insurance, creating serious difficulties with some agents. Gabbay also felt that Shanghai was in bad shape and "retreating backwards," as did his wife, Rachel, who likewise wrote to her uncle Suleiman the following day imploring him to go there and investigate some financial irregularities. Sensing criticism emanating from different branches, Abdallah wrote to a trusted employee in Bushir in Persia, "All my actions are for the sake of [our] work and trade, and for protecting our reputation, and not for enjoyment." Whenever the family intended to expand and open new branches, some tension arose until all issues were ironed out. In 1865, when a branch in Calcutta was planned, the oldest brother, Abdallah, traveled there with an employee—who was later put in charge of the new branch—to work out the logistics. But there was another reason for opening this branch: It was thought that taxes charged on opium trading would be lower if certain family members or employees became residents of Calcutta. Later, several family members moved to live permanently in Calcutta and even stayed behind when the others left India after the closure of the business during the Second World War.

Attempts to ameliorate some of the sources of enmity between the brothers were made. When Suleiman moved to Hong Kong early in 1867, he composed a document setting out the full responsibilities and rights of the office there, doubtless to avoid the kind of conflicts that had arisen during his tenure in Shanghai. Suleiman proposed that each main office have its own *amanat* (trusteeship), reflected in its accounting books as *amanat* Hong Kong, *amanat* Shanghai, and so on, giving each office greater independence in handling its own affairs. The document, which bears the pencil markings of multiple edits, suggests that trading profits earned in Hong Kong and Shanghai be split 50/50 with Bombay and that Suleiman would not take out any loans or risk the reputation of the firm without first notifying Bombay, and details how each branch should charge or pay agency fees to prevent duplication and ensure that all accounts would be transparent to all sides. This blend of practicality and diplomacy was characteristic of Suleiman. He tended to withdraw from his siblings' clashes, directing his energy instead toward expanding and developing the business.

Within months of Suleiman's move to Hong Kong, not quite three years after David's death, the simmering tensions between the two eldest brothers culminated in a permanent split. From then on, two global businesses, both carrying the family name, would compete head-to-head. Abdallah would remain head of David Sassoon & Co. and Elias would take charge of his own firm, E. D. Sassoon & Co. In contrast to Suleiman's attempt to rationalize the relationship between the various branches of the original firm, the family archives preserve few traces of this tectonic divergence. Indeed, they refer to it only after the fact, and exclusively in legalistic jargon about the division of assets and the need to inform counterparts that Elias and his son Jacob had left David Sassoon & Co. and thus lacked signing rights. Intriguingly, there are vanishingly few letters to or from Elias anywhere in the archives, even from prior to his departure. We can't be sure why.

Perhaps when the archives were first organized, his family, still separate from the rest, retrieved his papers. Maybe he took them with him when he left, or they were later deemed unimportant to the business and destroyed. How Elias's break with Abdallah really unfolded, what offers and entreaties were made and rejected, is therefore unknowable, but this absence in the archives seems in itself telling. There was no going back.

6

COMPETITION WITHIN THE FAMILY

1867–1871

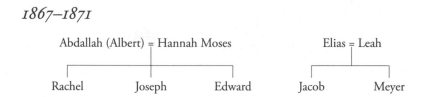

Abdallah (Albert) = Hannah Moses   Elias = Leah

Rachel   Joseph   Edward   Jacob   Meyer

Elias had been among the first Jews to enter China after the conclusion of the First Opium War and settle in one of the ports
in which foreign traders were permitted to live. Others followed in
subsequent years, and by the time Elias had established Shanghai as
the firm's primary hub in China, he was one of the figureheads of the
small but close community there, responsible probably more than any
other individual for "safeguarding the identity" of Baghdadi Jews who
had settled in Shanghai. Even when apart from his co-religionists, he
attempted to observe Jewish ritual; apparently every member of his
family was taught to slaughter chickens in accordance with Jewish law,
to enable them to eat kosher even when traveling to regions of China
where there were no Jews whatsoever. As in his father's firm, no work
was conducted on the Sabbath or during Jewish festivals.

Although their very presence in China was testament to the new
connections wrought by globalization's more muscular manifestations
in the nineteenth century, life in the treaty ports was an insular affair.
Foreigners had very little contact with the locals and a rigid set of
rules dictated their segregation. The favored legal status enjoyed by

expatriates codified this separateness, and the Chinese were often in-visible to them. Even commerce was conducted not directly but rather through compradors, Chinese agents who were knowledgeable about local trading and regulations and fluent in the local languages. The Sassoons, who sought to understand the culture and business prac-tices of all the regions in which they traded, failed to learn any of China's languages.

By the time of the split, Elias had been resident in China for a quarter of a century. In that time, he had likely contributed more to the firm's bottom line than anyone else, save his father, and after he set out on his own, he was determined to prove to all that he and his enterprise were the true inheritors of David's legacy. His first instinct was therefore not to differentiate himself but to signal continuity. This may have counted against him initially, as clients and counter-parts, particularly outside India, were confused by the two companies' shared name, leading the Chinese to differentiate between the two by calling the original firm "the old Sassoon" and E. D. Sassoon "the new Sassoon." Following in his father's footsteps, Elias made his eldest son a partner in the new firm. Jacob, aged twenty-four, had been posted to China two years before the split and had proved himself expanding the business into new cities across the country. His younger brothers would follow as soon as they reached the age of eighteen, and four of them were dispatched over the next decade to manage different locations in a network of branches very similar to the system set up by their grandfather. Only after they had distinguished themselves would they be appointed partners of E. D. Sassoon & Co. (Not all were quick studies: Meyer, Elias's fifth son, would work for three years in a number of locations before making partner.) Elias was a great believer, similar to his father, in the significance of philanthropy and gave to charities throughout his life. After he started his own company, he visited Calcutta in 1868 and gave a large donation to the local government to help the poor, and did the same two years later on a visit to Madras. In Bombay, he helped to set up a Jewish school and contributed to the Jewish cemetery in the city.

Elias was affected by his upbringing—by a dominant father—and he believed that the family did not appreciate his tremendous efforts in building the business and felt that it was totally unfair that Abdallah was crowned the head of the family after their father's death. Family tragedies shaped his thinking, particularly toward religion and charities. In late 1868, scarcely a year after Elias had broken off from the family firm, his third son, Joseph, died suddenly at the age of seventeen. According to *The London and China Telegraph,* the son had gone to sleep in good health but was found dead in the morning by a servant. Physicians and surgeons were called to investigate, and it was reported that the cause of death was "a highly congested state of the lungs" stemming from "a charcoal stove that had been alight in the room all night." The demise of this charismatic and entrepreneurial young man shocked the foreign settlement in Shanghai and the Jewish community beyond. It was the first test of familial ties after the severing of commercial ones. The family gathered around Elias and his wife, Leah, to offer their condolences and support: "His sudden death in Hong Kong caused pain for everyone. This is destiny and we have no say in it." Even Abdallah, dismayed by the recent split, expressed his deep sorrow. Tellingly, however, he made no mention of his brother: "We are extremely saddened by the death of Joseph. Pity his lost youth. We made a lot of effort that his mother does not find out as she sailed to Cairo. We all have to be strong to carry this heavy anguish."

The division of the family pushed both firms to be more competitive, not only with each other but also with their rivals. It forced both sides to think of innovative ways to reach new markets and trade lucrative products. Upon Elias's death in 1880, his four sons took over the business, but as tradition dictated, his eldest son, Jacob, aged thirty-six, took charge.

Abdallah had been at the helm of David Sassoon & Co. since 1864 and would remain there for the next thirty years, and under his leadership the firm was transformed into a truly global enterprise. He entered new ventures not only to meet Elias's challenge, but also to maintain the company's reputation as a successful international trading house. Abdallah's ambitions were not purely economic, however. He aspired to join the political and social elite, first in his adoptive home, India, and then in Britain. For him, politics were far more closely intertwined with business than for his father, and he was much more concerned with establishing himself in Indian society even before he turned his attention to Britain.

For the first three years after David's death, however, Abdallah had concentrated his energies on consolidating his position and, in accordance with his father's wishes, preventing a break with his brother. When this failed and Elias created a new firm, the challenges were multiplied: Abdallah not only had to deal with E. D. Sassoon as a competitor but felt the whole world looking expectantly at him to see if he, and not Elias, was David's true heir, capable of expanding his firm and furthering the interests of his family while preserving its prestige. As David's eldest son, he had been raised to eventually succeed his father as patriarch of the family and chairman of the business, to continue and further what David had started and bring to the firm new achievements in every sphere. Born in 1818, Abdallah must have been deeply affected by the family's sudden departure from Baghdad in 1830 when he was still a teenager. First, they were refugees in Bushir on the Persian Gulf, and then, after a year, they boarded a ship to an unknown foreign country in Asia where the family had no connections. Seeing his father struggle to create a business in Bombay and fighting to expand it while preserving the family's reputation at all costs marked the young Abdallah with a deep sense of a life mission. His mother died in Baghdad when she was only thirty-two after bearing four children. Abdallah was eight years old and learned early on the meaning of family responsibility and loyalty.

Though Elias's creation of the firm's business in China outshone Abdallah's achievements, they were by no means few or insubstantial. According to one source, he knew seven languages: Arabic, Hebrew, Persian, English, French, Hindustani, and Turkish. At the age of twenty he had married the Bombay-born Hannah Moses, aged twelve, and had three daughters and two sons. He traveled extensively for business and properly settled in Bombay only in 1862 to co-manage the business with his ailing father. He was shrewd, strategic, and sometimes ruthless in his dealings, but without ever losing the essence of the original company. From the middle of that decade on, Abdallah had to grapple with employees increasingly drawn from outside the traditional Baghdadi Jewish pool in increasingly far-flung offices, troublesome siblings, and the growing number of legal entanglements related to claims against agents and counterparties or the rebuttal of accusations against the firm. None of these problems were entirely new, but they were complicated by the growth of the business and, now, competition with E. D. Sassoon.

The management style did not appreciably change after Abdallah formally took charge. After all, he had been more or less running the show from 1862 given his father's poor health. He cared for all members of the family and all their employees much as David had, and likewise continued to rebuke, criticize, and second-guess them. His relationship with Suleiman, at the time based in Hong Kong, was particularly intense. The two corresponded almost daily and although Abdallah loved his brother, he could be extraordinarily hard on him. In one letter, he reminded Suleiman to follow procedure and copy him on all correspondence from Hong Kong or Shanghai about Persian opium. "Do not be negligent," he admonished, before proceeding to criticize his brother's handling of the opium shipments themselves: "For how long will we continue to send money to you and spend here when we have about 1200 chests for sale?" Remarkably, this rebuke was joined in the same letter by thanks offered to Suleiman for responding to his plea of a week earlier to send money as soon as possible to cover losses for the office in London. He declared, "We will never ask you for money anymore after this," underlining this promise. Yet, barely two months later Abdallah wrote again to ask for £10,000 to buy a house and purchase a shipment of butter oil, promising that this shortfall was temporary and "what destiny has imposed."

How Suleiman and the rest of the family reacted to these incessant criticisms and demands is difficult to judge, as every letter sent to Abdallah was courteous and obliging, as his position demanded. Sometimes Abdallah comes across as a compassionate manager concerned for Suleiman's well-being: "Oh, my brother, it has been a long time on my mind but I never wrote to you: I think you need a change of air and a holiday at least two to three times per year, each time for 15 days. If you do not want to do this, because of your commitment and since you do not like to move from home, you must do it for the sake of your health." In other letters, he seems defensive: Three weeks after berating Suleiman over Persian opium, Abdallah declared, "We do not interfere in your opium trade, and whether you decide to buy or not, that we leave to your judgment. We are only asking from time to time whether you bought and how the purchase has gone."

The use of criticism to manage and motivate the firm's partners and employees was not a new technique. David had been a master of the art, and Abdallah was far from the only member of the family to learn it from him. Complaints about the way other houses were handling trades, particularly ones that were not profitable, were unending, as one letter from London to Bombay clearly shows: "Stop complaining, and if you are grumbling, then prove there was a real reason and not just for the sake of complaining." Abdallah's micromanagement knew few boundaries: When he "advised" an employee in Calcutta to wear "English clothes" whenever meeting British officials on official business, he didn't stop at their professional attire: "Of course you decide what is best for you to wear but I think you should always wear English dress." As he aged, he grew even more fastidious; he sent detailed instructions on how parcels of letters should be packaged when sent from one office to another to cut costs and save time. Naturally, employees and other members of the family copied his style; one relative and a senior employee in Bombay counseled Suleiman in Hong Kong "to mix only with successful people."

As the number of offices increased, so too did the firm's head count, and dealing with employees became ever more time-consuming. Some employees, seeking to make fortunes of their own, ended up incurring substantial losses investing outside the firm, leaving Abdallah and the senior partners to decide whether to give them the opportunity to make some money back or decline to bail them out and risk souring relations with otherwise committed and competent subordinates. In all such circumstances employees reminded the partners of their steadfast commitment and loyalty. One pleaded with Abdallah to give him a share of a consignment, as this would "tidy [him] up for the rest of [his] career," and found his wish granted. This largesse didn't stop at traders: Staff who worked for the Sassoons in different capacities likewise had to be taken care of. The father of S.D.'s first English tutor, when discharged from the British navy after a career spanning thirty-five years, asked for a "suitable job in India," and his request was granted. When the overall business declined in the mid-1890s, management in London decided to reduce the salaries of employees in Calcutta by 20 percent, a decision that understandably led to anger and resentment and a petition sent from colonial outpost to headquarters in the metropole. The answer, written in the clipped English of one of a new generation of employees recruited from a province not in the Ottoman Empire but rather in England, was firm: "The Partners desire me to point out that this step was deliberately decided on in consequence of the marked decline of business passing the Branches relatively to former years." London did, however, assure Calcutta that the cut applied to all staff everywhere, and announced "a concession of 5% in favour of [Calcutta's] staff," so that their salaries were reduced by only 15 percent.

The subject of employee loyalty was always high on the agenda, particularly during the first decade after the split, when Elias pursued the family's employees as he sought to build his own firm. We can see one of Suleiman's nephews writing to reassure his uncle of his loyalty in the face of two direct approaches by Elias, who had even made overtures to Mozelle (his mother and David's youngest daughter), and to thank him for persuading Bombay to allow him to engage in more trades and thus grow his own wealth. The stick could also be used, and there was no mercy for those who crossed the line—especially when they weren't a member of the family. In a bizarre incident, Abdallah, in Pune for the summer, was informed that an anonymous letter alleging "betrayal by one of the clerks in London" had reached Bombay. Aharon Moshe Gabbay, one of Abdallah's sons-in-law and a senior figure in the Bombay office, was confident of the identity of the informant in London. He suggested that the partners there investigate and then exile the perpetrator to Fuzhou in China for two or three years until "he forgets all the secrets of our trades."

Trust in subordinates was invariably a major concern for all global merchants. After all, huge sums of money were at stake and competitors were willing to pay handsomely for any sensitive information about trades or inventory that would lead to profitable trades. In a confidential memo to London, one of the firm's representatives in Manchester reported paying a visit to the office of a competitor and coming across a Parsi employee "who divulges what takes place" in his office. He warned, "Bribery is going on to a large extent—as long as this exists, your interests cannot be served," and that leaks would mean losses.

The competition with E. D. Sassoon undoubtedly intensified such worries. Writing to Abdallah, Gabbay warned, "[Elias] will not sit on his laurels and is chasing our people either to recruit them or to ask them to spy for him. Meanwhile, we are sitting quiet watching all these actions," and that Elias would doggedly follow their footsteps and open branches in Calcutta and London—in fact, wherever David Sassoon & Co. was operating. Gabbay was a hawk, convinced of the need to stand up to Elias's firm and "fight him in every corner." In his letters to Abdallah, he repeatedly called upon him to block "the boundless greed of this Elias" and move "to constrain his activities and put him in his place." This was more than healthy competitiveness: Gabbay purposely procrastinated in refunding E. D. Sassoon a percentage of maritime insurance on one shipment of opium for which David Sassoon & Co. had acted as an agent and offered a different excuse to each reminder from Abdallah. Not long after, he implored Abdallah to rally his other brothers to the fight: "Elias is interested to

The Suez Canal opened in 1869, which dramatically changed
trading for global merchants such as the Sassoons
by reducing time and cost.

expand his business and to smash ours, but if the brothers make an effort, he would not be capable of hurting us." Gabbay knew that to get through to Abdallah he needed to scare him not only about lost trades but, more important, about the potential loss of employees.

For Abdallah, it was not so simple. The rupture had bruised him and he was anxious to avoid further strife within the family. And although he didn't want to lose business to his brother, he thought Elias's rapid expansion was reckless and was more concerned about the damage it might do to the family's reputation. "I am so sad to hear about the huge losses that Elias incurred from trading opium. This is a nightmare for me. His greediness will get the better of him." As we shall see, there were other things on Abdallah's mind. His political ambitions in India and the pull of London and English society may have lessened his appetite for the kind of confrontation Gabbay desired.

Eighteen sixty-nine was a landmark for global trade in the nineteenth century and beyond: The opening of the 101-mile-long Suez Canal brought Asia and Europe much closer. The length of a journey from Bombay to London via the Cape of Good Hope was slashed from more than 10,000 nautical miles to about 6,000, reducing shipping costs by 30 percent. A trip from Marseilles to Shanghai was cut dramatically from 110 to 37 days. The opening of the canal thrust new steamship technology forward and made it possible for steamships to compete on Asian routes. As a result, high-tonnage steamers, bound for ports across East Africa and Asia, could pass from the Mediterranean through the canal into the Red Sea and onward to the Indian Ocean. Economic life in Western India in general and Bombay in particular was transformed. The overland route to India, which entailed crossing the Sinai Peninsula by caravan, usually took four to six months, depending on the weather and the speed of the ships to Alexandria. The sea route took between one and two. With the opening of the Suez Canal, the world grew smaller, and the importance of India and Egypt grew, as did the stature of global merchants operating in and knowledgeable about these regions. The Sassoons, once again, were among the pioneers who understood these changes

Docks built by Albert in Bombay and opened in 1874.

and what they meant for global trade. Men such as Abdallah were seen as crucial to Britain's intention to dominate the politics and economics of these countries.

A more immediate consequence of the completion of the canal was a surge in demand for docks for the large ships now entering Bombay on a regular basis. Abdallah was quick to see the opportunity and purchased about 200,000 square feet of land in Colaba, at the tip of the Bombay peninsula, "at a very high price from the late Back Bay Company." In 1874, after three years of construction and excavating out of solid rock, the Sassoon Docks opened for business, easing the approach to Bombay, which was difficult because of the rocky nature of the area, and ships could anchor once a dock and wharf were constructed there, boosting traffic to the port meaningfully. The Sassoon Dock Company was formed and a 999-year lease obtained from the Secretary of State for India. By 1876, the year the Public Works Department (at Abdallah's encouragement) erected telegraph wires to connect the Sassoon offices to the Sassoon Docks, the moorings were bustling. A glance at a manifest of the freight passing through shows immense variety, each product specified by its landing and wharfage rate per week. Within a few years, the sheer volume of traffic at the docks led to calls for public ownership, and the Sassoons agreed to sell them at a substantial profit to the government, which issued in 1879 a public debt loan to finance it. Now under supervision of the Bombay Port Trust, the docks are perhaps the most visible extant sign of the Sassoons' presence in the city. They are still an integral part of the Mumbai scene today, operating as a huge market for hundreds of fishermen to gather and sell their catches five days a week.

The surge in shipping also had the benefit of ending the near-monopoly enjoyed by P & O, as French ships began docking in Bombay and prices dropped. Adroitly, the Sassoons managed through discreet negotiations with P & O (namely, the threat of taking their business to Messageries Impériales, a French company formed in 1862 to carry mail to Indochina and return with Chinese silk) to get a rebate of more than a fifth on maritime taxes—on condition of strict confidentiality so as to prevent other merchants from requesting the same. By the early 1870s, when David Sassoon & Co. was responsible for more than a third of the entire Malwa opium trade, it demanded and received further concessions from P & O, principally reductions on their general cargo, though it failed to persuade P & O to start trans-

Sassoon offices in Fuzhou, China, in the 1870s
for the transport and trade of tea and opium.

porting opium from Calcutta to China via Galle, a harbor in Ceylon, as the shipping company did not believe it would be profitable.

As the opium trade continued to boom, a major concern surfaced: oversupply. In the face of rising demand and unprecedented prices earlier in the 1860s, traders rushed to buy from outside India, and Chinese peasants, especially in Yunnan and Szechuan, were encouraged to produce locally. By the decade's end, Persian and Turkish imports, as well as Chinese fare, were threatening the Sassoons' profits. Although they complained about the glut, the family could claim some responsibility for it; they had been among the first to establish trade routes for opium from Persia to India and on to China. Abdallah had not only encouraged trading with Persia but had taken a personal interest in developing relations with a couple of major trading families in Isfahan and Bushir, nurturing these over more than two decades. A trade report about exports of Persian opium from 1869 indicated that "Messrs. D. Sassoon, Sons, and Co." were "the chief consignees" and referred to their close ties to Haj Mirza Mohammad Ali, a prominent trader in Bushir. The trade was not without its risks, however. The report mentions that the quality of the opium was poor and it was off-loaded in the coastal ports of Amoy and Fuzhou. One of Abdallah's senior employees, a nephew of his wife, reported after a visit to Bushir his strong concern that the involvement of the city's senior officials in the trade and the cost to the company of meeting their incessant demands might make the whole enterprise unprofitable. One trader, who claimed a connection to the Shah of Persia, requested a loan to purchase opium directly from the peasant farmers for sale to the Sassoons, meaning that he stood to make a large profit without taking on any risk. Nevertheless, trading with Persia would endure and continue growing until later in the century, supplemented by imports from Turkey, albeit on a smaller scale.

One of the most distinctive features of Abdallah's chairmanship was the strengthening of the firm's relations with Baghdad and other cities and ports in the Middle East. Applications for navigation rights to the Tigris and Euphrates were driven by his desire to see trade with his homeland increase across the board. It meant, for example, that when an agent in Baghdad in the 1870s was interested in acquiring coal (and was willing to pay handsomely for its delivery), he turned to

David Sassoon & Co., and they in turn were able to supply it. It also meant that friends and distant relatives of the family would write to ask for financial assistance or for help advancing their business in different locations in the Middle East. On one occasion, a relative requested that a shipment to Aleppo be registered in the name of the Sassoons to avoid potential problems with local officialdom. Despite his keen interest in all things British, Arabic remained Abdallah's primary language, and he insisted that his family and employees learn it well. In one letter, he mandated that all clerks in Bombay be able to write in Arabic. In another, he expressed surprise and irritation at the inability of any of the clerks in Hong Kong to write the language properly.

The firm's trading would still be dominated by opium, cotton, and textiles at the end of Abdallah's tenure, but the two decades following Elias's departure saw it shift from passive investments in shares and bonds to a more sophisticated approach. David Sassoon & Co. participated in a syndicate run by an American railway company (from which, given the demand for rail, it expected to make a quick profit of 6 percent) and bought national debt—chiefly of Hungary, which had a particularly high yield. Investments in banks continued at scale and the firm's properties in India continued to be rented to government officials—from 1868 in systematic fashion to ensure a steady stream of income and simultaneously strengthen ties to these officials.

The company took an increasingly modern approach to more and more of its business, whether hiring consultants to advise on entering the pearl market or by exploiting differentials in interest rates on the deposits for consignment in opium, say, between the different locations where the Sassoons operated. This blend of risk and innovation served Abdallah well, and these were the years when the company grew fastest and the door opened for it to become an international heavyweight.

INDIAN POLITICS

Abdallah did not waste much time after the death of his father to leave his mark on the family's properties. He added extensions to Garden Reach, the family house in Pune, turning a small mansion into a decidedly large one—such that handbooks for European travelers to India would later recommend seeking permission to view its sumptu-

The Sassoon family house Garden Reach, in Pune, c. 1870.

ous furniture and beautiful gardens. He justified the cost on the grounds
of prestige and the chance that he might one day live there (which he
eventually did, though only for a few years). Although sections of the
exterior of the house have been demolished, most of the original building still stands, only swallowed by the Sassoon Hospital as its campus
expanded to meet the demands of Pune's growing population.

The residence at Pune was complemented by another magnificent lodging in a hill station in India's forested Western Ghats range,
250 kilometers (160 miles) south of Bombay, acquired by Abdallah
before his father's death. The name of the station, Mahabaleshwar, is
derived from three Sanskrit words meaning "God of Great Power." Its
altitude, some 1,353 meters (4,438 feet) above sea level, makes it significantly cooler than the coast and thus an ideal summer resort. Hill
stations—towns located at a high elevation that offered respite from
the summer heat—are one of the less overtly controversial legacies of
Britain's involvement in India. Each local administration had its own;

Bombay's was Mahabaleshwar, and high government officials fleeing the heat decamped there between April and June before they moved on to Pune (120 kilometers or 75 miles northeast of Mahabaleshwar) until October. Abdallah, naturally, followed the same circuit.

The journey from Bombay to Mahabaleshwar took about eight days: one and a half by boat followed by six by land. It was a hard journey, often through dense rain forest—the British had used Chinese prisoners of war captured during the Opium Wars as labor to build the roads—but the invigorating air and beautiful scenery at the end of it more than compensated for it. Mahabaleshwar possesses one of the highest annual rainfalls of any town in India, and each monsoon season deposits incredible quantities of water there. The land is extremely fertile as a result, and the area is known for the delicious strawberries and mangoes that grow there. Visitors can take a breathtaking walk from town to a perch, called Baghdad Point, which offers stunning views of the mountains on every side. Abdallah had heard about the place from Sir Bartle Frere, the Governor of Bombay, and purchased seven acres of land overlooking a large forest there. The colonial-style bungalow he built on the property is still there and now serves as

The bungalow in the Western Ghats built by Abdallah in the 1860s, to be close to the British elites during the summer.

a small boutique hotel called "The Glenogle Bungalow." Abdallah's presence in Mahabaleshwar was a sign of his closeness to the upper echelons of the British Raj, and he spent the summer months rubbing shoulders with important officials and other members of Bombay's elite every year from 1865 until he quit India.

From the crisis of 1857–58 to the end of the nineteenth century, British rule in India was paramount and its hold in the country seemed secure. This total control led to a rise of national feeling. As all India was linked to one common administration, "it made it easier for people to conceive of the country as a nation." Abdallah's closeness to British officialdom, long both a personal and professional priority, grew increasingly pronounced during his time as chairman. He never missed an opportunity to socialize with British officials, and whenever he attended a function at the Governor's house or hosted him or other officials at his home, he was quick to recount the details to his brothers and, on occasion, senior employees:

> I decided to postpone my sailing to London given that when I met with the governor in Calcutta, he informed me that he was very sad that I am leaving to London because he prefers me to be close by. On the spot I told him I will defer my journey.

For the British, Abdallah was a valuable source—in touch with developments not only in India's trading scene and China (predominantly concerning opium in the latter), but in regions where they exercised less control, such as Persia. He could also offer them substantial resources: When the British began planning a military expedition to Abyssinia late in 1867, for example, the Sassoons offered to lease them ships. For Abdallah, the financial benefits of these relationships were clear. In a confidential letter to Suleiman, he wrote:

> I will do my utmost to reduce the tax on Malwa opium and will attempt to increase the quota for cultivating opium in Calcutta so the prices would return to a good level for us. I will be advising the governor of Pune to suggest to the Indian government to reduce these taxes when I dine with him in a couple of days.

Such attempts to influence policy relied primarily upon Abdallah's reputation as a businessman, though he also worked hard to make life pleasant for the British. Whenever an official needed help with anything, be it purchasing pearls or renting a bungalow, the Sassoons were ready to oblige.

Entertaining was key in building these relations, and as a memoir of one Englishwoman's time in Bombay attests, Abdallah excelled at it:

> The most splendid entertainment of all was, however, given by Mr. Sassoon, the worthy son of that David Sassoon whose name will be immortalized in this part of the world. . . . This ball surpassed anything I had seen or heard of. Looking down from an upper veranda on the garden, illuminated everywhere with jets of gas, one could fancy oneself in a scene described in the "Arabian Nights' Entertainments."

One traveler to Bombay in the 1870s wrote: "We were most kindly entertained by various members of the wealthy and influential family of Sassoon. Indeed, the genuine kindness which they showed us in a variety of ways, we shall ever most gratefully remember." Abdallah made himself a fixture in Bombay's social scene. When the Governor of Bombay hosted the King of Siam, Abdallah was one of the invitees. Hosting was not only about dinners and balls, however. When the senior British official Sir Rutherford Alcock, who served in China and Japan, was preparing to return to London, Abdallah invited him and his wife to stay at his house for a few days rather than at a hotel. Aharon Moshe Gabbay described the visit:

> One day we sat with the Governor and discussed with him all the problems in dealing with China and its opium policy. Abdallah pushed the Governor either to prevent the Chinese from allowing cultivation of opium in their country or allow the expansion of opium cultivation in Calcutta and reduce taxes. Later some Indian princes joined for lunch and we all had a fruitful discussion with him. Sir Rutherford was pleased not only with our hosting but with the reputation of our firm, may it continue forever.

The effort seems to have paid off. Upon his return to London, Sir Rutherford wrote to Abdallah to reiterate his belief that the British government had "to oppose the cultivation of poppy in China for the express purpose of driving the Indian drug out of the Chinese market."

Charity remained central to the family's reputation, and Abdallah gave generously. He continued to support the hospital in Pune founded by his father, and expanded and developed the reformatory in Bombay, as well as developing new philanthropic projects of his own. As one commentator put it: "A. Sassoon has thus been the means of reclaiming many youths, who but for the Sassoon Reformatory School would not have been what they are." He erected a public building in Calcutta, presented an organ to Bombay's Town Hall, and in 1870 established the Sassoon Mechanics' Institute in the city. The institute provided advanced education in technical subjects and boasted a large library (at the time more than ten thousand books and five thousand periodicals), still called the David Sassoon Library today. Besides Abdallah, another member of the Sassoon family was always a trustee. In short order, the institute became something like the equivalent of a modern think tank; by 1875 it had about 350 members and alongside its technical courses it offered lectures, which often addressed topics close to the family's heart, as with one talk on the cultivation of opium in India and the livelihoods it had offered for tens of thousands of farmers.

Charitable activities won the respect not only of Bombay's elites but also of the public at large. Abdallah was rewarded for them in 1867, when Sir Bartle pinned the Order of the Star of India to his chest. This honor paved the way for a more active role in local politics: He ascended to the Bombay Legislative Council and became one of the Governor's main advisers on educational and building projects. Abdallah developed a close relationship not just with the Indian and British elites; he also corresponded with the Shah of Iran, on the basis of the Sassoons' trade in Persia, and similarly with the Sultan of Oman and Zanzibar. The political clout he mustered made the firm's attempts to petition the British government to ensure favorable terms of trade for opium all the more effective. Under David, the firm would lobby the Governor in India and alert their contacts in London whenever a duty was imposed on opium. As early as 1864, the firm had petitioned for a reduction in opium duties from 600 rupees a chest to 400, claiming that a chest bought in Bombay for 1,500 rupees could not be sold in China for more than 1,575, and often fetched less; the government of India, having examined the prices of Patna and Malwa and the cost of transportation and insurance, rejected the appeal. A memo of 1870 written to the Foreign Secretary, the Earl of Clarendon, requesting his support for the firm's opposition to an increase in tax, from 30 to 50 taels per chest exported from India to China, indicates a more robust position:

> Our firm represents in this country the interests of one-third of the whole [opium] trade, and consequently we contribute about 300,000 [sterling] per annum to the revenues of the Chinese Government in opium duty alone, besides other large payments on a general import and export trade between England and China, so that we consider we are only discharging a duty to ourselves and our constituents, by humbly representing to your Lordship the probable effect which will be produced upon the opium trade by raising the tax.

The memo warned that higher taxes on Indian opium would only stimulate local production in China, adding:

> If Her Majesty's Government desire to discourage the trade in opium, this could be at once obtained by imposing a prohibitive duty, or by other more stringent methods, but so long as the revenues of India are drawn largely from this source, we humbly submit that is a grievous wrong to hamper the trade with such excessive export and import duties, as can only injure the Indian cultivator and merchant.

The same week a letter from a Shanghai merchant published in *The Economist* argued against the increase:

> A consideration of the ethical bearing of the opium trade is foreign to a discussion as to the effect of the proposed increase of duty, because the question does not lie between lightly and

heavily taxed opium—between the encouragement and discouragement of opium-smoking—but affects solely the success
of the competition between India and China for the profitable
cultivation of the poppy-plant; and deleterious as opium smoking may be, the suppression of the Indian trade would do nothing towards its discouragement, for opium is now produced
throughout the length and breadth of this country [i.e., China].

The memo and letter both made the same point: The British never
intended to discourage the trade of opium, but only to collect more
taxes. In this case Abdallah's lobbying was successful and the tax was
not raised.

COMPETITION AND COOPERATION

The two family firms had a shared interest in petitioning against taxes
on the commodities they both traded, but at least at first that would
have been all they agreed upon. The threat posed to David Sassoon
& Co. by Elias's operation fired the imagination of its partners and
employees in a way that Jardine Matheson never did. In September
1869, Bombay urged Hong Kong not to neglect their relationships
with any trader, lest their loyalties shift elsewhere. "If you will not try
hard as E. D. Sassoon is doing, our trade will diminish in comparison
to theirs." A month later, one senior member of the Bombay office
wrote a stinging letter to Suleiman in Hong Kong complaining bitterly that Shanghai had been functioning poorly since the split and
noting, "While E. D. Sassoon's trade is expanding, ours is shrinking
by the day." He was outraged that Elias's firm was managing to outsell
them in opium. "I am tired of continuously highlighting our failures
both in terms of quantities and prices, in comparison with them." The
new firm was aggressive in its pursuit of traders and agents, offering
traders a generous twenty-eight days to pay their debts, promoting
demands for David Sassoon & Co. to follow suit, and creating a serious predicament: "If we do not act as they are doing, no one will trade
with us. We have no choice."

The old firm also felt pressure to follow the new one whenever
E. D. Sassoon tried to undercut its competitors and grab a larger share

of the market. Writing to Suleiman from Bombay, Abdallah told him, "[Our] brother Elias, may God protect him and give him long life, has reduced the fee on selling opium, and as much as I hate cutting the price, please instruct the House of Shanghai to charge reduced fees, and for those who already paid higher fees, to refund them." These aggressive tactics doubtless boosted E. D. Sassoon's business and allowed it to grow at a pace, sometimes at the expense of profits or with increased financial exposure to agents or traders who reneged on payments. Though Elias claimed he would not poach any of the original company's clients, the realities on the ground were another matter: E. D. Sassoon was opening branches in all the cities and ports in which David Sassoon & Co. was established. Direct competition was unavoidable. Each firm watched the other closely, and the need to gather information was always critical; business, "whether ancient, medieval, or modern, needs information to function." Hence, gathering information became even more vital for David Sassoon & Co., which had more to lose and the resources to gather information about its upstart rival. Arthur, on a trip to London less than two years after the split, wrote that his first objective on arrival would be to meet an English trader who had been doing business with Elias in order to find out what he was up to and what his future plans were.

Even when E. D. Sassoon was not driving down prices, the different branches of David Sassoon & Co. diligently reported what they were doing and the prices they charged for different commodities. Criticism and friction between the branches intensified as each blamed the other for falling behind the new firm. "We are losing ground everywhere. Sales of E. D. Sassoon in Shanghai are outpacing us. It is incomprehensible how our trade is lagging behind. Inexcusable." The new firm was scrutinized at every juncture. London, checking E. D. Sassoon's balance sheets, found to their surprise that the shares Elias inherited from his father were included as part of the business, which obviously strengthened the firm's financial standing when dealing with banks. Sometimes interest gave way to obsession, and that in turn to paranoia; in one letter, an employee worried that E. D. Sassoon was setting them up to work with an agent who would betray them as soon as they signed an agreement.

The founder, David Sassoon, after his arrival in Bombay, c. 1850.

Farha, David's second wife, with whom he had ten children, c. 1850.

The gateway to Sassoon Docks in Colaba, Bombay, built by Abdallah Sassoon, opened in 1874.

Clippers were introduced in the 1850s. These fast ships were built to carry chests of opium and tea and significantly enhanced the trade. The Sassoons utilized them because they cut costs and reduced the travel time between India and China.

A typical business correspondence in Baghdadi Jewish dialect (reads from right to left), which family members used from the 1840s to the 1920s. "We wonder whether Abraham Shalom [Arthur] could use his influence in the matter of this [trade] but in the past you were hesitant."

The house that David Sassoon built in Bombay, which he called Sans Souci, with its expansive gardens.

Exterior and interior of David Sassoon's mausoleum in Pune.

The red brick Ohel David
(Tent of David) synagogue in Pune,
completed in 1867.

The Magen David Synagogue
in Byculla, Bombay, built by
David Sassoon near his home.

The blue interior of the Magen David Synagogue.

The Sassoon family crest, cast in iron, still adorns the interior of what is now Mumbai's Masina Hospital.

Labels printed by Sassoon mills. Cotton was as critical as opium in building the family's fortunes. By the early twentieth century, both Sassoon firms owned and operated numerous mills in Bombay and Manchester.

A portrait of Aline de Rothschild,
Edward's wife, by the painter
John Singer Sargent, 1907.

A cartoon of Edward Sassoon
in *Vanity Fair*, 1900.

An envelope that contained correspondence from
David Sassoon's agents in Karachi to the head office
in London, 1903.

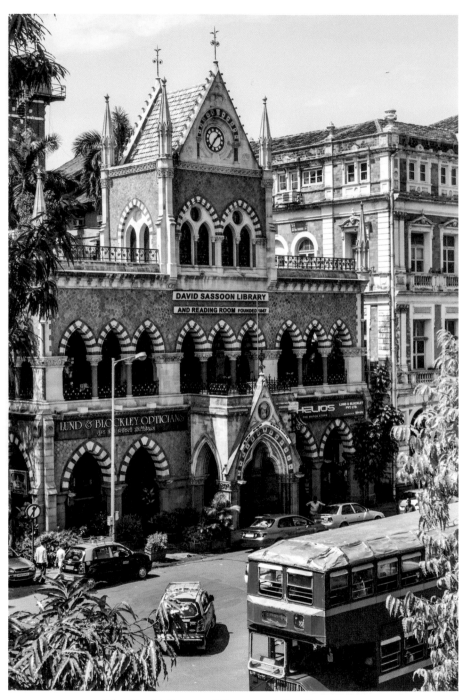

The David Sassoon Library and Reading Room
in Mumbai, completed in 1870.

Though both firms instinctively shied away from making the rift public, there were occasions when one side felt the other had gone too far. A case in point was a letter by David Sassoon & Co. to the editor of *The North-China Herald,* complaining about a certain Chinese employee who, as it was alleged, had provided details "of our opium and other particulars of our businesses to the editor and to Messrs. E. D. Sassoon," and accusing the editor of paying their employee a bribe for this information. The journal published the complaint and the editor's reply, in which he denied the allegation, pointing out the employee had been on E. D. Sassoon's payroll for the past two years, and that the arrivals and departures of steamers and quantities of opium they carried "was never information which was not open to anyone interested." He added, "Neither I nor Messrs. Sassoon had any idea that the man was in your exclusive employ." Evidently, the Chinese employee had taken advantage of the schism to draw pay from both competing firms.

Whether it was his intention or not, Elias managed to infuriate Abdallah in ways few others could. In one letter, Abdallah told Suleiman that Elias had written to him yet again about a refund of maritime fees, and mentioned that he was sick of Elias's barrage of letters on the subject. Suleiman, even-tempered as always, responded by telling him not to pay too much attention to it, as Elias was by nature pessimistic and given to ceaseless complaints. A few unsettled matters to do with their inheritance added to the enmity and suspicion. Three years after David's death, it emerged that a property he had bequeathed to the Alliance Israélite Universelle in Baghdad so that they might turn it into a school had not in fact been bequeathed. Some brothers suggested that the building should be gifted to the education institution and named David, but it seems there was no immediate agreement as Elias wanted to know how the charity would be run and who would be "directing" it.

Whenever a trade involving E. D. Sassoon & Co. went awry, however, recriminations or subtle accusations of mismanagement followed. Nor did the resentment directed at Elias ever fully dissipate. Ten years after the split, Abdallah bemoaned the fact that his brother remained as avaricious as ever:

Even as my brother, may God protect him, is advancing in age, his greed knows no limit. He is engaging in many activities that will not bring him (and the Sassoons) a good name. I have no idea why he is doing this when he has so much money now. I do support writing the banks that E. D. Sassoon has a good reputation but I worry that the bank would think we have an interest, apart from protecting the family's name.

Decades later, both firms continued to monitor each other's business. In a letter from 1889, eight years after Elias had died and the reins had passed to Jacob, the House of London reported, "E. D. Sassoon are imitating us: whatever we buy they buy, whatever we trade, they aim to trade, even if they make less money."

The animosity was felt up and down the hierarchy of the two firms, particularly in the original company. Correspondence between more junior employees in the final years of the 1860s indicates significant anxiety about their futures and incomes. After all, many had left their community and relatives in Baghdad to start a new life in the East, hoping that one day they might follow David Sassoon and build a great fortune. One senior employee in Bombay wrote to Suleiman in Hong Kong to complain about the situation:

I have to inform you that in these days, our revenues are not the same as in the past. If we reduce our trade further, you should know that we will have a problem dealing with the expenses of the Bombay office. This is at the time that Mr. Elias is expanding his business and building a trade network with his greedy tactics of offering discounts to try to gain a market share at the expense of reducing the overall prices. If this continues, we will be standing in the back watching the takeover of our business.

Resentment at the new firm's success deepened a sense of gloom that prevailed in all the offices in the first decade after the split. This pessimism abated only once it became clear that the business continued to be profitable and the forecasts of losing everything to Elias were proven false. Time, too, played its role. Both Abdallah and Elias were getting older, and Abdallah's attention turned increasingly from Orient to Occident, away from this regional conflict.

It would be a mistake to assume that fierce competition between the two firms prevented any cooperation in the business world, however, or that solidarity among family members entirely dissolved after Elias broke away. The two companies would later coordinate on critical strategic issues, namely those ensuing from campaigns to ban the trade of opium. More than twenty years after the split, both had representatives on the boards of the same banks, and where interests aligned they acted in tandem. And although Elias's departure and subsequent attempts to poach employees from David Sassoon & Co. stoked paranoia at the old firm, the brothers working there continued to trust and depend on one another. Even during the separation process, when no one could be completely confident where the loyalty of their kin lay, Suleiman wrote to Reuben in London empowering him to act as his attorney and agent on all matters in Britain. But it was not only in financial matters that trust prevailed; they confided in each other about their troubles, their unhappiness about their postings, Abdallah's leadership, or feeling marginalized in the decision-making process that their father instituted.

Philanthropy was another area where the two Sassoon firms worked in tandem. By 1867, the government of India had approved all the proceedings related to the construction of the Sassoon Hospital in Pune, and it was reported that the contributions from the two competing branches of the family exceeded the original budget. The government further contributed to the services of an assistant surgeon for the hospital and paid all expenses incurred by government officials admitted to the hospital. Despite finding themselves on opposing sides of the split, Elias and Suleiman maintained a cordial and respectful relationship. Only two letters from Elias to Suleiman survive, both from more than ten years after the separation, but both show that a fraternal bond persisted. In the first letter, Elias wrote:

> Your letter arrived yesterday with regard to the building I
> bought from you in Hong Kong to be a synagogue, I was
> taken by surprise by your statement that although you sold

me the building, you need now the opinion of Faraj Haim
[a younger brother]. Do you recall that when we took the
carriage together [in Hong Kong], you told me that you are
happy to sell me the building at any price because it is for
charity? Only because we are brothers, you sold and I bought
and there was no contract. It is inconceivable in our world
that a man changes his opinion after he agrees to buy or sell.

In the second letter, two days later, Elias warmly acknowledged Suleiman's response:

Your cherished telegram arrived yesterday informing me that
you are sending me in the mail a document. I would like
to emphasize, once again, that the only reason I want this
building is for charity reasons. I know this amount of money
we are talking is not significant and not relevant to you.
But I realize also that you are under pressure as they [other
members of the family, most likely Abdallah] are furious
about this deal and are intent on spoiling the relationship
between us, since they see that we are close, and they simply
cannot accept it.

Family solidarity was most apparent in times of sorrow. Eight
months after Elias lost his son, his and Suleiman's oldest surviving
sister, Amam, wrote to tell Suleiman that Elias was recovering and
that time was healing his grief. The death of Elias's son came only six
months after the untimely death of their younger brother S.D. at the
age of thirty-four in London—and we can again see Suleiman writing
to an elder brother, this time Abdallah, to console him and ask him to
take care of himself, particularly in the summer heat of Bombay. S.D.
was the first member of the Sassoon family to be posted to Britain,
and the children he left behind at Ashley Park had been raised (and in
some cases born) there and felt that England was their home, rather
than Baghdad or Bombay. They were the first Sassoons to identify this
way but they would not be the last, and whether he was driven away
by some combination of Bombay's scorching summers and family
infighting, or drawn to London believing it to be the center of the
world, it wouldn't be long before Abdallah joined them.

7

LONDON CALLING

1872–1880

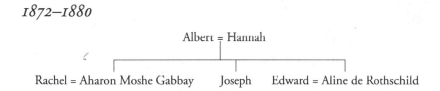

Not satisfied to entertain only those British officials who were actually stationed in India, Abdallah hosted seemingly any and every visiting dignitary too. He seized every opportunity to forge connections with the country's aristocracy and political elite, whether they visited the subcontinent or not. Overtures were made to prominent politicians from both parties, most notably William Gladstone. As early as 1865, Abdallah, in concert with S.D., donated £1,000 to a refuge set up by the then-Chancellor's wife to aid London's poor. She graciously accepted, and "expressed her high gratification to Messrs Sassoon for the confidence they placed in her." Later that year, Abdallah (or rather Albert, as he signed all the letters he wrote in English) wrote in turn to Gladstone of his pleasure at the circumstances that "place me in relation with you" and to say that they would be honored "with any command with which you or Mrs Gladstone might be pleased to favour us."

In 1872 Abdallah was rewarded for his public service with a knighthood, after which he became known as Sir Albert. (Though in his letters to his siblings and the rest of the family, he continued to sign himself as Abdallah.) It was a tremendous honor and seemed to mark the zenith of a remarkable ascent, from Baghdadi exile to accredited member of the upper crust in just four decades. When the new Viceroy of India, Lord Northbrook, first reached Bombay, Sir Albert and Lady Sassoon invited twelve hundred guests to a ball at Sans Souci to celebrate his arrival, combining that with a celebration of Albert's honor (although this was modestly omitted from the invitation). The grounds around the mansion were beautifully illuminated. Indian princes and maharajas mingled with the heads of merchant families and a crowd of British officials. Meanwhile, in England, Albert's family threw a large garden party at Ashley Park, where the band of the Coldstream Guard entertained the guests, among them Mr. and Mrs. Gladstone and their daughters.

Late in the following year, Sir Albert was presented with yet another honor at a large gathering at the Guildhall in London. The Freedom of the City, awarded in recognition of extraordinary success or celebrity, had overwhelmingly been received by those born and resident in Britain, so the award was a historic occasion, as the commemorative brochure made clear:

> This is the first time an East Indian merchant has been admitted to the honour highly prized by its possessor, and much coveted by the aspirants to City fame. . . . It is the first time that the freedom of the City of London has been presented to a Jew.

In the audience were the Chief Rabbi and Lord Mayor as well as several Members of Parliament, along with Albert's brothers Arthur and Reuben, both with their wives, and numerous merchants from the City of London's guilds. The Chamberlain, Benjamin Scott, addressed Sir Albert:

> You are, therefore, Sir Albert, the first subject of Her Majesty's Indian Empire upon whom that freedom has been conferred. The resolution makes allusion to your valuable public services as a member of the Legislative Council of Bombay and in other capacities—services which your sovereign has recognized by conferring upon you the Star of India and other distinctions.

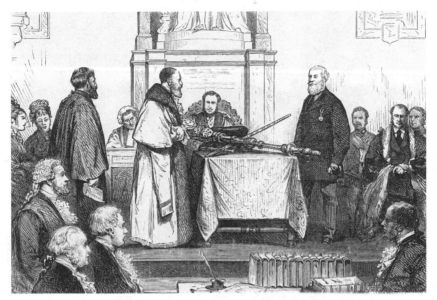

Abdallah (Albert) being honored in 1873 by the City of London
for his contribution to the British Empire.

It also refers to your munificent and philanthropic exertions
in the cause of charity and education, more especially, though
not exclusively, in our Indian Empire. It is the cosmopolitan
and unsectarian scope of your liberality no less than its extent
which has attracted the attention of this Honourable Court.
Schools for Indian and Jewish children; colleges for the higher
education of the native youth; institutes for mechanics; hospitals for the diseased; retreats for the convalescent; and reforma-
tories for the depraved; such are some of the numerous works
of charity which your judicious liberality has either founded
or fostered. Not only Bombay, the place of your residence, but
Calcutta, Pune, Madras, Persia and Great Britain have shared
in your wide-spread munificence, which was culminated in the
establishment of scholarships in connection with the school
founded by this Corporation, of which this Court is justly
proud.

In a slow, penetrating voice that only occasionally betrayed his
emotions, Sir Albert replied:

A golden casket presented to Albert
by the City of London, 1873.

It is an honour which . . . I may say I had never aspired to, and
which I had never hoped to gain; but it is an honour of which
I may be justly proud . . . the honour is perhaps enhanced in
my case as it is bestowed on me a member of the Hebrew community, and I accept it as a new proof of that religious tolerance which is one of the characteristics of your enlightened
corporation.

Albert was presented with a golden casket engraved with his name,
and to applause he announced that it would "remain with my family
as an heir-loom for ever."

Albert was then just a visitor to London, but the following year he
would move there permanently. The decision was partly pragmatic.
London's status as the capital of international trade had by the early
1870s been enhanced by advances in telegraphic communications, particularly undersea cables, and Albert believed that his proximity to this
world, and the locus of British imperial power and decision-making,
would benefit the firm more than his distance from the head office
would cost it. The price to his marriage would be more acute—his
wife didn't want to leave Bombay and would not join him—but this
too was tolerable, it seems. London promised some insulation from

the endless bickering between family members in the East. And if escaping these squabbles freed him to manage the other partners more closely, so much the better. Albert always felt himself to be a Baghdadi Jew but had long been fascinated by all things English, and reading the letters and newspaper clippings sent from his brothers in London induced some jealousy. However, to join them, he needed to appoint someone whom he could rely upon to run the business in Asia. High on the list was his younger brother Suleiman, who was managing Shanghai and Hong

Albert Sassoon, c. 1870.

Kong, and he brought him to Bombay several times in the run-up to his departure.

In 1874, when Albert took up residency in England, his wife, Hannah, remained at Sans Souci, where she would live until her death in 1895. She had by most accounts been "an uninspired hostess at his many dinner parties and receptions" in Bombay, and one wonders whether he was embarrassed by her: She had been born and raised in Bombay by a typical Baghdadi merchant family who had settled in the city before his father's arrival but never traveled outside India, having "pleaded ill-health to avoid accompanying him on his English visits." Or had he felt she could impede his integration into English society? Either way, it is unclear why Albert left his wife behind in India all those years and did not go back to see her in spite of his extensive travels. He obviously could provide her with anything she wanted, but she had no interest in joining David Sassoon's wife in Brighton, who was sending long letters about life in England.

Albert's sights were set altogether higher. Over the next two decades, his reach would extend from Britain's mercantile and political

elite to its aristocracy and even its royalty—as well as that of other
nations. In 1875, for instance, he gave a dinner for the Sultan of
Oman and Zanzibar at his new house in Brighton (1 Eastern Terrace,
Kemp Town). Despite moving in such rarefied circles, he never lost
his interest and involvement in business and continued to push the
firm's agenda whenever it was needed and manage its global affairs.
David Sassoon & Co.'s headquarters were at 12 Leadenhall Street, and
because of the global reach of the firm a staff of translators handling
bills of lading and marine insurance occupied the top floor of the

Statue commemorating the Prince of Wales's
visit to Bombay in 1875. Statue unveiled in 1879.

building and dealt with mail in Hebrew, Arabic, Persian, Chinese, and Hindustani.

One of Albert's first overtures to the royal family was also one of his grandest. When Albert, the Prince of Wales, visited India in 1875 as part of an extensive tour of the empire, his Sassoon namesake remained in London but ensured that Lady Sassoon would entertain the Prince at Sans Souci and meet other members of the family. After the Prince's return, Sir Albert obtained his permission to erect a statue of him in Bombay to commemorate his visit. A few months after the sculptor Joseph Edgar Boehm began work on the "colossal statue," at a cost of £10,000 (more than £1 million today), Queen Victoria herself inspected it. Two years later, at a party hosted by Mr. and Mrs. Reuben Sassoon at their home in Belgrave Square, London, the Prince, accompanied by his young daughter Princess Louise, viewed the finished statue—a bronze figure on horseback mounted on a granite pedestal, together stretching twenty-seven feet into the air—before it was shipped to Bombay. In June 1879, the statue was unveiled in Bombay by the Governor, Sir Richard Temple. Officials, merchants, and residents gathered in heavy rain to view it and hear Suleiman, now the presiding member of the Sassoon family in the city, speak.

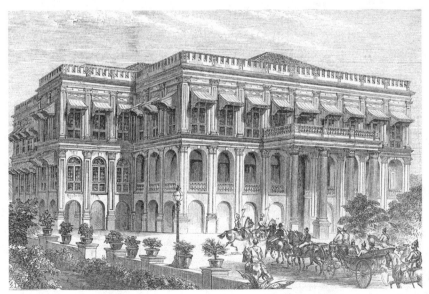

The Prince of Wales on his visit to the Sassoons' house in Bombay, 1875.

It had been a hugely expensive affair, though it had its rewards: Ever more articles began to appear in British papers praising Sir Albert and the "laudable spirit of true charity" he embodied. Whenever a dignitary visited Bombay and stopped at the statue, the media dutifully reminded its readers that Sir Albert had been behind this gift.

Suleiman was then passing two of life's milestones almost simultaneously. On one of his visits to company headquarters in Bombay back in 1873, he had found himself captivated by the charm and knowledge of Farha. After another trip, he overcame his lifelong shyness and social awkwardness and asked Abdallah, his half brother and Farha's grandfather, for permission to marry her. While marriages between first cousins were common in many cultures in the nineteenth century, a union between great-uncle and niece was generally held to be too close, and advice was sought from rabbis and legal experts. After some deliberation, Abdallah gave his blessing, hoping that this marriage would help cement his control of the family's business in Asia after his move to London. The couple married in Bombay in February 1876, when Farha was nineteen and Suleiman thirty-five. As the marriage deviated from tradition, Albert wrote from Brighton to Suleiman about the *sbahiyya* (dowry):

> You wrote and mentioned that you are not upset that there
> was no gift in any sense, and that you want absolutely
> nothing. You also said that it is not your style to keep things
> hidden inside and that you will make sure everything will
> work to the benefit of Farha. This is what is expected from a
> dear brother.

Their brothers in particular were relieved that Suleiman would be in charge of Asia, both because they saw him as entirely capable and because it meant they could continue to live in England. One letter from Arthur (as Abraham Shalom had Anglicized his name), on holiday in Hamburg, to Suleiman, in Bombay after his marriage, is revealing of the need to have Suleiman in this position:

> You mentioned that one of us head to Bombay to help in the
> business. But you know that our brother Abdallah is an old

man now. So how do you expect him to go there for a brief visit? I think you should stay in Bombay and take over the helm of the business. We can then send someone [a non-partner] to Shanghai for two to three years. This way we can reduce our costs also. I do not believe that partners should be in every office we have. Instead we can write more detailed correspondence to explain matters.

Unlike his twin brother, Aharon, who lacked any interest in the family business, had declined to participate in the apprenticeship program devised by David, and had escaped instead to Brighton (where he lived all his life, leaving all his assets to charities located wherever the family firm had branches), Suleiman had a head for business. He had been sent to China at the age of fifteen and been based in Hong Kong and Shanghai ever since. As we saw, his letters to Bombay tell first of his homesickness and then of his eventual acceptance of his father's instruction to stay there. Later ones show an unusual single-mindedness that was particularly evident in his ability to absorb massive amounts of data. He finally moved back to Bombay in 1875, twenty years after his departure and a year before his wedding, to run the office there and oversee the other branches in Asia. Eight months after his marriage, Suleiman was admitted as a general partner for all the branches. He was described as a "keen, active business man, always straightforward, with a generous nature, and his liberality made no distinction between the different nationalities who inhabit Bombay." In private, he felt his religious obligations keenly, giving generously to the Jewish individuals and organizations who wrote to him from as far away as Sana'a in Yemen to seek assistance. He set up a small private synagogue in his house in Bombay and contributed to the building of another in Hong Kong. He was fluent in Hebrew and studied the Talmud and Torah intensively, and many rabbis were frequently hosted in his house when they visited Bombay. In 1878, he asked the Supreme Court in Bombay to exempt Jewish judges from working on Saturdays. Nonetheless, like his brother and father before him, he took an active part in public life in Bombay, as a director of the Bank of Bombay, a trustee of the port, a member of the city's judicial committee, and at one point a member of the international committee organizing the Melbourne International Exhibition of 1880–81. As more and more of his relatives moved west, relishing their wealth and luxury in England, he threw himself into running the company's trade in Asia—to the extent that his health suffered as a result. Certainly, that was how Farha came to see it.

BUSINESS AS USUAL

Though physically removed from many of the levers of the business, Albert retained control over its direction and even steered it to new heights. The 1870s were years of healthy profits, as he wrote to Suleiman in Bombay: "Despite all the problems, our profits for 1877 were 15% and if 1878 continues at the same momentum they will reach 20%." That proved optimistic—the final number was just over 12 percent—but considering the sheer size of the company and conditions in which they were trading, such returns were more than decent. They were comparable to Jardine Matheson's a decade earlier, when the competition was not as robust and the risks of trading opium lower. Even a decade later, profits were still in the double digits—a remarkable feat given the economic turbulence that characterized the period. From 1873 until 1897 wholesale prices dropped precipitously; the expansion of Britain's economy, which had commenced with the Industrial Revolution in the late eighteenth century, slowed considerably in what became known as the great depression; and tariffs rose, adversely affecting the global commercial system.

Britain dominated global trade, so its depression was felt keenly in many countries, not least India, and revenues from the opium trade grew to be even more important. India, ruled by the British Crown from 1858, was required to pay a large annual sum, estimated at roughly fourteen million rupees in the early 1870s, to Britain to cover its military and administrative costs. India's exports were expected to cover this, as well as its own expenses. India's opium exports as a proportion of total exports ranged from 9 percent in 1839 to a high of 39 percent in 1858, and for the next three decades it rarely fell below 15 percent. Only from the 1890s would it drop to single digits, and only after the First World War would it slip to less than 1 percent. From 1862 until the end of the 1880s, India exported 80,000 chests per year on average, equivalent to 11.2 million pounds (5.08 million kilos) of opium, and this marked the trade's peak.

The two Sassoon businesses operated alongside each other, competing and occasionally cooperating, but both continued to grow. Their systems had been built up in a methodical, efficient manner, perfected over time, as a British trade report from 1874 described:

> Our principal importers are the two well-known Bombay houses of the Sassoon name. From these the Opium is bought wholesale for silver by Chinese, who repack it in smaller parcels and stamp it with their brands—chief among which are those of the Têk-sing and E-sim hongs [trading houses]. Thus marked, the Opium is ready for retail distribution.

A memo reveals the extent of the firm's activities in just one week in January 1874: 1,045 chests of Bengal opium, 250 chests of Malwa opium, 700 chests of Persian opium, and 20 chests of Turkish opium were shipped to Shanghai. Prices during this period stayed high enough to be profitable for traders, in spite of increases in supply. For high-quality Malwa opium, they actually increased.

As always, exporting to China meant operating through the compradors, who were the "Chinese managers of foreign firms in China serving as middlemen." A foreign firm's comprador was responsible not only for staffing in China but also for the credit of their customers, and thus always bore substantial risk. The compradors' success was tied to the ban on foreign traders from dealing directly inside China—they alone had access to distribution networks inland. Foreign trading houses relied on a system of guarantees to ensure a comprador's trustworthiness, while the comprador recruited his staff in accordance with China's traditional values. It was a complicated system, and compradors effectively acted as agents while simultaneously running their own businesses. Some achieved great wealth and high status with their parent companies—it was rumored that the Sassoons' comprador in Chinkiang sold 1.5 million taels (a unit of Chinese currency, roughly 1.3 ounces of silver and worth about four shillings and sixpence, which is about £22 today) of opium in a single year—and worked with them for long periods, while others faced financial difficulties that

frequently landed them and their foreign partners in the courts. They
grew ever more important after 1858, when the Treaty of Tientsin
enshrined free trade of opium in China and the opening of more of
its ports to foreign merchants. A case in point was Hoo Mei-ping,
comprador to David Sassoon & Co. in Tientsin from 1869 to 1884.
He also did significant business on his own account: He had trading
houses in Mongolia, a chain of shops in Peking, and a small bank in
Shanghai. Not only did his services substantially increase the firm's
overheads, but "he also gradually turned into their most effective rival
in China's commerce." The more audacious compradors could even
compete with foreign traders overseas, in Japan and elsewhere.

Outside China, agents played a critical role in international trade,
and global merchants therefore were obliged to invest in their relationships with them to ensure loyalty and honest representation. David
Sassoon & Co. had agents in Bushir, Isfahan, and Baghdad, among
others. The relationship between Albert and his primary agent in
Bushir, Haj Ali Akbar, was particularly close, and the Sassoon archives
are enlivened by numerous letters in beautifully scripted Arabic sent
by him to the family. While he addressed everyone as Their High Excellency, Albert was "our beloved Khawaja" (an honorary title), with
his knighthood appended from 1872. The bond between the two
lasted for decades, enduring considerable volatility in opium prices.
Haj Akbar was the exception, however. The family's relations with
most agents—including compradors—were often fraught. Indeed,
as both Sassoon firms expanded, legal disputes with them came to be
almost a component of the trade itself. Many of the cases centered
around liquidations, disagreements over clauses of trade agreements,
or marine taxes. On one occasion David Sassoon & Co. wrote to
the Secretary of State for India (who in turn referred the letter to the
British Political Resident in the Persian Gulf) to complain about their
inability to instigate the liquidation or settlement of the estate of two
merchants in Bushir with whom they conducted business, reminding
the official:

> Our firm have considerable business relations with the
> ports in the Persian Gulf, as well as with Baghdad, and we
> credit ourselves with having to a large extent assisted in the

development of British trade and influence in that quarter of the globe.

The Resident explained that the authorities in Persia were not treating the case as an insolvency, and that because the Sassoons' claims had been joined by other British firms, there was not much hope of receiving the full amount. Other times, they were more fortunate. The firm insured an opium shipment on a steamer, the *Delta,* sailing from Bombay to a port in China, for about 45 percent of its total value. When the shipment was lost, however, a British court ordered the insurer to pay almost 80 percent of the total. The case dragged on, gaining sufficient notoriety for *The Economist* to devote a long article to it, in which it revealed that the underwriters lost the case as they had not stamped the insurance policies properly.

In accordance with the privileges granted to foreign merchants in the treaties following the two Opium Wars, claims, counterclaims, and appeals by both David Sassoon & Co. and E. D. Sassoon against compradors in China were governed by British law and administered by British judges and juries. A perusal of law reports of the British Supreme Court for China and Japan indicates just how common they were and does nothing to disabuse the reader of any preconception that the British judicial system favored the merchants. It had, after all, been built to protect British subjects. The volume of cases was partly the product of China's unsettled economy, particularly after the financial panic of 1883 and the merchants' subsequent scramble to minimize their losses. "The coexistence of contradictory judgments, therefore, has the effect of undermining the credibility of the comprador system among the Chinese and Western mercantile people in China."

Not irrelevant, however, was the remarkable amount of time, money, and energy that the Sassoons were prepared to dedicate to legal wrangling. They believed themselves obliged to litigate every case that contradicted their interests or agreements, pursuing every agent or merchant who they felt had broken his word. Some of the claims were exceedingly small, and it is clear that what was at stake was the principle that each side must keep their part of the bargain.

But the law was not strictly for business dealings. Members of the family had to use the courts wherever they were based to deal with the complexities of the estates and trusts that their success had spawned. One filing, some fifty-five pages long and dating from 1879 to the middle of the following decade, gives a sense of the difficulty of blending fortune and family. One of Albert's daughters, Mozelle, had, at the age of seventeen, married Elias David Ezra, a widower who brought four children to the marriage, to which they added seven. A trust was formed upon the marriage of Elias and Mozelle, signed by Aharon Moshe Gabbay, husband to another of Albert's daughters, Rachel. (The Sassoons, Gabbays, and Ezras continued to intermarry throughout the next two generations.) Upon Elias David Ezra's death in 1886, it became clear that he hadn't paid the trustees properly and, worse, the trustees (one of whom was Aharon Moshe Gabbay) had failed to ensure that the trust complied with its requirements. The matter was complicated by the revelation that the sole executor of the estate was Ezra's eldest son from his first marriage, Joseph, who engaged in irregularities of all sorts and declined to tender proper accounts or give information to the entitled beneficiaries. It took almost two years, dozens of lawyers, and countless hearings to get to the bottom of the matter; the result was not to the satisfaction of all parties, and relationships between them soured.

As long as they did not encroach on business, Albert avoided getting entangled in family disputes. In practice, distinguishing between what was in the best interest of the enterprise and the relatives who worked for it was difficult. His eldest son, Joseph, for instance, gambled on a trade scheme that failed, effectively leaving him bankrupt. Albert hesitated as to whether or not to bail his son out but in the end decided to do so. His son-in-law Aharon Moshe Gabbay assured him that he had done the correct thing:

> First and foremost, the world will praise your action, second, the family would know that you protected its reputation, and third Joseph would not have endured being penniless. Money comes and goes, and I am sure God will compensate you ten times more than you spent.

Afterward it seems that Joseph took a less active role in the business than Albert's sons-in-law and younger son, Edward, who would in time inherit his father's title. Joseph had a troubled life and would pre-decease his father by almost a decade. Albert, in spite of his toughness in business, was a caring father. In an emotional letter to his daughter Rachel, he described feeling breathless and incapable of showing inter-est in anything while Edward, who had boarded a ship to Shanghai but sent no word of his arrival, remained silent. "Every hour seemed like eternity while waiting for some news to arrive." Only when he heard calming news about his son was he able to reply to his daughter.

Some especially rancorous disputes stretched familial bonds to a breaking point. One such case was that of Solomon Ezekiel, husband to David's third daughter, Kate, and thus a brother-in-law to Albert and Suleiman. Whether the vitriolic attack launched by Solomon Ezekiel against the family was justified is unclear, but evidently the resentment and bitterness ran deep. In a letter to David Sassoon & Co.'s lawyers, he claimed that some substantial losses applied against his personal account were unlawful—a charge the firm repudiated, attributing the allegation to Ezekiel's "bad motives." It seems that he directed transactions to an account he labeled as "Friends" but argued that the company was aware of it. He demanded compensation and said he would go public with his accusations if he didn't receive it; he wrote to a senior manager at the firm, "I am desperate, and shall not for a moment hesitate to sink the whole lot of them with me—from Sir Albert down to Gabbay and they will have to appear in the witness box." The tactic worked, and an agreement was reached five days later in the presence of a barrister. The firm agreed to clear Ezekiel's debt, and he in turn apologized unconditionally for his threats, withdrew his allegations, and resigned immediately as a representative of the company.

When the Sassoons had entered the opium market, the trade in western India was dominated by a few large Indian traders and British companies, notably Jamsetjee Jejeebhoy and Jardine Mathe-son, respectively. By the 1870s, David Sassoon & Co. had teamed up with two leading merchant families of Baghdadi Jews in Calcutta, the Gabbays (Albert's wife's family) and the Ezras, to influence opium prices in eastern India. It wasn't a straightforward association: The

Sassoons were obliged to defer to the Gabbays and Ezras in Calcutta despite the fact that they had their own branch there, and the archives indicate multiple disputes within this mini-cartel whenever the families could not agree on a strategy or one felt exploited by the other. But this alliance did allow them to control most of the trade emanating from Bombay and Calcutta. More important to the firm's profits, however, was securing control of the Malwa opium trade by the 1870s. They made cash advances to Indian dealers, who in turn financed the farmers cultivating and producing opium.

> This put Sassoon in a position somewhat analogous to that of the Indian Government in Bihar and Benares. The firm acted as the "banker" to finance the Malwa opium crop, making advances to an already established group of dealers and, in effect, purchasing the crop before it was even planted.

Insightful details about the competition between David Sassoon & Co. and Jardine Matheson can be excavated from the latter's archives. Jardine's directors were aware of the aggressive measures the firm had adopted to cut opium prices: providing loans to producers in India; making bulk sales at low rates combined with advances to Chinese dealers; and, probably most effective, advancing as much as three quarters of the costs to Indian dealers willing to consign shipments on a regular basis. The firm worked hard to maintain its relationships with its partners; Albert, discussing a deal with one of the big farmers, encouraged him to ensure that the quality of opium was high and promised to purchase even more chests of opium from him if it was. The strategy reduced the firm's costs and gave them an edge over their competitors—"[The Sassoons'] activities are seriously upsetting prices here," reported one panicked Jardine Matheson employee from China—thereby allowing them to control a large portion of the market by the mid-1870s. Dislodged by P & O's steamships and the competition from David Sassoon & Co. (and not, as was later claimed, due to "moral arguments"), by 1871, Jardine Matheson withdrew almost completely from the opium business and shifted its focus to banking, insurance, railways, and mining. Thus the two Sassoon companies were acknowledged as the major holders of opium in India and China, controlling 70 percent of all the stock according to some estimates. In reality, the number was between 30 and 50 percent, but it is undeniable that the two Sassoon companies were, by the 1870s, the world's most prominent opium traders, and by the early 1880s reports indicated that the opium trade with China was "nearly wholly in the hands" of Parsi merchants and the Sassoons.

How lucrative was the opium business? For companies such as Jardine Matheson, profits averaged about 15 percent of the firm's investments during the 1850s and 1860s, and about 4 percent on agency business during the same period. Jardine used these profits to build its structure and expand its trade to tea and silk. These numbers were relatively high, as from the 1870s onward opium cultivation grew at an astonishing rate, creating an oversupply. In a letter dated 1878, Albert wrote: "How long do we keep sending money everywhere and buying? We own now 500 chests of Persian opium and in China we are sitting on 1,200 chests? When are we going to sell these? When are we ever going to make profits and more importantly receive the revenues?"

Away from opium, one of Albert's major ventures was a foray into textile manufacturing. The potential was obvious: Cotton was abundant in India and labor was cheap. The only missing piece was the machinery. As soon as that could be exported to India, local manufacturing commenced. The first mill in Bombay was opened in 1868 by Jamsetjee Tata, a member of a leading Parsi family in Bombay. It was Tata's first venture into mill construction after having grasped the enormous benefit that India would derive from an expansion of the textile industry. Once the Sassoons saw that it could be profitable, they leaped into spinning and the manufacturing of textiles. David Sassoon & Co. was the first of the Sassoons, and a few years later E. D. Sassoon, slow off the starting line but quick to make up the lost ground, opened its first mill in 1883. Both Sassoon companies, particularly the upstart firm, would acquire control of numerous manufacturers of cotton goods over the next couple of decades, and by 1925, E. D. Sassoon would control eleven factories to David Sassoon & Co.'s two. As one British MP observed, workers at Indian mills processed cheaper raw material, over longer hours and more days per year for less pay than their counterparts in Lancashire, and within a few years of Tata's mill opening its doors, the Indian industry posed a real threat to British manufacturers. Moving into the textile business led to more cooperation between the Sassoons and some Indian families. For instance, the first board of directors of the Sassoon Spinning and Weaving Company was comprised of three Sassoons and four Indians. Most interactions were with another minority, the Parsis, who had arrived in Bombay from Persia in the mid-seventeenth century, well before the Sassoons, and had quickly established themselves. Parsis were renowned for their business acumen, and a bond developed between them and the Baghdadi Jews in India as soon as the latter arrived in Bombay. They were the dominant force in opium trading in the first half of the nineteenth century. Later, many Parsis acted as agents, brokers, or junior partners. "They entered into a symbiotic patron-client relationship with the British." Subsequently, they played a key role in shipbuilding and emerged as a capitalist class. This intercommunal cooperation was a striking feature of Bombay during that era, when India was enjoying an economic boom. The decade between 1875 and 1885 in particular saw the number of textile factories in India grow rapidly. Spinning generated high returns, and Albert was delighted with the profits and predicted even higher yields in the future. Following the early success of the spinning mills, the Sassoon Silk Manufacturing Company was created in 1876, chaired by Edward Albert Sassoon, Albert's younger son. The company later merged with another to form the Sassoon & Alliance Silk Mill Company, which would continue to turn a decent profit as late as 1941.

Nestling alongside textile manufacturing in David Sassoon & Co.'s commercial portfolio was agriculture. The sector encompassed some 90 percent of India's population—and one reason for the failure of British rule to revitalize the Indian economy was its unwillingness to invest meaningfully in agricultural projects. Taking advantage of the financial crisis of 1865 and the resulting slump, the family had purchased vast estates in southern Calcutta. Now, in a series of initiatives aimed at improving land yields and the organization of those who labored on them, Suleiman modernized production. A previous historian of the Sassoons claimed, somewhat fancifully, that "never before perhaps in the history of agriculture had work of this sort been undertaken so systematically and on so vast a scale." In reality, the enterprise involved about fifteen thousand farmers, but it did provide food at cheap prices to Calcutta, and its holding company, Port Canning and Land Improvement, would operate well into the twentieth century.

The 1870s also saw the London branch of David Sassoon & Co. achieve a kind of parity with Bombay in the firm's pecking order; later it would obtain preeminence. Even before Albert's migration, large

Per Str. " *Lombardy*," to Bombay

Per Str. " *Legislator*," to Calcutta.

HONGKONG, 21*st January*, 1874.

DEAR SIRS,

We continue our advices from the 13th instant, since when the arrivals have been: the French Mail steamer *Ava* on the 16th, and the steamer *Legislator*, from Calcutta, on the 17th instant, bringing 1,045 chests of Bengal Opium, and 3,411 bales of Cotton. Stock: 2,000 chests of Bengal, 250 chests of Malwa, 700 chests of Persian, and 20 chests of Turkey Opium. Cotton 12,000 bales. Shipments to Shanghai for the fortnight: 1,120 chests of Malwa, and 380 chests of Bengal Opium.

BENGAL.—The market has been dull throughout the week, and the business transacted has been in favor of buyers. Rates have gradually declined, Patna closing at $602½, and Benares at $600; the latter drug being in little demand at present.

MALWA.—The low rates ruling at the date of our last brought out more buyers, and the sudden fall in Rupee Exchange, coupled with the news of smaller shipments from India, has imparted more confidence to holders, and values have improved to $600. The English Mail steamer *Travancore*, due in a day or two, brings forward about 2,100 chests.

PERSIAN.—Sales of 10 chests best quality new drug are reported at $515 per pecul, which may be considered as the nominal quotation. About 200 chests of newly imported drug have been transhipped to Amoy and Coast Ports, but no sales have been advised up to the present time.

TURKEY.—35 chests of old drug have been placed at $565, showing a decline of $100 since last sales on 14th August. The stock of 20 chests, all old, meets with no enquiry There have been no arrivals of new drug.

COTTON.—The market for Indian staple continues exceedingly inactive, and without sacrificing, it is extremely difficult to effect sales at anything like the full value of the Cotton. The steamer *Legislator* brought forward a good selection of new Cotton, but no business has taken place, and sales are prohibited by the high limits placed on the majority of the parcels. Holders continue very firm, and as the next two Calcutta steamers are only bringing forward a limited quantity, (900 bales), we may reasonably expect more activity before long, when the stocks of China Cotton become somewhat reduced. Sales for the fortnight, comprise : 450 bales of Kurrachee, 350 bales of Bengal, and 150 bales of Madras; and we quote nominally $10 @ $15 for all descriptions, according to quality.

There have been continuous arrivals of China Cotton from the North, and sales have been made to a large extent, necessarily exercising a prejudicial effect on East Indian descriptions. At the close, however, there is a quieter feeling, and stocks are rapidly accumulating. Prices paid vary from $13½ @ $14½.

BULLION.—GOLD LEAF, $24.35; SOVEREIGNS, $4.75; SYCEE, 9 per cent premium; and BAR SILVER, 10 per cent premium.

EXCHANGE.—On London, Bank Bills, at 6 months' sight, 4/3½. On India, 3 days' sight, Rs 219.

Shanghai.—Latest quotations by telegram, are: Malwa, Tls. 460; Patna, Tls. 444; Benares, Tls. 446. Stock on 15th instant: 1,915 chests of Malwa, and 1,427 chests of Bengal Opium.

EXCHANGE.—On London, Bank Bills, at 6 months' sight, 5/10; on India, at 3 days' sight, Rs 302.

We remain, Dear Sirs,

Yours faithfully,

DAVID SASSOON, SONS & Co.

A typical correspondence in English between different offices of David Sassoon & Co., 1874, reporting on shipments and prices of "Bengal, Malwa, Persian and Turkey" opium and cotton.

sums of money were being moved from Bombay to London, rather than the other way around. (The transfer of £49,053 at the end of January 1874 would be a typical example.) London was charging the firm's branches and partners for the costs that the company incurred: one charge for the collective partners, and another for each individual partner, except for the chairman, Albert. Among the partners, Suleiman was the most active in the opium trade, and most of the accounting dealt with his purchases and sales. Each week shipments of 25–30 chests of opium, mostly Malwa, arrived in Hong Kong from Bombay or Calcutta to be sold in different locations in China. Even in the late 1880s the number of chests purchased was quite high; in 1889 Albert informed his brother that they had bought 3,600 chests of Patna and Benares and said, "With God's help, we expect to make a decent profit."

Each branch collected revenues and promptly sent them back to the main office in Bombay (for now). Deductions would then be charged and credit given at the end of each month, and again each year. Whenever an office was late sending revenues, Bombay was distraught and shot off terse memos to hasten the remittance. The accounts memos say little about the profit or loss incurred per chest but do give a sense of the astounding scale: For 1873, the House of Hong Kong had a credit of 4,572,513 rupees and a debit of 5,525,056 rupees. The difference of nearly a million rupees was derived from all the charges, including employee salaries, expenses, and internal charges of 4 to 5 percent interest on capital used by each office. So this didn't mean that the House of Hong Kong lost money that year. Far from it.

A NEW LIFESTYLE

Perhaps the clearest sign of the shift in the Sassoons' footing away from Asia and toward England came in the form of a wedding. In Bombay, marriage had cemented both the Sassoons' identity as Baghdadi Jews and their relationships with other commercial families. Marriages between Jews and gentiles in the mid-nineteenth century were rare to begin with, but the Sassoons' options were further constrained by their desire to maintain their difference from the Native Jewish

Caste, and if a spouse could not be found in India, the family looked to Baghdad. Marriages within communities played an essential value in sustaining heritage and tradition in society, particularly among the diasporas. As the family's star rose, however, marriages with eminent Jewish families from farther afield offered opportunities to enter high society in England. As in other communities, "members of these larger clans forged marriage alliances and . . . these alliances shaped their economic investments."

Eugenie Louise Sassoon, 1890s.

The first of these marriages both to reflect the family's international standing and to enhance it took place in Trieste on January 19, 1873, when Arthur wed Eugenie Louise Perugia, of an old Jewish family from Trieste. Louise, who would invariably be called Mrs. Arthur, became a noted socialite in London, hosting many memorable parties, and when her sister Marie married Leopold de Rothschild eight years later, drawing relatives from Vienna and Paris to London, she hosted a wedding breakfast for the bride and groom at the house she shared with Arthur on Albert Gate. Three days earlier, Arthur had hosted a sumptuous ball attended by the Prince of Wales, and many members of the Rothschild family, and though the day of the wedding itself saw London battered by a blizzard, it was no less well attended. Among the well-wishers at the synagogue on Great Portland Street was their friend the Prince of Wales on his first visit to a Jewish place of worship. The Prince was among the signatories on the ketubah (Jewish wedding contract) and toasted the couple at the wedding reception, also attended by Benjamin Disraeli, the former Prime Minister. Members of the aristocracy admired the Italian Louise as a "brilliant hostess blessed with 'magnolia complexion and chestnut curls, magnificent diamonds and French chef.'"

In sharp contrast to traditional Baghdadi weddings, little thought seems to have been given to negotiating the terms of Louise's dowry, and though David Sassoon & Co. would later trade with the bride's brother, what marriage to the Perugia family really offered the Sassoons was entry into the ranks of the European aristocracy. It was a life they would grow accustomed to. Altogether more traditional was the marriage of Mozelle, David's youngest, to Rabbi Jacob Hayim, who was twenty years her senior, that same year, also in London. In a dispiritingly functional letter, Reuben provided Suleiman with the details of her dowry:

> For the wedding of our sister, Mozelle, we gave a dowry of £10,000 [£1 million today], and we arranged for her husband to endow a similar amount in a fund. This way not much of the dowry would be spent. Simultaneously, we gave Mozelle her share of the will of our father, may his name and memory be blessed.

The Sassoons' foray into aristocratic circles would rely not solely on their financial assets, however. They knew how to entertain. The hospitality for which Arabs were famed was their calling card. It also helped to have beautiful wives, whose elegance and talents were commented on every week in the society pages. Attending balls and making generous donations to fashionable causes likewise elevated their status. "The results of the bazaar at the Duke of Wellington's Riding School last week were most satisfactory," *Vanity Fair* reported, and "Mrs Sassoon's stall was one of those that raised most in funds for the Convalescent Home, Ventnor." Sir Albert, meanwhile, became a trendsetter, fêted in the same pages:

> The grand feature of Sunday now is *luncheons,* which are to be found well spread at many houses. . . . Of these feasts none are more popular than Mr. Albert Sassoon's, . . . who gives a great spread nearly every Sunday.

Albert knew that such entertainment could provide opportunities for business; future generations would lose sight of the latter half of this

Reuben, like many other members of the family,
owned houses in Brighton. Photograph, 1896.

equation. For them it became vital to be seen in the right places with
the right people even if there was no benefit, direct or indirect, to the
family firm. Sir Albert's luncheons were held mostly at 25 Kensington Gore, originally built in the mid-1870s by Sir Samuel Montague,
where he had established himself. It was a house "to be seen and
remembered":

> There is a large dining-room covered with Windsor tapestries
> and inlaid panelling, a large drawing-room of the purest and
> most delicate style of Louis XVI, a grand staircase and con-
> servatory, and numberless rooms, beautified with plush, and
> silk, and modern cabinets. . . . The bedrooms are such that one
> wonders how anybody can sleep in them without dreaming

that he is Solomon in all his glory. The house and contents are altogether a surprising and magnificent specimen of modern art upholstery.

Albert shuttled between this marvel and his house in Brighton, away from the bustle of the capital. The Sassoons would establish strong ties to Brighton for years to come, and their name still lives on there.

Excepting Elias and Suleiman, all of Albert's surviving brothers were by now resident in London. Arthur lived on Albert Gate near Hyde Park. He was believed to have one of the best music rooms in any home in London, and one of the city's finest staircases. Frederick, the youngest, lived in Knightsbridge. Reuben, meanwhile, had settled at 1 Belgrave Square, amusingly described in a compendium of England's twelve most "beautiful houses" as modern, with "very little *Oriental* about it." In fact, many of its rooms were garnished with Chinese and Japanese embroideries, and every stool, ottoman, and table "glimmer[ed] with raised gold work on the new '*high-art*' plushes and velvets." Unusually for the time, the house had three elevators: one for dinner, another for domestic staff, and one to connect the stable with the street outside. It was seen as one of the most technically advanced homes in London—the numerous bathrooms had showers, and the elevator in the stables had been installed so that the horses could be housed above ground level to benefit from natural light. There were reportedly "so many ingenious mechanical arrangements in *Mr. Sassoon's* house, that an engineer is in residence to answer for their perfect working order."

As Sir Albert was settling into his new life in England, his brother Elias was contemplating a move of his own. He had spent almost his entire adult life in China, but his firm needed headquarters in Bombay and he took the opportunity to return to his adolescent home. When not traveling to visit his firm's various branches, he worked diligently at E. D. Sassoon's offices on Rampart Row. Perhaps, in Albert's absence, Elias was able to reconnect with some of his family, for he chose to live in the same neighborhood in Bombay as Suleiman, around the Kala Ghoda (Black Horse), and it is hard to believe they did not cross paths heading to their offices or at the synagogue. Elias never fully recovered from his son's untimely death, and when his wife, Leah, whom he adored, fell ill and died in 1878, the blow proved fatal. He tried to work even harder to soothe the pain, throwing himself into schemes to purchase old mills or badly run ones and turn them into modern factories. He purchased a site to establish a new factory close to the Sassoon Docks and called his son Jacob from the Far East to help. On a visit to a tea plantation in Ceylon, and at the same time attempting to recuperate from a persistent cough, he fell ill and died in March 1880 at the age of sixty. The family, for a time, forgot the antagonisms of the previous dozen years and mourned him in all branches.

8

HIGH SOCIETY

1880–1894

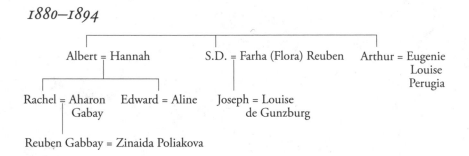

One of the defining elements of the refugee experience is the negotiation of old and new identities. The dilemma of whether to preserve the language and traditions of the land one has left behind or assimilate to one's adoptive home—and the difficult search for acceptance in both—faced every refugee in the nineteenth century, as it does now. As exiles from Baghdad who left behind a glorious past, David Sassoon and his family wanted to belong first in India and then in England. They invested much time, energy, and money in striving to become members of the English upper class, and for all practical purposes this high ambition was crowned with success.

The upward social mobility began in India, where upon arrival, the Sassoons had to deal with the issue of being Jewish and their relations with Indian Jews (the Bene Israel, the "Native Jew Caste") who had lived in Bombay long before their arrival. The Sassoons and other Baghdadi Jews in Bombay grew prosperous by aligning themselves and their businesses with the British Empire and its interests, and thus, in a move that was at once political, commercial, and social, sought to be considered European. They worked within the social valuations of the colonial order and brought some of their own to bear too, and thus spurned relations with Indian Jews, whom they saw as ethnically Indian and whose Jewishness they questioned. This attitude was imbued with a racist prejudice about color and pride in a tradition they believed was superior. This identification would become increasingly important after the uprising of 1857–58 and resulting institution of the British Raj, which by linking all India to one common administration both strengthened British rule and "made it easier for people to conceive of the country as a nation," and thereby led to a rise of national feeling.

The first generation of Baghdadi Jews to leave for India did not stray far from their roots. A rabbi visiting Bombay in 1859 described the Baghdadi community:

> The language of the Jews in their house and between themselves is Arabic, their mother tongue, and their customs and habits, their manners . . . [are] without any change or modification. They have neither changed their language nor their mode of dress, nor their way of living.
>
> They do not have a Rabbi here or a Teacher, either in this city or in the whole country, and every important question they ask by letter from the Rabbis of Baghdad . . . [as] they consider the Rabbis of Baghdad their authorities.

No wonder there was segregation between them and other Jews in the city. The 1881 census in Bombay distinguished between "Jews proper" (2,264) and "Beni Israel" (1,057). Baghdadi Jews were categorized as "Protected British Persons," which gave them valuable rights others lacked. Almost fifty years later, more than one hundred Baghdadi Jews in Calcutta signed a petition to the British government demanding that Jews of Iraqi origin, who were also British subjects, be included in Bengal's electorate, "based on a combination of their ethnic and racial background, European cultural practices, and unshakable loyalty to the British Empire." In reality, Baghdadi Jews were rarely accepted as properly European in India. For all their wealth and influence, the Sassoons were not allowed to enter Bombay's first hotel, the Watson, when it opened its doors in 1871 (nor were the Parsi Tatas). (Indeed, rumor has it that the two families aided the construction of the rival Taj Mahal Hotel as revenge.)

Despite the country's relative homogeneity and its rigid class system, England in some ways proved more hospitable to the Sassoon family. They arrived at a time when the liberalism of the Manchester School—and the idea that free trade would bring about a more prosperous and equitable society—was at its most influential, along with a wider package of beliefs about the dignity of the individual and acceptance of talent irrespective of creed. Edward, Prince of Wales, became the champion of this cluster of ideas, and the aristocracy grew more liberal in its outlook, showing greater tolerance to some foreigners and recognizing that restraints on their advancement should be reduced. There were limits to this tolerance, of course, and it could be argued that one reason why the Sassoons were viewed more favorably by the British aristocracy than the Warburgs or Rothschilds was that they weren't overtly in the moneylending business. (In fact, many of the merchants' trading activities were not dissimilar from banking activities, as "in their origins merchants and bankers were virtually indistinguishable," and only in the late nineteenth century did the boundaries become more recognizable.) It has also been argued that, for the British, social rank was then as important as, or even more important than, their color when it came to organizing the extra-metropolitan world. Thus, even religious and ethnic minorities could, with the right credentials, gain standing with and acceptance by the upper classes.

In spite of their accomplishments, the reality was that between "caste-conscious India" and "class-conscious British India," the British Empire was always "an international but closed world" to the Sassoons. Light-skinned Baghdadi Jews could rise higher than dark-skinned Indian ones, but they were "always beneath the British, whose schools they attended and whose citizenship they sought."

In principle, the British favored minorities in their colonies—their dependence on the colonial ruler ensured their loyalty—and the Jews

were undoubtedly a conspicuous minority. An examination of Sephardi Jews living in Hong Kong indicates that while "Judeo-Arabic
background led to social, economic and political exclusion," identify-
ing with British élites and their characteristics was "a means to overcome this exclusion." Families such as the Sassoons allied themselves
with the British and benefited from British rule, and commercial opportunities opened up for them as a result, not only in India but in
other colonies too. "Thus, a few elite Baghdadi families moved rather
quickly from their status as 'alien pioneers' to become key commercial
interlocutors for the British." The changes that took place over a relatively short period were staggering; even in 1865, the Sassoons felt they
were living in *balad al-ingliz* (the English state) and understood that
they had to abide by English rules in their dealings. More than thirty
years later, when most of the Sassoons had settled in England, India
was still home to some and was perceived as such. Writing to Farha,
who was about to leave on a trip to England, an employee reassured
her that all post would be held "until you safely return *lil-watan* [to the
homeland]." Yet, he went on to write that he would be sending his son
to London to study engineering, and most likely the boy would stay
there after his studies. England was the land of opportunity and there
was no contradiction. If asked, most members of the family right up to
the turn of the twentieth century would have described themselves as
Baghdadi Jews first and foremost. At the heart of this identity was the
bond of being "tied together by Jewish beliefs and religious custom," a
shared language, and more than two thousand years of history.

This bond found expression in the Sassoons' charitable works for
Baghdadi communities in the Far East and also for Jews still in Baghdad. When the latter suffered sporadic attacks in 1889, the family
sought to aid the victims and their families, and also to exert pressure
in London on the Sultan to remedy the situation—with success, as
Albert reported to Suleiman:

> As regards our people in Baghdad, we received good news
> about the Sultan firing the governor, may his name be
> tarnished. I hope that our brothers there will not engage in
> any measure that would ignite the anger of the masses by
> showing their delight in the dismissal of the governor.

On the other hand, they were criticized for not assisting Jews in other countries. When Jews in Jerusalem needed help in the late nineteenth century as Russian and Yemenite Jews began arriving in the Holy Land, Baron Edmond de Rothschild announced he would help only Ashkenazi (European) Jews and wondered why the Sassoons did not help their Sephardi brethren.

It was, as we shall see, much easier in Bombay or Calcutta to protect their tradition, religion, and pride in their Baghdadi heritage than in England, however. There these bulwarks of identity quickly eroded.

THE ROAD TO THE TOP

As Arthur's marriage to Louise Perugia showed, acceptance into the aristocratic fold relied as much upon the right marriage as upon riches or success in business. There are three principal types of marriages in commercial dynasties: intermarriages with other commercial families for the enhancement of the business, marriages for political gain, and marriages to boost social standing. The Sassoons started marrying for business purposes, but as their star rose, the emphasis shifted. By the 1880s, marriages with other wealthy Jewish families, mostly of Ashkenazi European stock, were common. One such wedding took place in St. Petersburg on November 19, 1884. Joseph, S.D.'s eldest son, had been born in Bombay but grew up in England. He took a degree at Oxford University and devoted his life to collecting rare books and antique furniture. Because his father had died when he was only eleven, it was his mother, Flora (not to be confused with Suleiman's wife in Bombay), who decided on the qualities his bride had to possess. She had to be young, rich, beautiful, and a practicing Jew. Louise, the eldest daughter of Baron Horace de Gunzburg of St. Petersburg, a wealthy banker, philanthropist, and bibliophile, proved the ideal candidate. Originally from Bavaria, Germany, the family had made their money selling vodka to the troops during the Crimean War and later became bankers for the Russian aristocracy. Louise grew up surrounded by luxury, in a home that hosted salons attended by such luminaries as Ivan Turgenev. Like Louise Perugia, she would play an active role in English society, and the couple would take up residence at Ashley Park.

Joseph, son of S.D.,
on the lawn of Ashley Park, c. 1890.

The marriage that tied the Sassoon and Rothschild families together more tightly than any other came three years later. The wedding was of Albert's second son, Edward, to Aline Caroline, daughter of Baron Gustave de Rothschild of Paris, on October 19, 1887. The Rothschilds were probably the most famous of all European banking dynasties and the most prominent Jewish family in Europe. They originated in Frankfurt and by the 1820s had established branches in the important European capitals and exerted great influence on the economic trajectory of Europe, and thus indirectly on its political direction also. The wedding itself, erroneously described by a French heraldic circular as between the daughter of an eminent family and "the son of Sir Albert Sassoon, from a family of Rajahs from India," was attended by seemingly every grandee in Paris. The Grand Rabbi of France conducted the ceremony to a packed synagogue on rue de la Victoire: "The flowers, the singing, the jewels, the presents, the oratory, the titles, the aroma of wealth, took away the breath of plebeian spectators . . . 'completely overpowered by the magnificence of the fête.'" At the reception, the guests, numbering around 1,200, were entertained by a chorus from the Paris Opéra, and the groom gave the bride a pearl necklace costing about £9,000 (more than £1 million today). Aline's charm, taste, wealth, and connections opened new doors for her husband and his family in French and English society, and her house in London became a center of literary and artistic life. From a business point of view, the marriage consolidated the relationship between the two families and ensured that if ever needed, the Rothschild banks would be willing to provide loans to finance the Sassoons' global trade. Twelve years after their wedding, Edward was elected as a member of Parliament in Hythe, Kent, a seat held by Meyer de Rothschild earlier in the century and where the family had a lot of property and influence.

Albert lost no time in taking advantage of this relationship. The same month, it was proposed that the two families float a sterling loan to finance the construction of railways in China. In the event, unlike its German counterpart, the British government did not show much enthusiasm for the scheme, and despite lobbying some influential MPs, their fear that they would be left out was realized. The family's relationship with the Rothschilds spread to other areas, such as charities. In a handwritten letter to Sir Nathaniel de Rothschild, one family member representing Albert thanked him for chairing a committee of wealthy families "to lend their effective aid to the growth of our less fortunate brethren." Though the Rothschilds' wealth outstripped that of the Sassoons, the relationship between the two families was not unequal—and neither were the benefits one-way, as the Rothschilds lacked the Sassoons' global reach. The disparity had been noted in 1881 by *The North-China Herald:*

> The name of Sassoon is less known in Europe than that of Rothschild, but among Arab or Banyan traders, even with Chinese and Japanese merchants, in the Straits as well on both sides of

the Ganges, it is a name to conjure with; and the strange ignorance of these facts (true and romantic at the same time) which once prevailed in England has long been dispelled.

Not long after his son's wedding, Albert did what thousands of aristocrats had done before him: he adopted a family crest. Around 1888, he commissioned the College of Heralds in London to design one. The Hebrew at the top, *Emet ve Emmuna* (Truth and Trust), was taken from the evening prayers, while the Latin at the bottom, *Candide et Constanter* (With Candor and Constancy), had first been used by the Earl of Coventry a century and a half earlier. David would doubtless have approved of the primacy of trust and reputation and perhaps also the palm tree that the crest carried, as a reminder of their Baghdadi roots, and because date palms were praised in the Bible (and the Quran) and became symbols of beauty and plenty. The coat of arms was later added to many of the family's buildings in Bombay and London, and also to the grave of the founder David Sassoon.

Another marriage that sealed the family's connections with European families took place in September 1891, and again to a wealthy European Jewish family. Albert's grandson Reuben (Ruby) Gabbay married Zinaida (Zina) Poliakova, scion of a family of Russian Jews who had grown rich building railways. The wedding was described as the grandest event of the Moscow calendar. Reuben had been born in China to Aharon Moshe Gabbay, head of the House of Shanghai, and Rachel, Albert's second daughter. The groom's father sent a detailed account of the wedding to Farha in Bombay:

Albert commissioned the coat of arms in the late 1880s with mottoes in both Hebrew and Latin and numerous religious symbols.

The day started at 11 a.m. when we went to the British Consulate to conduct a civil marriage. At 2.30 p.m., the couple were

married at the synagogue in a ceremony conducted by the
Grand Rabbi of Moscow, nearly 400 guests were at the
synagogue, women on the left and men on the right, 90
percent of whom were not Jewish. . . . I did not understand
the Rabbi's speech as it was in Russian but people said he
spoke beautifully. Then kissing started, everyone was kissing
everyone as I realized that men kiss each other as the custom
is here. Princes and princesses, and a representative of the
Tsar, all attended. Then we headed to a beautiful house in
the countryside surrounded by trees and magnificent flowers
all around. Champagne and cold starters were awaiting, and
toasting began, more than one hundred bottles of champagne
were consumed within one hour! What can I tell you? It felt
like all Moscow was there. More than 250 telegrams arrived
from the four corners of the world.

Then he turned to the business of marriage:

It is true Zina is beautiful, but somewhat vacuous like her
mother. Supposedly her father has allocated three million
francs (not rupees) for the dowry of his three daughters, so I
hope Ruby's dowry will not be less than one million.

Not long after, Gabbay wrote from Paris to tell Farha that the bride's
father planned to open an investment bank there, and said, "I hope
he would appoint Ruby to run it. Poliakov has built railways in Russia
and owned some of the lucrative lines, and his reputation here is more
prominent than the Rothschilds', and he owns properties everywhere
in Moscow." He wrote too of his third son, a student of German who
planned to add Russian to his roster on the grounds that "as long as
we are living in Europe we should master its languages, thus opening doors for a better life and business opportunities." In love as in
business, partnerships can all too easily come unstuck, and it seems
Ruby and Zina were a poor match, as her diary underlines the cultural
chasm between the two and her prejudices:

I always dreamed of finding myself a companion, but I erred in
my judgement. The point is that for complete mutual harmony,

above all, one needs to have, at the very least an equivalent
education. But that he [Ruby] absolutely did not have because,
when he was sixteen they sent him to get rich in Hong Kong,
where he spent the best time of his life, sitting at the table
smoking and selling opium. . . . [He has] an Eastern nature,
completely different from the European way and much of it is
incomprehensible to me.

Zina suspected, not without reason, that "Reuben had married her
only for money," and believed her father was not enthusiastic about
the marriage as he feared Reuben's "pockets are empty," but the gap in
culture and upbringing definitely made this marriage far less harmonious than the previous two.

Dowries seem to have been high on the agenda in most marriages,
but in marriages between wealthy and well-connected families, this
was not raised. There were other examples of a dowry being excluded
from the negotiations; when one of Reuben Sassoon's daughters was
engaged to the son of Mr. Raphael, a rich stockbroker, the papers
reported that no dowry was arranged as "both Mr. Raphael and Mr.
Sassoon are each credited with a fortune of something like £3,000,000.
Altogether, it seems a most suitable alliance."

The lavish weddings these marriages inevitably entailed were only
the most egregious examples of the capital families spent to integrate
themselves into British and European society. The balls and parties they
gave and attended, the weddings and dinners they hosted at their
homes week after week, required deep physical and financial reserves,
and their expenditure of both ensured that there was no issue of *Vanity
Fair,* the "Weekly Show of Political, Social, & Literary Wares," that
did not have a Sassoon giving or participating in a party of some kind.
Albert's home in Brighton was the place to be in the summers, and
"a large number of people availed themselves of the hospitality of the
Sassoons' there." It began with Albert, and other Sassoons followed
suit in living there, mostly as a second home. "Mr. and Mrs. Sassoon
had a very large party for Easter" in their Brighton house though
the weather was "capricious" with "raging" winds on Easter Monday.
Even at embassy functions, they were part of the scene; at a dinner
at the Austrian embassy it was mentioned that Mrs. Sassoon and

Arthur (Abraham Shalom), left, and Reuben, right, at the
Duchess of Devonshire's fancy-dress ball, London, 1897.

Mrs. Oppenheim "were immensely admired." When a London
monthly, *The Lady's Realm,* published an article about the London
season, it asked: "Then who are the great London entertainers?" The
answer, of course, was the Sassoons and the Rothschilds.

The press was not always kind—when one of the Sassoons threw
a ball at the New Club instead of at their home, *Vanity Fair* commented, "Two hundred guests scarcely fill the hall, and it was called a
dance"—but it recognized that the constitution of the aristocracy was
changing. In a commentary about the social scene in 1882, *Vanity Fair,*
unimpressed by the prospects for the coming season, claimed, "In
fact, there is but one class left to whom Society can look for entertainment and hospitality, and that is the great moneyed class, those whose
wealth arises more or less from commercial sources, quite independent
of land." Millionaires such as the Sassoons, Oppenheimers, Rothschilds, and Wilsons were the only families on which "Society [can]
pin its faith and hopes." By then, the City of London had become the
hub of wealth and the "single most important geographical unit," and
nearly all wealthy individuals were engaged in commerce.

Parties and ostentatious celebrations were not restricted to London,
of course. In Bombay, sixteen-year-old Rachel, Suleiman and Farha's
daughter, kept a diary of social occasions, in which she described "a

ribbon ball at Government House" that took place on February 7, 1893, in clinical terms:

> 350 guests were there: not a single native, except the Persian Consul. Lady Harris wore an old satin dress and very short puffed sleeves, black ribbons mixed with white at her waist. Very plain. Ellen Smith wore white silk with mauve ribbons. Plain. Mrs. Budgen had on white silk with yellow ribbons. Mrs. Acworth wore white silk with red, green, and pink bows. She is very stout. Mrs. Gabbay wore white silk with coloured ribbons. Ugly. Mrs. Forgett wore black with red bows. Very plain.

The teenager recorded visits and regular encounters with the Governor of Bombay and his wife, Lord and Lady Harris. In a mode less critical but no less observant, she wrote of the decor at one such dinner party at her parents' home:

> Ma had 4 tiny wood tables made, & they were arranged down the centre of the table, & white silk with silver stripes were draped over them, & and tiny gold dishes were put on them (the tables were covered) & at each end of the table were 2 enormous bunches of flowers, and small vases all over. Large sprays of maidenhair were strewn on the silk. It was lovely.

The diary carefully notes that some of these dignitaries were aware of and respectful toward Jewish laws for the Sabbath: "When Mamma was saying goodbye to H.E. [Her Excellency Lady Harris], [Lady Harris] said she was sorry that the [planned] fête was on a Friday, but she could not help it, as Lent is coming, and then the Bishop would get angry."

Occasions like these were an opportunity to show off the hosts' Baghdadi Jewish cuisine, a combination of Arab, Indian, Persian, and Turkish styles with Jewish restrictions on pork and shellfish and mixing meat with dairy. One menu: chicken kabob, *marag* of *kubba* (soup of meatballs), *hamod* with beetroot (meatballs with sour beetroot), *tabit* (a signature Baghdadi Jewish dish of stuffed chicken buried in rice, cooked overnight), a variety of rice dishes, *rishta* (cheese dumplings), and *kahee* (a kind of pancake) followed by custard pudding and peach tart. Desserts aside, Suleiman and Farha were clearly proud of their heritage. It would not always be so; a menu from a party held at Sir David Ezra's house in honor of Sir John Anderson, Governor of Bengal, in Calcutta in 1937 looks farther west than Baghdad to France, beginning with a *suprême du melon frappé* and finishing with a *soufflé de marrons*.

Houses too played an important role in the Sassoons' ascendancy. One that attracted attention was that purchased on Park Lane by Edward and Aline. It had originally been built for Barney Barnato, an entrepreneur who made his money in mining. Upon Barnato's death, Edward sold his father's house in Kensington Gore and paid £100,000 for the Park Lane residence, although unlike his brothers he preferred to spend most of the year in Brighton. The big house was "chastened and toned down by its present owner, and . . . is now quite one of the palaces in London, with a gorgeous suite of reception rooms and a magnificent square hall." *The Lady's Realm* was delighted that Aline, whom it considered a wonderful hostess, would have "this splendid, spacious house at her disposal," and wrote that she was "sure to give some royal entertainment."

Predictably, the real measure of the family's aristocratic credentials was not their town houses but their country estates. The most famous among them was Ashley Park in Walton-on-Thames, Surrey, bought in 1861 and where S.D. lived until his death in 1867. Later it was occupied by his eldest son, Joseph, and his (S.D.'s) wife, Flora, until her death in 1919. Its 430 acres had been part of the hunting grounds of Hampton Court Palace in Tudor times, and seemingly little changed in the next three centuries. The building, lost to a fire in 1986, was described in *Beautiful Houses:*

> The . . . hall, as we enter . . . , is very spacious, and occupies the entire height of the house, with a gallery at one end, and windows at both ends. . . . The two wings of the house are connected by a long gallery visible from the hall. . . . The furniture of the house is chiefly modern, with, of course, a decided dash of *Oriental* taste. Some portraits by a *Persian* artist of members

Edward and Aline Sassoon at their Scottish estate
with members of the Marlborough House set, c. 1895.

of the Sassoon family, in their *Oriental* habiliments, for a quaint
contrast with the *Renascene* and *Queen Anne* character of *Ashley
Park*.

The property was renowned for "its *Scotch* firs of unusual eminence
and girth," and had a pretty Italian garden "which in summer is a
blaze of colour." Other family members likewise acquired estates and
mansions as far away as Tulchan Lodge in the Scottish Highlands,
where Arthur and Louise "always have gay parties" and entertained,
among many others, King Edward VII. The estate was "the sporting
person's dream," boasting excellent hunting and shooting as well as
an eight-mile stretch for fishing on the river Spey. The fecundity of
the river was attested to by the *Evening Standard* when it reported
that "one of the finest salmons landed in Scotland was a specimen of
48 lb., which was secured by Mrs. Arthur Sassoon." She also excelled
at organizing grand picnics; the fifty-nine invitees to one held in a
deer park in Scotland included the Prince of Wales, Lord Macaulay,

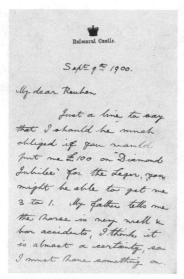
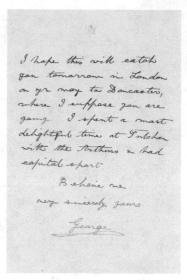

Letter to Reuben from the Duke of York, a few months before
his father was crowned Edward VII, 1900, asking him to place
a bet on a horse: "I should be much obliged if you would
put me £100 on 'Diamond Jubilee.'"

and members of the well-known Baring and Sykes families, a total of
thirty-one ladies and twenty-eight gentlemen of the British aristocracy
and upper class.

Horse racing, that most English of pastimes, became almost an
index of family members' fascination with and incorporation
into the British upper classes. By the mid-1880s, at least one Sassoon
would be in attendance at all the important horse-racing meets in
England. Reuben in particular had an appetite for horse racing—one
of the pillars on which his friendship with the Prince of Wales rested,
and which strengthened it, and it was rumored that Reuben was the
"'administrator of funds for his pastimes'—i.e., his unpaid agent
for his betting on the Turf," his "pearl-studded" "unofficial bookie."
Archives indicate that these rumors were true; in one letter the Duke
of York, the son of the Prince of Wales, asked Reuben: "Just a line
to say that I should be much obliged if you would put me £100 on
'Diamond Jubilee' for the Ledger, you might be able to get me 3 to

1." Interest in racing was not confined to England; as early as the 1880s, the Sassoons came to dominate the racing scene in Shanghai. One of Elias's sons, David, who was never interested nor participated in business, purchased a stable of thoroughbreds, when he was just twenty years old, and went on "to dominate the Champions' for the next decade," to the irritation of many of the English and the media in Shanghai. Another family member, Frederick, was heavily involved in the Hong Kong equestrian scene and on the committee making decisions about horse races in the city.

Royalty in Victorian Britain was immensely significant due to the reach and influence of the British Empire. The Prince had been acquainted with the Sassoon family since Albert had lavishly entertained him during a visit to Bombay. After Albert moved to London, the relationship continued, but the Prince was closer to Albert's two brothers Reuben and Arthur. Theirs was a bond founded on hospitality, sustained by their provision of expensive presents and (indirect) financial assistance, and also companionship—enjoying with him the shoots, races, and hunts the Prince loved. The eldest son of Queen Victoria was amiable and affectionate, though always a disappointment to his mother, who would describe him to his sister as "so idle and so weak"—hence her suggestion that he should travel her empire to occupy himself. Around Bertie formed a fashionable circle, known as the Marlborough House set, of young aristocrats, tycoons, society beauties, and others who shared his delight in betting and drinking. They did not always embrace Reuben and Arthur, as the Countess of Warwick recalled:

> We resented the introduction of the Jews into the social set of the Prince of Wales, not because we disliked them . . . but because they had brains and understood finance. As a class we did not like brains. As for money, our only understanding of it lay in the spending, not the making of it.

For the Prince, the group offered companionship and respite from his mother's endless moralizing, and from financial pressures too—a constant worry given his extravagant spending.

Reuben delighted in giving him gifts; he wrote excitedly to

Louise of the Prince's birthday, telling her, "He received many presents, among them my cigarette case, and there were five other similar cases, but mine was more appreciated as being uncommon." On another occasion he wrote giddily to his brother, "HRH thanked me over and over again for the treats I gave him." This generosity may have endeared him to the Prince, but Reuben was not universally popular. He was seen as Bertie's banker and drew acid comments about his manners during his many visits to Sandringham (his name was the second-most frequent entry in the visitors' book there), such as, "He never opened his mouth, except to put food into it." Nevertheless, even after the Prince was crowned King Edward VII in 1901, their friendship endured, as did Arthur and his wife Louise's with the King, and he would visit their home in Brighton to recuperate when he fell ill later in life. The Prince enjoyed the company of Arthur's wife, Louise, and liked Edward's wife, Aline, enough to name a yacht in her honor upon her marriage to Edward. Knowing the right people helped the family in many cases to become part of the aristocracy. Reuben was delighted when the Prince sponsored Edward, Albert's son, for membership of the Marlborough Club, known as the King's Club. It adjoined Marlborough House, and the Prince had exclusive use of a private entrance. Club members were elected only by consent of the royal family.

Albert realized that the focus should not be only on royalty, and while his half brothers were busy developing this relationship, he was playing a different role. When the Shah of Persia visited London in the late 1880s and the Prince was at a loss how to occupy him, Sir Albert came to his aid, renting the Empire Theatre to provide glittering entertainment that much pleased the Shah, as well as the British government, for whom a relationship with Persia was becoming vital for the empire, given its strategic location. Letters poured in after the event offering thanks and congratulating Albert for the splendor of the occasion. "We are not supposed in England to understand the science of spectacle as it is cultivated abroad. But in my life time I have never witnessed so fine a sight as you gave to London yesterday." The Prince and Princess of Wales expressed their thanks and congratulations on its success and felt sure that the performance gave His Majesty (the

Event hosted by Albert Sassoon for the Shah of Persia
during his visit to London in 1889.

Shah) much pleasure. Albert would later be rewarded with another
title partially due to his role in this episode.

The relationship between the Sassoons and Persia is fascinating
from the time the family fled Baghdad throughout the nineteenth
century. Persia was ruled by Nasr al-Din Shah for nearly fifty years.
It was a sovereign country with a strong identity but had difficulty
adjusting to European political and economic realities. Albert was well
placed to act as a mediator of sorts between the British and the Persians, especially with the arrival in Tehran in 1888 of the half-Jewish
envoy Sir Henry Drummond Wolff. The firm's stake in the opium
trade there as well as its early investment in the Imperial Bank of Persia
made Albert a substantial figure—enough to be made a member of the
Order of the Lion and the Sun by the Shah—and he maintained ties
with a number of powerful figures, such as Zell al-Sultan, a Prince and
Governor of Isfahan. Informing him of Edward and Aline's engagement, Albert wrote of "the good will evinced and extended toward
myself and family by his Imperial Majesty the Shah and your Royal
Highness [Zell al-Sultan] on the many occasions, together with the
extensive commercial relations between my different firms and Persia." Albert continued to correspond with Zell al-Sultan even when

he was on his deathbed. Zell lamented the fact that his position had prevented him from acquiring shares in the Imperial Bank of Persia, but he was willing to help direct some business to benefit the bank. Albert responded by offering shares in a nominee name designated by the Prince, or simply to receive bearer bonds (with no name), "in consideration of our friendship."

For these connections and others, Albert became a sage-like figure in London, consulted by British officials about matters in India, China, or Persia and wooed by foreign dignitaries for his links to the British government. In 1895, when the Sultan of Oman hoped to "use his influence to induce some member or members of the British Parliament to assist in his claim to the throne of Zanzibar," he naturally turned to Sir Albert. But by then Albert's health had begun to deteriorate, as one of his assistants explained to the Sultan. Given "the present temper of the House of Commons," however, Albert advised the Sultan, "Follow Sir John Kirk's advice to relinquish your claim to the throne of Zanzibar and urge the Government to assist you in recovering your legal rights in your brother's estates." In contrast to his half brothers, Sir Albert was styling himself as more of a statesman than a courtier. Albert also ensured that the reach of his firm was worldwide; wherever they operated, the Sassoons wanted to be an active and integral part of local society. When Shanghai celebrated its jubilee in 1893, David Sassoon & Co. hung its own flag in colored lanterns around the city to emphasize its presence and contribution. Albert sat on the London committee to raise money for the China Famine Relief, chaired by his friend Sir Rutherford Alcock, and when floods devastated the province of Guangdong in the mid-1880s, both old Sassoon (David Sassoon & Co.) and new Sassoon (E. D. Sassoon) donated cash to the relief effort. For his native Baghdad, Albert contributed toward a new school for the Alliance Israélite Universelle. In 1890, this school for boys and girls was described as spacious and had 139 pupils, and the British Consul General in Baghdad himself examined the pupils in English. Contributing to the Alliance Israélite Universelle put Albert in a small group of prominent Jews in Europe, such as the Camondo family and the Rothschilds, who were behind this project. Yet, the emphasis on charities in cities and ports they lived in rather than charity for its own sake was sometimes reflected in their refusal to grant emissaries from Palestine any donation; their Jewishness and strong adherence to religion did not translate into automatic donations to these envoys.

This mix of business, diplomacy, and charity was a delicate one, but the relationships on which it depended and which it facilitated could be capitalized upon, such as when Albert sought to cement the status of his line by acquiring a hereditary title. As Reuben told him:

> I had lunch with the Prince of Wales at the Marlborough Club, and when an opportunity arose, I showed him letters and documents relating to you getting a Baron title. He thought the letters most suitable for you to receive a baronship and [said] that he hopes that your son Edward would be worthy of taking his father's place. I assured him that Edward would make every effort to be worthy for the title.

The reward for Albert came in 1890, when Queen Victoria named him 1st Baronet of Kensington Gore. She had for the majority of her long reign opposed making any Jew a peer—"a step she could not consent to"—and it was not until 1885 that Nathaniel Rothschild was named in the Honours List. The Queen also had strong reservations about her son's friends in the Marlborough House set, including Reuben and Arthur, and advised him that once he became King it would be hard to break away from them. Despite this, her journals make many references to the Sassoons, particularly Mrs. Arthur, from the 1870s almost to the end of her life, when she attended a luncheon in honor of her 1899 visit to Folkestone organized by Sir Edward Sassoon, by now the MP for Hythe, Kent. Yet, *The Spectator,* reporting on the Honours List of 1890, revealed almost the full gamut of prejudices:

> The list of honours usually published at the beginning of the year is unusually short, and contains no remarkable names except that of Sir J. Lubbock, who is made a Privy Councillor, and of Mr. Savory, the President of the College of Surgeons, and of Sir A. Sassoon, who both [the latter two] receive baronetcies. The rise of this Jewish family in England has been remarkably rapid, as they were till quite recently strictly Indian Jews, almost

natives in their manner of life. They have long borne, however, a high character in Bombay, both for business capacity and a punctilious honour in dealing which has been in part the source of their wealth. Much of the Central Asian trade is in their hands; and this trade depends absolutely upon personal integrity. . . . Asiatics are supposed to be swindlers; but nobody ever saw an Indian "hoondee" dishonoured, and half the business of Asia is conducted on confidence alone.

LOOMING THREATS

Sir Albert's prominence in London drew proposals from unexpected quarters. One came from a British businessman who suggested that the firm join him to set up a new bank in Hong Kong to meet the needs of the Chinese, then remodel "their Army-Navy, constructing railways, arsenals." Another, from a Persian trader, advocated opening a branch in Isfahan, "the largest consuming market in Persia," and promised, "The advantages that would accrue by a branch of your house in Persia would be immense." Neither fitted the company's general strategy of the time, which prioritized stable investments in property to earn income and potential capital gains over other new ventures, and both were rejected. The number of properties owned by the firm increased substantially, and property management teams were hired to take care of maintenance and deal with tenants. Their team in Hong Kong, for example, reported that all their tenants were responsible and paying rent on time but also that there was substantial expenditure on extensive repairs. Property managers were also hired to handle family members' personal homes: A memo to Suleiman about properties he owned in Bombay detailed the rentals and renovations of each building and tried to dissuade him from selling any, arguing that they would appreciate substantially and continue to bring in a decent income.

The firm's expansion in the final decade of the nineteenth century was not only in their property portfolio but also in new products. While the Sassoons had traded pearls during David's era, this was a peripheral affair, undertaken in a way that would come to be seen as haphazard. How they planned to enter this market reveals the level of sophistication that began to characterize global merchants like the Sassoons. In the early 1890s, a consultant was hired by the firm to undertake a comprehensive study of the market surveying the types of pearls, indicating whether the market was well supplied in terms of their availability, price, and demand; summarizing the principles of the pearl business; and making recommendations about what to buy and how: "You should not hesitate for fear of offending a client to decline to receive common consignments of pearls. Let them go elsewhere if they like. Avoid getting locked [in] with a quantity of unsaleable stud which will take your time and give you trouble." The detailed twelve-page report induced the Sassoons to be more active in the pearl market, which they were until the early 1930s. Pearls were joined by diamonds, though here the company acted only as agents, charging a 2.5 percent brokerage fee as well as 1 percent for any diamonds not being sold and thus sitting on the firm's books. There was, for instance, more activity in trading diamonds in the 1880s and 1890s compared to the 1860s and most of the 1870s. There was a notion in London that Bombay tobacco might have some appeal in England, and the firm dabbled in importing it—but this was sporadic rather than consistent trading. Albert saw these auxiliary activities as a natural expansion of the business, though the profits were always modest compared to its core products, opium and cotton. Diversification led to new vehicles of investments; they were among the founders of the Persian Gulf Steamship Company in 1892 and maintained direct or indirect control of the company, whose paid capital was over £83,000, and its main assets were six steamships, all named after different places in Iraq, such as Basra and Amara. Even with this more diversified portfolio, we can see that they did not diversify enough and were dangerously reliant upon their two main products.

Profits from the opium trade, which in the 1880s had been healthy, started to decline in the following decade. Currency trading had steadily grown more complex and volatile over the 1880s and some traders began to use sophisticated tools, such as forward markets and arbitrage with Mexican silver dollars, to reduce their exposure. Fluctuations in the silver price affected traders; commenting on a sharp price decline in 1886, Albert wrote to his brother Suleiman asking for advice on whether to wait or to buy some silver at the depressed prices. In moments of extremity, the company sought governmental help. In 1893, David Sassoon & Co. wrote to the British government explaining its predicament and describing its trade:

> A large proportion of the trade of India with China has for many years been carried on by ourselves and others by the dispatch of yarns, piece-goods, and opium from Bombay and Calcutta, the return proceeds being received by Bank bills, telegraphic or demand. Since the uncertainty [regarding the opium trade], it has been impossible in Hong Kong and Shanghai to get any Exchange Bank to grant remittances on British India, and there was, therefore, during the uncertainty no other way for ourselves and others to get their funds returned from China to India except by the dispatch of silver bullion.

Given the depreciated market value of silver, the firm asked the British government for assistance shipping Mexican silver dollars back from China. A major reason for seeking assistance was the closing of mints that had allowed free coinage of silver, a service used by the Sassoons, who were in the habit of tendering small amounts of silver annually to the mint for coinage. E. D. Sassoon followed suit, though for a relatively small sum—£7,000 to David Sassoon & Co.'s £74,000. The flurry of letters and memos about this request within the British administration and with the two firms reflected the government's concern that if it approved it, it would leave itself open to more claims, and although some voices in the administration argued that David Sassoon & Co. should receive compensation, all claims were rejected. Payments in cash in lieu of bank orders became "in vogue during 1873" and continued for many years, adding to traders' prosperity. The glittering rewards held out by trading with China were always tempered by such risks; profitable trades were only half the battle: Could a trader sell his commodity for a profit and could he manage the currency risk?

A major challenge facing the opium trade in the 1880s was over-supply. As the price of opium declined, the family actually stepped up their lobbying to limit or lift any restrictions against the trade. The oversupply was driven by local Chinese production. Between 1879 and 1906, total Chinese production increased from 98,000 piculs (a Chinese weight equivalent to 133.3 pounds) to 584,000 piculs, as Chinese farmers discovered that "poppies yielded four to five times the profit of wheat." The Sassoons couldn't control production within China's borders, so they concentrated their efforts on reducing any taxes on Indian opium, particularly Malwa, in order to make their own product more competitive. Chinese demand for Indian opium remained relatively stable between 1870 and the late 1880s but then began to decline, and by the early 1890s, losses started to appear.

On New Year's Day 1890, a senior employee in Hong Kong wrote to Edward in London to apologize for the losses he had sustained over the previous year—his office originally expected a profit of more than £40,000—which he blamed on a combination of high bank interest rates and rising agents' fees. Albert bombarded all the branches with letters about the rising losses from opium, encouraging them not to shy away from risk altogether—"Everything you put money in, there is risk, and trading in opium is no different"—but as losses mounted, Edward was shaken:

> In the last few days, I am depressed and utterly dazed due to the large losses in opium. What kind of traders are we? Why are we sitting on a commodity instead of trading it? Is this a new strategy to keep the consignment in a warehouse and accumulate losses?

Part of his frustration was due to the high interest rates banks and traders had to pay on cash, which meant that any risky trade had to be weighed against secured cash deposits. By March 1890, losses had reached two hundred thousand rupees—substantial but dwarfed by profits previously amassed.

Attempts to compensate for these losses were made by finding new outlets for opium. David Sassoon & Co. tried to sell it to the French authorities in 1892. A letter from a French firm in Paris to the company expressed its regret as it had not succeeded "in the adjudication of the 31st August last, for the supplying of 1000 chests of opium to the French Government." It seems the consignment was supposed to be sent to Saigon in Vietnam, where a tender offer had been made. But the French firm felt it could not make any profit; it was willing to reimburse all expenses incurred by the Sassoon firm and hoped "to be more fortunate in the future." Interestingly, the French government in Vietnam then turned to E. D. Sassoon, which was able to offer 140 chests from Calcutta. E. D. Sassoon regretted that it could not sell the 500 chests that the French government in Hanoi wanted, because "the Government of India is reluctant publicly to increase the quantities of opium offered."

Losses continued to climb, however, and by the end of April they were estimated at between 500,000 and 600,000 rupees, and the House of Calcutta was selling chests of opium at a loss of more than 140 rupees per chest. A memo in mid-1893 indicated that total net losses after offsetting credit received were approximately £80,000: £24,000 from Persian opium and another £11,000 from Isfahan opium; £23,700 from shipments to China; and over £21,300 written off as a loss to January 1890 and placed as a debit on the books. Turkish opium, on the other hand, traded by the London office, contributed almost £26,000, and receivables from China were about £24,000, almost equal to the losses incurred. In a premonitory letter to Suleiman at the end of 1891, Albert described the state of the trade:

> Oh, my brother, what we are shipping to China is no longer profitable. We are losing 20 Rupee per chest and even when we make profit, it is no more than 5 Rupee. We have so much of this [commodity] in China and the more we ship, the more we depress the market. You are thinking of buying 1500–2000 chests via Calcutta. Well, the minute you do that, E. D. Sassoon will make sure prices decline. Our merchants are screaming that they have no more place in their warehouses to accommodate more chests. You heard that one or two merchants even kept the consignment on the ship due to lack of space. You are trying to control the Calcutta opium by buying 3000 chests out of a total production of 5000 chests.

One merchant we shipped to has not sold anything for two years and we have not received anything in revenue. How long is this going to be? Shouldn't we reduce our exposure and prevent more losses to accumulate?

One answer was to redouble the firm's efforts to reduce its tax burden, and the Indian National Archives preserve numerous requests by the Sassoons, who were adept at enlisting other merchants to support their cause, advocating against proposed increases in taxes on Malwa opium and for their reduction. The government of India was well aware that if it yielded to the pressure to reduce duties, exports of Malwa would increase considerably because of the large stocks being held by merchants in the early 1890s. Correspondence among officials indicated relatively static exports between 1888 and 1891 of around 40,000 chests, from a peak of 50,000 chests in the late 1870s, and most important, that the price of Malwa had stabilized around 1,200 rupees (down from highs of 1,700 rupees in the late 1870s). The Governor-General therefore informed David Sassoon & Co. and other merchants that they were "unable to make any reduction in the export duty on Malwa opium." It could be inferred that the firm's lobbying failed, but senior British officials in both India and England knew well that the Sassoons and other global traders were more than capable of marshaling their political connections to achieve economic objectives, and the pressure they exerted deterred the government from levying other duties or changing the system.

The status quo increasingly looked unsustainable, however. By 1893, even senior employees were beginning to doubt the profitability of opium; interest rates were high in Bombay, meaning returns shrank as supply increased. A report by David Sassoon & Co.'s Manchester branch of that year illustrates both its awareness of the interconnections between region, nation, and more that shaped its business and its concern that the opium trade was in decline:

Business of this branch has been depressed for several months of the year owing to the Persian market upheaval: depreciation of silver, cholera, and subsequent trade closed by quarantine. These influences combined with those of poor wheat and opium crops, leaving but little to export to pay for imports. This has been aggravated by the Imperial Bank of Persia raising the rates of exchange for homeward remittances.

A comparative statement of Manchester's profits from 1884 to 1892 shows that they had peaked at just over £17,000 in 1891 before falling sharply in 1892 to £12,500. The report contemplated introducing new goods—Turkey Red twills and other textiles—in order to diversify the business.

Why, when the realization dawned in the early 1890s that opium profits were dwindling, the company didn't seek to fundamentally diversify, to reduce their heavy reliance on opium in favor of other business, whether financial or industrial, is unclear. True, it was sitting on substantial stocks of opium and the rewards of the previous three decades had been the making of them. And in spite of the pressure on profits, we can see from Bombay's account for 1892 that the house's profits totaled £230,705 on a capital of £2.32 million, so roughly 10 percent after all expenses. Put in modern parlance and currency, Bombay's turnover was roughly £250 million with £25 million net profit. There was life in the trade yet.

OPIUM AND THE CHURCH

The biggest threat to the opium trade came not from taxation, over-supply, or currency fluctuation, but rather political pressure in Britain to put a halt to it. The trade's fiercest adversaries were a group of reformers from the Society of Friends, or the Quakers, as they are more commonly known. In 1874, a group of Quakers formed the Society for the Suppression of the Opium Trade, whose members included inter alios politicians, members of the aristocracy, and journalists. They succeeded in making prohibition the subject of parliamentary debate in 1881 when J. W. Pease, an MP who was also President of the society, put forward the following resolution:

That, in the opinion of this House, the Opium Trade, as now carried on between India and China, is opposed alike to Christian and International morality, and is instrumental in effecting the physical and moral degradation of thousands of Chinese, and ought not to be continued in the manner in which it is at present conducted.

Mr. Pease called for gradual development of resources in India to replace opium revenues, and for Britain to assist India if this caused a shortfall in its budget. That same week, the Society invited the Archbishop of Canterbury to speak at its annual conference. They had been encouraged by the U.S.-China treaty of 1880, which imposed restrictions on the opium trade between the two countries, and thought the moment ripe for "all Christian Englishmen [to] combine to free our country from the sad responsibility for this evil trade." The news in 1881 that the Inspector General of Customs in Peking estimated the number of opium smokers at over two million and rising annually intensified the moral argument to ban the trade. A two-pronged campaign was mounted, to convince public opinion of the need to halt this "evil trade" and MPs to support a change in the law. William Gladstone, in his second term as Prime Minister, had previously condoned the trade and would do so again, in part not to alienate powerful figures in his Cabinet, but he sensed that pressure was building up in Parliament for reform. A long letter to Gladstone, signed by dozens of MPs, members of the Society, university professors, schoolmasters, mayors, and retired army officers, denounced exporting opium to Burma from India and cited a report that painted "a painful picture of the demoralization, misery, and ruin produced among the Burmese by opium smoking." In regard to China, the signatories regretted the policy "that our fathers began, we their children are pursuing; and though we can never undo the irrevocable past, we have yet much we can do to lessen the result of our evil deeds in the future." The letter asserted that imposing high duties as a means of reducing exports would not solve the problem and claimed that:

The Government is at once the chief of growers, of manufacturers, and of vendors, and the tax which is levied for transit of the drug grown in native states is always adjusted to equalize the price of that opium with our own. It is in the power of the Government to stop the growth to-morrow in the British dominions.

The anti-opium lobby, which now included leaders from the Methodist, Unitarian, Baptist, and Presbyterian churches, was relentless. Although its campaign was gathering momentum, the lobby sought to avoid being a political movement. In its diverse publications, its leaders insisted that opium was a vice and that the habit of opium smoking was among the worst of vices. They enlisted senior Chinese officials to rouse public support for the cause and published their letters in magazines and pamphlets. Among these was a Chinese dignitary from Tientsin, who expressed the gratitude of his countrymen to the Society [of Friends] for its efforts to free China from "the evils of the opium traffic." He claimed that England and China could never meet on common ground: "China views the whole question from a moral standpoint; England from a fiscal." In his long letter, the dignitary referred to the "unlawful cultivation" of opium in his country and assured the Society that his government did not approve of this cultivation and treated it as any other crime committed in China. The anti-opium lobby denounced the trade in its literature and argued that there was no greater barrier to the spread of Christianity in China than the vice, and that the government was not an independent body but rather acting in its own interest, as it did not want to lose £6.5 million in revenues from opium taxation. Oddly, the Archbishop of Canterbury refused to ally himself totally with the Society in the early stages of the campaign because of what he saw as its political objectives, although he agreed in principle with the abolition of the opium trade.

The attention of the public having been drawn, the real battle took place in Parliament. In 1891, Pease put forward another motion in the Commons, urging the Indian government to stop granting licenses for the cultivation of poppy and the sale of opium, "except to supply the legitimate demand for medical purposes." The motion was nonbinding, and the House adopted it by a substantial majority of 160 against 130, but when the question of taxation was raised and how to replace opium revenue, the House could not agree and the matter was left unsettled. Among those supporting the status quo were the Conservative MP for Evesham, Worcester, Sir Richard Temple, a former Governor of Bombay who knew the Sassoons well. Addressing members of the Temperance movement in Parliament, he argued for the trade, defending Indian taxation of opium by comparing it to the excise system in England, and contended that, based on medical opinion: "Opium is not deleterious in reasonable moderation, and is, under all circumstances, far less deleterious than alcoholic drink. Either taken to excess is harmful." He vehemently disagreed with the idea that opium was a poison except as a concentrated distillation, which he asserted was a "wholly different thing to the substance sold in the Eastern bazaars under the name of opium. That opium is perfectly harmless if taken in moderation, and it is taken by many classes in Western India without any mischief whatever." He defended the traders of Bombay and Calcutta as "men of wealth, energy, and enterprise," and questioned those who supported taxation of spirits but not of opium. Temple's words later became the rallying call for all those supporting the trade: Opium was not harmful if taken in moderation and it was no different from alcohol.

A flurry of correspondence ensued between London and the Indian government after the debate, and the Cabinet discussed how best to deal with MPs who supported the suppression of the trade. Faced by political agitation in both the House of Commons and the House of Lords, the British government did what governments tend to when presented with irreconcilables: It formed a Commission of Inquiry to study the subject in detail, thus delaying the need for immediate action. In 1893, in Gladstone's third term, a Royal Commission on Opium was appointed, with a mandate to study whether the cultivation and sale of the poppy should be prohibited, except for medical purposes; whether any change in the existing system should be made; and the cost for Indian cultivators if opium were to be prohibited.

To counter the abolition movement in Britain, both Sassoon firms turned to the China Association, a lobbying group set up in London to protect British interests in China. A majority of its representatives were former government officials, mostly from the Foreign Office, who would lobby the Foreign Office or Parliament. Many of the letters addressed to the Association were signed by representatives of both Sassoon companies (and usually by another half dozen companies).

All these companies coordinated their efforts to ensure that exports of opium to China were not curtailed or—worse—banned.

A QUANDARY IN THE EAST

Albert's frustration with the state of the firm's trade, particularly opium, was deepening. His letters to Suleiman were full of complaints about and ruminations on E. D. Sassoon's purchases and sales. He was impatient if Suleiman failed to respond immediately or follow his instructions to the letter and expressed fury whenever he heard of anyone who owed the firm money failing to pay on time. He grew increasingly intolerant of dissent and began one letter to Suleiman by asking his brother to "please fulfil all these requests" rather than argue with him.

Although Albert retained overall control, since 1864 Suleiman had been effectively in charge of David Sassoon & Co.'s activities outside England. He dealt with correspondence from every corner of the globe. The sheer volume of it indicates that he worked long hours six days a week—as his father and Albert had, and as the majority of the family now didn't. He was never as captivated by the thrills of high society as his brother and never contemplated moving to London, knowing that without him, the business would falter. In addition to his immediate family—he and Farha had one son and two daughters—he found solace studying religious texts and strolling in the garden of their magnificent villa at Pune, Rose Bank. Farha, determined to help relieve the burden on her overextended husband, announced, in defiance of all taboos, that she would start accompanying him to headquarters in the city's grand Elphinstone Circle. Her announcement shocked many within Bombay's mercantile class, as no other woman dared to participate in business negotiations.

Adding to Suleiman's woes was the emergence of a new competitor, specializing in real estate and expanding throughout Asia. Silas Hardoon had arrived in Shanghai in 1874, one of many entrepreneurial young Baghdadis who aspired to work for the Sassoons and then create their own wealth. He was employed by David Sassoon & Co. but then left and in the 1880s joined E. D. Sassoon in Shanghai. Until then, the Baghdadi community had been his main point of reference, but in 1886–87 he broke with convention and married outside his community and faith. His bride was a half-French Chinese woman and a devout Buddhist, and their marriage led him to be interested in Buddhism and drew him closer to Chinese society. He eventually left E. D. Sassoon and founded his own real estate company; by the time of his death in 1931, he would be "Shanghai's major individual landowner and the richest foreigner in East Asia." At David Sassoon & Co.'s old foe, Jacob Sassoon was revealing predictions that Elias's death would precipitate the collapse of his business as wishful thinking. He was continuing his father's expansion into new territories and markets, and with him at the helm, E. D. Sassoon adhered as closely as ever to its internal dictum: "Wherever David Sassoon & Co. are, we will be; whatever they trade, we can trade." Jacob was relatively lonely as he felt he could rely only on his brother Edward. He had lost his only son when the boy was young and hence had no direct successor. At the same time, Suleiman's health was deteriorating and he felt less energetic as problems were piling up.

As the pressure on Suleiman mounted, even Farha's assistance was too late to save him. He died aged fifty-three in March 1894. Eulogies poured in, from Jerusalem to Baghdad to London. His death was announced in all major newspapers in India, China, and Britain—one went so far as to recognize that the "most active partner" in the firm of David Sassoon & Co. had died. In Bombay, as a mark of respect, all Jewish companies, schools, and mills owned by the two Sassoon firms, as well as the opium, gold, and silver bazaars, and the Oriental Life Assurance Company (where the Sassoons had an interest), were closed for the day. Obituaries praised Suleiman's achievements, his munificence, his commitment to his family and community, and his dedication to studying the Hebrew Bible. A large memorial service in Baghdad was attended by most of the city's Jewish notables, and Suleiman's untimely death was lamented in pamphlets published there. In London, his brothers had to balance their surprise and grief with the urgent need to find a successor. None of them wished to return to Bombay, to uproot their families and leave behind the glamorous lives they had built in their new home. They were English now.

9

THE MATRIARCH

1895–1901

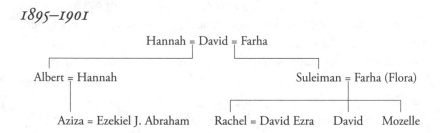

Hannah = David = Farha

Albert = Hannah   Suleiman = Farha (Flora)

Aziza = Ezekiel J. Abraham   Rachel = David Ezra   David   Mozelle

Many commercial dynasties in history have produced notable matriarchs. But until relatively recently, their power was almost always wielded behind the scenes. In managing a global business as the nineteenth century gave way to the twentieth, then, Farha Sassoon was unique in her time. Her background and upbringing were similar to that of most women of the time from privileged families. Women in the Jewish diaspora, and Sephardic women in particular, learned from a young age how to negotiate religious and socioeconomic boundaries and to exert influence or "soft power" behind the scenes. For the vast majority who were blocked from formal positions of authority, "women played a crucial if indirect role in the formation, transmission, and preservation of merchants' capital because of the legal customary rights they possessed over their dowries."

At the time Farha was growing up, women were at a considerable disadvantage in every respect. One of the first Indian girls to receive an English education wrote in her memoirs that the Baghdadi Jews in Bombay had followed the Parsis in allowing their daughters to be educated, and that Albert had exceeded David in his commitment to girls' education:

> He overcame the prejudices of his old sire, and thus strengthened he spread the light of many a beneficent principle, opening the gate of happiness to the women of his faith. It is within my memory that Jewesses never appeared in public without closely veiled faces. When the ladies of the Sassoon family came to visit [my house], they would never unveil till the male members of the household, servants included, had removed themselves and the coast was clear.

Farha's mother, Aziza, was one of Albert's five children, and by the time Farha was born in 1856, the family was well established in Bombay and enjoying the fruits of the firm's success. Her father was Ezekiel J. Abraham, a trader and businessman who had moved to Bombay from Baghdad. The eldest of twelve children and therefore familiar with leadership from a tender age, Farha was assertive even as a child, determined to get what she wanted. Her education exceeded her mother's in rigor: Reading Shakespeare was paired with the study of the Hebrew Bible alongside learned rabbis. She enjoyed studying and added French and German to the required English, Arabic, Hebrew, and Hindustani.

The dearth of archival material on the role of women adds to the quandary in research about nineteenth-century global merchants, and this was exacerbated by the paternalistic attitudes of some male researchers. For instance, Ben-Yacov's massive work on the Jews of Babylon dedicated more than four pages to Suleiman, Farha's husband, but a mere two sentences to Farha's groundbreaking management of the business. In spite of the scant information about the role of women among the Sassoons and other Baghdadi families, the accounts of those women who were not mainstream European or Indian "show us that they were active in both the public and the private domain as householders, travellers, traders, and businesswomen."

Women are mostly mentioned in the extensive correspondence in the Sassoon archives rather than the authors of it, often at the end of letters when a correspondent would inquire about the recipient's wife or mother and request that his best wishes be conveyed to her. There were a few exceptions. Hannah Gabbay, whom we met making recommendations to Suleiman about how best to end a compradors' strike, sometimes wrote business letters when her husband was traveling, and she certainly intervened in the business. A few letters survive from mothers to their sons, separated by great distances often for years at a time. David's wife, also called Farha, wrote frequently to her son Suleiman after she moved to Britain following the founder's death. Her letters always began with *"lil-walad al-aziz wa nur al-ain"* (to the dear son and the light of my eyes). In one letter she described being awed by London, though she found it cold and heard that it always would be. Her letters gave news about her family and told him of various relatives' travels and reminded him that she missed him and it pained her that they would not be together during the Jewish holidays. In fact, Suleiman was absent from the family in Bombay and from festivities for many years. An altogether different type of letter carried requests from employees' wives or mothers beseeching help or asking for opportunities on their behalf, presumably because it was felt that these pleas would be more likely to be heard coming from a woman. One wife and mother, however, would take matters into her own hands.

Suleiman and Farha's marriage was remarkably equitable by the standards of the time, perhaps almost a partnership. He often sought her advice on company matters and more, and he valued her wide learning. She loved him for his faith and his modesty: It was said that he was so unassuming that he used to slip into the synagogue he had built by the back door to pray. Farha's outgoing personality complemented and indeed compensated for her husband's. She was for her part comfortable with the rich and powerful men she regularly hosted at their home, from Indian royalty to senior British officials, able to talk freely with them and put them at ease. The Prince of Wales never forgot her charm or hospitality during his visit to India in 1875. When Reuben stayed with the Prince in 1891, some fifteen years later, the Prince reminisced about Farha and the two small gifts she had given him for the long journey back home: *amba* (homemade mango chutney) and *mishmish yabis* (dried apricots), and told Reuben that "he ate a spoon of *amba* every day on his boat from Bombay until he reached Suez." Farha had no shortage of confidence either. One anecdote, from after she moved to England, has her accosting a policeman, who was sweating in the heat of a midsummer's day in Hove, and with inimitable style, telling him, "What you need is a melon. It's the best thing to cool you on a warm day. Do you like melons?" Having confirmed that he did, she asked him how many policemen manned his station. "Sixty-four," was the answer, and the next day sixty-four melons were delivered to the local police station with Farha's compliments.

When Suleiman died in 1894, Farha announced she was ready to take over his duties. Accompanying him to the office in the couple of years before his death, she had learned the ins and outs of the business and already established relations with other merchants and agents with whom her husband collaborated. The Sassoon family was not prepared for a female leader. They couldn't look to the old country and Baghdad for a precedent, and though seemingly every day brought news of the suffragettes' activities in England, women did not run global companies there either. Even in Europe, women did not manage global firms, and although Queen Victoria was ruling over the largest and most powerful empire in the world, she was, after all, royal and hardly a role model for business. Albert, however, had few options: Reuben, Arthur, and Edward were too enmeshed in English society to leave it for Bombay or Shanghai, and they weren't necessarily qualified to manage the business in the East while he coordinated matters in England. His own health was fragile, and he had reduced his commitments to the minimum—even the number of letters bearing his signature had diminished. Furthermore, not long after Suleiman passed in Bombay, Albert's wife, Hannah, followed, and his brothers and son had to rush to Brighton to break the news to him. Zinaida Poliakova opined in her diary that Albert did "not pretend to be saddened by the death of his wife," but this has to be taken with a pinch of salt as Poliakova was far away and probably was projecting her own troubles with her husband.

Farha was self-evidently competent and effectively already in charge of the company's business in Asia. Despite his misgivings about having a woman run the business, Albert knew well how capable and determined she was, and thus acquiesced, as, even more reluctantly, did his brothers. Farha wasted no time and promptly immersed herself in the business. Aged thirty-eight, she wasn't satisfied just to raise her three children and enjoy the wealth left by her late husband. She had ambitions and was an avid reader not only of the stream of reports reaching her desk but of information about the different commodities handled by the company and the global events that might influence their prices. By the end of 1894, Farha was admitted as a full partner in all the offices of David Sassoon & Co.—India, China, and England—and enjoyed full signing authority.

The revised partnership is revealing. A fixed capital of £1 million (more than £110 million in today's value) was proposed, to be divided as follows: 41 percent to Albert; 15 to Reuben; 22 to Arthur; 12 to Edward; and 10 to Farha. Farha's smaller portion didn't reflect her contribution to the business, which she would in effect be managing, nor that of her husband, who had labored unstintingly for the family firm over three decades, but she was the first woman in its history to be named a partner. The formal document, however, left no doubt who remained in charge:

> The good will and right to use the style of David Sassoon & Co. [is] to be deemed the sole property of Sir Albert D. Sassoon and in the event of dissolution of partnership no partner [is] to be entitled to any compensation in respect of such good will or to have any right to interfere or carry on business under the firm of David Sassoon & Co.

The partnership agreement also made it clear that no partner could cash out unless their profits equaled the amount they sought to withdraw, and affirmed Albert's power both to fire any partner with two months' notice and to appoint new ones. Appropriately in the circumstances and given the chairman's advanced age, the agreement made numerous references to retirement and death:

> No retiring partner or executors of a deceased partner [are] to be entitled to force a general liquidation of the partnership affairs in which such partner may be interested but in the event of such death or retirement the liquidation of all transactions in which

he or she shall be or have been interested [is] to be conducted
by the remaining partners in the ordinary course of business.

From now on, the merchants, brokers, and agents with whom David
Sassoon & Co. did business would have to negotiate and even shake
hands with a woman. It was a daunting challenge, though Farha had
her supporters: One Indian friend in Pune told her, "May God assist
you in your deliberation to steer it to a haven of wealth and prosperity
and your leadership will be an addition to the prestige of the Prince
of Merchants," meaning David.

By the final years of the nineteenth century, the firm's route to
greater riches was not straightforward. As we have seen, the opium
trade was subject to pressure from prohibitionists in Britain and
increased production in China and elsewhere. The firm's textile mills
needed constant attention and the impact of rising competition from
Japan was beginning to be felt, and its cotton-pressing business was
waning: The directors' report of 1894 showed a loss, explained as the
result of "most of the cotton pressing business . . . now being done
up-country, and [due also] to the low rates charged owing to keen
competition." The pressing company was chaired for many years
by Suleiman, and upon his death, Farha took over as President and
Chairman of the Board, which was also unprecedented at the time.
The pressing company's profits improved somewhat under her leadership, although the company complained that there was little demand
for pressing in Bombay.

A letter to Farha from her younger brother Ezra at headquarters
in London a few months after her formal appointment indicates the
complexity of the issues she had to address as a managing partner.
Ezra expressed concern that the First Sino-Japanese War, which had
broken out the previous year, was taking a toll on the opium trade and
the financial situation in China was deteriorating, and asked Farha to
weigh the possibility of investing in an American bond and about a
senior appointment within the company.

Even the company's passive investments were unsettled. David Sassoon & Co. had in previous decades cherry-picked these investments,
mostly getting solid returns, but the shared interests and assessments
of opportunities that had made that possible were fraying. Albert's

influence was felt less keenly and other members of the family started
to clamor for the chance to make decisions. This state of affairs began
to develop in the 1880s, and its ramifications were being felt long after.
In one such incident, the partners sent a stinging letter to Frederick,
David's youngest son, in Hong Kong, castigating him for unapproved
and inappropriate investments:

> You participated in a syndicate for Oriental Bank, Fringe [sic]
> Hotel and another bank. We wanted to be only in the first
> one. You have no right to represent the firm in syndicates of
> offerings not approved by Abdallah and the other partners.
> You are not being considerate and are putting your personal
> interests ahead of the firm.

It would be another decade after this incident before Frederick would
be admitted as a general partner, in 1896. This didn't mean that investments came to a halt in the intervening years. In the half-decade since
Farha first entered the Sassoon offices as Suleiman's understudy, the
firm had expanded its operations in China beyond their core opium
business. The firm was represented on the board of the Hong Kong
and Whampoa Dock Company. It was chaired by Suleiman, and after
his death the chairman of the board became Shellim Ezekiel, son-in-
law of David Sassoon. The rest of the board was comprised of Indian
merchant families. The firm also acted as agents for the Pulsometer
Engineering Company in Baghdad and sought to supply pumps to
Bahrain capable of lifting water to a height of ninety feet. The company also attempted to obtain permission to employ steamships on
the Tigris and Euphrates to handle their increased trade with Baghdad
(the Sultan's court denied their request because the steamers would be
under a British flag and the firm's attempts to lobby the Ottomans via
Lord Salisbury, Foreign Secretary at the time, didn't come to much).
More successfully, the company acquired a controlling stake in the
Persian Gulf Steamship Company, created in 1892, which operated
in ports around the Gulf.

Challenges were met and opportunities were taken, then, and
Farha managed to juggle all these difficulties and decisions, much as

Suleiman had. Her attention to detail was likewise the stuff of legend, and it too was attributed to the study of the intricacies of the Bible and Talmud. Certainly, she earned the respect of her employees; one, in charge of building a bungalow, wrote sheepishly of her specifications, "You are right (as you usually are)." It wasn't long before some veterans began to compare her with her great-grandfather David. She even revived an old rule of his that had long fallen by the wayside: All correspondence must be dealt with the same day. Under her reinvigorated leadership, the locus of power in the company shifted perceptibly east, away from the Sassoons' headquarters at 12 Leadenhall Street in London.

Her achievements did not diminish the usual feuds and squabbles between branches about allocations and budgets, which now fell under her remit. Almost every memo in the aftermath of Suleiman's death referred to infighting among senior employees, both members of the family and not, and their attempts to carve out more responsibilities for themselves under the new leadership. Taxation was another issue that was becoming more intricate. An insight into income tax is gained from one of the memos: It explains that each partner paid their taxes individually, although if profits were accrued through the branch, then the branch had to pay. Tax inspectors in England did "not care if taxes were paid in Bombay already on trades and investments, unless [the partners could] prove that [they] paid for these gains or income in London. They might reimburse later for double taxation, but all the tax collectors really know looting."

Still less pleasant must have been the disposition of her beloved husband's estate, which was enveloped in bureaucracy that took many years to be resolved. At the time of his death, Suleiman's investments included mills, spinning companies, banks, real estate companies, and a share in the Royal Yacht Club in Bombay, all totaling more than 4.76 million rupees (roughly $15.6 million in today's value). His personal and company assets were hopelessly entangled, and some had been inherited from other members of the family, all of which added to the complexity of the estate. By the end of her first year in charge, Farha was inundated by directorships and company chairmanships she had accepted, including Director and President of the Sassoon &

Alliance Silk Mills Company, the Sassoon Pressing Company, and the Sassoon Silk Mills Company.

On her way home from the office at the end of the working day, Farha would often visit one of the textile mills the company owned in Bombay to talk to the managers there and seek their opinions on issues facing the textile business. She asked London to prepare every fortnight a "tabular summary" of mill returns owned by the family to assist her in supervising them, and Liverpool and Manchester to send reports on wool auctions and updates on the textile industry there. She sought information about the state of the competition, and memos were sent to her about the mill industry in Japan and the difficulties faced in Shanghai: "This business is not quite such a gold mine as the promoters anticipated and in spite of cheap silver."

Two decades after the Sassoon Spinning and Weaving Company was floated in 1874, the Sassoon & Alliance Silk Mills Company was established, which Farha presided over after Suleiman's death. It was

Rachel beside her mother,
Flora, 1902.

part of a larger reallocation of the firm's resources, in response to
E. D. Sassoon, which had acquired many mills and factories in India
in recent years and galloped ahead of its competitor David Sassoon &
Co. The Silk Mills Company prompted a visit from the Governor of
Bombay, Lord Sandhurst, guided by Farha. He was suitably impressed
by the methods used to process raw silk for weaving and the scale of
the mill he viewed, which employed a thousand men and women,
providing job opportunities for locals and producing a wide range of
silk garments, and he paid tribute to the high standard of working
conditions in the mill.

The demands of the business had to be balanced with the burdens
of motherhood, and Farha's commitment to her three children—
Rachel, aged eighteen; Mozelle, eleven; and David, fifteen—is evident in the letters that join the business correspondence in the family
archive. One note reveals her approving an invitation for the three
to go to a relative's house one afternoon to play with their children.
Others show her concern for Mozelle, who had suffered an injury to
her spine as an infant after a nurse dropped her and was left permanently disabled. A small flurry of correspondence shortly after the
turn of the century indicates that the family tradition of sending its
young men out to explore the world continued and had if anything
grown more lavish. Farha arranged in 1900 for David, then twenty
years old, to travel from Bombay to Colombo, Penang, Singapore,
Hong Kong, and Shanghai in a first-class cabin, with his tutor in
second class and two servants on deck, as well as "a small stock of live
fowls on board" to enable him "to keep kosher while aboard." The
age of the ocean liner had arrived, and such extensive travel could be
undertaken in several weeks, not months, and in complete comfort.
A letter from Farha's nephew Ruby to her son, David, describes a
journey with his parents from Shanghai on a German ship to Kobe
and their visit to "the celebrated Asaka Exhibition," where he was
awestruck by the innovations on display: a wireless telegraphy instru-
ment, an X-ray machine, a baby incubator, a refrigerator, and more.
He wrote to his cousin about the pleasures of being in Kobe and in
"a country place by the sea-side called Shioya" where he "passed a
very pleasant three weeks there swimming, fishing, walking, and train
excursions."

THE END OF AN ERA

In Farha's first year as a partner, the Royal Commission of Inquiry set up by Gladstone to advise on Britain's policy on opium published its report, some 2,500 pages of data and witness statements divided into seven volumes. The Commission had intended to start by interviewing witnesses suggested by the Society for the Suppression of the Opium Trade, but most of these were in China and it took the help of representatives in Hong Kong to collect statements there, so they began with officials in England who had served in India. "From the beginning the Commission was viewed with a suspicious eye in many quarters, as a meddling inquiry into Indian affairs imposed upon the government by faddists." From there, they proceeded to India, where they collected testimonies in Calcutta, Patna, Benares, Gujarat, and as far away as Burma.

Among those interviewed were employees of David Sassoon & Co. At the end of 1893, the Commission interviewed an R. M. Cohen, who had held positions in Singapore, Shanghai, and Nanchang, in southeastern China. Asked about the effects of opium on Chinese users, Cohen responded enthusiastically: "After they smoke they never seem any the worse. It calms them and they transact their business cheerfully." He claimed that all his servants smoked opium and he had never dismissed anyone for being unfit due to the habit. Rather than as an addiction, Cohen characterized the smoking of opium as a "luxury" and a "fashion," used for such "a long time it has become a sort of necessity of life." Summing up, he argued that depriving the Chinese of the Indian drug would be an "injustice, especially to high class people." The Commission found out that about 1,200 chests of Bengal opium were exported monthly to China by David Sassoon & Co. In his final statement, Cohen asserted, "It is the duty of the Government of India to give its support to the opium trade," and said, "Morally, Government will be held responsible for the loss of this trade."

Cohen's testimony was joined by that of E. S. Gabbay, "manager of the opium department of Messrs. David Sassoon & Co." After complimenting the Chinese as a "set of intelligent and most industrious people," he denied that smoking opium could "render them inferior, either mentally or physically, to those that abstain" and declared his firm belief that:

> the consumption of opium is perfectly harmless to the constitu
> tion, and very often a moderate use of the drug far from having
> a depreciating has a favourable effect upon the intellect, the wit,
> and the system, enabling people to undertake and go through
> more work and fatigue than they could otherwise. An excessive
> use of the drug is of course injurious, but such cases are very
> rare when compared with the abuse of alcohol.

It was a sentiment echoed by a manager at E. D. Sassoon, who proclaimed that opium in moderation was beneficial, "especially to people suffering from certain diseases, and also in old age," and that in Bombay, "all classes of Hindu and Mahomedan communities eat opium, and a very small percentage smoke it." Despite their professed belief in the beneficial properties of opium, none of the interviewees were asked if they consumed it themselves or recommended its use to their family or friends, and the prejudiced nature of the questions prepared by members of the inquiry, replete with derogatory references to the "Asiatic race" and its dependence on opium, is hard to avoid. The Commission's concern over the potential loss of revenues to the British government is equally clear. According to their data, the annual net revenue from taxes on opium over the previous fourteen years was on average 7.44 million rupees, although this had dropped to just over 7 million in the last five years. It was a colossal sum, and it looms large over the Commission's closing statements:

> As the result of a searching inquiry, and upon a deliberate
> review of the copious evidence submitted to us, we feel bound
> to express our conviction that the movement in England in
> favour of active interference on the part of the Imperial Par-
> liament for the suppression of the opium habit in India, has
> proceeded from an exaggerated impression as to the nature and
> extent of the evil to be controlled. The gloomy descriptions
> presented to British audiences of extensive moral and physical
> degradation by opium, have not been accepted by the witnesses

representing the people of India, nor by those most responsible for the government of the country.

It was an extraordinary conclusion. The Commission's report effectively "removed the opium question from the British public agenda for another fifteen years." Criticism from the anti-opium campaigners was immediate and severe, and the proceedings developed "into a tournament between two points of view, with both sides determined to state their case in as extreme a form as possible." The fact that China received little attention in the report was not the fault of the Commission, which simply followed parliamentary guidelines that barely mentioned China. Ultimately, despite the political and public support the prohibitionists had mustered, for many MPs, the report relieved them of the burden of continuing to pay the issue any attention. Although the battle was lost in 1895, the war was not over. Both sides geared up to get the public and politicians behind them for the next fight, which began in the early twentieth century and continued after the First World War.

Albert was by now in his late seventies and frail. He spent his days in Brighton, away from the bustle of London. After the Commission published its findings, however, he went to London to call on the Chinese ambassador, likely to discuss the restrictions on opium sales from India. It was one of the last acts he would perform for the family firm. When he died a few months later on October 24, 1896, he was buried in a mausoleum in Brighton specially built at his instruction four years earlier in an off-kilter Indian style reminiscent of the Royal Pavilion. Not only did all the offices and mills of David Sassoon & Co. close for the day as a mark of respect, so did those of E. D. Sassoon, and many merchants and Parsi bazaars in India followed suit. In Shanghai, the flags of the opium fleet were flown at half-mast, as were those on the roof of the P & O building.

By then Albert's surname was known all over the commercial world. His three decades at the helm of David Sassoon & Co. would prove to be the firm's golden age, and the networks he had built, be they with traders in Persia or the King-in-waiting, would continue to function and enrich his siblings and descendants after his death. He achieved his dream of mingling with the upper classes and finished his life an aristocrat, a far cry from his early days in Baghdad and Bombay. Albert learned the art of trade from his father and was very sensitive to the cultural and religious backgrounds of others. As the award of the Freedom of the City declared, it was the cosmopolitan nature of his liberality that endeared him to the citizens of Bombay and made him a totemic figure of his age, "a polymath engaged simultaneously in finance, trade, politics, art and philosophy—'part businessman, part politician, part patriarch, part intellectual aesthete.'"

From his will, we know that his final share of the company was 35 percent. This was down from 41 roughly two years before (the difference likely went to his brother Frederick when he was admitted as a general partner), and the majority he presumably had after his own father had died, but the value of the whole and his own personal wealth had grown almost immeasurably, and the taxes due on his estate were themselves the size of entire fortunes. His lawyers dutifully claimed for tax purposes that his main residence was Bombay, where he still had a large portfolio of property and assets, as the taxes would be lower there than in England, where he had lived for more than two decades, but the case went to court. The Chief Justice in Bombay, Sir Charles Farran, concluded that the business "cannot be said to be carried on at both places," that "London is the locality in which the business which is the property of the partnership is situated," and the proof was that each year's profits and losses, although private, were entered in London and credited to each partner. Worse, the lawyers believed Indian duty on any property would not be deductible from the English sum unless the land was owned in partnership, which would cost the estate still more money. As we shall see, poor planning of this meant that the wealth the family had built up over the nineteenth century would start to slip through their fingers in the twentieth century. Edward, Albert's son and the will's executor, fearing disagreements and squabbles within the family, instructed the lawyers to pay all death duties before allocating the balance of the estate.

Albert's death marked the beginning of the end; though the business in China and India was in capable hands, most family members were keen on monetizing their wealth rather than investing and were less enthused to work hard to maintain the prime position of David Sassoon & Co.

CONSPIRACIES

Albert's death came as a blow to Farha, as he was her guarantor in England and she could not count on the support of his surviving brothers for the changes she was pioneering in Bombay. She had reorganized the Bombay office into nine departments, each with a clear management line: opium; local properties and the textile press company; bills of exchange; cotton and cotton mills; import and export, Europe; import and export, Persian Gulf; business in China; bookkeeping; and finally, a general department. She implemented strict rules for borrowing and lending, imposing order on what had been essentially a free-for-all whereby the office lent or borrowed money according to the needs of each trade by setting maximum and minimum borrowing balances and interest rates, ensuring that the balance sheet of each office had to be scrutinized. Reports under her management were arranged systematically and clearly rather than in the previous erratic system, which had usually jumped from one subject to another seemingly without reason—showing, for example, a breakdown of each commodity traded by the office, its quantity, prices, and major news, or a table for each type of opium, with the number of chests and estimated stock available. Similarly, Farha asked that letters sent to her or dispatched from Bombay be in the form of memos with subject headings, as this allowed her to address each topic separately, and then to ask for anything left unresolved to be followed up. For the historian, the difference is akin to a break in the archaeological record, when one ancient society is conquered or displaced by another; for the business, it meant the professionalization of methods and practices that had gone unchanged and unquestioned for half a century.

These changes came as a shock to several members of the family in London, and doubtless the fact that they had been introduced by an ambitious and effective woman didn't help. Outside the family, however, Farha's reputation was expanding far beyond Bombay's mercantile class. When the U.S. General Consul to Singapore visited India to study its cotton industry, he turned to her to "afford him assistance and information," and news that she had in 1897 been elected as director of the Grain Trading Company, formed to help relieve famine in Bombay, was reported as far away as New York. Farha basked in the Indian and international attention, which did not please the men of the family.

After Albert's death in October 1896, she was, in effect, the senior partner in the company and certainly the most experienced. It left her vulnerable to her opponents but also afforded her opportunities, chief among them to heal some old wounds. She concluded that the rift with E. D. Sassoon was not helping either firm, and since the rift's antagonists, Elias and Albert, were now deceased, she managed to reach a truce with E. D. Sassoon: an end to the poaching of employees, competition for buyers of opium and other commodities traded, and attempts to dislodge a trading house from specific areas of commerce. The armistice benefited both companies and allowed them to better coordinate their efforts to counter the lobbying of opponents to the opium trade and reduce the fallout from its decline. The partners in London, typically, were less inclined to congratulate Farha on her achievement than remind her, "Its success will depend on you."

As the business became more complex, the number of lawsuits against the firm increased in almost every region where it operated. Farha was known for her stubbornness and insistence on minor points, which exacerbated these conflicts. She reacted sharply, much like David, to any hint of disloyalty or cheating, even if the cost to the company was negligible. Through her lawyers, she was relentless in pursuing cases until she felt justice had been done. A story circulated that a garage owner cheated her over the sale of a car and she sued him for breach of warranty, winning the case after extensive correspondence. She also pushed London to be tough on anyone who she felt was double-crossing the firm. A letter sent to two Baghdadi Jews who worked as agents for the Sassoons illustrates this:

> We regret to find that you do not see your way to accept the
> proposals made by us for your future connection with our
> firm but have formulated conditions of your own which as
> men of business you must have known would be altogether
> inadmissible by the Partners.

Despite all her voluminous responsibilities, Farha didn't relinquish her involvement with charities that interested her. Here too she introduced innovations, such as the concept of endowments—funds invested in stocks and bonds in order to deliver higher returns to the charities and sustain them in perpetuity. She also assumed the role of mediator within the family, as can be seen in a letter from the wife of an employee based in London pleading with her to intercede on behalf of her husband so that Frederick might allow him to stay in London with their children: "As the time is drawing for us to leave for Bombay, you who are a mother, can well understand what my feelings are. The idea of another long separation from my children does indeed make me miserable as we are obliged to leave them behind to finish their education."

In England and India, meanwhile, her family was also involved in charities. All the charitable initiatives of David and then Albert were maintained by other family members, and sponsorships continued unabated. In perusing *The Jewish World* for 1897–98, the range of charities, in both geography and areas of interest, is astounding: In England, Edward, Albert's son, contributed to the building of an annex for Stepney School in East London in memory of his father and attended numerous charitable dinners, one in aid of the City of London Hospital, of which he was treasurer; another at a hotel to raise money for the Westminster Jews' Free School; and another in support of the City of London Hospital for Diseases of the Chest.

In India, Jacob, Elias's son and the senior partner at E. D. Sassoon, gave a handsome sum of one hundred thousand rupees to the St. George Hospital Nursing Fund in India, and a donation to fight a plague raging in Pune. On one occasion, he distributed Passover matzo to all members of the Baghdadi Jewish community in Bombay and donated to a central nursing association named after Lady Lamington, whose husband was the Governor of Bombay from 1903 to 1907. He also contributed a large sum to establish the Central Institute of Science in Bombay, which was perceived by Indian educators as innovative in educating and equipping young Indians with adequate resources.

In spite of all of Farha's achievements, innovations, and everything she brought to the family, clouds were gathering. The Sassoons in London, most of whom preferred the comforts of a life of leisure to the demands of work, had tolerated her leadership in part because none of them was willing to replace her. The exception was Frederick, who had moved from Hong Kong to London early in the 1890s and managed the head office well. He was married to the daughter of a rich Baghdadi family and had settled in an elegant house in Knightsbridge. Like his older brothers, he couldn't fathom how a mother of three could manage a global business, and reports of Farha's success and modernizing zeal riled him. Unlike them, however, he fancied running the business himself. He found a co-conspirator in Charles Moses, Farha's brother-in-law and an employee in the Bombay office who aspired to run it. Together they worked to undermine her authority throughout the company network. By 1899, even Farha's younger brother Ezra, her primary interlocutor in London, was growing hostile. In a letter of May of that year he reproached her for not informing London about an opium trade made in conjunction with another local firm, for failing to send London the profits accrued in Bombay, and more. London was looking for anything to discredit Farha and show that she was not managing the business properly. To ease Farha's ire, her brother would sometimes divert to subjects unrelated to business. For instance, he wrote to her about the Dreyfus affair and how he was hoping that soon the tribulations of this "poor man who did nothing wrong" would come to an end, as no one deserved to undergo such a torturous episode.

When she complained to him that London was not consulting her about affairs related to Bombay or on major business decisions, Ezra's answer was:

> Oh, my sister, the answer to that is that you turned down everything we [London] asked, and to every reform we enacted to which not only you rejected but at no point you expressed gratitude to London. You have to accept the vote of the majority and that's it.

These were harsh words for an older sister, never mind a boss, and the tone was markedly different from the businesslike memos he had sent Farha immediately after she began running the business. There are remarkably few letters in the archives from the partners in London to Farha at the end of the 1890s; it seems they had assigned Ezra to deal with a partner whom they viewed as stubborn and uncooperative. When, in a letter to Farha from Sandringham, Reuben mentioned that trade was slowing down, it was in passing before he reached main topics: the Prince of Wales's upcoming birthday party, a dinner Reuben had hosted attended by the Duke and Duchess of Devonshire, and his uncle's appointment as head of the Chamber of Commerce in Foxton, England. Though he was addressing the operational head of a global company, he dispensed with the usual formalities and instead deployed a few, cloyingly patronizing adjectives: "To the dear and gentle Siniora [Mrs.] Farha Suleiman Sassoon, the most blessed woman."

The steady drip of criticism continued. A terse memo sent from London in December informed Farha of the existence of mortgages on properties in China belonging to her husband's estate, "but standing in the names of some of our employees," emphasizing that the firm would not assume any responsibility for the debts, and asked that she transfer them into her name. She was even sent a small bill to cover the legal costs. It was abundantly clear that the partners in London wanted to tie up loose ends before making their final push.

In 1898, a year before the plot to remove Farha was hatched, Frederick was already laying the ground for her unseating. Writing to his nephew Edward, who was on holiday in Egypt, Frederick asked for his support:

> Our people [in Bombay] will realize that we are in earnest
> and they must reorganize the office. Albert Moses [an
> employee helping the conspirators], we can discuss on your
> return what position we can give him and in the meanwhile
> we shall hear what Farha has to say in reply to my letter
> [about reorganization].

By "reorganization," Frederick meant ousting Farha and reshaping the Bombay office to suit the needs of the Sassoons in London. He set about questioning Farha's every decision to other partners, portraying her as uncommunicative, lacking in understanding of trading and prices, stubbornly refusing London's advice, complaining unfairly about the firm's overall policy, and altogether lacking the focus neces-

sary to run the business: "I really do not understand Farha when she
writes to say that we induced her to buy Rupee papers," Frederick
wrote to Edward, and proceeded to criticize her for buying them at
too high a price while they "sold in London at a profit." The fact that
his two brothers Reuben and Arthur held larger shares of the company
than Farha and were far from focused on the business escaped mention. Meanwhile, Ezra pressured Farha to sell the family's properties in
Bombay and Calcutta, as it became obvious to the Sassoon brothers
that none of them would be going to India and they did not want to
spend money on their upkeep.

One way of clipping the wings of Bombay and its chairman was to
curtail the system laid down by the founder, David, whereby branches
traded for their own accounts as well as on behalf of the firm as a
whole. This had been the source of tension in the past, as each branch
sought to make more profits for itself, and had been one of the causes
of the split between Albert and Elias, but it had been retained because
it enabled branches to make swift decisions and encouraged the partners to be more entrepreneurial. Frederick had tried to convince
Suleiman to abandon the system in the previous decade in favor of
centralizing control in London, but to no avail. In 1899, however,
London announced:

> Owing to the disastrous results attending the Bombay trans-
> actions on the firm's account we are greatly disturbed at the
> manner in which this business must have been carried through
> and have definitely decided that all business in yarn and malwa
> opium must cease on our acct. . . . We feel confident that trad-
> ing on our acct. cannot proceed satisfactorily & simultaneously
> alongside of a good commission business.

Then came the real reason for this abrupt reversal of a policy that had
stood for almost six decades:

> As our dealings in yarn & opium in Bombay will be given up,
> your staff will be in excess of requirements and you will be en-
> abled to make further reductions in the numbers, as you must
> acknowledge that such a business as we can contemplate can

only be successfully & profitably earned on by strict attention
to principles of economy.

Even before this memo reached Bombay, Farha was aware that London was working against her. She knew too that her brother-in-law
Charles had been sowing animosity against her in Bombay and sending slanted reports to London. The pressure of being undermined at
every turn eroded her trust in her own employees, and she increasingly
took on responsibilities that should have been theirs, giving London
grounds to criticize her for failing to delegate. The final blow came
at Christmas in 1901, when she was told that the firm of David Sassoon & Co. would be incorporated, forming a limited company with
a capital of £500,000 in £100 shares, with a mission to "carry on
the business of dealers in any kinds of goods and produce . . . bankers, general merchants, commission agents, importers, exporters, and
charterers of ships and vessels, ship and insurance brokers. . . ."

The company was kept private in the sense that there was no initial
public offering. The directors held all the shares, £200,000 of which
were ordinary shares, with the balance in the form of preferred shares
carrying a 5 percent dividend. Its board comprised Sir Edward Sassoon, MP, as chairman; Arthur, Reuben, and Frederick as permanent
directors (as long as they held a minimum of £5,000 in shares) along
with David Gabbay (one of Albert's grandchildren); and, for the first
time, two gentile employees, J. Owens and C. J. Longcroft. Farha's
name is striking by its absence, and the last two were nothing short
of an insult: They weren't even part of the family. The chairman was
an active MP and therefore only part-time, and his two uncles were
scarcely businessmen. Only Gabbay, a talented accountant with a legal
background, had contributed to the company. This was not a disagreement between partners in a global business; it was a putsch, intended
to push Farha out of the firm altogether. The incorporation caused
bewilderment in London and Bombay. Outside observers could not
fathom why a profitable company run by family members would
voluntarily give up these advantages, but many believed that the Sassoons, who had always seemed to possess impeccable timing, might be
onto something. What they didn't know was that most of the family
was keen to extract capital from the company to fund their lifestyles

and avoid being actively involved in business, and it would be easier to hire top professionals in a corporation.

Rumors circulated in Bombay that Farha would follow in Elias's footsteps thirty years before and create her own, rival company. The reality was less swashbuckling: She announced her retirement, telling a friend, "I do not think I can any longer drudge all day while the others take a superficial interest only, doing more harm than good when they suddenly awake." Farha felt that there was no purpose in staying in India and decided to leave Bombay for London, where she hoped to find doctors able to help treat her disabled daughter, Mozelle. Her final days in Bombay were unpleasant. As a reward for the role he had played in the affair, Charles was appointed by the new firm to be in charge of Bombay business. He moved with indelicate speed into her office and set about pressuring senior employees to stop bemoaning Farha's departure and support him instead.

With Farha leaving, Frederick grabbed the reins of David Sassoon & Co. Farha's chapter in business ended, and with it the brief burst of innovation and good management she brought. But it should be said that Farha did not manage to reproduce the tight cohesion in the firm that prevailed under David and Albert, and on many levels the firm, by the time she took over, had lost its vision and willingness to innovate to stem the slide of the business. The bickering among the family's members significantly reduced the chances of revitalization. Furthermore, in spite of her religious beliefs and charity work, she was not dissimilar from other Sassoons who saw opium as another commodity and believed that if there is demand, then there should be supply. Farha never questioned the trade and like others abstained from any discussion of the morality of it, even when the Commission of Inquiry was going on. She decided to leave Bombay as soon as possible. Even in victory, her brother-in-law and Frederick could not resist imposing one more humiliation: On the pretext of cost cutting, Charles ordered that local newspapers would not be forwarded to her in England. The spite was however drowned out by her well-wishers in the city. She had always been popular in Bombay, maintaining good relations with everyone she dealt with, irrespective of religion or caste, and one Indian woman wrote to express her family's "warmest acknowledgments," saying, "No words of ours can adequately convey to you how deeply grateful we feel for your extreme kindness." On the day of her departure, Farha and her entourage of assistants, servants, and even a rabbi were seen off by a crowd of former staff, as well as officials and friends. One story tells of a Parsi girl presenting her with a garland inscribed: "Her Majesty, the Queen of Bombay and Empress of Malabar Hill."

10

A NEW CENTURY

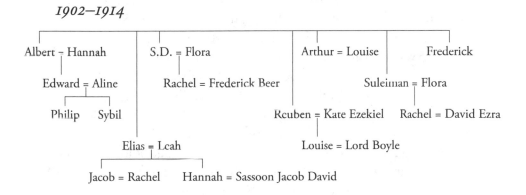

1902–1914

Albert – Hannah   S.D. = Flora   Arthur = Louise   Frederick

Edward = Aline   Rachel = Frederick Beer   Suleiman = Flora

Philip   Sybil   Reuben = Kate Ezekiel   Rachel = David Ezra

Elias = Leah   Louise = Lord Boyle

Jacob = Rachel   Hannah = Sassoon Jacob David

The arrival of the twentieth century was telegraphed, a year late, by the death of Queen Victoria. Her sixty-three year reign encompassed a series of momentous industrial, cultural, political, scientific, and military transformations in Britain and the world. The passing of the Victorian age and dawn of a new century ushered in another wave of advances. Travel grew faster and more efficient; India's rail network grew so rapidly that by 1910 it was the fourth-most extensive in the world. Hundreds of thousands of miles of cables were laid under the ocean, a laborious feat that revolutionized international communications. Information now traveled substantially faster than people, which radically influenced global trade networks and allowed traders to make faster and more informed decisions.

The first decade of the twentieth century also saw the two Sassoon firms slip from one epoch to another, undergoing changes that would dictate their destiny. After ousting Flora, David Sassoon & Co.'s board in London turned to Sir Edward, Albert's son and the inheritor of his baronetcy, to chair the newly incorporated firm. The heir to the firm's longest-standing chairman and an elected official, Edward brought stature, respectability, and impeccable connections in the City of London to the firm. He had since 1899 been the MP for Hythe, and for a time he balanced both positions, drawing on his knowledge of India and trade to comment from the backbenches on anything relating to Britain's most important imperial possession, especially the need to improve telegraphic communications with India and to avoid unnecessary charges that could impede commerce. He argued, for instance, that the Marconi Company's development of communication lines gave the British considerable strategic and commercial advantages. Edward was a clear voice in Parliament on the Sultanate of Brunei and took up the cause of its people. In a letter to the Foreign Office, he underlined the negative opinion that prevailed among the chiefs and people of Brunei regarding their harsh conditions and called on the British government to ameliorate their situation. He also proposed a debate in Parliament to discuss the Baghdad Railway before the government committed itself on the project. He never seems to have shared his father's appetite for business, however, and his health was not robust. After the death of his beloved wife, Aline, in 1908, any remaining interest he had in the firm's affairs was quenched and Frederick, aided by David Gabbay, "who stood barely five foot but was already a giant in the counting house," and Cecil Longcroft, was effectively left in charge of the company.

Opium profits continued to decline, and outside observers increasingly felt the company was lethargic and past its prime. Research undertaken by a couple of banks is telling:

June 1906: Kleinwort, Sons and Co: The general opinion among the Eastern Banks is that this firm is perfectly good but at the same time they regard them as a more or less declining firm.
September 1908: Chartered Bank of India, Australia and China: Of course, they do not possess the same standing as before

Brighton mausoleum where both Albert and his son Edward
were buried, in 1896 and 1912, respectively.

they became a 'Limited Company' but he [the manager] was
of opinion that Sassoons, outside the money in the business,
would protect their name. No fears need to be entertained.

Although entirely uninvolved in the running of the business, by his
presence Edward did add stability. In May 1912, however, he died at
home, having suffered a serious injury motoring to the golf links earlier in the year on holiday in the south of France when his chauffeur
took a sharp turn to avoid a restive horse. Edward was succeeded in
the baronetcy by his son Philip Gustave Sassoon, who had even less
interest in the business than his father but accepted a directorship,
and Frederick was duly appointed chairman. Edward was buried in
the family mausoleum in Brighton where his father had been laid to
rest. He had been President of London's Spanish and Portuguese Jews'
Congregation, and rabbis from Brighton and London conducted the
funeral service. Given his prominence in the City of London, the
Financial Times published his will. He left an estate just in excess of
£1 million. After various bequests to relatives, friends, and domestic

servants, the remainder was held in a trust for his son, Philip, and his daughter, Sybil. Unusually, Edward left nothing to charity:

> I desire to state that I have made no bequests for charitable purposes—first because I give and intend to give during my life according to my means; and secondly, as a protest against what is in my view the impolitic and prohibitive legacy duty prescribed by law on charitable legacies. Any impost that tends to discourage charitable bequests, especially in a country like Great Britain where healing agencies altogether depend on voluntary contributions, must in my humble opinion, be radically unsound.

In fact, duties on his estate amounted to only £160,000 because of the careful way it had been arranged. As well as offering his children riches, his will made solemn demands of them:

> I impress on my said son the desirability of attending to the interests of the business of David Sassoon and Co. Ltd., so that its reputation and standing so laboriously built up by his ancestors for close on a century may not be tarnished or impaired by the possible neglect or mismanagement of outsiders.
>
> I further earnestly impress on [my children] the necessity of avoiding all extravagance or gambling, and I earnestly hope they will devote some part of their time and money to objects of benevolence.

As we shall see, it was advice that neither would follow.

Farha's departure from Bombay signaled the end of her involvement in the business, but her arrival in London opened a new chapter of her life. She seems to have been determined not to be resentful of her treatment at the hands of her former partners, however deeply she detested their maneuverings. She busied herself meeting old friends from Bombay such as Lady Reay, the former Governor's wife, and making new ones, from Prime Minister Balfour to dukes and duch-

esses. She was at ease with all the board members' wives, particularly
Aline, Edward's wife, whom she frequently joined in her box at the
opera house in Covent Garden, but took against Reuben and Arthur
for what she saw as their desperate fawning over the King. Reuben
was by then ill with rheumatism and mostly confined to his home in
Hove, East Sussex. She also befriended members of the E. D. Sassoon
side of the family such as Edward (Elias's son) and his Egyptian wife,
Leontine, whom she found less haughty than her own side.

While Farha abstained from interfering in the business, she continued to manage her own assets and even deal with legal cases. Her
accounts of 1911 and 1913 with Chartered Bank of India, Australia
and China indicate income from a number of companies, such as Tata
Iron, though only a minuscule dividend from David Sassoon & Co.,
along with substantial expenses incurred maintaining properties and
repaying mortgages. She maintained her interest in financial markets
and can be seen buying and selling shares and government bonds,
though her primary motivation was to protect her wealth rather than
grow it. She continued in her forthright way to fight for her interests
whenever they were threatened—as in the case of a dispute over the
sale of some land in Bombay's Malabar Hill, which stretched from
1920 to 1928, when it finally reached the High Court in Bombay and
was decided in her favor.

She settled in London at 32 Bruton Street, Mayfair, and, like the
rest of her family, Anglicized her name, to Flora, though, unlike the
others, the westward move (or at least freedom from the demands of
running the business) strengthened her connection to the language of
her religion, as she now had the time and energy to explore her interest
in Judaism and Jewish texts more deeply. When a Jewish journalist on
a visit to London from Palestine was invited for lunch at her house,
their conversation was conducted in Hebrew and he was astonished
by her knowledge of rabbinical texts. Flora was a strong believer in
women's rights and saw no contradiction whatsoever between a devout
adherence to religion and the role of women in societies.

In time, she came to exercise the kind of authority over relations
within the family that she had had over the management of its business,
and members turned to her for advice, direction, and adjudication.
A twelve-page letter to her from Dr. Ariel Bension's wife complained

bitterly about her disrespectful treatment by Flora's daughter Rachel and son-in-law, Sir David Ezra, then living in Calcutta. Dr. Bension had been on a fundraising mission for the Zionist cause but was given a cold reception by Ezra, who had not only spurned his advances but actively "urged people not to give to our cause." His wife complained that Rachel was "living with a brute, whom she has not been able to impress with her own goodness," and even though their home was open to gentiles, the Bensions were not invited. According to her, Dr. Bension was "spitting blood. My heart is bleeding. I accuse David Ezra of being responsible for his illness." The letter is testament both to the range of attitudes toward Zionism that a single family could contain, all sharing a deep commitment to the Jewish faith and its institutions, and also the role Flora came to play in London, solving and resolving crises of a different kind to those she had labored over in Bombay. The archives do not indicate any strong support of Zionism by any family member, and even individuals such as Suleiman were far more interested in helping rabbis in Palestine create religious schools rather than for political reasons.

The steely compassion she brought to the family was on display on her visit to India in 1911. While she was staying in her house in Malabar, a relative died while visiting her. She wrote movingly to his widow to inform her of the news, and told of how he fell ill and, on his deathbed, asked to see letters of the family from Baghdad to remember the city of his birth. "His wish was to die in Bombay, be near my husband, so we have put him as near his grave as possible. . . . We had everything done which devotion & friendship could think of & thus comes to an end the loyalty & love of a lifetime, & you have lost a devoted husband, your children, a most loving Father, & we, our sincerest well-wisher." Flora instilled this love and respect for others in her children, and it runs through the letters they wrote to one another, particularly David and Rachel. Genuine affection and devotion to one another's needs prevailed. David paid attention to his sister's accounts after she moved to Calcutta and diligently informed her of every dividend and transaction. He addressed most letters to "my own sweet and darling sister Rachel," and occasionally when he wanted to write something confidential about financial affairs, he inserted a few lines in Judeo-Arabic in the English letter, signing off with "your devoted & grateful brother."

Retirement also afforded Flora the time to travel. A book written by David and published many years later records a remarkable expedition undertaken by Flora and her three children, with David and Rachel both accompanied by their spouses, in 1910 to their ancestral homeland in central Iraq. They visited Baghdad and Basra, along with many other cities and small towns, almost retracing in reverse David Sassoon's flight eight decades earlier. (The tidy symmetry was disrupted by a visit to Muscat, a gesture to the family's relationship with the Sultan of Oman.) A large retinue accompanied them, including a kosher butcher, a chef from Cochin, and a number of servants, with one dedicated solely to care for her disabled daughter, Mozelle. A photograph shows the family with two guards and a few Baghdadi dignitaries in the city. The intention was to see as many synagogues as possible (Baghdad had some thirty-seven at the time) as well as the tombs of ancient Jewish prophets and famous rabbis, while David was out hunting for antique books and Bibles. David wrote the book from an almost anthropological viewpoint, with very little expression of sentiment about seeing the homeland, and it reads like the travel writing of an outsider, describing the temples and methods of prayer in the places they visited with sympathy and understanding but little sense of belonging.

Not long after Flora gave up Bombay for London, another member of the family who had reached unprecedented heights in her profession was also approaching retirement. At the age of thirty, Rachel, S.D.'s only daughter, fell in love and married Frederick Arthur Beer. The Beers, originally from Frankfurt, were converts to Christianity, and the day before her wedding at Chelsea Parish Church, Rachel went so far as to be baptized—the first Sassoon to do so. Frederick's father had bought the *Observer* newspaper and possessed a lot of political clout—Mr. and Mrs. Gladstone were signatories of Rachel and Frederick's marriage certificate—and not long after they wed, she started writing for the paper. Rachel, who strongly believed that women "had duties greater than matrimony and motherhood," was in short order appointed assistant editor and then promoted to editor in 1893, making her the first woman to assume control of a national newspaper—and at a time when women lacked the vote. When *The Sunday Times* came onto the market, Rachel acquired and edited that too. Her biggest scoop came in 1898, when Charles Esterhazy disclosed to her that he had forged the documents used to convict the Jewish army captain Alfred Dreyfus of treason. Early the following century, however, Frederick fell ill and died (reportedly of syphilis) at the age of forty-five. Rachel nursed him to the end, all the while continuing to write for *The Sunday Times,* but her own health deteriorated afterward, and when she was hospitalized in 1904, both papers were sold.

In contrast to the distracted leadership of David Sassoon & Co., the chairman of E. D. Sassoon was going from strength to strength. Jacob seemed almost a replica of his father, Elias, down to the spectacles both wore. He had started his working life traveling all around Asia and the Persian Gulf but moved to Bombay. He never settled in England and worked diligently despite having seriously deficient eyesight and an invalid wife, traumatized by the death of their only child (a boy, named after his grandfather) two months after his birth. These misfortunes made Jacob reclusive, and he never sought the kind of public life enjoyed by his relatives in England. His energies were instead channeled into his faith and charity, and one newspaper wrote: "His simple ways of piety and benevolence are in striking contrast to his colossal fortune and high position in life." Jacob gave so generously to Bombay that a newspaper pleaded with him to extend the favor to Calcutta so it could also benefit. He contributed to the building of a synagogue in Hong Kong in 1902, calling it the Tent of Leah in memory of his mother; it still functions today, sitting atop a cliff with stunning views of the city. In Shanghai, he built another synagogue, called the Tent of Rachel, to commemorate his wife after her death in 1911. Yet, he broke away from a tradition that stretched back to David Sassoon and beyond, that the firm's offices closed on the Sabbath, wherever they were. From 1914, all E. D. Sassoon's employees in Bombay were required to work on Saturdays and all Jewish festivals, save the New Year and the Day of Atonement.

Jacob donated money to David Sassoon Hospital in Pune to build an extension (he timed it to coincide with the visit of the Prince and Princess of Wales to India in 1905), and work was completed in 1909. Both the hospital and the extension are continuing to function today as a public hospital mostly catering to the poor and needy in the city. The hospital benefited from the fact that a medical school was erected nearby, and the two function in tandem. He also gave money to Bombay University.

Jacob was supported in Bombay by his brother-in-law Sassoon Jacob David, a talented partner who was recalled to Bombay after Elias's death (Elias had fathered nine children and this proved to be an asset in the long term). Jacob proved a capable manager of the firm's mills, returning them to profitability, and later became chairman of the Bombay Millowners' Association. Sassoon Jacob David served as Sheriff of Bombay in 1905 and was instrumental in efforts to reduce overcrowding in the city's slums. He was rewarded for his services to the city in late 1905, when he was knighted during a visit by the new Prince of Wales (later George V), and in 1915 he received a baronetcy. Jacob and his brother-in-law oversaw a dynamic period at E. D. Sassoon, as can be seen in research reports commissioned by the London-based merchant bank Kleinwort in 1906:

All the Eastern Banks look upon this firm as quite A1. They are very keen energetic people reported to possess a capital between 1¼ and 1½ million [pounds]—spending very little money. They possess considerable property in Hong Kong & other Eastern centres & do a very large trade in opium. The Banks buy their clean drafts to a large extent.

The family's involvement in banking stretched back half a century, but it had always been at arm's length, as board members or investors. Now they were directly involved. One sizable new investment was made in 1909, when Jacob played a key role in founding the Eastern Bank, an exchange created to facilitate short-term loans in regions undergoing rapid industrial expansion. Two million pounds was raised, headquarters were opened in London, and branches were opened in India, Baghdad, and Singapore. E. D. Sassoon, "the moving spirit of the enterprise," capitalized on the new bank by raising loans for itself to grow the firm, guaranteeing overdrafts for plantation owners and building contractors from Malaya to Shanghai. Thanks to these arrangements, E. D. Sassoon was positioned to profit handsomely from the substantial rise in rubber prices that followed the onset of the First World War. Besides Jacob, the Eastern Bank's first board of directors included Lord Balfour of Burleigh (not to be confused with the Foreign Secretary who would issue a statement of support for the establishment of a home for the Jewish people in Palestine in 1917); a director of a Belgian bank named Emile Franqui; a representative from the private bank Brown Shipley in London; and a senior employee of E. D. Sassoon. (Through Franqui, the firm would gain a seat on the board of Banque du Congo Belge, which had many branches across French Africa.) The bank was successful from the start, reporting profits of £55,000 in its second year and in 1911 declaring a dividend, and according to the *Financial Times* had by its fourth year "acquired a substantial share in the business proceeding between Indian and foreign countries," a feat the paper attributed to the fact that "this Bank represents the firm of Sassoon, which has a greater power in the East than ever before."

OPIUM IN DECLINE

In the decade following the Opium Commission's report, the drug continued to flow from India to China, although local production continued to grow and constituted serious competition. In fact, from the 1870s until 1906, the Chinese production of opium increased more than twelvefold, and by 1906 it was nine times greater than opium imports. Momentum was gathering in China for a rejection of outside interference in its affairs and assertion of its right to control its own polices, however. The impetus began with the Boxer Uprising of 1900–1901, an anti-foreign, anti-imperialist movement initiated by peasants and militia groups (who practiced Chinese martial arts and hence became known as boxers), but the revolt, seen as China's "awakening," was also supported by the government. In 1906, an imperial decree, known as the Opium Edict, cosigned with India, promised that within ten years, "the evils arising from foreign and native opium be equally and completely eradicated." China agreed in 1907 to ban the domestic cultivation of opium on the understanding that exports of Indian opium would decline and cease completely within a decade. A year after the Edict, a British report indicated that progress had been made in India, but that enforcement in the Chinese provinces, where the loss of revenues from opium sales was felt the hardest, had proved challenging. It expressed doubts as to whether China could curtail its opium industry, both native grown and imported, without more forceful government intervention.

In England and India, opinion increasingly coalesced around the belief that the trade was morally indefensible. Parliament was once again open to suggestions of reform, and a motion to halt the trade was introduced in May 1906 on the same grounds that formed the anti-opium movement in the last decade of the nineteenth century. In India too, attitudes were shifting as revenues from taxes on opium were becoming less important for the treasury. Lobbyists for the trade gathered themselves, and the China Association, mobilized once again, circulated memos and letters to politicians and officials to defend British interests and oppose any policy that would impinge on trade with China. One letter, sent at the end of 1908, claimed that if the Edict was enacted, "the number of dealers in raw opium will dwindle to a very small number, healthy competition will cease, and the British merchant will be at the mercy of the few native shops left in the trade." Predictably, among the signatories were David Sassoon & Co., E. D. Sassoon & Co., Tata & Sons, and others. Although E. D. Sassoon's opium trading was declining, it still constituted about 40 percent of its total business in China, a revenue stream it sought fiercely to protect. The China Association archives clearly show that the two Sassoon firms cooperated in this effort, contrary to claims that their schism was total. The reports of the Hong Kong Chamber of Commerce between 1907 and the First World War contain dozens of letters that the two firms jointly sent. Others were sent with traders such as the Tatas. The Chinese were for their part beginning to implement the Edict. By 1909, supplies from India could only be imported under special permits, the number of which would be reduced annually by one-ninth, so that by 1918 it would come to a total halt.

By 1910, the government had begun closing shops in Canton and

Peking that were selling opium without a license, a move protested by foreign merchants as "undue interference with the trade" and an infringement of the Nanking Treaty of 1842. A typical appeal was that if the Chinese closed the outlets for opium, then "we shall suffer enormous losses, and whom shall we look to for compensation?" Each time a new Chinese regulation was announced or punitive taxes imposed, both Sassoon firms were swift in their condemnation and demands for support by the British government. It was a relentless campaign, heavy with claims that the merchants were suffering unprecedented losses. When a new opium tax was imposed in Canton, E. D. Sassoon & Co. petitioned the Foreign Office "to obtain assurance that similar measures will not be imposed" in other treaty ports and to support the merchants in their "legitimate trade during the remainder of the term agreed upon." In other words, the end was nigh, and the merchants wanted to make as much profit as possible before the trade folded.

The China Association fully supported the Sassoons and took the matter farther with the Foreign Office in London. In fact, what was happening on the ground during 1909–10 was beneficial to the two firms: As the opium system in India and China adjusted to the changing regulations, the prices of opium—especially Malwa—soared, ensuring high profit margins and fat receipts for India's treasury. The rope, however, was tightening, and any optimism accrued from this reprieve wilted in the face of a stream of new levies and regulations to limit the trade through the Chinese Opium Prohibition Bureau.

In Britain, the campaign for prohibition was gathering momentum. Churches and Christian organizations around the country labeled opium the greatest hindrance to missionary work in China. In 1908 National Anti-Opium Sunday was proposed, when "at the united request of the Archbishops and the leasers of Nonconformity, the story of the facts on the Indo-Chinese Opium Traffic may be told from the pulpit in every Church and chapel in the land, and the Nation called to Repentance." The Archbishop of Canterbury, however, felt that a National Anti-Opium Sunday would not help the cause, as Parliament stood with the government "in doing the very thing we ask for," and therefore nothing would be gained by applying further pressure.

By 1912, the Indian trade had reached a crisis point. During a

Farha (Flora) and Suleiman at their wedding in Bombay in 1876.

VANITY FAIR.

"The Indian Rothschild."

The second generation: David's eldest son, Albert (*top*), continued on the path of his father and expanded the business. Elias (*bottom left*) created a competing business; his enterprise prospered and lasted longer than the original one. Reuben (*bottom right*) was utterly Anglicized and indulged in upper-class activities, such as racing.

A portrait of Philip Sassoon by
John Singer Sargent, 1923.

The dining room at Port Lympne
(the estate of Philip Sassoon), painted by
Winston Churchill on one of his visits,
1921.

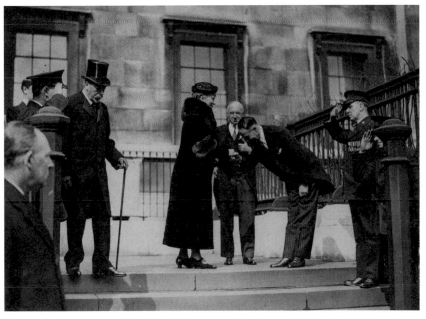

Philip Sassoon, a trustee of the National Gallery, welcoming
King George V and Queen Mary to the gallery, 1934.

A rare set: a gilt silver-cased Torah scroll (*left*) and a Haftarah scroll, property of Flora Sassoon, 1893.

Flora Sassoon, granddaughter of Albert, in London, 1907.

A parcel-gilt silver-and-enamel Torah shield (front and back) from 1782, purchased by Reuben Sassoon. It was sold by Sotheby's in December 2020 for about one million dollars.

period of four months, the price of export permits for Malwa opium dropped by more than 70 percent as buyers in China vanished, and bank loans exceeding £3 million were outstanding as more than 20,000 chests worth upwards of £10 million were stuck in ports. This was an opportunity for the two Sassoon firms to sound the alarm: "This is an exceedingly grave state of affairs, threatening not only British merchants interested in the trade, but the banks, and the whole Hong Kong and Shanghai trade as well, and calls for immediate and strong action if a financial crisis is to be averted." By this stage, the merchants and their lobbyists in London were fighting a losing battle. For all the Sassoons' clout, they couldn't reverse government policy or the overall direction of the Foreign Office, and officials there grew wary of their pleas. One official recommended to his colleagues: "Be very careful as to how you commit yourself to the representatives of Messrs. Sassoon and Company in regard to our general line of policy . . . only telling them generally that you have received instructions to protest against interference with the wholesale trade in foreign opium." The Foreign Office, for its part, wrote to E. D. Sassoon that it could not support its claim to hold the Chinese government liable "for losses sustained through the illegal restrictions on the opium trade," although strong messages were delivered in Peking and London to China's representatives.

The next critical phase was set on May 7, 1913. The Under-Secretary of State for India announced during a parliamentary debate that the British government was willing to commit to halting all exports of opium to China on the single condition that China would be steadfast in pursuing its policy of suppression. In fact, the Under-Secretary announced to Parliament, "For the first time in [the] modern history of India . . . we are selling not an ounce of poppy for China and for the Indo-Chinese opium trade at all." If the Edict marked the beginning of the end of the trade, this signaled its terminal decline. The Sassoons desperately attempted to modify some of these changes. In a detailed joint letter from both companies to the Foreign Office, it was pointed out that China had already abrogated the Opium Treaty and therefore Britain had no further obligations. The memo begged to differ about the statement that "opium is not a wasting security" and claimed that Malwa, in particular, suffered from shrinkage in weight if left in storage as it dried out, and this should be taken into consideration when deciding on weights allowed to be shipped to China. Two months later, with no reply received from the Foreign Office, the two firms sent another letter requesting clarification and warning that the provinces intended to be closed to Indian imports were far from free from local produce. By then, however, British policy-makers wanted only to wash their hands of the trade and the embarrassment it brought them. Meanwhile, in China, ceremonies were being held everywhere to burn opium and to declare different provinces free of opium. There were rumors, however, that senior officials in Peking were taking advantage of the supply shortage for personal profit.

The anti-opium lobby leaped into action. Even before the declaration in Parliament, a group of churchmen and politicians wrote to the Archbishop of Canterbury urging him to seize the opportunity and declare a ban on the opium trade. Following a letter from the Archbishop to the Foreign Secretary, Sir Edward Grey, Lambeth Palace (residence of the Archbishop of Canterbury) received a handwritten letter from an assistant of Sir Edward, two days before the announcement in Parliament, expressing his thanks for the Archbishop's message and adding: "No pressure is in his [Sir Edward Grey's] opinion necessary in regard to the Opium question. His Majesty's Government fully share the desire to see China rid herself of the opium habit." During 1913, pamphlets were distributed all over the country emphasizing the importance of ending the opium trade for the Christian faith. The Archbishop rejected as impractical the suggestion that the churches raise a sum of £8 million throughout the empire "in order to destroy the stock of opium lying in

Pamphlet issued by the anti-opium lobby, January 1908, during the last chapter of the opium trade.

China unsold." The opium stockpile in China and smuggling of opium from French colonies in the region and from Hong Kong continued to dominate the scene, but the wheels were set in motion.

While the trade waned, both Sassoon firms continued to trade the drug, and prohibition provided opportunities for profiteering. It has been estimated that the two companies between 1907 and 1914 made profits of almost twenty million taels. Whether these numbers are accurate or not, it is clear that the Sassoons mustered all their resources to ensure that the last chapter of opium trading was still profitable, or at least that their exposure was limited. They turned to the British government and Viceroy in India to assist them whenever they felt that the Indian government or, more important, the Chinese were not abiding by the terms of the different Anglo-Chinese opium agreements that stipulated a reduction in Chinese production and in Indian exports to China. Furthermore, they claimed that the Chinese authorities had seized and destroyed certified opium on which duty had been paid, thus inflicting severe losses on the dealers.

INDIAN EMPIRE

In India, perhaps for the first time since 1858, British rule looked uncertain. In the summer of 1905 the *Swadeshi* or "Make in India" movement was born and a boycott of British goods was launched. India had become by 1913 the main export market for British goods, including machinery, textiles, and other products. The seed of nationalism had been planted two decades earlier when the Indian National Congress, comprising about seventy English-educated Indians, held its first meeting in Bombay. The spread of nationalist ideas and aspirations for self-rule from the topic of intellectual debate to popular sentiment was accelerated by natural calamities that struck India in the final years of the nineteenth century, triggering famine and epidemics that led to a decade of extreme suffering and killed millions, and the inability or unwillingness of British administrators to remedy the situation. Confidence in the Indian Civil Service, considered the "steel frame" of the British Raj, was shaken. Lord George Curzon arrived in India in 1899 (serving as Viceroy until 1905) convinced that "efficient administration by benevolent autocratic rulers best served the country." Hindu nationalists evoked a sense of pride in the country, but that led to clashes with Muslims. The Indian economy, however, continued to be dominated by private enterprise, and the role of the state was modest indeed. All decisions on what to produce and who produced what were made by private individuals. Mobilization of workers demanding higher wages emerged; though organizations defending workers' rights were not developed enough to protect the workers, they managed to establish a consistent influence that would prove to be critical years later.

In India, textile mills were becoming a cornerstone of both Sassoon firms' business, and for the first time the family could credibly be labeled industrialists as well as merchants. The number of cotton mills in Bombay had been increasing since the 1870s, most of them emulating British industrial methods using imported British machinery, with the result that by the century's end "India has taken almost the whole of Japan and China trade in yarns from Great Britain." Concern about competition from India led the Manchester Chamber of Commerce to set up the Bombay and Lancashire Cotton Spinning Inquiry in 1887. One of those who came before the committee of inquiry was a C. J. Sassoon, most likely Elias's son Charles. When asked about the mill business in India, its profitability, and whether he expected its

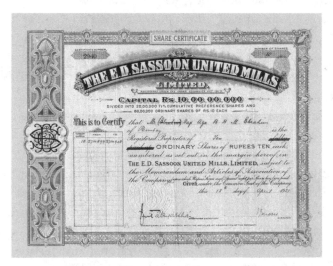

Share certificate issued for one of the
E. D. Sassoon mills in Bombay, 1921.

expansion to continue, his answer was prophetic: "In about ten years from now, there will be over two hundred mills in Bombay," he told the committee, and said that new markets, in addition to China and Japan, would be reached, such as the Persian Gulf and Zanzibar. He refused to speculate on whether a revaluation of the rupee (at Britain's request) would enable Lancashire to compete on equal terms with Bombay, but when pressed by the committee he would say that more mills would be built regardless. In spite of the increased competition, however, in 1911, "140 years after the establishment of the first spinning mill, 40 per cent of the factory cotton spindles in the world were still in Britain; of those outside Britain 22 percent were in the United States or Canada."

As industrialization gathered momentum, electricity became another trading opportunity. Edward Sassoon was a member of the board of the Bombay Electric Supply and Tramways, incorporated in 1905. Industrialization in India drove demand, and in 1909 the company sold shares to the public to increase its capital. Anxious to bring electricity to E. D. Sassoon & Co.'s mills, Sassoon Jacob David supported large-scale hydroelectric schemes proposed by Jamsetjee Tata; "Sir Sassoon's guarantee gave considerable impetus to the progress of the scheme," and a license was granted in 1907 to launch the project. By the end of the First World War, the E. D. Sassoon mills in Bombay would have their own generators to keep the spinning and weaving departments running.

HIGH LIFE

The accession of the Prince of Wales after Queen Victoria's death in January 1901 naturally drew speculation around the world. What would this new monarch, the King of the United Kingdom and Emperor of India, be like? Winston Churchill, on a lecture tour in Canada to promote his account of his exploits during the Boer War in South Africa, wrote sardonically to his mother upon hearing of the news:

A great and solemn event . . . but I am curious to know about the King. Will it entirely revolutionise his way of life? Will he sell his horses and scatter his Jews or will Reuben Sassoon be enshrined among the crown jewels and other regalia? Will he become desperately serious?

The obsequious nature of Reuben and Arthur's friendship with the King was common knowledge. To be friends with the King of the strongest empire in the world was no small thing, but the closeness of the relationship was no aberration. Indeed, the new Prince of Wales and future George V too maintained a close friendship with Arthur and Louise. Less than three weeks after Edward VII's death in 1910, George wrote Louise a long, handwritten letter, filled with intimate details about his grief:

> You know what my beloved father was to me & therefore you can understand what a terrible blank there is in my life, we were more like brothers than father & son & I consulted him in everything & always asked his advice. He was so fond of you and Arthur & I know you will miss him. . . . Please thank dear Arthur for his kind sympathy, I know his sorrow is real.

Louise was officially asked to assist at "the Interment of His Late Most Sacred Majesty of blessed memory in the Royal Chapel of Saint George, at Windsor," and the Rothschild archives in London contain numerous letters between her and George V. When Arthur died in March 1912 at the age of seventy-one, he wrote to her:

> I cannot tell you how shocked & grieved I was to get your telegram this morning telling me that I should never see your poor husband again. I can't realise yet that I shall never be able to chaff him again. I feel that I have lost a real good & true friend in dear Arthur whom I had known for so many years & from whom I had received so many kindnesses.

When George himself fell sick in 1929, he told Louise that she was "one of my oldest friends." And when he died in 1936, his daughter

EARL MARSHAL'S OFFICE,

NORFOLK HOUSE,

ST. JAMES'S SQUARE,

S.W.

The Earl Marshal has it in Command to invite

Mrs Arthur Sassoon

to assist at the Interment of His late Most Sacred Majesty
of blessed memory in the Royal Chapel of Saint George, at
Windsor, on Friday the 20th instant.

May, 1910.

Gentlemen : Full Dress with Trousers.
Collars and Orders to be worn.
Ladies : Morning Dress.

An immediate answer is requested in the enclosed envelope, to enable the
Earl Marshal to forward the necessary ticket.

Letter to Louise (Arthur's wife) inviting her to
participate in the Interment of Edward VII, 1910.

Princess Mary added a handwritten note at the end of a typed letter
to her saying "how much my father appreciated your friendship as he
often talked to me about it."

The royal embrace did not dispel or shield the Sassoons from criticism and anti-Semitic attacks, but actually invited them. One book
published in London in 1904 under the pseudonym "A Foreign Resident" tells of the author visiting the capital after a long absence:

> Say what you will, the Jews are the salt of smart Society, and
> the City the one intellectual stimulus that its faculties know. . . .
> The possible demoralization of a high-minded and virtuous
> aristocracy by the new mammon-worship . . . had no sooner
> somewhat receded than one heard about the Judaising [sic] of
> the West End and the degrading materialism of its spiritually
> minded denizens which was sure to follow.

He explained how the Jews, in order to ingratiate themselves into the English aristocracy, imitated them and began "to farm, as well as to sport," and that "Sassoon, of Tulchan Lodge, Advie, is bracketed among Highland deer-stalkers," and added: "The Sassoons, originally presented by Bombay to Britain, occupy a strip of Sussex and a larger area in Kent. Thence they have in a manner, extended themselves to remote parts of the United Kingdom." Describing the Prince of Wales's relationship with the Jews, he claimed: "The rich men from the East are to-day only where he found them on his accession. With the tact which keeps Jew and Gentile alike in high good-humour, he has contrived to make them pay in philanthropy for what they have received in honours."

The Sassoons attracted negative attention not only in England but also in the United States. A predictably terrible novel based around the family, titled *The Salamander* and serialized in *McClure's Magazine,* depicts Sir Albert as a greedy tycoon, once a malign power in New York, entrapping young women attempting to make a name for themselves in show business in the city.

In India, as in England, anti-Semitism was commonplace, and Jews were often prohibited from joining European clubs. In 1907, David Ezra was barred from the Bengal Club, a European gentlemen's club in Calcutta. Amusingly, the members did not realize that he controlled a large real estate portfolio in the city, including the land on which the club was built. In retaliation he ordered them to vacate the premises, ultimately rejecting the membership that was hastily offered to him but allowing the club to continue renting the property.

Actually, the name of the Sassoons was seldom out of the society pages. In a collection of photographs from *High Society* for 1897–1914, Sir Edward Sassoon and his wife, Aline de Rothschild, were photographed with the Marlborough House Set in a country house, together with the Prince of Wales, and the photographs were part of a feature on "Politics and the New Establishment" in Britain. There were plenty of other ways for members of the family to spend their money, however; lavish expenditure on parties, marriages, and mansions persisted, and an almost obsessive interest in horse racing prevailed everywhere from Hong Kong and Shanghai to England. Even more expensive was the world of art. The exhibition catalogs of the Royal Academy of Arts

and other institutions indicate that numerous works of art and historical artifacts were being lent by members of the Sassoon family from
the late nineteenth century on. They attended the openings of plays in
London theaters, and when a well-known soprano performed a song
recital in London, it was under the patronage of Sir Edward and Lady
Sassoon. The ledgers of members of the family at the time indicate
extravagant spending on all fronts. One "Racing Account" shows bets
on horses totaling thousands of pounds per year, out of a total budget
of £33,000—an enormous sum at that time (equivalent to about £1.9
million today). Charities were not forgotten but donations diminished
as time went by, and Louise Sassoon can be seen giving 312 pounds
10 shillings 7 pence to miscellaneous charities over six months, a sum
comparable to a single day's bets at the races.

There were many sumptuous marriages in the family, and the celebrations grew even more elaborate and the guest lists ever more selective. When Sir David Ezra married Rachel in London in 1912, *The
Times* gave the wedding extensive coverage. The ceremony took place
in Lauderdale Road Synagogue in Maida Vale:

> The bride's dress was of plain white satin, Princess style, with
> long, close-fitting sleeves and a bodice of chiffon and tulle. The
> bride carried a shower bouquet composed of lilies of the valley
> and white carnations. The bride wore a single row of pearls—
> her hair was simply but most becomingly done. She looked
> sweet & tremulous during the service & when it was over her
> colour rose & she left the synagogue with such a happy smile.

Prior to the wedding, Flora, who by then had settled in England, held
an engagement party for family members with a sit-down dinner
for thirty-six (and was even able to telephone some of her guests
to confirm their attendance). A two-page spread in *The Times* was
devoted to the wedding gifts the couple received, from which we can
see that the Baghdadi Jews in attendance mostly wrote checks (no
sums mentioned), while the English guests offered vases, silver, pots,
crystal, sets of dishes, and clocks. In Shanghai, the marriage in 1907
of one of the granddaughters of Sir Albert to another Baghdadi was
described as a magnificent occasion, where the ceremony took place

in an "overflowing synagogue under a white silk canopy supported by four holders." Many guests attended the reception, and more than two hundred gifts were displayed in the billiard room.

As in other dynasties, the premarriage discussions within the family were not just about dowry negotiations but also about safeguarding the bride's future. David advised his sister Rachel about the details of her marriage settlement, explaining for example the legal ramifications for the trust set up in her name were she to move to England and be subject to English law. Marriages to other wealthy and well-connected families ensured that the Sassoons would continue to be a dynasty to reckon with globally, and they tended to intermarry less often than the Rothschilds, for example. David's children had married either wealthy Baghdadi Jewish families or their own cousins. The next generation extended their range, marrying into Baghdadi families or Europe's prominent Jewish families, such as the Rothschilds and Gunzburgs, or—controversially—aristocratic families who were not Jewish. By the fourth generation almost all marriages were to British and European families, Jewish and not. The migration to London brought with it marriages outside the faith. Sybil Sassoon, Edward's daughter, was married in 1913 to George Cholmondeley, the future 5th Marquess of Cholmondeley and Lord Great Chamberlain. According to one source, the Rothschilds, by then joined by marriage to the Sassoons, expressed disquiet about Sybil's marriage on religious grounds. Their uneasiness and others' was likely the reason for the modesty of Sybil's wedding, which was held at a registrar's office in London with only ten guests in attendance. Marrying "out" sometimes led to serious fractures within the family, even though most of the marriages were into the British aristocracy. Young men or women were shunned or boycotted by the older generation. When Reuben's daughter Louise married Lord Boyle, twenty-four years her senior, in 1914, it caused a rift in the family. Flora cut off all relations with Louise, relenting only when Lord Boyle died suddenly two years after their wedding:

My dear Louise,

I could not muster courage to write you, but I have been told that I might do so & that you would not take it amiss. You know what my feelings towards you have always been & you will believe that I feel <u>very very</u> sorry for you & send you my sincere sympathy & condolence. I had often hoped to meet you but it did not come off.

With love & sincere sympathy again,

Yrs afftly.,

Flora Sassoon

The problem was neither new nor unforeseeable. None of S.D.'s children, the first Sassoons to be raised in England, had married Baghdadi families, and two had married out of the faith.

The family found it easier to resist assimilation in India, and it was there that their commitment to the community in their ancestral home was most evident and persistent. One telegram of 1917 asked the senior British official in Baghdad to pass on a donation of fifteen thousand rupees from E. D. Sassoon to the Chief Rabbi to distribute among needy Jews during Passover. As benefactors and a superlative example of a local family making good, the Sassoons enjoyed substantial celebrity in the city's Jewish community. When one young Jew needed to pay a *badal,* a sum owed to the Ottoman government in lieu of army service, he turned to the Sassoons for help. He wrote to the House of Bombay about the suffering of recruits and promised to work for the family in return for their assistance, offering up his fluency in the Baghdadi Jewish dialect and accounting experience as credentials. The war from which he sought an exemption had begun a year earlier in a small European country not much closer to Baghdad than Bombay, but a network of international alliances meant that the great powers of Europe, and thus their imperial possessions all around the world also, were dragged into the conflict. Whether or not it was the world's first, it was indisputably a global war. Men from Britain, India, and Ottoman Baghdad would all be mobilized, fight, and die in its course, and every map of the world would look different in its wake.

11

WAR AND UNCERTAINTY

1914–1924

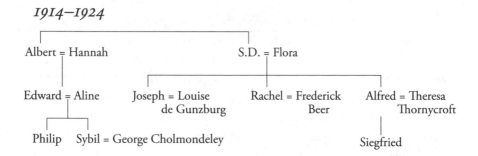

Albert = Hannah   S.D. = Flora

Edward = Aline   Joseph = Louise   Rachel = Frederick   Alfred = Theresa
                        de Gunzburg   Beer   Thornycroft

Philip   Sybil = George Cholmondeley   Siegfried

July 1914 marked the start of the First World War, which led to seismic changes to the British Empire and impacted the Sassoons wherever they lived. It brought an abrupt end to the relative peace and prosperity of the Victorian era, and the war and its immediate aftermath signaled the beginning of deep changes to both branches of the family. Though Britain emerged from the conflict with greatly extended imperial possessions, 1918 was high noon of the British Empire before its gradual decline. In the postwar world, controlling and placating the various strands of the empire proved an increasingly difficult task.

No one in the family epitomized the suffering of millions of soldiers around the world during the war years better than Siegfried Sassoon.

Siegfried Loraine Sassoon was named by his non-Jewish mother after Wagner, whose operas she admired, and an esteemed canon called

Loraine. Siegfried had no connection to the family business, nor did he pay it any attention. His father, Alfred, was S.D.'s second son and the first Sassoon to be born in London. He suffered from consumption and remained weak throughout his life. He married Theresa Thornycroft, an English sculptor and painter who had exhibited at the Royal Academy. She was Catholic, and the union led to a complete break with his family. At their mother's encouragement, Alfred's elder brother Joseph (who married into the aristocratic—and Jewish—Gunzburg family) declined to see him. Their sister, Rachel, refusing to cave in to her mother's pressure, developed a lifelong relationship with Theresa and (as we saw) followed Alfred and married out. Alfred and Theresa's marriage was neither long nor happy, and they separated when Siegfried was four years old, with Alfred moving to London and his wife and three sons staying in their home in Kent, as Siegfried would describe in his memoir of his childhood, *The Old Century and Seven More Years*.

The children were never told the reason behind their parents' split and were essentially raised by their nurse, Mrs. Mitchell. "Such were the bare details," Siegfried wrote, "which serve to show that my early awareness of the world began with a confused knowledge that I was living in a family story which did not promise to have a happy ending." They were taken from time to time to visit their father, "a dark-haired youngish man with large sad brown eyes and a moustache which tickled when he kissed you." Siegfried described a visit from his grandmother Farha (not to be confused with his great-grandmother, David's second wife, or Suleiman's wife), who, after not seeing her son for more than a decade, had come to say goodbye to Alfred, on his deathbed at the age of thirty-four in 1895. "She was talking very fast in a foreign voice. . . . She was very lively and seemed kind and was delighted at seeing us." Siegfried was too devastated to attend the funeral, and had to hear about the unfamiliar Jewish rituals of burial from his elder and younger brothers—they had been raised as Christians. "Two old men in funny looking hats walked up and down saying jabber-jabber-jabber was how my elder brother described the rabbis. . . . We knew that Pappy had given up that sort of religion a long time ago."

Siegfried had little contact with other members of the family throughout his early years, but sometime after his father's death he learned about the Sassoons and their history from his great-aunt Mozelle (David's youngest daughter). He saw himself as "a poor relation, and relatively speaking, he was." S.D.'s estate had to be divided between his wife, Farha, and his four children, and it could not be claimed, as Albert's inheritors sought to, that he was a resident of Bombay and therefore eligible for reduced death duties, so Alfred lacked the wealth enjoyed by many of his cousins. Siegfried's "attitude towards the family's money was both disdainful and apologetic." In 1927, he summed up his feelings about the family in a letter to the poet Robert Graves:

> They made it in the East by dirty trading, millions and millions of coins. They spent it all in draper's shops and jewellers and pastry cooks and brothels. They hire large mausoleums and get cremated at Golders Green. They smoke Coronas and worship German royalties and dissolute peers.

He also referred to "Semitic sovereigns none of which I have the least right to call my own." There is no doubt that Siegfried was ashamed of his family and his oriental roots. He totally identified with the Thornycrofts. The scorn and cynicism cannot be attributed to his childhood alone. His experience on the Western Front had changed him, his politics, and, of course, his poetry. The swell of patriotic feeling that saw him sign up on the day war was declared was shattered by the horrors he witnessed in the trenches; he became one of the war's most prominent opponents, and his wartime experience witnessing horrible deaths of less fortunate soldiers in the trenches disillusioned him about money and luxury.

Siegfried became famous for his poetry and was among the leading pacifists of the First World War, such as the philosopher Bertrand Russell and the poets Wilfred Owen and Robert Graves. He suffered from trench fever and a neck injury and was later decorated for bravery, which allowed him to criticize the war publicly with relative impunity. He began to sink into depression when he saw no end to the massacre. The dead and wounded haunted him, and this was reflected in his poems, which, with those of Wilfred Owen, Rupert Brooke, and

Robert Graves, came to define how the British public remembered
the war, whether lamenting the fallen—

> But death replied. "I choose him." So he went,
> And there was silence in the summer night;
> Silence and safety; and the veils of sleep.
> Then far away, the thudding of the guns.

—or the deceptions of those who remained:

> . . . and how, at last, he died,
> Blown to small bits. And no one seemed to care
> Except that lonely woman with white hair.

Siegfried struggled hard to come to terms with his sexuality, and
not until 1967, the year he died, was homosexuality between two
consenting adults legalized in Britain. All his life he was full of con-
tradictions and felt pulled between two directions: his homosexuality
and social pressure to marry and produce a son; his Sassoon ancestry
versus his English ancestry; his well-off wider family against his utter
contempt for wealth; and "his innate self-distrust combined with a
passionate longing to trust." Yet, and maybe because of all these conflicts, "no poet of his generation has been better loved by his fellows."

Siegfried had a strong relationship with Rachel Beer, his paternal aunt who also became famous for being an editor of a national
journal. Unlike Siegfried, Rachel (born in Bombay) was proud of
her Eastern ancestry and in many costume parties she dressed as an
Arab lady, swathed in strings of coral and pearls, but at the same
time she felt absolutely English and made sure she was perceived
as such. When she died in 1927 from stomach cancer at the age of
sixty-nine, neither Siegfried nor his older brother Michael attended
her funeral even though they were named in her estate. Siegfried
was attached to his aunt, who "shared many of his father's qualities and, incidentally, his own. All three were witty, charming and
volatile." Yet, Siegfried did not see her in the last twenty years of her
life. Rachel was very kind to Siegfried when he was growing up and
left him a quarter of her estate. This allowed him to buy his house

in Heytesbury, Wiltshire. Ironically, the day she died he published a poem attacking the wealthy, not knowing he would benefit from his family's riches even more:

> I accuse the Rich of what they've always done before—
> Of lifting worldly faces to a diamond star.

Ten years before his death in 1967, Siegfried became a Roman Catholic, and "his conversion gave him peace." More than anyone among the Sassoons, Siegfried in his Englishness symbolized the full immersion in English society and the total disconnect from oriental roots.

Whether in business, art, or journalism, all the Sassoons felt the impact of the First World War and shared its burdens. During the war, "at least fourteen of David's grandsons and great-grandsons held commissions in the British Army." Siegfried's younger brother Hamo, a second lieutenant with the Royal Engineers (the only one of the three brothers to complete his university degree as an engineer), was killed at Gallipoli in November 1915 along with more than twenty-five thousand Allied troops. Reginald Sassoon, one of Elias's grandsons, was so nearsighted that all believed he was ineligible for service, yet he became a captain in the Irish Guards and was awarded the Military Cross for "conspicuous gallantry and devotion to duty." When he died in 1933 from a riding accident, one of his military friends wrote in *The Times* about how he had gained the respect of officers and soldiers: "Then the test came and Captain Sassoon never altered his gait, but kept going steadily on—in bad times or good times, they were all the same to him; obstacles, why, they were just made to be scaled." Reggie was not known for his acumen but was far more interested in horses, and therefore played no real role in the family's business. His cousin Victor joined the Royal Flying Corps and was wounded, as were several other members of the family. The Sassoon women of the family also played their part. Some, such as Mrs. Arthur Sassoon, joined the Queen's Work for Women Fund, which helped women during the war, while others participated in numerous voluntary charities aimed at helping the soldiers and particularly the wounded.

No branch was unaffected. One "positive" consequence of the war is that members of the two sides of the family, David Sassoon & Co. and E. D. Sassoon, showed signs of unity in the face of calamity as both had encountered the atrocities of the war and had suffered their share of wounded soldiers. Each side offered messages of sympathy whenever the other suffered.

BUSINESS IN WARTIME

The First World War offered opportunities in certain commodities, but it caused severe dislocation in the global financial sector, and merchants trading across borders found themselves subject to scrutiny. The Sassoons' involvement with the Hongkong and Shanghai Banking Corporation grew anxious during the war, when it was suspected of having close ties to the Germans. Although the German members of its board were compelled to resign, there continued to be "an undercurrent of suspicion, of intercepted documents and charges and counter-charges." In one letter, Flora's son David informed his sister, "The Crown is suing David Sassoon & Co., of Shanghai for trading with the enemy, & the case is now being heard before the British magistrate there. I need hardly dilate here on the subject." Most likely the enemy here was the Ottoman Empire, where the Sassoons had long and deep relations with many of the Ottoman provinces, particularly their former home Baghdad. Ottoman provinces had, with the Persian Gulf, been growing in both firms' estimations in the years before the war, as they looked for new regions and commodities to compensate for the impending loss of the opium trade. Even the pearl business was declining by the end of the nineteenth century: "The trade in pearls seems to have been destroyed, and one cannot see any improvement in the near future." Before the war, David Sassoon & Co. can be seen requesting the Foreign Office's support in pressing the Ottomans to allow them to purchase more steamers for the Euphrates and Tigris Steam Navigation Company, while E. D. Sassoon was indirectly linked with the National Bank of Turkey, part of an attempt to expand their business in Iraq, moving into grain exports and establishing a river service between Basra and Baghdad. The war complicated these activities and others but rarely halted them altogether. Ten thousand pounds was seized by the authorities from the Eastern Bank's Baghdad branch, but it remained operational. Unlike the Rothschilds, the Sassoons had little exposure to Europe, and their relations with German entities were almost nonexistent; hence there was no direct impact on their overall business.

Both Sassoon firms were pushing into new territories in the Persian Gulf, such as Sharjah; they were well established in Bushir in Persia, from where they sent their goods to Shiraz. They continued to export goods to Baghdad and Basra: One report indicated their intention to export tin from Karachi to Basra, another concerned permission to ship motor tire covers and inner tubes, a third dealt with shipping wheat to the Persian emirates and exporting dates from Basra to Asia and Europe. Even before the end of the war, immediately after the British captured Baghdad from the Ottomans in March 1917, E. D. Sassoon was requesting permission for its employees to travel there for trade purposes. Indeed, the E. D. Sassoon accounting books in the archives include an analysis of their Persian Gulf commissions and Persian Gulf goods, indicating a wide variety of products from sugar to matches, and a stream of respectable profits.

While the two Sassoon firms were trading across borders and allegiances in the Gulf, in India they were pushing for more protectionism. Sir Sassoon David Sassoon lamented that the Indian government's policies advantaged outsiders at the expense of India's own industry. Whereas David Sassoon & Co. was largely concerned with preserving its business, E. D. Sassoon took more initiatives and even considered entering banking after the war. In January 1921, E. D. Sassoon was incorporated in India as a private limited company, as David Sassoon & Co. had been nearly two decades earlier, with a capital of one million rupees. The company embarked on a major reorganization, prompted by high taxation in Britain. Elias's son's Indian domicile allowed him to transfer some of the firm's assets by creating an elaborate system of trusts that could channel assets between them. The Bombay Trust was incorporated in September 1920 and the Hong Kong Trust in July 1921. The latter had "a paid-up capital of nearly £5 million [roughly £250 million in today's value], plus a similar amount in reserve, with very wide powers to lend money in all parts of the world." These trusts also enabled E. D. Sassoon to benefit from differentials in interest rates between Bombay, Hong Kong, and Shanghai, but more important, it gave the firm flexibility.

INDIA AFTER THE WAR

The First World War brought many changes in India, where nationalism was on the rise, and "by 1918, most Indians were convinced that independence was more important than the reform of their society." India's contribution to the war was substantial. More than half the 2.5 million subjects of the British Empire to serve during the First World War were Indian volunteers. Advocates of Home Rule in particular believed that Indians' participation in the war would allow them to demand greater freedoms from the British after it ended. As the war dragged on and the resulting disruptions to India's economy and politics grew more acute, however, disaffection and anti-British sentiment spread. British promises of greater self-government, embodied in the Montagu-Chelmsford reforms of 1919, were contradicted by the fact that the ultimate power still lay in the hands of the Viceroy and the India Office in London. That year, *swaraj* (self-rule) became the dominant demand of the nationalists. Meanwhile the spread of the influenza epidemic and a wave of strikes organized by the nationalists fostered unrest, leading to a cycle of crackdowns and civil disobedience. In April 1919 in the city of Amritsar, British troops opened fire on a peaceful, unarmed crowd, killing hundreds. The massacre turned millions of Indians into nationalists who would never again trust British "fair play." The postwar years were depressing and frustrating to India's great expectations from a British win, and Mahatma Gandhi began organizing the Congress Party to resist many British policies, including their economic policy.

For those whose interests and loyalties lay with Britain and her empire, such as the Sassoons, 1919 was a watershed moment, as the independence movement proved its power and popular appeal. The war years themselves, however, were a boon for the cotton and textile industries in India, as global demand increased exponentially at the same time as production elsewhere was disrupted. Between 1916 and

1922, the cotton textile industry experienced its biggest boom since the American Civil War in the 1860s. According to an Indian survey, by 1920 the two Sassoon companies between them owned fourteen factories (eleven of which belonged to E.D.) with 652,000 spindles and 13,500 looms, and in the decade following 1914 the book value of both firms' operations more than doubled. India offered many advantages to industrialists: Its weekly wage was far below that in the United States and England ($0.78 versus roughly $7 and $5 respectively); its manufacturing costs were less than half those of most other producers except China; and most important, the profit margin was much higher in India than among American or European manufacturers. Under Jacob, E. D. Sassoon had grown by finding unprofitable mills and acquiring them. He followed the trailblazing Jamsetjee Tata, one of the first Indians to enter manufacturing, by investing in quality machinery, expensive in the short term but more profitable in the long run. "Jacob had adequate capital, organizing flair and the supreme asset of plentiful labour," and he was the first owner in India to have a conveyor belt installed in one of his mills. Alongside native Indians, numerous young Baghdadis were recruited to work in the firm's mills, their families promised free schooling, medical care, and even plots at a cemetery. By the end of the war, a few thousand workers were on the firm's payroll with a combined output ranking among the highest in Bombay. The main challenge at the time was to keep up with demand, and because new factories took years to build, the larger mill owners began purchasing semi-derelict factories to meet the rising demand. One outcome of the First World War that impacted the business was a result of the withdrawal of British shipping from the Bombay–Hong Kong route. The Sassoons and a few other industrialists warned that the trade in cotton yarn had dropped since the beginning of the war and that the Japanese mill industry, a serious competitor to the Indian one, would be the main beneficiary, and surely that could not serve British imperial interests. The cancellation of the route was due to the requisitioning of ships for war purposes by the comptroller of shipping in London, but as a result of lobbying by the Hong Kong General Chamber of Commerce, the British government decided to allow P & O to retain four ships on the route.

One of the distinctive features of modern industrial India was the rapid formation of joint stock companies. By 1916 about 2,400 of them had been set up, including some 200 in cotton mills. E. D. Sassoon was among those utilizing the new structure, and they floated many of their mills successfully. By 1922, however, growth began to splutter; the number of looms in Bombay declined and the value of imported machinery dropped sharply. The mill owners then faced three problems: having to replace imported machinery at a time when their currency had depreciated in value, which meant higher costs; overcapitalization of many of the mills, forcing owners to write down their capital substantially in the middle of a slump; and increasingly adversarial labor relations. In November 1920 more than five thousand workers in E. D. Sassoon's mills went on strike in the hope of improving their wages and reducing the length of their shifts. The company retorted that shorter hours of operation and higher wages would reduce their competitiveness with Japan and China, though they undertook to improve working and sanitary conditions of the factories. When they and other mill owners launched rationalization schemes in 1922, it was feared that more than half of the workforce would have to be dismissed for the mills to survive, and the workers immediately went on strike. E. D. Sassoon's rationalization program was particularly aggressive and it liquidated several of its mills (and some of these were snapped up by David Sassoon & Co.). Yet an inquiry into mill conditions at the time noted that although wage rates in the Sassoon mills mirrored those of other factories, the reasonable working conditions in the Sassoon mills would be hard to replicate in other mills.

As the slowdown grew more severe, however, the mill owners began to scale back their operations. Raw cotton was no longer cheap and the exchange rate had shifted against Indian merchants exporting to China. Investing in new mills was now deemed inadvisable. While the cost of setting up cotton mills in India was relatively high—three times that of starting a new mill in England—once they were up and running, Indian operations had the advantage of being integrated, so that raw cotton went in one end of the mill and came out as a finished product ready for shipment, unlike in Lancashire. As efficiency increased and labor hires decreased, wages actually rose by about 13 percent, and the industry was lucrative enough to draw entrepreneurs to it. Attractive too was the prestige of owning factories employing thousands of workers. One newspaper wrote about "Sir Jacob being fairly entitled to be called the father of the Bombay cotton industry." But by the mid-1920s, E. D. Sassoon was feeling the squeeze in the cotton market. Its cotton department reported that the market was weak and it was struggling to compete with American cotton. Given the frequent fires that engulfed buildings in Bombay, the recurrent strikes, and the pessimistic futures market, bearish sentiment prevailed as stocks were accumulating.

THE FINAL CHAPTER OF OPIUM

During most of the First World War of 1914–1918, the British government shifted its focus to the more pressing needs of the war and was reluctant to assist opium traders who were saddled with stock they were no longer able to sell, as there was no political gain to be made by alienating the Chinese. There is a paucity of documents pertaining to opium from 1914 to the end of 1916. Similarly, the Sassoon archives contain almost no reference to opium from the early twentieth century onward. Early in 1917, a representative of David Sassoon & Co. wrote to the Foreign Office, on behalf of a group of merchants who became known as the "Opium Combine," that "the one and only desire of the opium merchants was to get rid of their stocks and be quit of the opium trade for good and all." The Combine was in effect a cartel, formed to take over accumulated stock and control supply in the hope that doing so would push prices up, backed by Chinese banks and the Hongkong and Shanghai Banking Corporation to the tune of 1.5 and 2.5 million taels respectively.

On behalf of the Combine, David Sassoon & Co. reached a direct agreement with the Chinese government to sell the residue stock of Indian opium, 2,100 chests in total, at 8,200 taels per chest, generating total revenue equivalent to about $13 million. The British, who hadn't been consulted, were hesitant to approve the deal, and the opium remained on the merchant's books until October 1918, when it was exchanged for bonds quoted at 36 percent, provided by the Superintendent of Chinese Maritime Customs. Even though the curtain had fallen on the trade in China, entries for opium can be seen in

E. D. Sassoon's accounts of 1923, and it wasn't until after 1927, when the export trade came to a complete halt, that they were free of it.

The Sassoons continued to focus on petitioning British officials to allow them to get rid of their opium stock. The total value of the stock held by the Sassoons at the end of the First World War was about $15 million (roughly $300 million today), hence their dogged pursuit of the matter at all levels. A typical letter from their representatives warned that when losses in the rubber trade reached about five million taels, it brought a blight on Shanghai's trade for a long period, and hence "it does not need much stretch of imagination to picture what the effect of the attack on opium would be." The firm begged to inform the British government that if the retail shops were closed before the stock could be absorbed, "the opium would have to be sold to other markets than China in which case it would not realise one-tenth of its value." It seems that the Sassoons were trying to get rid of their opium stock in novel ways; a letter from E. D. Sassoon to the Director-General of Posts and Telegraph of India indicates these new arrangements:

> We have the honour to address you with regard to transmission of opium samples by parcel post to London. . . . We have frequently to make shipments of opium to Taipeh in Formosa [Taiwan] and New York (U.S.A.). The sales are made on the basis of certain percentage of Morphia which is guaranteed to be contained in the drug according to the London Standard analysis.

It was not easy to get permission to transfer these samples, and the Post Office agreed only after many requests to allow the shipments if "the samples are sealed with the British Consulate seal and are addressed to a recognized laboratory in London." Even after the opium ban became official in 1917 (per the 1907 agreement that stipulated the end of trade after ten years), E. D. Sassoon continued to be active in the market, and reports by government officials from 1924 showed that they were attempting "to drive other merchants out of the market," with the intention "to effectively manipulate the auction buying of opium at Calcutta so as to compel us to reduce our prices."

Opium was now being sold officially to French Indochina, but not to China, and Indian officials were anxious about "the cornering of the opium market by Messrs. Sassoon." The government was holding monthly auctions of opium to be sold directly at fixed prices to importing governments in the French colonies. The Finance Department of the Indian government warned, "It is understood—though there is no official confirmation—that Messrs. Sassoon have recently come to an arrangement with the Saigon government under which the latter now obtain their opium solely through that firm." There was concern that "the effect of this arrangement has been to give Messrs Sassoon almost complete control of the opium export trade." The other merchants were "either unable or unwilling to outbid Sassoon and to hold the stock." The officials warned that what had happened in one auction would repeat itself:

> At the January sale this year [1924] 250 chests were offered. Messrs Sassoon purchased the first 200 chests put up to auction. As soon as the representative of the firm said that he did not want any more, everyone cleared out and no bid was got for the other 50 chests, no one daring to buy them, as they have no means of disposing of the opium.

The official counseled that the prices in these auctions "have been the result simply of Messrs Sassoon's demand." A summary of monthly sales from January 1923 to the end of January 1924 shows that he was not exaggerating. During the first six months, other firms bought just 10 or 20 percent of the stock at auction, and nothing at all in the second half of the year. Meanwhile, the Indian government was also battling against smuggling and illicit sales of opium, and some of that, it seems, was being financed by a Chinese company, with certain ships being diverted to engage in the smuggling.

As pressure mounted from all sides, more legal cases were brought against merchants or brokers. One report indicated that the Supreme Court in Shanghai was preoccupied with a case in which a Chinese opium merchant sued Messrs. E. D. Sassoon for damages due to the nondelivery of eight chests of opium, but the judge sided with the

Sassoons, arguing that all parties knew that opium not cleared by March 1918 would remain in the hands of the Chinese government.

It was a squalid end to a trade that carries a singular moral charge, and it is hard to make moral judgments from a contemporary point of view, given that opium was legal in London and New York for so long and its trade became fully legal after the Opium Wars. Opium trading during the nineteenth and early twentieth centuries "bound Indian peasants, British and Indian governments, a vast mass of Chinese consumers, and an array of Western, Parsi, Sephardic, and most of all Chinese merchants together in an immense revenue-generating system." Not all these participants were willing, and certainly they didn't benefit equally from the trade, though even here there are surprises. The argument that opium sustained Britain's industrialization and the expansion of the world economy in the nineteenth century is complicated by analysis that suggests even China benefited economically and the treaty ports actually strengthened its trading relationships with its Asian neighbors. Needless to say, Chinese consumers paid a hefty price for consumption of opium.

In spite of the stigma attached to it, the Sassoons and others defended the opium trade through the nineteenth century and well into the twentieth, going so far as to marshal opposition to the restrictions imposed by China and subvert the campaigns of prohibitionists in Britain. The drug was traded freely when David arrived in Bombay, and though the consensus changed around them, the family continued to see it as a commodity not much different from any other until they could trade it no longer. There is no trace in the Sassoon archives of any doubt over opium's effects or the ethics of their involvement in the trade. In this they were not alone. *Israel's*

A portrait of Rachel Beer, daughter of S.D. Sassoon, c. 1900.

Messenger, the only Sephardic journal to be published in China, has nothing to say about the drug—a glaring omission, given the extent to which it was debated and discussed in other local publications at the end of the nineteenth century. It seems that moral arguments did not arise when fortunes were at stake, and even members of the family who took no part in the business, though they disagreed over and even campaigned for many of the social and political issues of their day, were united, either standing on the sidelines or actively supporting the trade. S.D.'s daughter, Rachel Beer, editor of *The Observer* and *The Sunday Times,* commented on the appointment of the Opium Commission of Inquiry in 1895 that "great injustice was done in India by the appointment of the Commission" and predicted that its report would shatter "the case of the anti-opiumists." Her nephew, the poet Siegfried Sassoon, who often introduced himself, facetiously, as coming from the poor side of the family, wrote about his ancestors but overlooked the main source of their wealth:

> Behold these jewelled, merchant Ancestors,
> Foregathered in some chancellery of death;
> Calm, provident, discreet, they stroke their beards
> And move their faces slowly in the gloom,
> And barter monstrous wealth with speech subdued,
> Lustreless eyes and acquiescent lids.

Opium trading and its control by Parsis and Jews ignited many snide remarks by their competitors who were desperate to acquire a larger slice of the cake. Jardine Matheson's correspondence shows a blatant "us and them" attitude in a letter sent to the firm of John Purvis, which collapsed as a result of its trading, reprimanding it for its borrowing tactics: "What are you ever likely to do in competition with the Jews in your settlement who are content with the smallest possible advance on cost & charges?" Later, anti-Semitic propaganda claimed that the Jews were the force behind the Opium Wars and responsible for destroying the lives of many Chinese, ignoring the fact that before the Jews arrived, the East India Company was in control of all trade from India, including opium. The fascist Arnold Leese, a virulent anti-

Semite and a founding member of the Imperial Fascist League, wrote about "the Jewish Rotting of China" in a pamphlet claiming that the Chinese hated foreigners because of the Sassoons and comparing this to other situations where all the blame lay only with the Jews.

NEW PROSPECTS IN CHINA

The Qing dynasty ruled China from 1644 until 1911, when it collapsed as a result of corruption, peasant unrest, and food shortages. While certain classes and groups in China thrived from economic dynamism, nationwide poverty, famines, and floods fueled a growing national-ism that accused the mandarins and the Emperor of acquiescing to foreigners and selling China to them. Unfortunately, the Republic of China, declared in 1912, suffered many trials and tribulations as it was ruled by disparate elements such as warlord generals and foreign powers. China during the First World War sided with the Allies and was promised that the German concessions in the eastern province of Shandong would be returned to the Chinese. (Humiliatingly, at the end of the war, these concessions were passed to Japan.) One-third of China's imports came from Britain, which in turn imported one-fifth of China's exports, and the Sassoons were well placed to take advantage of this.

Economically, laissez-faire policies in China extended not only to the commercial arena but also to monetary policy, and merchant guilds extended their power in both Chinese and foreign trade. Both Sassoon firms continued their involvement with the Hongkong and Shanghai Banking Corporation as directors. The biggest postwar change was that Jardine Matheson was given representation on the board, after decades of being blocked by the Sassoons since the bank began operations in 1865. As a consequence, E. D. Sassoon decided not to continue relations with the bank and resigned from the board at the end of 1922, while a representative of David Sassoon & Co. remained. The bank regained its position after the war and expanded profitably.

Once the war ended and strife grew in India, E. D. Sassoon, ner-vous about the rise of Indian nationalism, began to consider transferring assets abroad. The profits accrued by their mills during the war had shown what investments in manufacturing could deliver, but it grew increasingly concerned about its future in India. Its focus was drawn to real estate in China, principally in Shanghai, China's first cosmopolitan city and its economic powerhouse. Trade in the city had grown by an astonishing 400 percent in the final two decades of the nineteenth century, but as the opium trade stuttered and finally ceased, the Sassoons' attention shifted in real estate's favor. This was a case in point for the dynamic changes globally in the nineteenth century, where "Industrialization and the rise of the huge, impersonal metropolis" took place. Bigger cities led to the emergence of "new social relationships and speeded up the passage of information."

At the beginning of the twentieth century, Shanghai contained sovereign concessions belonging to fourteen different countries and was divided into four separate units: the Chinese City, which from the late 1920s was ruled by the Nationalists under Chiang Kai-shek; the International Settlement, in which foreigners had extraterritorial privileges and were subject to the Shanghai Municipal Council, made up of representatives of eleven Western countries; Hongkou, which was governed exclusively by the Japanese; and the French Concession, governed by the French Consul. The Shanghai Municipal Council represented groups with substantial real estate holdings in the International Settlement, and from their records we know that between 1877 and 1920 the two Sassoon companies bought twenty-nine properties, mostly at bargain prices, and it has been claimed that in the intervening period the value of the two largest properties acquired appreciated more than twenty-five-fold. Increasing their property investments in Shanghai in the period around 1910 proved to be propitious; two decades later they had climbed by more than ten times in value.

The Sassoons protected their assets in Shanghai the same way other residents did: by lobbying the municipality to deny undesirables the right to live in parts of the city, or to shelve infrastructure plans— widening roads, for example—that would encroach on their properties. The *Municipal Gazette* of Shanghai is full of stories of the two Sassoon firms' legal battles with the Shanghai Municipal Council over such matters. In one case, they argued against granting more permits allowing locals to live in districts in which they had interests:

> A large number of foreigners reside In the above Districts and it is our opinion that the houses already licensed are very detrimental to property interests in general and objectionable to the residents in particular, the wives and children of the latter being continually compelled to witness sights and scenes against all rules of order and decency in addition to their running the risk of being insulted in passing through the streets.

The precise nature of these "indecent" and "disorderly" sights and scenes wasn't specified, but the intent was clear: to police who was and who wasn't allowed to live in a neighborhood to avoid anything that might dampen the rapid increase in property prices that was under way.

Alongside its properties, E. D. Sassoon sought to grow its trading arm in Shanghai by acquiring in 1923 a considerable interest in a firm called Arnhold & Company (and later taking it over entirely). The rationale was to use Arnhold's extensive network of branches to expand into regions in China where E. D. Sassoon had no foothold, such as Peking, Hankow, and Mukden. Arnhold had been set up by three scions of Jewish trading families from northern Europe in the 1860s to export Europe's manufactured goods to China and import tea, silk, wood, and oil in return. It became one of the largest European traders operating in China and had a virtual monopoly on lumber exports—a lucrative business while the country's armament and railway construction programs were under way. By the time E. D. Sassoon bought into Arnhold, it too owned a valuable property portfolio in China, and the consolidation was a union of equivalents. The amalgamation was warmly received by the markets: Two trading firms with different areas of expertise and in different locations joined to form one of the "largest undertakings in the Orient." E. D. Sassoon left the management of Arnhold & Co. intact, although later the acquisition afforded E. D.'s chairman, Victor Sassoon, a powerful voice in the political affairs of the International Settlement, since

Interior of the Japanese morning room of Edward and Leontine at
46 Grosvenor Place, London, filled with opulent silks and antiquities, 1896.

H. E. Arnhold was also chairman of the Shanghai Municipal Council
for many years.

CHANGE OF GUARD

E. D. Sassoon had undergone a change of leadership itself. Jacob,
Elias's eldest, who was running E. D. Sassoon from Bombay, lacked
an obvious successor. Of his brothers, only Edward (not to be confused with Albert's son and successor) enjoyed his confidence. In 1915
a law was passed by the Governor-General of India to create a trust
"so as to accompany and support the title and dignity of a Baronet"
specially for Jacob's benefit, with the result that when he died a year
later, Edward not only succeeded him as chairman but also inherited his baronetcy. Unlike Jacob, who spent most of his working life
in India and China, Edward was more of an Englishman. Born in
Bombay, he was sent to China young and later headed to England to

ensure a high-quality education for his children. He lived in London's fashionable Grosvenor Place and owned a country house in Brighton. He paid one visit back to Bombay in the winter of 1907–8 to confer with his brother Jacob, inspect the textile mills, and meet with large clients of the firm, but otherwise largely remained in England, from where he masterminded the firm's incorporation and decentralization (and thus the reduction of its tax liabilities).

Edward's health deteriorated in the early 1920s; he suffered a number of strokes, leaving him wheelchair bound, and the death of his youngest son, Hector, from an emergency abdominal operation, left him paralyzed by grief. Both he and his brother Meyer died in 1924, leaving substantial assets to Victor, Edward's heir, and Mozelle Gabbay, Meyer's widow. While Edward left only half a million pounds, as a result of his successful tax strategies, Meyer left an estate estimated at $28 million today. Victor also inherited his father's title, to become the 3rd Baronet Sassoon of Bombay. In a manner typical of him, he did not confirm the estate sums, but remarked lightly that "high estimates are always good for one's credit." With no alternatives in sight, after his father's death, Victor became the new chairman of E. D. Sassoon. He would be the face of the Sassoon family in its last phase.

Victor had been born in 1881 in Naples, where his parents were celebrating their first anniversary. His father, Edward, was the fourth son of Elias, and his mother, Leontine, the vivacious and cultured daughter of a prominent Jewish merchant from Cairo. She had a strong influence on Victor as a child and her views remained important to him well into adulthood; he was delighted that one of his women friends, Yvonne Fitzpatrick, made a good impression on his mother. From her he learned the art of entertaining and hosting large parties. Until her death in the mid-1950s, she was his first port of call whenever he visited London.

Unlike most of the Sassoons of his generation, Victor studied not at Eton and Oxford but Harrow and then Trinity College, Cambridge. There he read history, gaining a degree in 1903. He became known as "Eves," after the initials of his full name, Ellice Victor Elias Sassoon. An aeronautical enthusiast from an early age, he joined the Royal Flying Corps during the First World War and was injured when his plane crashed in circumstances that are unclear. (There are conflicting accounts of his being shot down by enemy fire or of his plane crashing during a training flight.) He would use a walking stick for the rest of his life. His sensitivity about his disability never diminished: The image of his stroke-afflicted father in a wheelchair haunted him, and he "vowed never to take to a wheelchair, even if he had to spend the rest of his life on crutches." After the war, he worked for E. D. Sassoon around India and China until he was posted to Bombay in 1922 to take over the management of the company's business in India.

At David Sassoon & Co. too the guard was changing. Frederick, David's last surviving son, died in 1917 and was replaced by the founder's great-grandson David Gabbay. He was a competent businessman known for his financial shrewdness, particularly when it came to accounting, and stayed at the helm until his death in 1928. As we shall see, the innovation or vision that might have enabled the firm, now approaching its centenary, to survive and indeed thrive in a world that was changing rapidly was absent. From this side of the family neither of the Sassoons who rose to prominence in the twentieth century were known for their business undertakings. Though, unlike Siegfried, Philip Gustave Sassoon, Edward Sassoon and Aline de Rothschild's heir, was formally employed by David Sassoon & Co., and indeed would be nominated chairman, he scarcely played a larger role in its business activities.

Philip was raised in the utmost luxury (totally different from the other famous Sassoon, Siegfried). His lack of interest in the business that supported it was similarly unadulterated. He grew up in London and Paris, one of the first members of the family to be schooled entirely in England, with no stint abroad or practical taste of business. He spent his childhood with his sister, Sybil, at his parents' home on Park Lane and his holidays on the Kent coast, with regular visits to their maternal grandparents on the avenue de Marigny in Paris and to the Rothschild château at Chantilly in northern France. Philip had a strong relationship with his sister, which did not alter even after her marriage. Sybil was mostly educated in France and tutored privately in languages, music, and drawing; the two shared a deep love of art and both were close to their first cousin Hannah Gabbay. Neither

Philip nor Sybil was as interested in charities in comparison to other Sassoons; art was more predominant than charity.

Philip studied at Eton and then Oxford, where he read modern history at Christ Church. Both his parents died when he was in his early twenties, and in addition to his share of the cash estate, he inherited the mansion on Park Lane; a country house at Trent Park, north of London; and a lodge in Kent. Furthermore, there was property in India, including his great-grandfather's house in Pune and his father's shares in the Sassoon firm, making him "one of the wealthiest young men in England." He enlisted, as per his father's wishes, in the East Kent Yeomanry and became a second lieutenant in 1907. During the

Philip Sassoon's house on Park Lane, London, 1918.

Philip Sassoon's house combined oriental
(Persian) carpets and occidental art and furnishings.

First World War he served as Private Secretary to the Commander in Chief of the British Forces, Sir Douglas Haig, from 1915 until 1919, experiencing the war from behind the lines and away from the horrors captured so unflinchingly in Siegfried's writing. After his father's death, he fulfilled his undertaking to follow him into politics, and with financial support from his parents' families, he won the Hythe seat occupied by Sir Edward from 1899 in the by-election that followed Edward's death in 1912.

He was then twenty-three, one of the youngest MPs of the age, but it was art that most animated him. His love and knowledge of the arts was legendary. He was known as an aesthete, connoisseur, and patron. In 1921 the Prime Minister, Lloyd George, acknowledged Philip's expertise and selected him as a trustee of the National Gallery, making him probably the youngest man to be nominated for this position, and in 1933 he was appointed chairman. He also became a trustee of the Tate Gallery and the Wallace Collection—a hat trick of appointments to some of the most important art institutions in the country. He was a prolific collector, principally of eighteenth-century painting, and led a revival of interest in it. A patron of John Singer Sargent and other artists, Philip adorned the walls of his home on Park Lane with many fine paintings, including Sargent's portraits of his mother and sister. Kenneth Clark, the famous art historian and a director of the National Gallery, described Philip as "a kind of Haroun al Rashid figure, entertaining with oriental magnificence in three large houses, endlessly kind to his friends, witty, mercurial, and ultimately mysterious."

In his capacity as Lloyd George's Parliamentary Private Secretary, he played a role in the San Remo Conference in April 1920, which decided on the allocation of League of Nations mandates over the former Ottoman provinces of Palestine, Syria, and Mesopotamia. The conference affirmed the Balfour Declaration's assurance to Lord Rothschild of Britain's support for a national home for the Jews in Palestine. Chaim Weizmann, President of the World Zionist Organization (later Israel's first President), who attended the conference, was furious that Philip took no interest in Palestine or Jewish affairs, remarking: "The only man to ignore the whole business [of Palestine] was Philip Sassoon, another of Lloyd George's secretaries, and as it happens, the only Jewish member of the British delegation." Other Sassoons were also not supporters of Zionism, and although they gave some donations to charities in Palestine, these were mostly for religious purposes. In spite of being a member of a synagogue, Philip "appeared unmoved by the faith of his forebears. Instead he found spiritual release through his devotion to the most beautiful images made by man." Superstitious by nature, Philip insisted on having "a cobra mascot in his cars and aeroplanes." Sybil likewise kept Judaism at a remove and shared her brother's skepticism of Zionism, declaring that if Zionism was meant to "serve as an opening for our poor co-religionists in Russia who have to suffer so much, I am all for it—but personally I do not believe in the regeneration of our people in their ancient lands."

Philip showed rather more interest in the theater of high politics and put his mansion Port Lympne (built in 1913–14 in the Cape Dutch architectural style), near Hythe, at the disposal of the Prime Ministers of Britain and France, Lloyd George and Alexandre Millerand, for their discussions of German war reparations. It is doubtful

A serene Philip Sassoon is contrasted with his
bellowing colleagues on the front bench of the Houses
of Parliament. Cartoon by Max Beerbohm, 1913.

that Philip played any significant role in these negotiations but he was
obviously delighted to host on a few occasions such two central personalities. Some derided his role, and the British fascist Oswald Mosley thought Philip "rather a joke among the younger generation for
serving Lloyd George as Private Secretary in peace directly after he had
served during the war in the same capacity to General Haig." Mosley's anti-Semitism was part of the spirit of the times, and an article
published about the appointment of Lord Reading, who was Jewish,
as Viceroy of India, took approximately the opposite view of Philip's
capacities:

> The real danger is that another Jew is added to the many Jews
> who are taking part in the government of our empire. Behind
> all of Mr. [Lloyd] George's actions is the hidden hand of Sir
> Philip Sassoon.

More common, however, were criticisms of Philip's servility to the
great men of the time, Lloyd George and Winston Churchill. C. K.
Scott-Moncrieff, the translator of Proust, even penned a poem on
the subject:

Sir Philip Sassoon is a member for Hythe
He is opulent, generous, swarthy, and lithe,
Obsequious, modest, informal and jejune . . .
The houses he inhabits are costly but chaste
But Sir Philip Sassoon is unerring in taste . . .
Sir Philip Sassoon and his sires, it appears,
Have been settled in England for several years
Where their friendly invasion impartially brings
To our cabinet credit, and cash to our Kings . . .
Sir Philip was always a double event,
A Baghdadi banker, a yeoman of Kent
But now in four parts he's appearing at once,
As a lackey, a landlord, diplomatist, dunce.

Philip spent much of his time in Lloyd George's coalition government angling for a ministerial job and was finally rewarded with
one by a later Prime Minister, Stanley Baldwin, who appointed him
Under-Secretary of State for Air after the 1924 general election. He
occupied this post for a total of eleven years, from 1924 to 1929 and
again from 1931 to 1937. He was delighted, believing, rightly, that
flying would flourish and air power grow ever more important. He
liked his superior, Sir Samuel Hoare, and as Philip knew all the Air
Ministry chiefs from his war service he felt comfortable fulfilling his
duties. "The Prince of Wales rang me up to say he'd drink a cocktail
on the strength of the appointment."

Philip wrote a book summing up his first period in the government titled *The Third Route,* about air travel in general and his own
travels around the world as Under-Secretary to review British forces
across the empire and examine possible sites for air bases. Among the
countries he visited was Iraq, his paternal grandparents' homeland and
now a British mandate. "Iraq was the first country in which was tried
the experiment of maintaining peace and order by air power. It was
an experiment that was forced upon Great Britain by the immense
cost of maintaining adequate control by ground forces." The Royal Air
Force had bombed Iraqi towns and villages in the early 1920s to put
down rebellions against British control. While there, Philip desired:

Philip Sassoon during his travels as
Under-Secretary of State for Air, 1928.

to see something of Baghdad itself and to absorb some of the
spirit of this strange and wonderful country. Little time, indeed,
is needed: for Iraq takes you by the throat the moment you
enter it, saturated as it is with history and legend, religion and
fable.

He observed that Iraq had been fortunate in "her British servants"
as well as in King Faisal, whom the British had placed on the throne
in 1921. When they sipped coffee together and watched the boats on
the Tigris, Philip found him charming and surprisingly knowledgeable about French literature. What is remarkable (or perhaps not,
given his upbringing in England, where high society was imbued with
orientalism) is that, unlike Flora and her family, he did not seek out
distant relatives or ancestral roots in Baghdad. He was there on official business, though he found time to visit the city museum, "full
of entrancing things from the excavations at Ur and elsewhere." His

private papers too are devoid of any personal connection or reflection on the city that had been his paternal grandfather's birthplace. He came as an Englishman and a junior minister, "as if he wanted to downplay his eastern heritage."

Philip expressed little interest in the family business either, despite being nominally chairman of David Sassoon & Co. Despite his father's wishes, the archives contain not a single letter to or from him about it, and his biographies contain scant reference to his family's business or to any interest he had shown in its affairs. His interests were politics, art, and his mansions. He spent a fortune acquiring art and furniture from the Louis XIV and Louis XV periods, and from the mid-1920s many of Britain's most glamorous social gatherings were held at Trent Park estate near Barnet in North London. Philip never married and most likely was gay, but given the era he lived in, when the subject was taboo, this was never public, although many suspected it. Most of his friends in the interwar period were either gay or bisexual, but these relationships were not romantic and were "based on mutual interests and an easy personal rapport."

One important side effect of the war was a further push in the Anglicization of both parts of the family, which most likely ensured the final severing of links with their Baghdadi roots. In many ways, Philip's disinterest in Judaism was characteristic of his generation of the family. In a brochure about the history of Ashley Park, a picture of the Sassoon crest appears shorn of the Hebrew motto *Emet ve Emmuna* (Truth and Trust), while retaining the Latin words *Candide et Constanter,* and the family is identified as originating from Toledo in Spain, whose exiles were evidently more prestigious than their counterparts in Babylon. A desire to avoid association with "the Orient" and even with Jewishness became detectable. Stories circulated that other members also wanted the Hebrew words removed from the family emblem. Whenever a relative arrived from India or China, "the Society Sassoons would be slightly disconcerted," as it was "an untimely reminder of their past non-Society existence," of their origins far from the Occident, of the heavily accented English of their parents and grandparents, their rituals, and their heritage.

By the mid-1920s, the Sassoons had fully achieved their dream: They considered themselves English, had developed close relations with royalty, had been elected to Parliament, had received titles, and were, on the whole, accepted by most of the British aristocracy. The price of assimilation was the loss of ties not only to an old faith or old home, but also to the global business that had brought them to England in the first place.

One member of the family continued to adhere to tradition, however: Flora. She stuck by her promise and avoided involvement in the business, focusing on her family and her religious studies. In 1924, she was accorded the honor of addressing Jews' College in London on its annual Speech Day, when a new cohort of rabbis was ordained. It was the first time in the college's sixty-nine-year history that a woman had done so, and therefore only natural that Flora's speech centered on the role of women. She wondered why no woman before her delivered a speech to the College. She referred to the invitation informing her that she was "the ablest person" to give a speech and asked whether that meant that there were no other able women before her? Quoting from the Talmud and Torah, she noted that in biblical times, whenever the men in charge seemed to be out of options, they turned to women for assistance, citing as evidence the story of Barak, who "in troublous times" had "led an Israelite army against Sisera, commander of the Canaanite army, [and] asked the prophetess Deborah to join him and give support: 'If thou wilt go with me, then I will go, but if thou wilt not go with me, then I will not go.'" It was an allusion that could be applied just as well to the years after Suleiman's death, when Albert and his brothers, unable to find a solution of their own, turned to her to manage their business, as this particular event at the College: "I will apply this to the present occasion, when the men invited me to take the lead today, for which I say bless the Lord."

The strength of Flora's attachment to her religion was such that her children inherited it. Late in 1921, her disabled daughter, Mozelle, died in London. A letter from Flora's daughter-in-law to her parents described the family's trip to Egypt and Palestine in December 1924, three years after Mozelle's death, to find her grave in the Mount of Olives, the cemetery just outside Jerusalem's Old City, where observant Jews are traditionally buried. Jews are generally buried as quickly as possible, often within twenty-four hours of death, and it was unusual for a family to embalm a loved one, let alone keep them for so long. A couple of years later, Flora commemorated her daughter's death by establishing a charitable trust (for £285, roughly £17,000 in today's value) in her name to assist pupils in need at Tree of Life College, a Jewish college in East London.

By then, her son, David, had achieved quiet renown as a collector of Hebraic books. His house was described "as truly a unique library even in a city such as London." A journalist, who was given a tour of it over two evenings, wrote of a treasure trove of medieval Hebrew Bibles from all around the world and in many languages, such as a Persian translation from the early sixteenth century. He grew into a committed bibliophile and in 1902, aged twenty-two, he traveled to Damascus to buy a rare Bible dating back to the late fourteenth century. He was willing to travel anywhere in order to buy rare books and manuscripts and scoured most of the Arab world searching for old Bibles and antiquarian texts. In 1914, one of the greatest Hebrew bibliophiles characterized the 412 manuscripts then in David's collection as "of the highest importance, both from the artistic and literary point of view." The library would later have more than 1,200 Hebrew and Samaritan manuscripts.

Flora's daughter Rachel Ezra, who was living in Calcutta, continued the tradition of traveling. She took a trip across the Syrian desert in 1925 and, in a note titled "From Damascus to Baghdad," wrote: "We have been amply warned of the folly of our enterprise in undertaking this hard journey, one of the reasons being that the time of our projected journey was not all together propitious." But the trip was not all tough; a Cadillac driven by the chauffeur of Sir Herbert Samuel, the High Commissioner in Palestine, collected the passengers from the Damascus Palace Hotel on their way to Baghdad via the Syrian desert. "Between tea and dinner at 8, when we stopped, we did 100 miles, thus completing 250 miles—an endless straight track. Another camp fire was lit and we had more tea. Next morning dawn was very beautiful in the mysterious desert." The group crossed the Euphrates and witnessed cotton fields being plowed. Her conclusions: "To anyone in search of a unique experience, I can recommend a cross-desert trip to Bagdad [sic]—which is now only nine days from

Europe." Sadly, Rachel does not tell us in her notes about her feelings about visiting Baghdad, the city of her ancestors.

B y the end of the war and in the early 1920s, it was becoming obvious: Leadership at David Sassoon & Co. had lost its bearings and there was no obvious person within the Sassoons to take over the helm. More professional outsiders were hired and assumed senior responsibilities. Both Philip and the other Sassoons saw the firm merely as a source of income to underwrite their activities and lifestyle. The death of the first generation of the family and some of its second generation depleted the family's wealth due to heavy death duties in Britain and the splitting of the estates among many children and their spouses. The net result was that by the 1920s, David Sassoon & Co., which had not fully diversified during the previous two decades in spite of the global upheavals, lost its focus and zeal. Another significant factor was the rise of new competitors and family firms, such as Hardoon and Kadoorie, whose founders had once worked for the Sassoons but then created their own dynasties and successful businesses in Hong Kong, India, and Shanghai. By the mid-1920s the powerhouse of the Sassoons had shifted to the firm of E. D. Sassoon, where a new leader, Sir Victor Sassoon, had emerged to lift his family into new orbits.

12

FROM BOMBAY TO SHANGHAI

1925–1949

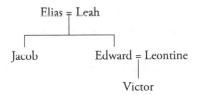

Victor Sassoon arrived in Bombay in 1922 to work at E. D. Sassoon, then chaired by his ailing father, Edward. When Edward died two years later, Victor succeeded him as head of one of the city's most valuable companies and de facto head of its Jewish community. Even in waiting, he was a natural choice for the Bombay Millowners' Association's representative in the Indian Legislative Assembly, and he served in this capacity twice, from 1922 to 1923 and again from 1926 to 1929. The Assembly was the lower house of the Legislative Council, formed by the Government of India Act in 1919 (and dissolved in 1947), which was targeted to appease nationalist demands for greater self-governance during the First World War. Victor now had to learn the business in greater detail and contend with the political and economic challenges of running a trading company in India. Among the political issues were the rise of nationalism and communal riots. In the economic arena, he had to deal with the slump affecting the textile mills that E. D. Sassoon had significantly expanded. Victor was known for his forthright views. In one fiery speech at the Assembly in

1928, he attacked the Communists in India, warning that "if the Red contingent was not expelled now, it was bound to train Indian leaders into propagandists who would work internally to disrupt society." Recounting his experiences in China, he erroneously predicted that Bolshevism could never flourish there, before declaring that India was dealing with "the most dangerous national enemy" in its history, and that the Communist influence in India was a national enemy that "aims to bring about the suffering of all the cultured classes." Victor, like many others during that era, perceived Communism and nationalism as two sides of the same coin, twin threats to business and empire, and this was not surprising given that both were the dominant anticolonial movements at the time.

At E. D. Sassoon, Victor saw the barrage of strikes and demands from workers as symptoms and products of the newly energized, assertive nationalism and, worse, the popularity of Communism among workers. In reality, the final few years of the preceding decade (1917–1920) had witnessed the cost of living in India rise more than 50 percent, which, combined with a poor monsoon season and the influenza epidemic of 1918, led to "the emergence of class-based protest movements" and the formation of India's first trade unions. The situation was exacerbated by the increasing competition from Japanese mills. The mill owners in Bombay argued that there were only two ways to counter this competition: the repeal of excise duties on textiles and the reduction of their workers' wages (the mention of which provoked the announcement of more strikes). Victor advocated efficiency, encouraging his fellow owners to cut their overhead wherever possible, and at the same time to "strain every nerve to increase the efficiency of the men." He told a journalist that "the efficiency of the labour force is the vivid interest of everyone interested in the prosperity of Bombay." Despite this febrile atmosphere, E. D. Sassoon's mills continued to offer the highest wages and best working conditions in Bombay. Victor even went so far as to support India's first Workmen's Compensation Act (which provided compensation for accidents in factories) in spite of his fear that it would not be enforced outside Bombay and Calcutta, giving factories and mills elsewhere an unfair advantage.

One of the main subjects that occupied him in the Assembly was the rupee. From the beginning of the twentieth century, the Indian rupee had been relatively overvalued, and the government was hard-pressed to respond to variations in commercial needs. When a plan emerged to stabilize it at one shilling sixpence, up from one shilling fourpence, the trading community was vocal in its opposition. The policy served to increase Victor's frustration with the Viceroy, Lord Reading (a judge and the first Jewish Lord Chief Justice of England before his post in India), whose liberal policies were, he believed, being thrust upon a nation that was not yet ready for them, and Reading's finance minister, Sir Basil Blackett. Victor found himself uncomfortably aligned with the nationalist Congress Party, as both argued that foreign interests would be the main beneficiaries of the increase in value of the rupee.

Often more revealing than the Assembly record are the letters Victor wrote to Yvonne Fitzroy, a former actress and nurse who came to India in 1920 as the private secretary to Lord Reading's wife, in which he poured out his thoughts about India and the choices it faced. Victor's friendship with her was unusually close—he signed all his letters to her as "Daddy"—and when she returned to England in 1926 he gave her the use of West Green House in Hampshire, a stately manor he had purchased but rarely visited, where she lived until her death in 1971. The letters consisted of political and economic observations rather than overt romantic declarations, and it is unclear whether the two had an affair; as we shall see, Victor enjoyed the company of beautiful, glamorous women, seemingly for their beauty and glamour alone. In a letter from 1923, he told her of his first debate at the Assembly in Delhi, confessing that he knew nothing about the art of debating, having never set foot in the House of Commons, but had still shuddered at Blackett's lackluster performance. His letter bristled with detail on the ins and outs of the Assembly, so much so that he pitied her reading it:

> Poor you. How do I inflict my moans on you. And with
> it pouring outside and the new Portable Remington I am
> trying, what chance have you got? Perhaps that is why you are
> getting two lots of stockings. You have earned them.
>
> Yours
> Daddy

His criticisms of the government centered on matters directly relating to trade and finance: the salt excise, for example, or the legal status of the Alliance Bank, and his bête noir, the value of the rupee. He told Yvonne that the proposed revaluation would benefit his family but run against Indian national interests, hence his vehement opposition to it. He disagreed with her view that he had been fighting the Viceroy too much and maintained that most of the fights were with the Finance Ministry. His criticisms did not always go down well in the media or the Assembly. A letter written to *The Times of India* opines that Sir Victor and others in his lobby group, the Indian Currency League, were simply operating on behalf of mill owners. The letter mocked Victor's so-called sympathy with India's agriculturists and stated that these "cotton magnates have in the past done all that lay in their power to wrest as much money from the poor agriculturists as they possibly could." The same newspaper criticized "the pathetic appearance of Sir Victor Sassoon in the House. . . . He insisted on taking his seat wearing a grey top hat," a theatrical gesture to underline the "Assembly's ridiculous indefiniteness."

Victor exited the Assembly at the end of 1923 but returned for a second term of three years after Lord Reading left India in 1926. He distrusted the *Swadeshi* movement, which believed in self-rule for India and encouraged buying Indian-made goods rather than British imports, and he also doubted Mahatma Gandhi and his tactics. Even though the strikes that bedeviled his factories annoyed him and made him impatient, he tended to oversimplify the causes of India's malaise. He was convinced that all the problems emanated from Communism, which had practically captured the trade union movement in Bombay due to assistance from abroad, and that its opponents lived in terror of their own lives.

Unlike David Sassoon & Co., which was gradually retreating from India, E. D. Sassoon's operations between 1914 and 1924 witnessed significant expansion not only in number of looms, but in machinery and plant investments. Thereafter, problems mounted. At a meeting of shareholders of the E. D. Sassoon mills it was resolved to reduce capital and the rights of holders of ordinary shares. Shouts of "Shame, shame" accompanied the exit from the meeting hall of some shareholders who were dissatisfied with the way the management was running the company. One Indian shareholder told Victor: "The Sassoons were Rajas of Hindustan and people trusted them," but he argued that the chairman's scheme was simply to protect those with preferred shares — the Sassoon family. As competition was increasing both from elsewhere in India and from abroad (mainly Japan), Victor repeatedly sounded the alarm in the Assembly. In late 1927 he foresaw a dumping war between India and China; he argued that the authorities in India were treating the mill industry with contempt and were taking serious risks by doing so. He compared the industry to "a wounded man lying in the road" and warned that unless conditions were protected, the industry would be hit hard.

Another major concern, not only for the cotton industry but for the whole Indian economy, was the rise in communal riots between 1924 and 1930. Many were triggered by sectarian incidents between Muslims and Hindus, and they spread fast across large parts of the country, disrupting business. Hindu-Muslim riots had intensified from the early 1890s, fueled by the spread of the telegraph and newspapers across India carrying news of riots, which in turn sparked more acts of revenge. Whenever communal tensions exploded, often around the religious holidays of either Muslims or Hindus, the British found themselves hopelessly attempting to broker peace and coexistence between the two dominant religious groups.

While the cotton industry was experiencing difficulties, the opium business was in its terminal phase. A memo to E. D. Sassoon in 1924 from the brokerage firm Samuel, Samuel & Co. (another trading group that was set up in 1878 and incorporated in 1907) is illuminating. Samuel's office in southern Manchuria had been approached by the Kwantung government, administrators of the territory leased to and controlled by Japan, to supply them with Indian opium, and Samuel in turn asked E. D. Sassoon whether they could provide it, "presumably on much the same lines as the Persian opium supplied by you to our Taipei office." Opium was the mainstay of Samuel's business in Taiwan and to a lesser extent in southern Manchuria. Unfortunately, there is no reply to this request, but it is very doubtful that E. D. Sassoon had any further access to Indian opium at the time unless there was some unsold stock.

In spite of these economic and political problems, Victor, a true bon vivant, knew how to enjoy life's luxuries and indulge in his hobbies. His love of horse racing knew no bounds. After his father died, he bought dozens of horses from an Indian cotton magnate whose business had fallen victim to the slump, and built a private racecourse in Pune, at a cost of more than £110,000, to train them. At a time when mills were struggling to pay their employees, hospitals were accruing debt, and schools were closed for lack of funds, it was an indiscreet extravagance, described by *The Times of India* as "preposterous and deplorable." He was undeterred, however, and races were held there every Wednesday and Saturday. Whenever he was in town, he drove to the course from his bungalow in Pune, named Eve, in a grand yellow car with the personalized number plate "EVE1." The grand prize, however, lay in England, and he used to joke that "there is only one race greater than the Jews and that's the Derby." He came close in 1927, when he was beaten by his friend Frank Curzon, and would go on to win it four times. As with his predecessors, expenditure on leisure was balanced with philanthropy, and in the same year he built the racecourse, he set up a fund of six hundred thousand rupees (roughly half the cost of his indulgence) to be distributed among local charities in India.

Victor's private diaries reveal a hectic blend of business and political commitments, further complicated by extensive travel. He took at least one luxurious cruise a year, and in advance he would receive, like other first-class passengers, a booklet from the liner detailing the route and naming his fellow passengers. Without fail, he would mark those whom he already knew and those whom

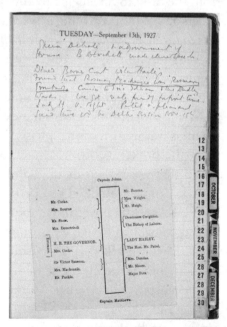

Victor regularly held dinners at home and carefully arranged the seating plan. An example of one dinner plan from 1927.

he wished to know. It was a relentlessly social existence, but he had the appetite and stamina for it, and his diaries are filled with a stream of lunches and dinners unbroken for weeks at a time, for both business and pleasure. In a talk he gave on "Isms," he argued that people overwhelmingly passively accepted ideas and opinions from what they read or heard rather than their own powers of reason. He posited that his generation, unlike all previous ones, had lost the time to think, and that this pandemic of hyperactivity was a "form of mental disorder which is likely to lead to complete mental atrophy unless it is checked."

When he was home, Victor's time was spent organizing and hosting dinners. From his diaries we can see the care with which he planned them, choosing and arranging his guests to maximize their returns. One dinner held at his home in September 1927 included the Governor of the Punjab and officers from the military, politicians, and businessmen, as well as friends from the British contingent in India, though no Baghdadi Jews. For another, in December 1929, an instruction card was printed, giving a short description of each guest and a glimpse into the social life of India's elite: "Sir Courtney Terrell, Chief Justice for Bihar, an authority on the law of patents, who took a keen interest in the Boy Scout movement and the Olympic Association."

By the end of the decade, Victor was spending less and less time in India. He was visiting Shanghai for two months every year and came to view the city as the locus of both his business and his social ambitions, while he grew bitter about the inflexibility of India's taxation system and the burdens it placed upon him—especially the obligation to pay income tax while appeals were being heard. His value to the Exchequer was such that when rumors spread that he was contemplating leaving India, the Central Board of Revenue sent a 1929 memo to the Commissioner of Income Tax in Bombay informing him that they suspected Victor would move his money abroad and conduct his business in India with loans, and suggested that this needed to be investigated.

In his final speech in the Legislative Assembly, he addressed the irrationality of the tax regime, the weight of government bureaucracy, and the threat posed by Communists to India. He fully believed that the government was not doing enough to alleviate the burdens on businesspeople and opined, "Considerable elements in the Legislature are too busy snatching evanescent political advantages to deal with the serious economic interests of the country." He admonished the government for not supporting industry in general and the mill industry in particular.

The Wall Street crash of 1929 and the ensuing economic depression had a severe impact on India, reducing both its exports and its imports and affecting, in particular, its agricultural sector and its internal trade. As a result, by the decade's close, a number of E. D. Sassoon mills were reporting heavy losses and the depletion of their reserves. Exacerbating their woes was a boycott led by the Congress Party. Victor claimed it was "undoubtedly based on racial lines; no other explanation could account for the fact that foreign-managed mills have been boycotted from the beginning" and exempted only if they undertook to improve working conditions and abstain from importing foreign goods, while Indian mills were obliged to do neither. Labor relations in Bombay remained tense; as a result of the unions' pressure, the Labour Commission recommended a fifty-four-hour week, while labor unions strove for forty-eight hours and Victor, with a few other industrialists, for sixty. He believed that Bombay appeared "to be heading towards economic suicide which can only lead to a lowering of the standard of living to that existing in other parts of India."

In July 1931, Victor announced that within a few months he would leave Bombay for Shanghai, which henceforth would be his principal commercial base. He claimed that he felt comfortable leaving India given that the textile mills, the main business left behind, had their own management, but most likely this was for public relations as he was now convinced that India did not offer him or his business the vitality of China. He believed that China was relatively stable after its civil wars and unrest, and that Chinese banks were keen to engage in joint schemes to develop Shanghai. He admitted that his family's mills, similar to other businesses in Bombay, could not compete with Indian-run firms, which had much lower overhead. In one interview, he admitted that the decision was primarily because "the outlook for the foreigner in India did not seem to be bright." He foresaw considerable trouble from the *Swadeshi* movement and, like many in British politics, had realized "the hollowness of their long-held assumption that self-rule for India would be pushed off into an indefinite future." He contrasted the situation with China, which, he thought, welcomed the assistance of foreign capital and development proposals despite its humiliation at the hands of the British and others in regard to the unequal treaties. Apart from the mills, Victor decided to leave his racing establishment intact until someone came forward to take it over, as he did not want to cause dislocation for the large number of people employed in the racing business.

The announcement was an international event, reported by media around the world, from *The China Mail* to *The Irish Times,* and caused some anxiety among the banking establishment in India, leading British politicians to make reassuring noises about Victor not cutting all ties to India but simply avoiding new commitments. It was a tone echoed by Victor shortly before his departure that October, when he told *The Times of India,* "If political disturbances can be guarded against, my views of the position of India are anything but pessimistic," and called for everyone in India to "invest in efforts to avoid communal tensions and to effect compromises between the different communities."

SHANGHAI

The Sassoon family had maintained a presence in Shanghai in one form or another since the 1840s. After Elias split off, both firms expanded their presence and activities in the city, and as other Baghdadi Jews flocked to China to find their fortunes, Shanghai became a lively trading nexus for opium, silk, and tea. The Baghdadi Jewish community in Shanghai was small—in 1895 there were 175 registered with commercial licenses in the city—but tight-knit, tied together by marriage or business or both, and their influence was far greater than their number might suggest. They were for the most part loyal British subjects, and a prayer for the royal family became a feature of Sabbath services there. The community was a consistent, staunch supporter of Britain and its policies around the globe. Not all were affluent, and there was a clear social divide within the community between those who lived in the International Settlement and French Concession, and the lower-middle-class residents in the Chinese neighborhoods. Many of the leading families owned impressive houses with large gardens, such as the Kadoories and their palatial mansion, Marble Hall, and the wealthy Baghdadis were known for their lavish entertainments. Anglicization of the community began with ensuring a thorough English education for their offspring (both boys and girls) and an identification with anything British.

Unlike in India, the Baghdadi Jewish community was not inclined to mix with the locals. Whereas in Bombay they tended to learn Hindi, in Shanghai only a very few mastered Mandarin, the main language of the city at that time. Victor, a late entrant, kept his distance from the Baghdadi community; he was drifting away from the religious observance that had characterized his upbringing and early childhood. He still participated in the major Jewish holidays—in London for Yom Kippur in 1938, he attended services at the Liberal synagogue in St. John's Wood, though his diary suggests a rather relaxed approach to the fast, mentioning "lunching with A," and it is plausible that "the laxity of his religious observance might have, to some extent, impacted his relationship with the Baghdadi Jewish communities in Southeast Asia." Nevertheless, some of his closest friends in Shanghai, such as Ellis Hayim and the Kadoorie family, were Baghdadi Jews, but he was never a community leader in China in the way that his great-grandfather had been in Bombay.

E. D. Sassoon too was losing its distinct Baghdadi flavor. A letter of 1931 from the wife of a Baghdadi employee in Shanghai to Lady Ezra, Flora and Suleiman's daughter, requests that she ask Victor to give her husband a second chance after he had been fired, and mourned the chairman's distance: "Lady Ezra, the Jews here have no influence on Sir Victor Sassoon." Increasingly, the business was made up of outsiders or relatives who had married out of the faith. Such unions could replenish the firm—Violet, Victor's cousin, married Captain Derek Barrington Fitzgerald, an officer from an old Irish family who had been badly wounded during the war and who would become one of Victor's most trusted lieutenants and a senior director of the firm's office in London—but they also signaled a shift in its character.

After a rare meeting in 1937 with some leaders of the Baghdadi community in Bombay about opportunities with the company, Victor reminded them that the main criterion for hiring was not religion but merit—"If any Jew was efficient, he was given a job"—and that his firm was "not a charitable institution for his co-religionists." The link between the firm and the faith of its leadership, and indeed between its leaders and their faith, slowly weakened throughout the twentieth century. Jacob had discontinued the practice of closing the business on Saturdays, and the move from India to Shanghai, where the Jewish community was smaller and the family's ties to it less robust, only accelerated the process.

At least initially, Victor's very public crusade against India's tax system and the way he carefully limited the time he spent in Britain so as to avoid liability there made his integration into Shanghai society somewhat rocky. The taipans (heads of business concerns) of Hong Kong and Shanghai invariably believed "the British Empire worked like a club and that it was unfair to enjoy all the privileges without paying the membership fee"—namely taxes—and they didn't look kindly upon his avoidance of it. Prejudices too played a role. Though Victor may not have felt as connected to Baghdad as his predecessors, that didn't stop the biases of others. When a woman at a party he attended wondered about the best way to get home and he began to answer her, her friend interrupted to ask: "Don't you go by camel?"

He couldn't be ignored, however. One estimate put the assets he transferred from India to China at $28 million, or at least half a billion dollars today. In spite of China's problems, Shanghai was booming: Victor had noticed the meteoric rise of Hardoon and concluded that investments in bricks and mortar were delivering substantial returns, and thus real estate development became Victor's first priority and the repository of much of that $28 million. He was a pioneer of high-rise buildings, drawing architects and engineers from Manhattan and creating a new enterprise called the Cathay Land Company to build what were some of the first skyscrapers in the Far East. The completion of the new Sassoon House, later known as the Cathay Building, caused great excitement in Shanghai. It was the city's first eleven-story building, utilizing the most advanced construction technology of the age, on the Bund, still the main street in Shanghai. The first and second floors consisted of offices that were rented out, mostly to medical and legal practices, while the third housed E. D. Sassoon and Arnhold & Co. The upper part of the building, crowned by a

Sassoon House, later the Cathay Hotel, under construction in the 1920s.

distinctive 240-foot-high pyramid jacketed in copper, was used as a hotel, intended to be "the Claridge's of the East," boasting a floor for private dining and a banqueting hall. The top floor became Victor's penthouse. (Today the building operates as the Fairmont Peace Hotel, and the penthouse has become the "Sassoon Presidential Suite.") From his bedroom, Victor could enjoy panoramic views over the harbor and city. The building was designed by George Leopold "Tug" Wilson of Palmer and Turner, where his ideal combination of "proportion, mass and form with simple interior decoration, colour and lighting was epitomized."

The building was opened in August 1929 to great fanfare, and was labeled "the Number One building in the Far East." Its voguish pyramid and obelisk, details typical of Modernist and Art Deco designs of the 1920s, as well as its sheer scale, quickly made it a landmark. From the air, passengers could see the letters V and S engraved into its sides, for Victor was "the first man in history to have monogrammed his initials into an entire city." The building provided headquarters for E. D. Sassoon until the Second Sino-Japanese War in 1937, but for Victor

THE GREATEST FLOOR SHOW
AT

Ciro's

No. 441 Bubbling Well Road   Tel. 34340
NIGHT CLUB and BAR
BALLROOM
PRETTY HOSTESSES. CONGRATULATIONS
TO ALL ALLIED NATIONS,
SWING MUSIC EVERY DAY
Ballroom & Bar From 2:00 p.m.
靜安寺路四四四號   電話三四三四〇

Ticket for Shanghai's first purpose-built nightclub, Ciro's, opened by Victor in 1936.

and his milieu it was above all a venue for the extravagant parties, music, and dances that characterized Shanghai in that heady decade. The hotel was known to have the smartest cabaret in town, where leading impresarios imported from Europe fronted the nightly shows, and was famous for one of its bars, the Horse and Hounds. Alongside the Cathay Hotel was the Sassoon Arcade, offering exclusive antique and clothes shops and a popular tea shop. However, navigating the different cultural and racial biases in Shanghai at the time was not simple; one toilet on the first floor of the Cathay was marked "Gentlemen" and the other "Chinese," which provoked an immediate uproar, quelled only when the signs were changed.

Before long, Victor laid the foundation for another hotel, the Metropole, this time with sixteen floors, two hundred rooms, and two hundred bathrooms. His next project was residential apartment buildings "to relieve the taipans of the onus of maintaining big mansions heavily staffed." One such building was Hamilton House, which became an apartment hotel. By the mid-1930s, he was described by *Fortune* magazine as "Shanghai's No. 1 realtor," and as the value of land on the Bund more than tripled between 1927 and 1935, he grew substantially richer. By 1937, he had more than thirty companies in Shanghai and had built six of the twenty-eight buildings that exceeded ten floors in height.

According to the company's archives, the total value of twenty-two plots, including the site on the Bund, on which it owned property was 2.65 million taels by the beginning of 1933, roughly $1 million, or $55 million today. This may be a serious underestimate. One recent Chinese estimate values the firm's portfolio in 1921 at 13.3 million taels, $11.2 million then and more than $220 million today. If this is accurate, and given the meteoric rise in property prices over the course of the decade, E. D. Sassoon's properties could have been worth in today's values nearly $2 billion by 1937. (My own estimate is more conservative but the figure is nonetheless startling: about $1.2–1.5 billion today.) The general strategy was to build a vertically integrated empire of properties and services in the city, controlling everything from the suppliers of the materials with which the firm's buildings were constructed to the web of businesses they needed to run when open. A common joke in Shanghai held that you could ride a Sassoon tram to a brothel housed in a Sassoon building and then drink a beer made in a Sassoon brewery. Victor did, in fact, acquire interests in a brewery, in the laundries that serviced his hotels, and in the transport companies used by his employees. In spite of this appreciation, the Sassoon company refused to raise its workers' salaries, which led to frustration and anger among the Chinese workers represented by their labor union.

Victor was assisted in Shanghai by his first cousin Lucien Ovadia. Like Victor's mother, he had been born in Egypt and educated in France. He had joined E. D. Sassoon in Manchester in the early 1920s but grew bored and left to work in a Belgian bank in London, where he learned about international finance. As the world's foreign exchange markets entered a period of extreme volatility, he became a leading expert on exchange. He was brought in to run the firm's financial side, and although Victor would occasionally attempt to intervene when something caught his interest, Ovadia effectively took charge of the firm's financial operations and was able to deflect any questionable projects by insisting that decisions be determined by the numbers rather than emotion. Ovadia joined his cousin at an opportune time in the early 1930s, when the firm began prioritizing banking and oil ventures, alongside real estate. Victor was convinced that the days of substantial profits earned through manufacturing textiles were over, particularly when he observed his competitor, David Sassoon & Co., wrapping up their textile business by closing down their Manchester branch and announcing that their other branches in Shanghai, Calcutta, and Karachi would stop trading textiles. While E. D. Sassoon's mills continued to operate, no new investments were made—though they were to flourish during the Second World War as demand soared.

While David Sassoon & Co. held its seat on the board of the Hong-kong and Shanghai Banking Corporation, E. D. Sassoon departed in the early 1920s to set up its own bank. The firm began in London and commenced operations in a few branches, most notably Hong Kong, but its assets, some £7.5 million, or roughly half a billion pounds today, were dwarfed by those of the existing commercial banks. Even where the bank specialized—in real estate transactions in the Far East, for example—it presented only modest competition to the established banks, not least the Hongkong and Shanghai Banking Corporation. A perusal of E. D. Sassoon's banking archives highlights that their business in Shanghai was mostly with other regional medium-sized banks (in terms of both credit and debit), and then in transactions with some individuals (mostly Baghdadis) or companies. There were some notable achievements: lending the Huai River Commission £238,000 to build a water-flow regulator, for example, and taking a controlling interest in the Yenangyaung oil fields, as well as a considerable share in the British Burmah Petroleum Company, which was developing these fields based on initial geological drilling indicating a high potential for oil.

Because of the foreign exchange volatility, Ovadia reduced the firm's nonbanking business in rupees and taels and bought sterling and dollars. According to a Chinese study, pound-denominated invest-ments for the Sassoon group hovered around £700,000 during the 1936–1940 period. The study's authors, who wrote about the Sassoons, claim that prior to Japan's surprise attack on Pearl Harbor in Decem-ber 1941, E. D. Sassoon managed to transfer out of China more than $7 million (roughly $130 million today).

Exchange rates continued to be one of Victor's preoccupations. He fully immersed himself in the currency debates in China, and because his views carried such weight in the financial markets, they continued to be widely reported in the media. He supported China's policy to reduce its exchange rate, as this would make its exports more competitive at Japan's expense. Although China remained on the silver standard, which tied its currency to the silver price, its currency weak-ened as international traders worried about the political situation in the region. Victor's "palliative solution" at one point was for China to receive a sterling loan from Britain, but the Chinese authorities and media criticized the plan on the grounds that it would advantage British trade. He also advocated issuing "Shanghai Pounds" yoked to the value of sterling to ease the stringent financial situation in China and particularly Shanghai. He continued to support the silver policy and blamed the United States for the crisis, because its silver-purchasing program had caused a rise in the price and a serious outflow of the commodity from China, with disastrous results for the country and its main trading hub, Shanghai. The U.S. Silver Purchase Act of 1934 was intended to revitalize the silver mining industry in the Midwest, but as a consequence China was pushed into an economic depression.

Victor saw himself as a globalist, offering political and economic advice about and to every country in which he had experience or interest. He proposed that the United States should buy Indian silver and predicted that China's recession would lead to a war in the Far East, though not as soon as some imagined.

It was a lifestyle as much as anything—involving lunches with politicians, businesspeople, journalists, and film stars visiting Shanghai and, above all, incessant travel. His diaries reveal his different travels in the United States; his annual trip to London and Europe, and expeditions to his firm's branches. In 1930, he sailed from Hong Kong to Kobe, Yokohama, and then Vancouver; in 1931 he spent many weeks traveling across Europe; in 1932 he visited Japan and then sailed to the United States; in 1934 he toured Cairo and Port Said. The voyage to the United States involved what he thought was a humorous incident. While the steamer was anchored en route to Honolulu, it was boarded by a customs officer who, when she searched his stateroom, found beer and wines in a trunk of his. The officer seized the alcohol and placed Victor under arrest. "It was really funny," he commented to the media, "I was frightfully embarrassed, for I had no idea I was busting any of your jolly old United States laws." He paid a fine of $150 and was allowed to return to the ship. Victor was a consummate businessman who adroitly combined business and pleasure across almost all his interests. By the late 1930s he had traversed most continents, crossed the Atlantic dozens of times, and visited almost every major European city, for reasons that ranged from sightseeing to the recruitment of European engineers to aid China's industrialization, and was received in the highest quarters wherever he went. Victor loved the life of luxury; he built a country house in 1934 outside Shanghai called the Rubicon Garden. It was designed by the architects Messrs. Palmer and Turner, who not only had a free hand in the building but transformed the land into "one of the most beautiful gardens in Shanghai." Taking advantage of a creek that ran through the property, they created an artificial lake. The house was designed in the style of an old English cottage, with rough timber exposed and a spacious living room that featured a large fireplace.

Victor's other great passion was photography, which developed more in the 1930s and became another obsession. At home or on his travels, Victor was rarely seen without a camera hanging around his neck or not in the company of one of many women he dated. It was rumored that his fascination with photography was a tactic: Whenever his eye was caught by a beautiful woman, he would offer to take her picture and ask for her address to send it to her. In his private papers at Southern Methodist University (SMU), there are thousands of such photographs, many of them portraits of women whom he met by chance, and a few in swimming suits, sparsely clad, or totally naked. One socialite who knew him at the time recalled that "women were intrigued" by him "partly because of his wealth, partly because he is an enigma that piques their curiosity." She described her excitement when Victor presented her with two dozen pairs of French stockings, and her disappointment when she found out that this was a routine offering made to any woman he liked. To those with whom he became enamored or whose company he enjoyed, such as the writer Emily Hahn, the gifts could be impressive—in her case a brand-new Chevrolet coupé in blue. Hahn was a journalist who became close to Chinese politicians and to Victor before the Second World War. She published her memoirs, titled *China to Me,* in 1944 and described giving the manuscript to Victor for his feedback, only to be shocked when he wrote bluntly of a few chapters: "This is dull." After some redrafting, it all ended happily: She felt he had done her "an enormous favor." Victor faithfully cut out a review of her book and stuck it in his diary.

He was not by nature romantic and could be coldly evaluative in his diaries or letters about his encounters with the women he photographed. In one letter to a Giulia, an Italian princess, about whom we know only that Victor asked his London office in 1936 to arrange a

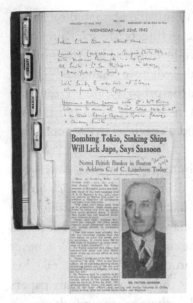

Example of a press cutting, April 22, 1942, inserted into Victor's diary. He added any articles about himself.

mortgage for her home in France, he wrote: "I tried to take some of Angela but I am afraid she is not a good subject, the same can be said of Helen McBain, but Marjorie Beith on the other hand takes very well." Enclosing a nude in another letter to her, he was still more blunt: "The model looks a great deal better in these photographs than she does in real life."

These photographs intermingle in his diary with clippings from papers, menus from dinners he attended, and manifests from cruises he enjoyed. On one of the trips back to Europe, he cut out a newspaper article claiming (erroneously) that the Sassoons were from Toledo in Spain and that one of them had been a Cabalist in Venice. Whenever there were news items about him or a cartoon depicting him taking pictures of a beautiful woman, he made sure to add it to his diary. Any time a newspaper published the names of guests attending a party or a gala and his was mentioned, the cutting would be attached to that day's entry.

Every year on January 1 he wrote in a recipe for the cocktail of the year (a retrospective selection rather than forward-looking resolution). One, for a "Green Hat," consists of 2/9 gin, 2/9 Cointreau, 2/9 French vermouth, 2/9 crème de menthe, and 1/9 lemon; another, called a "Barbara," of 1/2 vodka and 1/2 sour cream with a dash of crème de cacao. Flicking back a few pages reveals a list of his Christmas gifts and cash bonuses, ranging from £5 to £1,000, for everyone from "girlfriends" who found their way onto the payroll to regular staff. His banking expenditure underscores the large amounts of money he spent on hotels and entertainment.

Other entries are revealing of his appetites and the fashions of those interwar years, as his diaries contain recipes for dishes he liked, such as curried trout and orange pancake. His famous, very spicy "Sassoon curry" can be found today in a couple of restaurants on the Bund, the main boulevard in Shanghai, along with some of his cocktails. He told one journalist that as a bachelor he was always looking for recipes he could cook in a hurry or that could be kept, hence his curry sauce that improves if kept in the fridge. In spite of his love for good food, he was weight conscious—his younger brother had died obese at the age of thirty-four—and his diaries include diets and slimming techniques. His attitude toward women and life in general was very much influenced by his handicap, and many believed it was the reason he did not marry until very late in life. His leg injury and using a cane might have left him with a compulsive feeling that he needed to prove that he would be popular with women. Given his love of parties and music, he was frustrated that he could only dance, ride, or swim with a painful effort. Only in 1959, at the age of seventy-seven and two years before his death, he married his American nurse in Nassau, Evelyn Barnes.

Shanghai in the early 1930s, with its "sky-scrapers, neon lights, nightclubs, jazz bands, air-cooled movies and warships in the harbour," was a better fit for this fun-seeker than somber, business-minded Bombay. Victor was active in cultural life, attending concerts and hosting gala dinners. He threw a large garden party for two hundred people as part of the International Arts Theatre celebration of the return of a famous Chinese artist who had just toured the Soviet Union and Europe. He also became enthusiastic about Chinese art, particularly jade and ivory, which he collected. Later, after he left China, he privately published three bulky volumes of his Chinese ivories with comments by a well-known expert on ivories from London, Sydney Edward Lucas, a trilogy described in *The Times Literary Supplement* as "the most sumptuous of books printed in Britain since the war." Volume 1 was dedicated mostly to Buddhist figures, historical and mythical figures; volume 2 to vases, plaques, and hand rests; and volume 3 to pots, trays, and snuff bottles. According to the preface, Victor collected these items, often purchasing them from Manchu families who had received them as gifts from the imperial court, between 1915 and 1927; by then his collection was estimated to be worth £127,000, or £7.5 million today. Some are kept at the Victoria and Albert Museum in London.

His biggest love, however, was horse racing. It had been inculcated in him from a young age by an uncle, David Elias (Elias's youngest), known as Nunkie, who had no interest in business but loved horse racing and was himself a good horseman. Nunkie had a reputation, lurid even in liberal Shanghai, as a serial philanderer. When he died at the age of seventy-two, Victor was traveling in South America and could not attend the funeral. It seems that Nunkie nonetheless received an appropriate send-off, for he left instructions that he should be buried in an "elegant casket of crystal and gold." At the same time, and despite his playboy lifestyle, he followed procedure and left a donation to the Baghdadi Jewish community.

Victor at a race meeting, 1953. He adored racing, and his horses won the English Derby four times.

Victor too was upholding the family tradition of philanthropy. He contributed a large sum to a national medical college in Shanghai, gave donations to encourage foreign students to study Chinese, and helped establish a hostel in 1935 to assist women who had fled Russia and settled in Shanghai. As with his forebears, charitable giving was often tied up with power and the powerful. Victor became a close friend of the brother-in-law of Chiang Kai-shek, the leader of the Nationalist Party who directed the purges of the Communists late in the 1920s and managed to unify most of China under his control. In 1935, at a reception at the Cathay Hotel, Victor would be honored with a First Class Gold Medal by the Nationalist government. Later, Victor's closeness to the Nationalists would color his judgment about events in China and the rise of Communism in the region.

In London, Flora was getting her affairs in order. Late in 1935, she drafted her final will. Likely for British tax reasons, she emphasized her Baghdadi ancestry and Bombay upbringing: "I still own and maintain [as] my permanent residence the house in Bombay in which I lived with my husband during his lifetime." She appointed her son, David, as sole executor of her will and listed the following legacies: £2,500 to her daughter Rachel; £5,000 to her son-in-law, Sir David Ezra; £2,500 to her daughter-in-law, Selina; to each of her grandchildren from her son the sum of £2,500 upon reaching the age of thirty; to each of her three siblings £500; to her nephews and nieces £100 each. To any domestic staff in India and England who had been in her employ for six years or more, she bequeathed six months' wages. To her son, David, she left the sum of £2,500 to handle any obligations she had prior to her death, as well as "all property whether real or personal or immovable or moveable and including property over which I may have a general power of appointment."

Two months later, on January 14, 1936, Flora died in London. In her obituary, the *Hongkong Telegraph* mourned a "Great Scholar, Hostess, and Woman of Business," commending her "tremendous knowledge of commerce and the affairs of the world." The Chief Rabbi of England eulogized her as "a living well of Torah, of piety, of wisdom, of goodness and charity." Her house in Bruton Street was described as "a salon" for scholars of all nations and a link between London and India. She had opened her house to many visitors, and lonely students in London were always welcomed there, and every Saturday afternoon she threw her house open to anybody wishing to visit. It was said that she "walked like a queen, talked like a sage and entertained like an Oriental potentate." She was known for her banquets and receptions with her famous Eastern dishes, and she insisted that her guests taste from all of them. She was a matriarch, in every sense of the word. "Her greatest joy was to arrange a match between a young couple, adroitly brought together from far ends of the earth," when her house "would resound to the hilarity and music of a Jewish wedding in the Oriental style, just as though it were in Baghdad or Rangoon."

Photos of her in the last three decades of her life highlight her role and appearance as the grande dame in every sense. "Silver-haired,

imposing, dressed with a regal elegance and always wearing the celebrated seven-roped pearl necklace," she was a great conversationalist,
asking the right questions in a tactful manner, aided by an exceptional
memory. The singular nature of her professional achievements and her
talents as a business manager was acknowledged, too late, unfortunately, for the men of David Sassoon & Co., who had been so reticent
to accept a woman in a leadership role. In a piece titled "Women and
Their Emancipation" in *The Westminster Review*, her abundant capacity in business was approvingly noted: She "managed entirely alone
the large banking business of Sassoon & Co. in Bombay for six years
with great success." It was not banking, of course, but the *Review* made
the usual mistake. After Flora left the business, her role in protecting
the family's values and traditions had been critical. She held first the
business and then the family together, and neither would be the same
without her.

THE JAPANESE INVASION

In China, the Nationalists' success at suppressing their Communist
enemies drew the attention of a foreign power. A unified China threatened Japanese control of the Korean Peninsula and the South Manchuria Railway Zone to its north. Britain's policy toward China, as
opium was no longer on the agenda, was favorable and supported by
the British public. In 1931, in a prelude to later events, the Japanese
military had manufactured a border incident, providing itself with a
pretext to invade and occupy Manchuria. Later it managed to expand
its influence in a series of secret deals with Chiang Kai-shek in 1934
that, when they became public, gave ammunition to the Communists
to rally the population against him. From then on, Japan's expansionist ambitions overshadowed the strong economic relations it had with
Shanghai. Japan had invested more than a billion yen there over the
years and exported a wide variety of goods to the city. In July 1937,
a minor clash between Chinese and Japanese troops close to Peking
gave Japan the ostensible justification to invade again, and on a larger
scale. As news spread, an outpouring of public outrage and patriotic
fervor took place in Shanghai. A boycott of Japanese goods was organized, by this stage an essentially symbolic act, and the authorities

mobilized volunteers across the city. By mid-July Peking and Tientsin were in Japanese hands. The Battle of Shanghai, between China and Japan, began on August 13 and lasted until late November, and was the first key battle between two major Asian powers. While foreigners in the city watched and followed the fight, the world at large realized the importance of this battle, which would be described later as the "Stalingrad of the Yangtze." The Japanese erroneously expected a swift battle, but their casualties reached one hundred thousand, with soldiers fighting house to house.

On August 14, 1937, Shanghai, home to three and a half million people, was bombed by the Japanese. The world's fifth-largest city was caught unprepared: More than two thousand lives were lost in what became known as Bloody Saturday, and the city was cut off from its hinterland. Several bombs hit the International Settlement, causing carnage. One landed at "the Bund end of Nanking Road" just outside Sassoon House, and "dead and dismembered bodies littered the street." Lucien Ovadia, Victor's right-hand man, was hurled across his office in the Cathay Building by the explosion, and the adjacent Sassoon Arcade was wrecked. Ovadia and the hotel's senior manage-

Victor documented with his camera some of the scenes
from the Japanese invasion of Shanghai in 1937.

ment rushed to evacuate the upper floors of the building. Despite this onslaught, however, staff managed to open the restaurant and bar the following day, while the arcade was guarded against looting until its shops could be properly secured. In the chaos, the cost of food in the city rose sharply, and investors' confidence plummeted.

The attack augured the end of Shanghai's golden days. The Shanghai branch of E. D. Sassoon cabled their London office in late August to inform them that the situation was calmer and business had partially resumed. Foreign banks returned to work, but British property had suffered damage of more than £6 million since the outbreak of hostilities, and all were aware that even if the conflict were to come to an immediate halt, business would not return to normal for many months. By October, the effect of the disruption on Shanghai's trade was clear: Shipping collapsed to less than 20 percent of normal levels, most factories ceased to operate, and the scarcity of food drove up prices. Victor had been on his way to Europe for the summer when hostilities broke out but had by now returned. Early in 1938, he wrote from Shanghai to one of his directors in London, "The situation here appears to be more serious and dangerous than it ever has been, both from a political and financial point of view," and a few days later he expressed his fears that "the Japanese will throttle all foreign trade as only Japanese goods will enter China." One year after the attack, there was no significant improvement. Although daily hostilities had died down, it was reported that trade arteries had shriveled, and the overall value of British investments in the city had been decimated. Victor's diaries, on the other hand, demonstrate that the city's elite enjoyed a measure of normality; parties, dinners, and shooting trips continued as usual, at least until 1940.

The International Settlement and French Concession had been left largely intact by the invaders. These enclaves were surrounded first by a war zone and then brutal occupation, as the Japanese sought to impose order on the Chinese sector. The Japanese military appointed "experts" to deal with Shanghai's various communities. One of the two "Jewish experts" argued that "Japan should embrace Jews under the country's national spirit of universal brotherhood," though this was motivated less by altruism than by the anti-Semitic notion that America was beholden to the Jews, and their generous treatment in

Shanghai would encourage sympathy for Japan in Washington. The Japanese also pressed hard for a greater share in the Shanghai Municipal Council in order to handle local administration. They demanded guarantees from the council that anti-Japanese and political broadcasts from within the International Settlement would be "brought to an end." Even before the invasion, the Japanese, who had harbored imperial ambitions toward China since the end of the nineteenth century, insisted on being granted a seat on the council.

As a wealthy businessman with global connections, Victor precisely fitted their image of a Jew, and he was thought a figure who might be used to shape opinion not only in the Jewish community in Shanghai but also in Britain and America. Victor in turn wanted Japanese assistance to control the flood of refugees arriving at the International Settlement. The migration had begun in 1933, when Hitler became Chancellor of Germany. As persecution became the official policy in Nazi Germany, the numbers seeking haven elsewhere increased—reaching a peak in the wake of *Kristallnacht* in November 1938, when tens of thousands of Jewish homes and businesses, schools, and synagogues were damaged or destroyed. The number of Jews fleeing Germany and Austria prompted many countries to bar their entry, with the result that Shanghai had become a magnet for Jewish refugees, since they could go there "without visas because of its unique status as a city under the control of foreign powers." (In fact, the Japanese invasion and resulting chaos actually enabled a significant number of Jews to enter the city unhindered.) Many had been stripped of their assets and hoped that Shanghai would be a transit point to their new homes in Australia or North America. Meanwhile the condition of the refugees arriving in Shanghai continued to deteriorate. Between November 1938 and the following summer, there were an estimated twenty thousand Jewish refugees in the city, which was already suffering economic distress. Victor was anxious to both ameliorate the plight of the refugees and avoid overburdening Shanghai. News circulated in 1938 that he had purchased ten thousand square miles of land in Brazil to settle Jews from Germany and Austria. The Brazilian government, however, stipulated that only Jews with useful skills would be granted entry, and the scheme came to nothing.

Until late 1940, Victor attempted to act as a mediator between the

Japanese and the British to represent the Jewish Sephardic community in its dealings with the Japanese authorities. In May 1939 Victor and his friend Ellis Hayim met the Japanese "Jewish experts" to discuss the refugee problem, now exacerbated by the arrival of hundreds of thousands of Chinese displaced by the war unfolding inland. They asked the Japanese to halt immigration, as they believed the city could no longer cope with the influx. Representatives on the Municipal Council likewise urged their respective governments to "do everything possible to discourage persons of little or no means from emigrating to Shanghai," but though countries all around the world had closed their doors to European Jewry, in Shanghai they remained open a little while longer. It was, and is, a credit to the city and to the Chinese people who gave them refuge that, despite the hardships Shanghai faced, thousands of Jews would survive the war years in its midst and emigrate to other countries afterward. Though he was anxious to see the number of new arrivals fall, Victor strove to improve the circumstances of refugees in the city, donating $150,000 to assist them. He also devised an employment scheme and supported a number of Jews in opening businesses. He calculated how much it cost to feed one refugee in Shanghai—about ten shillings a week, or £26 per year—and used that figure, much as charities still do today, to persuade other donors to help.

Throughout, Victor's allegiance to Britain remained steady, and as war broke out in Europe, and Japan grew closer to Germany, the chances of his being able to maintain a cordial relationship with the occupiers diminished. At the beginning of the war, Victor announced he planned to donate £1 million (over £60 million today) toward the war effort, but it is not clear whether he did so or what the amount was. The chasm between him and the Japanese administration became public when, on a trip to the United States early in 1940, he criticized Japan and predicted that an impending economic collapse would see the Japanese turn on their military. Japan launched a bitter attack on Victor, describing his statements as "a grave slander not only against the Japanese Army but against the Japanese people," and his comments were immediately condemned by the Jewish community in Shanghai. Even Ellis Hayim joined them in coming forward to criticize Victor's statements and express their appreciation for "the sympathetic and courteous attitude" displayed by the Japanese officials in Shanghai toward Jewish refugees. For the Japanese "Jewish experts," this was proof that their strategy was working: The Jewish community understood the precariousness of their position well enough, and Japan could exploit their professed gratitude on the world stage. The Japanese felt shocked and betrayed by Victor's statements, and clearly signaled the end of the "cozy" relationship between the two sides.

Unable to return to Shanghai, Victor headed instead to Bombay, where he found a changed India. In the years following his departure from India, the nationalist drive for independence had gathered momentum; millions of Indians had been mobilized to engage in acts of civil disobedience, British institutions were regularly boycotted to express dissatisfaction with the Raj, and despite the frequently violent reaction of the British government, Mahatma Gandhi was determined "to lead the revolutionary movement to the path of nonviolence." In 1935, another Government of India Act, laying the framework for a system of autonomous provincial governance and expanding the franchise, had been passed in an attempt to ensure the survival of the Raj. On the outbreak of war in Europe in 1939, the limitations of this reform were exposed to all when the Governor-General informed India's political leaders that they were at war with Nazi Germany, enraging the Congress Party's high command and prompting large protests that culminated in the "Quit India" movement. As he had on his trip to the United States, Victor issued pronouncements on world affairs, mounting analyses and making predictions. He resumed his criticism of the Congress Party, declaring that India should help Britain before it aspired to independence itself: "Every Indian must realise that this country can avoid being a slave nation only if we beat Hitler." He was critical too of Gandhi's policy of "passive resistance," believing it would be futile against Britain's enemies. When Victor argued that handing power to the people in India would be a disaster, the retort, printed in *The Times of India*, was, "No one will take Sir Victor's advice seriously, but it indicates how much darkness can prevail in certain men's minds when the greatest amount of courage and wisdom is called for." As far back as 1930, Victor had attempted to insert himself between the Indian leadership and the British. At that time, he was friendly with some Indian politicians (such as

M. R. Jayakar, a barrister and one of the leaders of the self-government movement, who was close to Gandhi and Nehru), and from them he learned the ins and outs of Indian politics. It was only after 1939 that Victor was learning about the nationalist movement, unlike his days at the Assembly, when he was surrounded by pro-British Indians and representatives of the Raj. India paid a heavy price during the war; toward the end of it, almost two million Indian soldiers were fighting both Nazi Germany's and Japanese troops around the globe. Meanwhile, Bengal witnessed in 1943 a massive famine as a result of supplies of rice from Japanese-occupied Burma being stopped, and administrative failure to deal with the famine led to the death of two million people.

Victor continued issuing grandiose predictions. His record was decidedly mixed: In August 1941 he pronounced Japan too afraid to enter the war, and over the next few months he repeated this wherever he went, offering assurances that Japan would never fight against the United States or in Southeast Asia. He spent five of the first six months of 1941 in the United States touring and giving talks, though he claimed he was there to sell jewels to raise money for the Royal Air Force, of which he was a veteran. The real reason was to establish himself as a global commentator. The appeal to his vanity is obvious enough, but he also hoped to connect with politicians and business-people alike to shape the world that would emerge from the war. Wherever he went in the States, he made sure that his views were covered by the media, and cuttings from American and Canadian newspapers adorn his diary of 1942. In a speech he gave to the Boston Chamber of Commerce, he concluded, "It is not for me to try and give you advice," but he nevertheless urged his audience to place victory before everything in a war that he called "the war of survival . . . For the survival of the right of the ordinary man to live his own life and think his own thoughts." His economic projections were similarly flawed, though prescient for him and his family. In an interview in Memphis, he predicted, "[After] this war is over no man will be very rich anymore," and said, "Irrelevant [of] whether the West wins or loses, the economic system is going to be changed." His trips to the United States also provided opportunities to reconnect with the celebrities who had visited him in Shanghai in happier times and stayed in the Cathay Hotel. On a visit to Hollywood in 1940, Victor attended a party for the actor Basil Rathbone together with Charlie Chaplin, Laurence Olivier, Reginald Gardiner, Arthur Rubinstein, Bette Davis, Marlene Dietrich, and Vivien Leigh; one photo of the event shows him being embraced by the actress Paulette Goddard. (There were rumors of liaisons with Dietrich and Goddard, which Victor never deigned to deny.)

Meanwhile the conditions in Shanghai were growing desperate. The tone of the minutes of Municipal Council meetings approached panic, with discussions ranging from the desperate need to raise more income to the scarcity of rice. All this would change late in 1941, though not for the better. On December 8, a day after the attack on Pearl Harbor, Japanese ships fired on a British gunboat near Shanghai. The American and British navies had historically maintained a small presence near Shanghai, but by 1941 it had been reduced to one gunboat apiece. This was followed by Japan's rapid occupation of the foreign concessions. (Hong Kong came under attack the same day, falling into Japanese hands on December 25, where it would remain until the end of the war.) It marked the final chapter on a corner of Britain in Shanghai that dated back to when the First Opium War ended a century prior, and "Britain found herself in full retreat from China." Any notion of the innate superiority of Europeans over their Asian subjects was likewise finished. The Japanese occupied the Cathay Hotel and other opulent foreign clubs, which "served not only to accommodate the new conquerors, but also to convey to the Chinese open defiance of the rule of the White Man." Jews with British citizenship found themselves in a double bind. In addition to occupying the Cathay, the Japanese interrogated several of E. D. Sassoon's executives, including Henry Arnhold. Lucien Ovadia was fortunate to have been abroad, trying to sell the Metropole Hotel to an American consortium; when news of Pearl Harbor came, the deal fell through. He would travel with Victor around the United States throughout 1942 and later play a major role in strategizing and planning for the postwar period.

Victor had fortuitously left Shanghai before the Japanese fully occupied the city. The Japanese authorities closely followed Victor's anti-Japanese outbursts in different parts of the world. They were aware that some of his statements were repeated by Russian refugees, but there was also anti-Semitic propaganda distributed by some Russian agents in China about the sinister role of world Jewry, claiming that Victor was part of this cabal, which had to be opposed and defeated. The Jews who remained in occupied Shanghai found their free movement restricted, as the Japanese, under pressure from their German allies, imposed a series of punitive measures upon them. On February 18, 1943, the Japanese military authorities forced the Jewish refugees into a ghetto, where they remained until the end of the war. Other Baghdadi Jews, such as the Kadoorie family, who had been interned in Hong Kong, made it to Shanghai only to be interned a second time, now as British subjects. Life in the camps was harsh, food was minimal, and health conditions were abysmal, and they spent more than four years interred, having lost everything.

Victor's optimism about the future of China was steadily eroded over the course of the war. In its last couple of years, he spent more time in India, hoping to resurrect some kind of life there. Presiding over an all-India textile conference, he advocated the establishment of an industrial research institute similar to one in Manchester. In reality, however, he was groping in the dark and trying to figure out what to do next. In a discussion at a luncheon in early 1943 with an American businessman, he held forth on South America. He argued that the continent's natural resources and favorable climate made it the only place in the world that was attractive to immigrants. He thought the United States in the long run had "to marry South America" and worried that Brazil was insufficiently welcoming to immigrants, explaining that he had met with the Brazilian President, who had told him that Brazil wanted only "the right sort of people to come." (By which he meant races "like Danes and Scandinavians with no imagination, no brains, but with a great capacity for tilling the ground because the Brazilians do not want to till the ground.") Victor believed that South America was Hitler's final goal, the real prize. He predicted the creation of a "United States of Europe" on the grounds that the continent's countries could not defend themselves or grow economically unless they did so together. Turning to India, he stated that he had always believed Britain would have to give India its independence, but the question for both sides was timing. He also advocated a federation between Britain and the United States, though he thought the question of whether the federation would be ruled by the King or President unimportant.

GIVEN UP BY CHINA

By the end of a bitter eight-year war (1937–45) with Japan, Chinese society was left in chaos, with its economy in tatters and much of its infrastructure destroyed. Victory did not bring peace, and the reestablishment of political order was fragile as neither the Nationalists nor the Communists were in full control of the country. The Guomindang (GMD) central government technically regained control of areas occupied by Japan, but in fact in many of the small towns and villages of northern China it was the Chinese Communist Party (CCP) that took control. Manchuria was under the control of Soviet armies.

The end of the Second World War in 1945 dragged Victor's attention back from speculative solutions to the world's problems to his business. In a statement made during a visit to Bombay, he said he had adopted a "wait and see policy" for his vast property and utilities empire in Shanghai, now nominally under the control of the Nationalists. He believed that by 1947 it would become clear whether the Chinese government was prepared to guarantee foreign investments, and that China would face the same challenges as India had if it tried to discourage or limit foreign businesses' activities that had been put together for more than half a century. He called for India to build up its export markets for cotton textiles to take advantage of postwar demand and said that the prospects for the Indian textile industry were very bright. He advised that this industry should not be concentrated in just a few cities but spread across the country. As a result of the war, the Sassoon textile mills had reported their best year ever in 1943, and there were hopes that once the war was over investments in new machinery and expansion of mills would take place. From a press cutting in his diary, it seems that Victor took advantage of the increased demand and profitability to sell some of the mills in 1943 to an Indian family, the Marwadis, at high prices. In spite of his concern about the future of his company, Victor's postwar diaries in India are full of gossip and details about horse racing. He proposed that a Jockey Club be set up in India and suggested splitting the country into four racing zones, each with its own club. During the war Victor did not change the style of his diaries; the list of his 1942 Christmas gifts seemed more modest than before, but he continued to describe his cocktails and champagne mixtures.

Meanwhile the economic situation in Shanghai continued to deteriorate: Inflation was skyrocketing and the currency was depreciating. The cost of living in 1946 was more than 4,000 times that of 1935, and renting houses and apartments was extremely hard as "key money" had to be paid in advance. Furthermore, ambiguous tax laws were hastily imposed on foreign businesses, adding to the uncertainty in trading circles. It was becoming clear that the Nationalists were not in charge. Corruption had spread among their ranks and Shanghai was plagued by a black market. This added to the popularity of the Communists, who were waging war on the Nationalists for control of the country. The Cathay Hotel was in a bad state. Fighting had broken out there between the Nationalists and the Japanese in 1945. The Japanese had already ripped out boilers and radiators for scrap, and fittings were ruined. Victor was still hoping against hope that the situation would improve in China. He assumed that "the main stumbling block in China's return to normality was her unstable currency," and he believed that the Chinese were fundamentally sensible and understood that impinging on foreign businesses centered in cities like Shanghai would harm the Chinese themselves. He even talked about transferring some of his large interests from Bombay to South China and looked at the prospects in Hong Kong, which was enjoying a swift postwar recovery. That same week, he donated money to a school there and received a letter from its President, Horace Kadoorie, thanking him for his support. Victor was no doubt thinking that the Kadoories would be extremely useful. One piece of good news came during that time: Victor was awarded the Knight Grand Cross of the Most Excellent Order of the British Empire (GBE), considered the highest rank for the British honor system, in the January 1947 Honours List.

While optimistic in public, behind the scenes Victor and Ovadia were desperately attempting to liquidate the company's real estate holdings in China to reduce their exposure. They maintained a veil of secrecy and there was endless speculation in the media and the business community about their plans. Rumors circulated in the summer of 1947 that Wellington Koo, the daughter of a Chinese tycoon, had purchased the Cathay Hotel and Cathay mansions, or that a group of Russians was willing to buy the properties at bargain prices. But the following year saw the course of the civil war turn decisively in the Communists' favor; they proved they could fight effectively and their soldiers now numbered more than half a million. The value of real estate in Shanghai shrank as the Communist armies advanced; one estimate of the Sassoon properties after the Japanese occupation was £7.5 million (about £350 million today). Victor returned to Shanghai in 1948 to find disorder and chaos, amid a steady stream of Communist military victories, and clearly understood that "the commercial empire his grandfather Elias had established almost a century earlier was disintegrating."

In India too the outlook for foreign businesses was gloomy. The sectarian contagion that had escalated in the years before independence paled by comparison to the explosion of violence and the trauma of forced migration that followed Partition in August 1947, and the war between India and Pakistan over Jammu and Kashmir that began shortly afterward. Newly independent India's economy was overwhelmingly rural, and its policies focused on the immediate threat of severe inflation and encouraging the spread of manufacturing from the industrial centers of Bombay and Calcutta to all around the country. As a result, about a year after independence, E. D. Sassoon in Bombay was put into voluntary liquidation after mills were sold at low prices, thus ending more than a century of commercial activities in the city.

After a few months in Shanghai, Victor left to visit Argentina with the intention of helping to finance a pharmaceutical company there. Asked about it, he was noncommittal: "I'm rather trying to retire from my own business. . . . I just keep these small things going to keep me busy, you know." He returned later that year to Shanghai for one final attempt to salvage what he could from his properties. In the meantime, he put on a brave face to journalists. He told the *Los Angeles Times* that he had managed to liquidate many of his prewar holdings after the International Settlement had been returned to China at the end of the Second World War, and all that was left was his "hotels, a brewery and a trading company." Once it had dawned on him that China would not return to its prewar state, he had conducted a series of meetings with bankers, corporate lawyers, and brokers in New York and came to the conclusion that the Bahamas would be the ideal place in which to settle, given its negligible income tax and death duties. He had visited Nassau in 1946 and purchased an estate on East Street, where he allowed his representative in Nassau, J. P. Hart, to reside. By late 1948, on his return to Shanghai, he started moving employees to Hong Kong and announced that he would be transferring the bulk of what remained of the Sassoon fortune to the Bahamas. For many, abandoning Shanghai meant the loss of everything they had built up or aspired to build, and by now the "almost total eclipse of the British presence," first in China and then in India, was clear to everyone. Victor was still showing or attempting to show confidence in the future, telling journalists that his return ticket on Pan American Airways was for spring 1950. It was another prediction that missed the mark. Although he recognized that the Communists were there to stay, he was convinced that the

> Reds will be doing business with the United States and the British Commonwealth. First, because only the West has the goods they must have; second, because there are Chinese who are always ready to do business by circumvention, and third, because their leaders impress me as intelligent, though a ruthless outfit.

He did not realize that the Soviet Union would supply China with the goods it needed, or that Mao Zedong was utterly committed to class struggle. Victor was, however, absolutely correct that the Nationalists and Chiang Kai-Shek "by an endless procession of selfish ineptitudes lost any chance of regaining the support of the Chinese people, who are now ready to welcome the Communists as the lesser of two evils."

He sailed to the United States with a heavy heart, a lost empire behind him. The gamble he had taken, diverting his wealth and business from India to China, had cost him multiple fortunes. On May 27, 1949, Shanghai fell to the Communists. Fighting continued, and Nationalist planes even bombed the city, but the remnants of the empire established by Victor's grandfather almost a century earlier were now irrevocably in Communist hands. He was in his lawyer's office in New York when the news came. "He closed his eyes for a moment, then managed a smile. 'Well there it is,' he said quietly. 'I gave up India and China gave me up.'"

13

THE FINAL COUNTDOWN

1949–1982

Edward = Leontine
|
Victor = Evelyn Barnes

A few months before the German invasion of Poland in 1939, Philip passed away at the age of fifty. He had never married, and the baronetcy that had been conferred upon his grandfather Albert became extinct. At the time of his death he was still a principal of David Sassoon & Co. but seemed indifferent to fluctuations in his net worth. He left behind "a legacy of beautiful objects and an intriguing career. His public achievements were not sufficiently satisfying to him, and he seemed to be depressed toward the end of his life." His estate was valued at roughly £2 million, and he bequeathed money to some hospitals and £5,000 to the Royal Air Force College in Cranwell. Port Lympne was bequeathed to his cousin Hannah Gabbay, who was the only family member, apart from his sister, whom he was close to. It was sold by the family after the war and acquired by John Aspinall in the 1970s. Today, it serves as a hotel with a wild animal reserve on its grounds. Though Philip was always detached from the running of David Sassoon & Co., his death nonetheless sealed its fate, for it marked the end of the involvement of that part of the family in the business.

The decline of David Sassoon & Co. had begun long before that of its estranged sister company, E. D. Sassoon. The ambition and energy that characterized Flora's era would never be recaptured. There were some bright spots after her departure in 1901, particularly under David Gabbay, who succeeded Frederick in 1917, though his financial acumen faced severe headwinds. By the 1920s, the opium trade had been banned and the competition for textiles had sharpened from Indian local manufacturers as well as from China and Japan.

When Gabbay died in 1928, active management of the company passed for the first time outside the family, to Cecil Longcroft. He had joined the London office as a junior clerk and worked his way up, and was seen as a safe pair of hands—loyal, reliable, and lacking any appetite for risky speculation. His term was blighted by the 1929 stock market crash and the ensuing depression and fall in global trade. The firm tried to diversify and opened an office in Buenos Aires to trade commodities but lost money and quickly closed it down. Longcroft's time in charge was characterized by a pervasive caution: "From Manchester to Canton, every branch of David Sassoon soon became uncomfortably conscious of this extreme cautiousness at head office level." Unsurprisingly given his reliability, Longcroft was appointed the executor not only of Sir Edward's will but also of Philip's. Longcroft came from an old English family, remained a lifelong bachelor with austere habits, and "seemed to live only for success in business." He died in harness in October 1947 at the age of eighty-one, his twenty years running one of the world's most famous trading houses distinguished by its lack of innovation.

There are almost no records of the firm's activities from 1947, but it continued its modest business of exporting textiles to the Middle East and other parts of the world, and capitalized on some investments in shares and bonds. It is hard to hold Longcroft accountable for this state of affairs; he was appointed by, and for the first decade of his tenure answerable to, a chairman who never expressed any interest in the firm's business or intervened in it. Although the company presided over a large business in India, the only time that Philip visited the country was during an official trip to inspect all the Royal Air Force stations outside Britain, and it seems he didn't take the opportunity to visit the firm's offices or meet with any of its staff.

Philip's greatest impact was in the art world, where exhibitions at his lavish Park Lane residence and other venues caused reviewers to wax lyrical about his art collection and connoisseurship. His appointment as chairman of the National Gallery was the conclusive proof that the Sassoons were part of the British upper crust. Kenneth Clark considered him his mentor and felt he owed Philip a great debt. Philip's collection opened "the eyes of many people to the charm and excellence of British genre-painting." Similarly, his house at Port Lympne received many accolades, and its elegance was described time and again as an extraordinary creation. "The interiors were an eccentric jumble of rooms . . . converging around a Moorish courtyard." Clark thought that Port Lympne was somewhat ridiculous but admired the architectural gardens, "which contained the longest and deepest herbaceous borders."

Tellingly, the only document connecting Philip to the family firm isn't any request for information about the price of some distant commodity or instructions to subordinates, sent by his predecessors in their thousands. Indeed, it isn't even from him, but was sent from the Karachi branch in November 1934 to the Eastern Bank in Bahrain, confirming a remittance of fifteen thousand rupees for some cultured pearls he had bought for himself or his sister during a visit there. Philip's contribution to the art world was substantial, and his achievements in that field make his neglect of the family firm all the more stark. He was chairman of a company in which he had no interest and that he made no effort to lead. It is unclear, given his inclinations and tremendous talent, why he wanted to be the chairman. The first and second generations of the family had strived to reclaim the status they had lost in exile and reach the pinnacle of society, though never at the expense of the business, and each complemented the other. By the third and fourth generation, however, one side of this harmonious union of aspirations had been lost.

What happened to the other famous Sassoons mentioned previously? Siegfried Sassoon succumbed to social pressure, given his homosexuality, and married, in late 1933, the much younger Hester Gatty, whose family had produced many distinguished lawyers.

His wedding was small and attended by close friends such as T. E. Lawrence. Philip did not attend but sent a letter of congratulations. Within a few years and after producing one child, George, Siegfried's marriage ended in a friendly separation, and as he grew older he opted for solitude and a quiet life in the countryside, where he devoutly practiced his Catholicism. He concluded by the late 1940s that solitude "compels one to discover what one's mental resources amount to." He suffered from stomach cancer and died in September 1967, one week before his eighty-first birthday, stoic to the end.

Among the dominant characters in David Sassoon & Co.'s heyday were Suleiman and then his wife Flora. Both were innovative and effective in developing the business and taking it to new heights. Yet none of their three children followed suit. Mozelle died young, and her older sister, Rachel, married a businessman, Sir David Ezra, who was absorbed in his own affairs and local politics in Calcutta and never joined the family firm. Their brother, David, was well versed in the financial world, judging by his copious correspondence with Rachel, but took no interest in the family business, preferring more scholarly pursuits. In the early 1930s he published a two-volume catalog of the Hebrew and Samaritan manuscripts he had painstakingly collected in various parts of Asia and Africa. One reviewer stated that David owned one of the finest collections of Bible manuscripts in the world, including probably the oldest Yemenite manuscript. David's son Solomon became a distinguished rabbi and moved to Israel, where he dedicated himself to religious activities and scholarly writings. The archives contain his extensive correspondence with his aunt Rachel. Some correspondence between him and David Sassoon & Co. in London survives from 1969 and was the last communication under the company's letterhead in the archives. It relates to a donation of £40 on behalf of a trust set up by Aharon Sassoon to the sister of a Sassoon living in Israel who was in financial difficulty; Rabbi Solomon decided to help her.

The family's investments in India continued to provide a modest income to some living members, mostly from real estate, even in the mid-1970s, though Indian bureaucracy and English currency laws hindered and delayed these small transfers. Like his forebear David Sassoon, who maintained a strict Orthodox Jewish household, Rabbi

Solomon kept an open house for visitors from distant places and for scholars and bibliophiles, but without involvement in the mercantile world.

Without active leadership, the decline of the firm was uninterrupted. David Sassoon & Co. continued to function, though as a shadow of the firm it had been at the turn of the century. In 1952 one of its subsidiaries, the African Mercantile Company, issued shares to increase its capital to £650,000, which diluted the Sassoon firm's holdings to 44 percent. African Mercantile operated in East African countries in which the British were still the controlling power. In 1956, it withdrew from Hong Kong, and its representative on the board of the Hongkong and Shanghai Banking Corporation, H. D. Benham, resigned. This was a significant break; David Sassoon & Co. had been the only firm represented on the board since its first meeting in 1864 (except for the war years). Interestingly, the company's seat was taken by another Jewish firm with Baghdadi roots, Sir Elly Kadoorie & Sons.

Over the next two decades the firm retained one lingering family link, although distant—Lord John Cholmondeley (Sybil's son) was chairman for a few years. David Sassoon & Co. appeared in a list of banks and licensed deposit takers published in 1981. In 1982 Gerald Panchaud, an outsider who was running the firm, negotiated its sale to stockbrokers Rowe Rudd for around £2 million. The once flourishing merchant house had finally fallen off the financial map of London; its total deposits had sunk to a few million and profits were just over £100,000. Although the firm was now controlled by Rowe Rudd, it continued to operate independently from an office in Haymarket, in London's West End, with its own conditional license as a deposit taker. However, in August 1983, its license was revoked by the Bank of England as it was concerned about the liquidity ratio of the Sassoon banking arm, and that such a small bank should be engaged in project financing on an international scale. The company initially appealed against this last humiliation, only to accept it a week later and restrict its activities to merchant banking. In 1988, the Department of Trade and Industry declared that two ex-partners of Rowe

Rudd, including Tony Rudd, were "totally unfit to be directors of any company whether private or public." Precisely when David Sassoon & Co. formally ceased to exist is unclear—there are no records of its liquidation. An ignoble end for a powerhouse of global trade, a firm that had competed with the Tatas and once bested Jardine Matheson.

The nationalization of E. D. Sassoon's assets in China in 1949 and its forced departure from Shanghai dealt a heavy blow to the firm, but it limped on. Victor once again sought to limit his liabilities and chose the Bahamas as a base for continuing his businesses away from the traditional hubs of China and India. Once there, he returned to his old habits. An American newspaper reported that the "young British-born actress, Virginia Field," and her young daughter spent the winter of 1950 in the Bahamas, and that Victor had bought the child a red bicycle. His diary of that year contains photos of them on expeditions around the Bahamas and on a fishing trip to the U.S. Virgin Islands. The relationship with Virginia Field didn't last, however, and his diary has a press cutting of an article about her long romance with the American actor Willard Parker (whom she later married). He was still taking pictures of people he met or vacationed with, including some models, but not as much as in his Shanghai days. Horse racing continued to occupy a lot of his attention, and in this arena at least he was able to monetize some of his assets: A retired champion stud was syndicated for breeding for $294,000 ($3 million today), though he had previously declined an American offer to buy the horse for a million dollars. A report in a sporting newspaper stated that Victor had "more horses in the stable than any other patron" and detailed the qualities of each one. His passion for horses and racing was lifelong. He wrote an article and gave interviews about the question of racehorse doping, and carefully followed the racing news in several countries. "Racing was more than a millionaire's hobby with him. He applied himself to it with a dedication which often had a touch of ruthlessness."

Victor's diaries of the early 1950s show he did the exact opposite of what *Fortune* magazine predicted in the 1930s—that he would "build the Sassoon edifice up to new heights." There was almost no mention of the firm's business or of any new projects. Even his powers of foresight were waning: On a tour of the United States, he told journalists, "In the old days I could understand the economic picture," but said that in the new postwar order he could "no more predict what will happen next than we can predict what a woman will choose for her next hat." He was feeling the loss of Ovadia, his right-hand man, trapped in Shanghai until the summer of 1952 by the Chinese authorities, who were preventing executives of foreign firms from leaving the country until all taxes had been paid. On his release, Ovadia flew to Hong Kong and on to London, where he met Victor and resigned on the spot. He had long planned to retire to the south of France but took the opportunity to criticize Victor's decision to hand E. D. Sassoon Banking Co. control of the Hong Kong branch and subordinate it to headquarters in Nassau, like he did to the Manchester and London branches (the latter was managed by Captain Derek Barrington Fitzgerald, who was married to Victor's cousin). Ovadia saw a bright future for Hong Kong and believed it would be a mistake to relinquish any ground held there, particularly as the branch held lucrative agencies on behalf of some major international firms. Nassau, however, aspired to expand in the Bahamas and to launch merchant banking operations in Europe and Asia, and sold real estate in Hong Kong, and though Arnhold & Co. did focus its attention on the city, it too was sold, in 1957, to the Green family. This recoil from owning assets in Hong Kong proved in the long run a strategic mistake, and E. D. Sassoon excluded itself from what would become one of the great economic success stories of the latter half of the twentieth century.

Victor, now in his early seventies, suffered a painful spinal injury in 1953. The accident also caused damage to his good leg and forced him into a wheelchair, anathema to him since the days when his father had been confined to one. As soon as he could, he began using walking sticks—a pair rather than the single one he had depended on since the First World War. Apart from the pain, Victor was made irascible by the realization that he had to reconcile himself to the fact that his trips from the Bahamas to Britain and around the world were no longer feasible and that he would need constant care. While receiving treatment in New York he was struck by the "brisk efficiency" of one of the nurses, Evelyn Barnes, nicknamed Barnsie, from Texas. This new relationship injected excitement and energy into his life, and her patience and understanding won his heart. The following April, the couple paid a visit to her family's ranch in Dallas, where Victor was always fêted with barbecues. He was suffering from periods of depression—one particularly bad episode followed the news that the Chinese State Enterprise had seized his firm's properties in Shanghai and renamed the Cathay Hotel the Peace Hotel. Barnsie understood that the way to his heart was through horses and threw herself into learning about racing and bloodstock. The gossip pages entered into a frenzy of speculation over whether this would be yet another fling or something more: "Several international beauties are worried about Sir Victor Sassoon . . . considered the richest bachelor in the world," declared one, while another carried the headline "Sir Victor's Nurse Is Beauties' Nemesis." By the end of the year, Barnsie was his constant companion, mentioned almost daily in his diaries. Victor was growing increasingly frail, however, and in 1957 he had a fall at his home in the south of France that led to health complications. The following year, he was taken ill at Ascot and advised by his doctors to stay away from racecourses and cut down on cigars. He was spending several days at a time either in hospitals or bedridden but he never lost his sense of humor; in his diary he stuck a get-well card, depicting a large duck lying on a bed and stating: "Grounded? That's a crying shame. But just relax awhile . . ."

There was a lack of movement too on the business front. A Bahamas trust company was formed in Nassau. Its main sponsors were Barclays Bank, Royal Bank of Canada, and E. D. Sassoon Banking Co., all with branches based in Nassau. Banks and trust companies proliferated in the Bahamas to serve overseas companies and individuals taking advantage of the islands' tax-haven status. There was no income tax, no capital gains tax, and no annual tax on companies.

Victor was a typical wealthy man who was delighted by the absence of taxes in the Bahamas but said that if he were a young man he would head to South America to make his fortune. The Bahamas had been under British control for more than three centuries, gaining independence only in 1973, and it seems telling that a family whose fortunes were so completely tied up with the British Empire ended up in a British colony. Tax havens are a distinctly modern phenomenon whose origins were in the late nineteenth century. Only after the First World War did countries begin to develop comprehensive policies to become tax havens. With the collapse of the British Empire, Britain created a new, more hidden financial "empire" of tax havens, which handled huge sums of money, not least from former colonies or those that would shortly gain independence.

The inflow of capital and growth of the tourist industry in the Bahamas triggered a major boom in real estate and construction. Development was geared to the very rich, with luxury hotels and exclusive clubs springing up. Apart from banking, the only imprint of the Sassoon business on the islands was real estate. It was announced that Victor and a Florida developer would build a five-story apartment building in the Cable Beach area of Nassau, with properties ranging in price from $35,000 for a one-bedroom to $400,000 for a penthouse, at a cost of $5 million. He bought land at Lyford Cay Club, as had Henry Ford II and Roy Larsen, executive chairman of *Time* and *Life*. By the end of the 1950s Victor had consolidated his fortune in the Bahamas, far from the despised tax authorities, although it is doubtful he was making significant money anywhere else.

A decade after the Communists' triumph, attempts by foreign companies to reclaim or liquidate their assets in China were finally winding up. British assets lost to nationalization were estimated at $600 million or even higher, and many of the affected companies were compelled to remit large sums to China to pay local taxes and their employees' wages even though they had lost control of their businesses. Although relations between China and Britain began to improve in the late 1950s, with Britain's total exports to China reaching £25 million, there was absolutely no indication that the Chinese were willing to pay any compensation or to allow the owners of properties to sell them. By October 1958, E. D. Sassoon and its eight affiliates had been forced to hand all their sixty or so large properties to the state-operated Chinese State Enterprise. The best known were the Sassoon House, the Cathay Hotel, Cathay Mansions, Grosvenor House, the Metropole Hotel, Hamilton House, Embankment House, and Cavendish Court. As Victor told a newspaper on his visit to Miami, he had written off all his properties in China. The glorious days of the past had gone; one journalist who managed to get to Shanghai described the Sassoons' former Cathay Hotel, which had been converted into offices: "Above the great doorway of one enchanting house, the Soviet insignia proudly gleams; inside there is inevitably nothing but dull, unilluminated Communist offices."

In spite of the heavy losses, Victor managed to preserve significant wealth (see Afterword) and increased his charitable contributions in England, India, and the Bahamas. Because of the state of his health, he became interested in cardiology and donated heart machines to several hospitals in the United States where he had received treatment. To his credit, he continued funding the education and medical care of the Baghdadi Jewish community in Mumbai through the Sassoon Family Trust and donated funds for a new Jewish community center.

On April 1, 1959, Victor's marriage to Barnsie, aged thirty-eight, was announced. Asked why he chose this date, he joked that he wanted one he could easily remember, and April 1 happened to be the anniversary of the founding of the Royal Air Force. His diary that day has a picture of him with a big smile on his face, putting a simple, unpretentious ring bought off the shelf at a Neiman Marcus department store on Barnsie's finger. The *Miami Herald* carried pictures of the wedding and he was seen standing to cut the cake. The couple spent their short honeymoon in Miami and attended the Florida Derby. A year later, in England for the Derby, the "radiant and sun-tanned" Lady Sassoon (as she became when they wed) told the *Daily Mail* of their utter delight and how for the first fifty-three weeks of their marriage they celebrated it weekly, only then moving to monthly. Victor was euphoric after his horse won his fourth Derby, and with it a record prize of £33,000. His previous wins in the English Derby were with Pinza in 1953, Crepello in 1957, and Hard Ridden in 1958. He was hoping he could beat the Aga Khan's record of five wins. A few months later St. Paddy, ridden again by leading jockey Lester Piggott, won the St. Leger at Doncaster, and for 1960 St. Paddy's wins topped £100,000 (about £2.5 million today). Yet his dreams of winning another Derby did not materialize.

On a trip to San Francisco early the following January, Victor suffered a major heart attack and was hospitalized at St. Luke's Hospital. His condition stabilized and the media was informed that he was in "a satisfactory condition." He did improve and was soon back in the Bahamas. Over the next seven months, he remained boisterously cheerful, determined to enjoy life despite the fragility of his health. In August, in spite of his wife's reservations, he arranged a dinner party for the Governor of the Bahamas. The dinner guests enjoyed themselves, but the effort left Victor in an oxygen tent. He kept a brave face to the end. "When the time came for another injection, he looked with a faint smile and murmured, I'm not going to need that one, Barnsie." On August 13, 1961, at the age of seventy-nine, Sir Victor died, taking his title with him. A rabbi from Miami conducted the funeral service, which was held at the Anglican Christ Church Cathedral in Nassau.

Obituaries were published in newspapers around the world. *The New York Times* referred to his proposal in 1941 to create a federation of English-speaking democracies consisting of Britain, Canada, and Australia together with the United States. *The Times* of London reminisced about early 1945, when the arrival of a surge of British troops in Bombay and Pune depleted local furniture supplies and Victor came to the rescue, not only donating £50,000 but, knowing that the military authorities would be slow to act, assembling workers from around India to produce thousands of chairs, tables, and beds in a matter of a few weeks. The two stories capture both Victor's pretensions and his aspirations to be a global figure, advising governments on the management of the world, and his practicality and energy.

Victor Sassoon was undoubtedly a unique personality. His accomplishments in the business world, particularly in real estate in Shanghai, were impressive; his dedication to horse racing and his successes in the Derby and other races were remarkable. A narcissist, he loved attention no matter whether it was based on rumor or fact. He aimed to be in the news as much as possible, and hosted many parties and VIPs in his houses in Shanghai, in Pune, and on Cable Beach in Nassau. He did not allow the plane crash that injured his leg to deter him, and in later life an article even noted, "At times one wonders if his wheelchair is not a great source of energy for this man."

E. D. Sassoon continued to function after Victor's death, but without a Sassoon in charge. In the Bahamas it existed only as a banking trust with Barnsie as its director until she sold her interests in

1963. In 1967, a century after it had been founded, E. D. Sassoon made a final attempt to extend its interests and operations beyond its branches in London and Manchester. The E. D. Sassoon bank's capital remained a modest £500,000, but Ralph Yablon, a well-connected English industrialist (whose mother was a Sassoon), was added to its board in the hope that he would inject more cash. Later that year, the Crown Agents for Overseas Governments took a 40 percent interest in the firm and its headquarters were moved to London, with Nassau reduced to branch status. The plan was that the bank would expand its merchant banking activities and in particular develop export finance in European markets. By the autumn, the bank was capitalized at £2 million: 40 percent held by the Crown Agents, 25 percent each by Continental Illinois (which had extensive contacts in Africa) and Yablon, and 10 percent by Captain Fitzgerald, a relative of Victor and the bank's chairman at that time. The bank obtained authorization as a foreign-exchange dealer and tried to attract new clients to its investment management division, while an affiliated company called The Sassoon Trustee and Executor Corporation, owned not by the bank but by family shareholders, gained authorization to act as a trustee to settlements, executor to wills, and administrator to estates. Fitzgerald had married into the family, but no director carried the Sassoon name. The bank also invested in properties in the Bahamas, and in 1969 it was reported that a seven-hundred-acre plot of land would be developed by Sassoon Property Developments and Wonton Estates. It is not known whether this took place.

The investment of the Crown Agents in E. D. Sassoon aimed at expanding the bank's activities, reflecting the Crown Agents' business of about £80 million by the end of the 1960s, mostly for international orders placed in Britain. But the relationship soon soured, with both sides being dissatisfied with the results. The Sassoon company felt that the Crown Agents were giving business to competitors, and the Crown Agents, as the largest shareholders, realized that their investment in E. D. Sassoon had fallen below expectations. In the late 1960s the Crown Agents and Continental together purchased Yablon's 25 percent for £880,000. During the early 1970s, with profits flagging, E. D. Sassoon was sold to a merchant bank, Wallace Brothers, and the new combined company was called Wallace Brothers Sassoon Bank

Ltd. This new entity had deposits of £56 million and its paid capital was about £5.7 million. By summer 1972 total profits were a modest £500,000. Even at home in the Bahamas, when the government raised a medium-term loan of $10 million, E. D. Sassoon was only among the junior underwriters. In 1978, Charterhouse Japhet Ltd. announced the acquisition of the remaining outstanding interest in E. D. Sassoon Bank & Trust Ltd. in both the UK and the Bahamas. It was renamed Charterhouse Japhet Bank and Trust International Ltd. The Sassoon name slipped from the annals of global trade, banking, and finance.

AFTERWORD

The arc from unassuming beginnings to spectacular success and ignoble end took the two Sassoon companies less than a century and a half to traverse. The sheer rapidity of the opening and closing acts draws the obvious question: Why? Why did they thrive where so many other trading families merely subsided, or even failed? And having reached the heights that they did, what went wrong?

The roots of their triumph run in multiple directions. They were made by their allegiance to British colonial interests and the rise of global trade and commodity prices in the second half of the nineteenth century, though they were hardly alone in this. What distinguished them from their rivals and enabled this family to build a truly global trading firm? The merchants of the nineteenth century cared about one thing above all others: trust. In a world that was growing steadily more interconnected but where the primary methods of communication were slow or insecure, trust—and its talismanic partner, reputation—was as much the lifeblood of trade as capital and credit. Unlike many of their counterparts in Europe, who could depend on written contracts, the Sassoons had to rely upon their personal relationships with traders, suppliers, and buyers to do business. They had to choose carefully and were aided in this by the information nexus they built around their offices in Asia and Britain, and the network of agents, brokers, and more they cultivated in India, China, and beyond. From the beginning, the trust that existed within the Sassoon firms was projected outward. David deployed his sons as his agents and representatives and built a workforce he could likewise depend upon, mostly from other Baghdadi Jews—keepers of the "coded" dialect used by the family in business correspondence, which fostered trust within the firm by ensuring that their communications were impenetrable to rivals. He knew his employees' families, and by providing them with free education and health care, through the schools and hospitals he funded, he ensured their loyalty when his competitors struggled to trust newcomers. The weight David gave to the family's good name encouraged him and his sons to be risk-averse when assessing new projects and trades, helping to sustain the business in times of crisis and proving them worthy of the trust placed in them by their partners in business. Finally, David's core principle of donating to the poor sustained the family's cohesiveness as well as brought tremendous respect from outsiders and political clout. Risk was an integral part of trade, but the firm David built systematically avoided speculation and thus survived the financial crisis of the 1860s, which decimated many of its competitors.

We do not have to look far to find the seeds of their downfall, however. The system of independent branches, each with its own trading books and accounting, encouraged an entrepreneurial spirit and keen understanding of risk among David's sons, two invaluable assets that would see the firm flourish for decades. At the same time, however, it led to unnecessary competition between the branches, which sometimes worked to the detriment of the whole. A long analysis by Frederick after a visit to the Far East indicates an awareness of this flaw:

> In my opinion, partners in the Houses of China and Calcutta should receive a monthly salary. If you want to give them a further incentive, well give them a bonus if there are profits. It is clear that the partners do not care if Bombay loses or not, and sometimes they are willing to destroy the market in order to get rid of their opium chests or just to make a small profit.
>
> When I was in Hong Kong, we suggested that Shanghai House sells the few hundred chests they owned, but they declined fearing that their own market will weaken thus impacting their own profits.

Frederick appealed to his brother Suleiman to institute an alternative system whereby each branch would have its own allocation of opium chests for sale. He advocated an end to the branches' rampant opportunism, which was as likely to come at the expense of other branches as that of other companies, not least because the two Sassoon firms controlled so much of the opium market at the time. Frederick concluded by imploring his brother "to consider these proposals objectively and reach the right conclusions." Unfortunately, Suleiman did not heed his younger brother's timely advice. The system of internal competition remained in place until 1901, when the company was incorporated. But by then it was too late.

What really did stifle entrepreneurialism among the Sassoon dynasty was not the prohibition of competition between them but an altogether more protracted and subtle shift: Anglicization. As more and more of the family moved to England, they grew enamored with the aristocracy, fell under the spell of English upper-class life, and strove to join them. In this they were mirroring a mood that affirmed the primacy of landed gentlemen over industrial entrepreneurs by the end of the nineteenth century, as "the disruptive force of the industrial revolution" led to growing suspicion of material and technological advancements. Even *The Economist* changed its tune. In 1850, it had not looked kindly on capitalists purchasing land in order to acquire status. By 1870, however, it was trumpeting that "social consideration is a great and legitimate object of desire . . . that it would pay a millionaire in England to sink half his fortune in buying 10,000 acres of land. . . . He would be a greater person in the eyes of many people."

Industry was pushed aside, even disdained, and leisure assumed a higher priority than business in English refined circles. Making money was eschewed as common. The Sassoons accordingly abandoned the work ethic laid down by the founder and diligently followed by Albert and Suleiman. These men had worked long hours six days a week. They saw money as a means of gaining power and security, of contributing to their communities; they bought and built sumptuous houses and were generous hosts to the benefit of their business rather than its detriment. The same cannot be said of their successors. One letter from Arthur to his nephew Edward is revealing of a typical day at the office of David Sassoon & Co. in Leadenhall Street in about 1890 and the loss of the zeal that had driven its founder:

> We [Arthur and his brother Reuben] went to the office yesterday
> at 11 and remained there till 1, while we signed the Hebrew and
> Arabic letters. While we were there, [an agent] called and offered
> some Persian opium and he said there was a margin of more than
> $100 between the price here and that in Hong Kong, so we thought
> we might as well buy a small lot and make a little money. We went
> afterwards to Sandown [racecourse] with the Prince [of Wales] and
> [Lord] Rosebery in a special [train] and were grieved to see Ladas [a
> horse] beaten. I had a plunge on him £40 to win £70. Better luck
> next time!

How distressed David would have been to know that his two sons arrived at the office at eleven in the morning and stayed for only a few hours before heading to a racecourse to place bets! It was roughly the opposite of the way David and Albert conducted their lives. As one commentator put it: "Nothing suppresses an appetite for commerce more than a diet of gentlemanly pursuits." The fact that this letter was written in around 1890 while Abdallah (Albert) was still alive and Suleiman was working hard in the East with the help of Flora tells us that the decay had already begun then, and it gathered momentum after Albert's death and the dislodging of Flora.

For Albert, "Society life was an incident," but for Arthur and Reuben, "it came to be their principal, if not their sole, absorption." Commerce fell by the wayside. Arthur's neglect of the business has been attributed to his union with a European Jew—all his siblings had married other wealthy Baghdadi Jews who shared the same values and traditions—though this misses the way the Sassoons' fate differed from those of the aristocratic European families they married into. Anglicization was not by itself a core reason for the fall, but it definitely distracted members of the family from focusing on the business. Aspiring to British titles was also not in itself a reason to lose an empire; another Jewish immigrant to Britain, Marcus Samuel, founder of Shell, wanted a peerage, a prominent role in politics, a country house, horses, and the finest education for his children, and he obtained all of them. Over the course of his life, his interest in the business declined, but his family has retained its wealth and Shell is a valuable part of one of the largest oil companies in the world.

One key difference between the Sassoons and the family to which they are most often compared, the Rothschilds, was the transmission of wealth and knowledge between generations. David instituted a "training program" for his sons to learn the ins and outs of trade, but this enterprise was short-lived compared to the Rothschilds' equivalent, which diligently trained their offspring for generations. For those raised in it, the preservation of family ownership was an overriding principle of business. They created well-protected trusts and skillfully ensured that the family's wealth did not get diluted from one generation to another. The Sassoon family, by contrast, split into two after the founder's death, competing rather than forging ahead as a single entity. Niall Ferguson in his monumental work on the Rothschilds underlines the importance of fraternal harmony, quoting the founder of the Rothschild dynasty, Mayer Amschel, who told his sons long before his death and two decades before the Sassoon family's split that "acting in unison would be a sure means of achieving success in their work." But competition within the family was never so fatal to their interests as complacency. Take as a counterpoint the Tata family, who were similarly active in opium and textiles as opium prohibition loomed and textile production shifted to India. By 1917, Tata Sons, quick to adapt to the new trading conditions, had found success in India's industrial, trading, and financial sectors and owned the first modern iron and steel works in the country. Both Sassoon companies were comparatively slow to change. At the time when they gradually, and conservatively, were adding more mills to the already overcrowded Bombay cotton mill industry, J. N. Tata spent a few months touring Alabama and Georgia to study the latest cotton production techniques and then headed to Pittsburgh to learn about iron and steel plants. The Sassoons meanwhile never saw themselves as fully Indian, which lessened their commitment to their business in the country and blinded them when times changed. With their foothold in London, they had a clear advantage over their competitors in India from the 1860s, but this comfortable situation was overturned as ambitions became increasingly focused on the glitter of British society.

Or take the Kadoorie family. They too had been nourished and protected by the British Empire, and their activities were likewise facilitated by the elevation of free trade to a principle of its policy. And they too suffered massive financial losses both during and after the Second World War as a result of the Japanese invasion of China and subsequent Communist nationalization. Unlike Victor, however, they managed to rebuild a huge fortune and remain a powerful dynasty today, with major holdings in Hong Kong, including the luxury Peninsula Hotels chain. The twilight of the British presence in India and their dislocation from China did not condemn them to the same fate as the Sassoons.

The Sassoons, unlike more enduring dynasties, did not plan for the long term as they cherished harvesting the fruits of their existing businesses, such as opium and cotton. As one historian succinctly described the success of another family of this period, John Swire & Sons: "Key to Swire's development remains the ethos of investing for the long-term—a strategy that has carried the group through different periods of economic volatility and political turmoil."

The demise of these merchant princes stemmed also from the small pool they recruited from. As employees had to be able to correspond in the Baghdadi Jewish dialect and have knowledge of accounting, they were for the first three or four decades of the business mostly recruited from Baghdad. Some of these young men were extremely talented, others were not—but the pool was always small. Unlike the Parsi community in Bombay, who also hired from their own ranks but whose pool was larger given the size of its population. Only toward the end of the nineteenth century were outsiders with expertise employed by the Sassoons in management roles, but by then members of the family were less involved and often unwilling to be posted to China or India, so these outsiders were not directly supervised. As a result, David Sassoon & Co. was run by outsiders from the late 1920s onward, as was E. D. Sassoon from the mid-1960s. In both cases the results were abysmal. Families such as the Rothschilds had outside experts, but the difference was that executive positions were held by family members.

Paradoxically, one reason for the Sassoons' collapse is a lack of heirs. Theirs was a close business, centered around loyal, dedicated family members and near relatives at the top, and by the early twentieth century the lack of candidates—motivated or otherwise—had become acute. Unlike David, who had eight sons and six daughters from two marriages; Albert, who produced two sons and three daughters; or Elias, who had six sons and three daughters, later heads of the family were bachelors (Philip) or married very late in life (Victor), and neither of these two had children. One observer called it the "extinction of the house of Sassoon" as so many were childless or had no male heirs to carry on the family name. After their deaths no one emerged to take the helm, and no member of the family was interested in reengineering the businesses to meet the challenges brought by a changing world.

Outsiders perceived the decline of the Sassoons long before they themselves did. In 1940, the Colonial Office deemed the family a spent force and not a suitable partner for new ventures in the West Indies:

> So far as the . . . U.K. Sassoons are concerned there is not I think much "big business" left. Sir Philip, who got most of the family money, never did anything. Other members of the family are Siegfried, who is an impecunious writer . . . [and] Sir Victor Sassoon . . . [who] has been singularly unfortunate in his judgement of events. . . . He came to the conclusion that with the advance of self-government in India opportunities for making unlimited profits were diminishing. . . . He decided to restrict his interests in India and transfer his main activities to Shanghai.
>
> The Sino-Japanese war has of course made a complete mess of his business, and I imagine that it was in the hope of finding honey elsewhere that he took the golden road to Buenos Aires. . . . However, S. America, as those better acquainted with the situation could have told him beforehand, has proved a disappointment owing to currency and transfer restrictions.

Siegfried Sassoon *(second from right),* age nine, with his father,
Alfred; his older brother, Michael *(far left),* age eleven;
and his younger brother, Hamo *(far right),* age eight.

Philip *(left)* and Siegfried Sassoon in their service uniforms during
World War I, c. 1915.

Victor Sassoon with four glamorous women in Hollywood, California, in 1940. (*From left*) Lili Damita, Mrs. Peabody, Contessa di Frasso, and Marlene Dietrich.

Victor with Charlie Chaplin at a party in Hollywood in 1940.

A photograph of the Japanese invasion of Shanghai, taken by Victor Sassoon in 1937.

Victor and his wife, Evelyn Barnes (Barnsie), in the Bahamas after his retirement, 1961.

A modern view of Shanghai. Victor's Cathay building, now the Fairmont Peace Hotel *(center)*, with its distinctive green, obelisk-shaped roof, was completed in 1929.

The statue of David Sassoon by Thomas Woolner, 1865, which greets visitors to the David Sassoon Library and Reading Room in Mumbai to this day.

(*Left*) A stamp featuring Siegfried Sassoon, issued by St. Helena in 2008, included lines from his poem "Aftermath." (*Center*) A stamp issued by the Indian government in 1998 commemorated the David Sassoon Library and Reading Room in Mumbai. (*Right*) A stamp featuring Victor Sassoon, issued by the Bahamas in 2011, marked the fiftieth anniversary of his death in 1961.

The writing was on the wall, though at David Sassoon & Co. there were no members of the family present to see to it. A penetrating and hard-hitting verdict on those critical years after the Second World War is provided by Sir Michael Green, a Hong Kong–based businessman whose father worked with Victor after the union with Arnhold & Co:

> I would say that Sir Victor was casual about the empire he inherited. He didn't realise he was playing with real bullets. It didn't happen in a week; it happened over many years . . . a series of blunders and omissions. He can be held responsible for a lack of foresight, keeping not all but far too many eggs in one basket. According to my father, there was a series of irresponsible investment decisions or partnerships with the wrong people. Victor's [cousin] married into Irish aristocracy called Fitzgerald, and one of the Fitzgeralds was brought onto the Board [of the company] and was telling them what to do in England. The Sassoons were irresolute, unprepared for the changing world. You can't blame Sir Victor for the war. But you can hold him responsible for the failure to diversify and the failure to rebuild. He frittered away what he was left with.

In retrospect, the decision to leave India was fundamentally wrong. The notion that India, once independent, would not provide a safe haven for Jews was faulty. One Baghdadi Jew who stayed put, a Lieutenant General Jack Jacob, born in Calcutta to a kosher household, served as chief of staff of the Indian Eastern Army during the war of 1971, when Indian and Pakistani troops fought in what would become Bangladesh, and later as Governor-General of Goa and subsequently Punjab.

Another more recent magnate, Sir Michael Kadoorie, summed up why families such as his succeed: "It is about obligations and not just privileges. Leading by example is the only way to keep it going from one generation to another." The Sassoons partially failed to do so in the second generation and utterly bungled it in the third and fourth generations. Dynasties are, of course, more enduring than any one individual. But their survival is dependent on their leaders' ability to instill resilience and the capacity to adapt to changing circumstances in their organization. In the case of the Sassoons, this leadership faltered.

Remnants of the Sassoons' glory are still visible today in the many parts of the world where they did business. A visitor to Shanghai can stay in the

Presidential Sassoon Suite at the Fairmont Peace Hotel (for just $14,000 per night), while the neighborhood of Kala Ghoda in Mumbai is served by the beautiful David Sassoon Library. The wealth that built these monuments is more elusive, however. Where did the money go? Even wills, usually a reliable tool to assess wealth, here come with caveats. Some members of the family, notably Edward, divided most of their assets between their children before they died, so their estates were not reflective of their true wealth. Others, typified by Victor, siphoned off most of their wealth into offshore companies in places such as the Bahamas, rendering their wills almost symbolic.

David's will did not value his estate, though there were vague reports in the local press after his death in 1864 that he had left over £2 million. In England, his estate was valued at £160,000, while in Bombay estimates based on his real estate holdings and the value of his company ranged up to £5 million. This may be exaggerated by as much as a fifth, though £4 million would be roughly £400 million today, or £3 billion calculated by labor or income value. This had been accumulated in about thirty years; it would vanish relatively quickly. An heir to two dynasties in America, Oliver Wendell Holmes, succinctly explained the problems facing wealthy families who attempt to pass their wealth to their children and grandchildren: "It is in the nature of large fortunes to diminish rapidly, when subdivided and distributed."

A key to explaining the dissipation of the Sassoons' wealth is the lack of tax planning and the absence of trusts, such as those set up by the Rothschilds, that would have prevented wealth from being divided with each generation, and after the split likely in two directions also. Here, the adage that "the difficulties of the family business begin with the founder" is absolutely true. There was no long-term strategic planning that would have protected and secured family assets to the benefit of all. Wealth was eroded by Britain's high inheritance taxes, which in the late nineteenth and early twentieth centuries ranged from 30 to 50 percent for estates valued at more than £1 million. In 1939, Philip Sassoon's estate was estimated at about £2 million (roughly £125 million today), on which a crippling £800,000 or so was paid in death duties. Thirty years later his cousin Hannah Gabbay also left an estate of about £2 million, including assets in South Africa, Australia, and Holland, on which £1.2 million had to be paid. (She left £300,000 to the National Trust, and a source close to the family told the media that she had been furious that even this bequest to a respected national organization would not be free of estate taxes.)

Some wills were extremely detailed. Flora and Suleiman's daughter Lady Ezra, for instance, left a four-page list of beneficiaries, mostly locals who worked for the family. Other wills were complicated to execute and took many years to distribute, as the assets were varied and in several geographical locations. Arthur held assets in London, Bombay, Hong Kong, and Shanghai, and courts in each jurisdiction had to approve probate. In his case most of the assets in England were shares and bonds, which had to be liquidated prior to distribution, and the timing did not always realize best value. Other estates took a long time to be distributed because of appeals against the taxes levied, and in certain cases the dispute went all the way to the High Court to resolve conflicts between the Inland Revenue and the estate's executors. The amounts paid in inheritance taxes in today's values were colossal. Other families, such as the Kadoories or Gulbenkians (Calouste Gulbenkian, an Armenian, owned 5 percent of the Iraq Petroleum Company and was one of the richest men in the world when he died in 1955; his Lisbon-based foundation is still active along with his eponymous art museum), shielded their assets either by locating themselves in tax-free jurisdictions such as Hong Kong or by creating foundations. Victor did this, but only after he had suffered severe losses in China.

We don't know how much money E. D. Sassoon lost in China or what Victor was worth at the time of his death. His estate in England was tiny—just £12,000—though he left £300,000 to his three nieces, a yearly allowance of about £7,000 to each of his two sisters, and a few thousand pounds to some friends and to the RAF Association in Nassau. The rest of the trust benefited his wife, Barnsie. The press was predictably shocked that Victor's assets seemed so modest considering his wealth before the move to China. *The Daily Telegraph* called the Bahamas figure "sensationally low." Barnsie sold her interest in E. D. Sassoon Bank in the early 1960s, the Eve Stud Company in 1970, and the Sassoon Studs, originally called Beech House Stud, a year later. Precise figures for these sales are not available, but they are estimated at between one and two million pounds, at the very least.

How much was sheltered in Victor's Bahamian companies and trusts? According to one source, when Victor asked Lucien Ovadia at the end of the 1940s how much he was worth, he was told that he had "the Hong Kong Trust Corporation money, some five million dollars' worth of first-class securities in America [worth roughly $60 million today], as well as the Shanghai properties, plus the assets in India." As we saw, the Shanghai properties were valued at the end of the war at about £7.5 million (about £350 million today), of which Ovadia managed to sell £1.4 million. The rest was lost. It is worth keeping in mind here that Victor's assets in China in 1928 have had a value in our terms of about a billion dollars, and by 1937, this had probably doubled, or amounted to at least 1.5 billion. It is not clear how much was raised by selling the mills in India; they were booming at the end of the Second World War but the sale took place years later. In any case, Victor left China with substantially less than he arrived with, though we can be certain that this, combined with capital in America and that raised in India, amounted to a sum in the hundreds of millions of dollars in today's terms. Although this wasn't supplemented by any meaningful income from any business, neither was it subject to the expense of running one, and his wealth at the time of his death, and the value of the assets left to his wife, would have been significant. As Barnsie had no children, her nephew and niece were her inheritors, and an Eves Holdings Limited still operates in the Bahamas today, though its holdings are not known.

For other members of the family, inheritance taxes forced their inheritors to sell their properties and divide the proceeds. With so few children earning enough to buy out their siblings, the grand houses in London passed out of the family as one generation gave way to the next. As early as 1917, S.D.'s son Joseph and his wife, Louise, "could no longer afford to live in Ashley Park" and moved to a house on Rydens Road in Walton-on-Thames. Prime real estate in Belgravia, Hyde Park, and Grosvenor Square was sold over the decades; Philip's house in Park Lane would become the site of London's Playboy Casino. It would, however, be a mistake to assume that taxes alone depleted the family's resources. More significant was the combination of conspicuous consumption and lack of interest in business that led many to squander their fortunes. Some could not afford their lifestyle but maintained it anyway, and extravagance was a hallmark of the family well after David Sassoon & Co. ceased to be an engine of wealth. When Joseph's son, Arthur Meyer Sassoon, filed for bankruptcy in 1950, he told the court that his household expenses in previous years were £39,000 (about £1.4 million today) and that he had spent another £33,000 on jewelry and furs for his second wife (an actress twenty-five years younger than him). Asked why his wife had not come to his rescue, he admitted that since his financial difficulties began they had quarreled, and this was the reason he had filed for bankruptcy. At some point he had to pawn jewelry in order to pay bills.

Large sums were also poured into art and entertainment. Philip's three mansions and lavish balls and banquets were part of the reason for his fame. So many minor royals and celebrities were invited to his parties that a woman allegedly sent him a telegram at Easter informing him, "Christ is risen. Why not ask Him for lunch?" Philip also spent an inordinate amount of money on art, most of which was inherited by his sister, Sybil. She lived in Houghton Hall in Norfolk, considered to be the "quintessential and best-preserved Palladian house in England," where some of Philip's art collection is still displayed. She and her husband, the 5th Marquess of Cholmondeley, spent huge amounts of money restoring the house to its former glory. Later their descendants sold 160 works, mostly eighteenth-century French pieces from Philip's collection and from Houghton, at Christie's to raise funds. *The Times* reported that the sale, in December 1994, raised more than £21 million. Artifacts of the family expenditures are still coming to the surface today. Exotic Judaica and an eclectic array of possessions from descendants of Suleiman and Flora were auctioned at Sotheby's in Tel Aviv in 1999, and again in December 2020 in New York. Among the items on sale were oriental carpets, richly embroidered textiles, oriental porcelains, and even Chinese and European fans. Some of the religious items, such as scrolls and a rich Torah mantle, carried price tags of over $150,000. At the 2020 auction, there were two Torah shields from the eighteenth century that Sotheby's described as "the most important pieces of Judaic metalwork to appear at auction in a generation," estimated at $900,000 apiece.

The Sassoons' story is part of the globalization that took off during the nineteenth century. The interconnection between trade, finance, and people became more intense as time went by. Their 130-year story happened at a time when dramatic changes were taking place worldwide: the end of the East India Company; the two Opium Wars; the American Civil War; the opening of the Suez Canal; the First World War and the end of the Ottoman Empire; the 1929 Depression; the Second World War; the rise of Communism in China; the independence of many of the hubs they operated in, most important, India; and the end of the British Empire. Some events were advantageous to them (the Opium Wars and the American Civil War), while other events shattered their business (the Communist takeover of China). They embraced technological changes, and in many cases they were at the forefront of the transformation that was taking place. When the steamship arrived, they immediately changed their fleet; when the telegraph began, they immediately put it to use, as they clearly understood the critical role of information; when banking, finance, and investments became more sophisticated, they not only implemented new ideas but actually were among the pioneers in developing investments and trades that were globally oriented rather than local (from arbitrage in currencies and metals to contributing to banking activities across continents). Even in philanthropy they were innovative, allocating 0.25 percent of each trade to charity.

The Sassoons refused to be parochial; on the contrary, they were attuned to world events, be it the silk harvest in France or the rice crop in Asia. Their business model adopted vertical integration: They mostly controlled their supply chains and dominated the trade of certain commodities (opium in particular), which led to increasing efficiencies and higher profitability.

The story of the Sassoons tells us that globalization was transforming the world on every level, and businesses had to decide whether to keep up with the dramatic developments or to stand still. They chose the former. However, being at the forefront of globalization did not mean, as we have seen, having the ability to invest for the long term or to undergo fundamental changes of the business. The Sassoons were prophetic about the changes that would be brought by telegraphs and steamships but incapable of foreseeing the end of the opium trade and the need to divert into new areas. An important factor that aided them in adapting to global changes was their background: They left Baghdad knowing the meaning of security and insecurity, spoke different languages, understood cultures, and were respectful of all religions and sects wherever they traveled or traded. This allowed them to feel connected to the global world, which was beginning to be smaller with better transportation and communications. And most critically, their being refugees who were willing to change, adapt, and be integrated within different societies and cultures is the ultimate witness to their openness to globalization as we perceive it today.

The Sassoons' story is also a lesson on how refugee families contribute to the welfare of the world. The first book about the Sassoons was published in April 1941, during the darkest days of Europe; at the start of the text, its author, Cecil Roth, addressed Adolf Hitler and any leader who misled their people into believing that their race was superior. His conclusion was clear: "The absorption of gifted foreign families cannot be other than an advantage for a civilized state," and families such as the Sassoons and others proved that rudimentary supposition.

At the beginning of this book, Thomas Mann's *Buddenbrooks* was cited as a cautionary tale. To this we might append, at the end of the period covered in this book, the story of Lehman Brothers, another company founded by a family of migrants whose first generation lived frugally, worked hard, and created immense wealth. The decadence and disinterest of their third generation echoed that of the Sassoons, and the relinquishing of control of the company also augured the beginning of its end, though in this case the fallout was altogether grander. "No, things are not going well for this family," says one of Mann's characters as the family business began to founder.

Unlike the fictitious Buddenbrooks, the Sassoons' decline stemmed in part from their success—the titles, social and political standing, and friendship with royalty they sought and obtained, seemingly at the cost of what had brought them riches in the first place. David Sassoon had always been adamant that the family's reputation was of the utmost importance and demanded that his children work to enrich themselves; less than a hundred years after his death, his descendants enjoyed these riches while the firm he built became marginal in every sphere, managed by outsiders who were eventually declared unfit by the Bank of England. The desire for acceptance and status was not particular to the Sassoons. Between the founder and the fourth generation, something more than money had been lost. One astute observer likened the shape of the dynasty to a diamond, "starting at a point, widening out rapidly, and tapering disastrously towards the bottom. In [the fourth] generation, moreover, there is little left of the specific quality of the Sassoons of a previous age." The final curtain on the global merchants, or "the Rothschilds of the East," came down.

Outside Mumbai or certain districts of Shanghai, few today have heard of the Sassoon family. The name calls to mind only the famous First World War poet Siegfried Sassoon, in Britain, and the hairdresser Vidal Sassoon (whose origins were Syrian and had no connection to the Baghdadi Sassoons), in Britain and the United States. I know this because I too carry the Sassoon name, and I too scarcely gave the legacy of my extended family a thought until I began writing this book. My great-great-grandfather Benjamin, one of David's younger brothers, stayed behind when David and their father, Sassoon, fled Baghdad. In the twentieth century, most of my father's older brothers left Iraq when they reached the age of sixteen to study and then work abroad. When my father's turn came, however, his father fell sick and died, and as tradition dictated, my father was obliged to stay to take care of his mother and sisters. Much like the Sheikh and his son, he and I were forced in the 1970s to flee our home by dark political and cultural winds—in our case, the emerging tyranny of the Ba'th Party and Saddam Hussein in the late 1960s—to the other side of Iraq's eastern border. Like David, I was fortunate to find work and achieve a degree of success in exile. They say, "Once a refugee, always a refugee," and researching and writing this book has led me to reflect on how this too is part of the Sassoon legacy. I carry with me not just my own experience of leaving my homeland behind, but also that of generations before. And while I am safe and secure in my new home, and my children and grandchildren are too, I try not to take anything for granted.

ACKNOWLEDGMENTS

This book started with a letter in 2012 from Joseph (Joey) Sassoon in Scotland, and to him and his children, Tania and Peter, I owe a big debt. In the last nine years I have accumulated more debts to many people and institutions, and I ask for forgiveness from and offer sincere apologies to anyone I have overlooked.

My journey for the sake of the book was not unlike the Sassoons' passage in the early nineteenth century: travel in many countries and cities, but this time to undertake research and to work in archives. It began in London, then continued to Jerusalem, Mumbai, Pune, Shanghai, and other locations. This book, I believe, is the first full-length work to make significant use of the David Sassoon Archives at the National Library in Jerusalem, which are mostly in Baghdadi Jewish dialect. For the support I received, my gratitude is especially due to the National Library and to Rachel Misrati, who was phenomenally helpful. The assistance of other archives and archivists was also invaluable: the Sir Ellice Victor Elias Sassoon Papers and Photographs at the Southern Methodist University, Dallas, and the archivist, Anne Peterson; The Rothschild Archive, London, and its archivist, Melanie Aspey; and the Collection of Kenneth and Joyce Robbins, and its owner, Ken, who has been extremely generous with his time and knowledge. Other archives and libraries were instrumental as well in making the book possible: Babylonian Jewry Heritage Center Archives (Tel Aviv); Brighton and Hove Archives; British Library (London); British National Archives (London); China Association Papers (School of Oriental and African Studies, University of London); Church of England Archives (London); Indian National Archives (Delhi); Kadoorie Archives (Hong Kong); Metropolitan Archives (London); Otto-

man Archives (Istanbul); Shanghai Municipal Archives—and to all of them
I am truly grateful.

A number of wonderful assistants helped me along this long road. I was
extremely fortunate to have met Doron Goldstein, a true polymath who
proved a genius at decoding every letter and article and assisted me in deci-
phering the handwriting and some of the jargon in thousands of documents
in the David Sassoon Archives. He is fluent in Hebrew, and his knowledge
of Arabic and its different dialects, as well as of Persian and Turkish, was
priceless. Benan Grams and Fatih Çalışır helped with the Ottoman Archives
and Turkish manuscripts, and Yaqiong Wang with the Shanghai Municipal Archives. In Washington, D.C., Rebecca Murphy worked with me in
gathering much of the data and scouring newspapers, and Kaylee Steck was
not only a great researcher but showed organizational skills and a depth of
knowledge about the material that were simply astonishing; without Kaylee,
it is doubtful I would have been able to master the immense amount of
information collected for this book. She also helped me with sketching the
family trees, with maps of Bombay and Shanghai, and with the initial search
for pictures. Lauren Stricker indexed many documents and other material to
make everything more accessible while I was writing. Sydney Roeder helped
in later stages of editing.

In some places, locals who became friends offered me information. Simin
Patel in Mumbai, an expert on the city, aided me with some of the locations
and put me in touch with people who knew about the Sassoons. Kayan
Ghyara in Pune provided me with details of the Sassoons' properties in
the city. Cyrus Patel and Nevil Patel not only helped me with my research
in Mahabaleshwar, but thanks to their wonderful hospitality I spent three
nights at beautiful Glenogle (the Sassoons' house in the mountains), a stunning location—it was an incredible experience to be in the place where some
of the main characters in this book spent part of the year. In New Delhi, Max
Rodenbeck and his wife, Karima Khalil, were fantastic hosts while I stayed
in their house; and Max joined me on my first trip to Mahabaleshwar. In
Shanghai, my nephew, Omer, who lived in China at the time, accompanied
me to all the Sassoon buildings; and the staff at what is now the Fairmont
Peace Hotel (premises owned by the Sassoons in the 1930s) were most welcoming and even provided me with plans of the building and books about
its history. In Dallas, I had the pleasure of dining with Evelyn Cox (niece
of Barnsie, Victor's wife), who shared with me what Victor Sassoon meant
to her family during the times they spent with him in Dallas, England, and
the Bahamas.

Virginia Myers helped with editing in the first phases of the manuscript.

Some members of the Sassoon "clan" supplied me with incredible pictures, letters, and an extensive family tree: Sybil Sassoon, Hugh Sassoon, Joanna Sassoon (Perth), and Edwina Sassoon (London). I also discussed the topic a number of times with James Sassoon (London), who made useful suggestions and recounted family stories.

I am deeply indebted to many friends and colleagues who offered much support and insight, and read parts of the manuscript: John McNeill, Charles King, William Clarence Smith, Diana Kim, Stefan Eich, Paul French, Harold James, Nancy Berg, Kevin O'Rourke, Zvi Ben-Dor, and Emma Rothschild. Eugene Rogan, Richard Ovenden, and Dina Khoury have been wonderful with their advice, encouragement, and friendship, as they were for previous books. John Makinson gave me invaluable advice and suggested sending a proposal to Penguin that ended up being this book. Once again, I discussed the text and expressed my satisfaction or frustration at every stage of research and writing with my childhood friend Terry Somekh. Evan Osnos, who knows China well, introduced me to people who lived or live in Shanghai and was most supportive of the project. With Robert Worth, I bounced around many ideas about the writing of the text. To all those friends and colleagues, a million thanks.

I would also like to express my deepest appreciation to the different institutions that invited me to talk about the book or aspects of it. I greatly benefited from the comments and questions raised by the academics and audiences who engaged with this research: Princeton Workshop of Telling Histories of Families; Harvard Business School; Jewish Country Houses at the Modern Jewish History Seminar, Oxford University (run by Professor Abigail Green); Peking University Middle East Seminar; Brandeis University; the Jewish Museum in London; St. Antony's College, Oxford; and, last but not least, my home university, Georgetown, where I gave two talks over the last four years at the superb history department and where my brilliant colleagues read and commented on every phrase, as well as the Center for Contemporary Arab Studies, which has been my immediate home for more than a decade. I thank all my friends and colleagues at the center and at Georgetown University. I had the good luck of being a fellow at the Katz Center for Jewish Studies at the University of Pennsylvania, which allowed me to write and exchange ideas and create friendships with fellows there.

I am much beholden to Stuart Proffitt from Penguin Random House, who championed the idea for this book when it was just a proposal, and Ben Sinyor, also from Penguin, who accompanied the manuscript from the start, edited this book, and discussed every word. At Pantheon, I am indebted to Victoria Wilson, who is a force of nature, for her support and encouragement for this book. My thanks also to her assistant, Marc Jaffee. My agent, Felicity Bryan, was an incredible woman who offered her advice even during her illness and in the last few weeks of her life. I am fortunate that her colleague Catherine Clark took over the project, and she has been a staunch advocate from day one. Cecilia Mackay has been most helpful with all the images in this book, a huge task indeed.

My family has remained as supportive of me as ever in more ways than one: my ninety-six-year-old mother (Victoria) kept an eye on what I was doing until she passed away In February 2022. She was a truly remarkable woman and the family's grandchildren gave her the title Queen Victoria. My daughter, Rachel, contributed by reading a number of chapters and commenting on them; her husband, Daniel, also read parts of the manuscript and shared some interesting insights. But my greatest support has been the same person who has accompanied me at every stage of my last three books: Helen Jackson not only was my true partner throughout these years of research and writing but joined me on a trip to India and gave me invaluable help in my research in London and Jerusalem. It is hard to imagine that I would have been able to do all this without her.

Finally, in the last three years, a new person entered my life: my granddaughter, Aya, to whom this book is dedicated. Her laughter and smiles melted my heart and made me forget all the difficulties of the book and the pandemic. I call her my *fidwa,* a term of endearment in Baghdadi dialect that can be freely translated as "someone whom you love so much, you are willing to sacrifice your life for them." So, thank you, *fidwa,* for all the pleasure and joy you have brought into my life.

APPENDIX

Value of Indian rupee (₹) in British pounds sterling (GBP) and United States dollars (USD), 1850–1910

Year	GBP/INR	USD/INR	GBP/USD
1850	£1 = ₹9.88	$1 = ₹2.02	£1 = $4.87
1855	£1 = ₹9.92	$1 = ₹2.02	£1 = $4.89
1860	£1 = ₹9.23	$1 = ₹1.90	£1 = $4.85
1865	£1 = ₹9.74	$1 = ₹2.27	£1 = $7.69
1870	£1 = ₹10.49	$1 = ₹1.88	£1 = $5.59
1875	£1 = ₹11.07	$1 = ₹1.98	£1 = $5.59
1880	£1 = ₹12.02	$1 = ₹2.48	£1 = $4.85
1885	£1 = ₹12.96	$1 = ₹2.67	£1 = $4.86
1890	£1 = ₹13.14	$1 = ₹2.79	£1 = $4.86
1895	£1 = ₹17.78	$1 = ₹3.64	£1 = $4.89
1900	£1 = ₹15.00	$1 = ₹3.09	£1 = $4.86
1905	£1 = ₹9.75	$1 = ₹2.00	£1 = $4.86
1910	£1 = ₹9.52	$1 = ₹1.96	£1 = $4.86

Sources: A. Piatt Andrew, "Indian Currency Problems of the Last Decade," *Quarterly Journal of Economics* 15, no. 4 (1901): 483–516; Stefan Eiich, "The Problem of the Rupee," in *The Cambridge Companion to Ambedkar*, eds. Anupama Rao and Shailaja Paik; Brij Narain, "Exchange and Prices in India, 1873–1924," *Weltwirtschaftliches Archiv* 23 (1926): 247–92.

NOTES

PREFACE

xvi Following the advice: Robert A. Caro, *Working: Researching, Interviewing, Writing* (New York: Alfred A. Knopf, 2019), 141.

xviii In it he charts: Thomas Mann, *Buddenbrooks: The Decline of a Family*, trans. John E. Woods (New York: Vintage, 1994). The novel is regarded as Mann's greatest work and was cited as one of the main reasons for his winning the Nobel Prize in Literature in 1929.

1. BAGHDAD BEGINNINGS, 1802–1830

3 He traveled through: Walter J. Fischel, ed., *Unknown Jews in Unknown Lands: The Travels of Rabbi David D'Beth Hillel (1824–1832)* (New York: Ktav Publishing, 1973), 11.

3 He spent a whole: Fischel, *Unknown Jews in Unknown Lands*, 82–83.

4 Its reputation for: J. R. Wellsted, *Travels to the City of the Caliphs Along the Shores of the Persian Gulf and the Mediterranean* (Philadelphia: Lea & Blanchard, 1841), 176.

4 The incessant conflicts: Bruce Masters, *The Arabs of the Ottoman Empire, 1516–1918: A Social and Cultural History* (New York: Cambridge University Press, 2013), 30–33.

5 There were thriving: Bruce Masters, *Christians and Jews in the Ottoman Arab World: The Roots of Sectarianism* (Cambridge: Cambridge University Press, 2001), 48.

5 A later traveler: Wellsted, *Travels to the City of the Caliphs*, 178.

5 He went on to develop: David Solomon Sassoon, *A History of the Jews in Baghdad* (1949; repr., London: Simon Wallenberg Press, 2007), 123–24.

6 Many honors were: Naim Dangoor, "The New Ottoman Empire," *Scribe* 29 (October 1988): 4–5.

6 Such Jews were: Fischel, ed., *Unknown Jews in Unknown Lands*, 83.

6 It was a position: Avraham Ben-Yacov, *Perakim Be-Toldot Yehudei Babel* [Treatise in the History of Babylonian Jewry] (Jerusalem: Olam Ha-Sefer, 1989), 1:20.

6 This system of two: Nabil al-Rubai'i, *Tarikh Yehud al-Iraq* [The History of Iraq's Jews] (Beirut: al-Rafidain, 2017), 107–10.

6 One gentile traveler: Wellsted, *Travels to the City of the Caliphs*, vol. 1, 277.

7 This delicate balancing: Marion Woolfson, *Prophets in Babylon: Jews in the Arab World* (London: Faber & Faber, 1980), 89.

7 He grew up in: Ben-Yacov, *Perakim Be-Toldot Yehudei Babel*, 22.

7 Sassoon was known: Ben-Yacov, *Perakim Be-Toldot Yehudei Babel*, 22.

7 Sassoon was by this: Justin Marozzi, *Baghdad: City of Peace, City of Blood— A History in Thirteen Centuries* (London: Da Capo Press, 2014), 226.

8 The sheer pace: Tom Nieuwenhuis, *Politics and Society in Early Modern Iraq: Mamluk Pashas, Tribal Shayks and Local Rule Between 1801 and 1831* (The Hague: Martinus Nijhoff, 1981), Appendix 1.

8 Sa'id Pasha was in control: Nieuwenhuis, *Politics and Society in Early Modern Iraq*, 18–22.

8 A talented writer: Stephen Hemsley Longrigg, *Four Centuries of Modern Iraq* (Oxford: Clarendon Press, 1925), 239.

8 Ezra in turn: Zvi Yehuda, *The New Babylonian Diaspora: The Rise and Fall of the Jewish Community in Iraq, 16th–20th Centuries C.E.* (Leiden: Brill, 2017), 138.

8 Shortly after Dawud: Ben-Yacov, *Perakim Be-Toldot Yehudei Babel*, 22.

8 It was a neat echo: Ben-Yacov, *Perakim Be-Toldot Yehudei Babel*, 22.

9 A British political agent: Political agent in Turkish Arabia to Bombay, October 13, 1817, papers relating to the political situation in the Pashaliq of Baghdad, British Library, IOR/F/4/574/14025.

9 The British had other: See, for example, Abdul Aziz Nawwar, *Dawud Pasha: Wali Baghdad* [Dawud Pasha: Governor of Baghdad] (Cairo: Dar al-Katib, 1967), 327–29.

9 Even Dawud's closest: Political agent in Turkish Arabia to Bombay, March 11, 1818, papers relating to the political situation in the Pashaliq of Baghdad, British Library, IOR/F/4/574/14025.

9 Dawud was supported: Nieuwenhuis, *Politics and Society*, 92.

10 In reality, greed: Anthony N. Groves, *Journal of a Residence at Bagdad: During the Years 1830 and 1831* (London: James Nisbet, 1831), 285.

10 When some of Baghdad's: Nawwar, *Dawud Pasha*, 139–40.

10 Between them, "this": Sassoon, *A History of the Jews in Baghdad*, 124–25.

10 Unable to face life: Sassoon, *A History of the Jews in Baghdad*, 125.

11 It was sage: Sassoon, *A History of the Jews in Baghdad,* 125.

11 Violence in the province: Nieuwenhuis, *Politics and Society,* 96.

11 The Pasha cordially. Mehdi Jawad Habib al-Bustani, *Bağdad'daki Kölemen Hâkimiyetinin Te'sisi ve Kaldırılması ile Ali Rıza Paşa'nın Vâliliği (1749–1842)* [The Establishment and Decline of the Mamluk Rule in Baghdad and the Governorship of Ali Rıza Pasha (1749–1842)] (PhD dissertation, Istanbul University Faculty of Literature, 1979), 82–83.

11 "danger was balanced": Longrigg, *Four Centuries of Modern Iraq,* 263.

11 He initially sought: Al-Bustani, *Bağdad'daki Kölemen,* 83.

12 The city went into: Journal of Major R. Taylor, British political agent in Basra, October 6, 1831, papers relating to the political situation in the Pashaliq of Baghdad, British Library, IOR/F/4/1455/57333. The journal describes the events of June 9, 1831.

12 At the height of: Longrigg, *Four Centuries of Modern Iraq,* 265; Marozzi, *Baghdad: City of Peace,* 234–35.

12 One English traveler: Wellsted, *Travels to the City of the Caliphs,* 205.

13 One local depicted: Hatt-i Hümayun [Imperial Decrees] (hereafter cited as HAT), April 30, 1831, 00462_22645_E_001, Ottoman Archives.

13 Another reported that: HAT, June 12, 1831, 0046 2 2 2645_D_001, Ottoman Archives.

13 It was estimated: Charles Issawi, *The Fertile Crescent, 1800–1914: A Documentary Economic History* (Oxford: Oxford University Press, 1988), 104. These estimates differ from Wellsted, but the real population of the city was most likely around eighty thousand, dwindling to fifty thousand.

13 The Pasha and his: Longrigg, *Four Centuries of Modern Iraq,* 266.

13 According to one: HAT, May 11, 1831, 0046 222642_A_001, Ottoman Archives.

13 Another informed the: HAT, September 3, 1831, 00404 21157_C_002, Ottoman Archives.

13 Constantinople sought to: HAT, October 20, 1831, 00389_20705_C_001, Ottoman Archives.

14 The investigation generated: Al-Bustani, *Bağdad'daki Kölemen,* 154–55.

14 In an extraordinary: Longrigg, *Four Centuries of Modern Iraq,* 274.

14 Eight decades after: Sir Edward Sassoon, "The Orient," a lecture given on November 16, 1907, *Israel's Messenger,* February 7, 1908, 9.

14 In a letter to one: David Sassoon (London) to Mr. Rothschild (not clear whom), March 13, 1917, Rothschild Archive.

2. EXILE AND A NEW LIFE, 1831–1839

17 Rabbi Hillel described: Fischel, ed., *Unknown Jews in Unknown Lands,* 118.

18 Already by 1794: Sharada Dwivedi and Rahul Mehotra, *Bombay: The Cities Within* (Mumbai: India Book House, 1995), 28.

19 As the historian: William Dalrymple, *The Anarchy: The Relentless Rise of the East India Company* (New York: Bloomsbury Publishing, 2019), 394.

19 Already in the early: Dalrymple, *Anarchy,* 13–14.

19 The East India Company's: C. A. Bayly, *Indian Society and the Making of British Empire* (Cambridge: Cambridge University Press, 1990), 106.

19 While Bombay boomed: Amar Farooqi, *Opium City: The Making of Early Victorian Bombay* (New Delhi: Three Essays, 2006), 9.

19 British monetary policy: Stefan Eich, "The Problem of the Rupee," in *The Cambridge Companion to Ambedkar,* ed. Anupama Rao and Shailaja Paik (Cambridge: Cambridge University Press, forthcoming).

20 These agency houses: Geoffrey Jones, *Merchants to Multinationals: British Trading Companies in the Nineteenth and Twentieth Centuries* (New York: Oxford University Press, 2000), 227.

20 Sometimes there were: See, for example, letter from Hong Kong to Shanghai, May 9, 1861, David Sassoon Archives, National Library, Jerusalem (hereafter cited as DSA), 1808, and from London to Shanghai, September 9, 1864, DSA, 1862.

20 Economic growth drew: Mariam Dossal, *Imperial Designs and India Realities: The Planning of Bombay City, 1845–1875* (Bombay: Oxford University Press, 1991), 22.

20 Jardine had since: Freda Harcourt, "Black Gold: P & O and the Opium Trade, 1847–1914," *International Journal of Maritime History* 6, no. 1 (June 1994): 18–19 (article 1–83).

21 Jejeebhoy was famous: Jesse S. Palsetia, *Jamsetjee Jejeebhoy of Bombay: Partnership and Public Culture in Empire* (New Delhi: Oxford University Press, 2015), 7.

22 Only in 1841: Cecil Roth, *The Sassoon Dynasty* (1941; repr., New York: Arno Press, 1977), 44.

22 The first mention of: *The Bombay Times and Journal of Commerce,* November 18, 1843, 739.

22 We do not: *Bombay Times and Journal of Commerce,* October 16, 1844, 663.

22 This mix made for: Tristram Hunt, *Ten Cities That Made an Empire* (London: Penguin Books, 2015), 273.

23 The first of these: Walter J. Fischel, "Bombay in Jewish History in the Light of New Documents from the Indian Archives," *Proceedings of the American Academy for Jewish Research* 38/39 (1970–71): 119–44.

23 When he visited: Fischel, ed., *Unknown Jews in Unknown Lands,* 119–20.

23 By the early 1830s: Joan G. Roland, *Jews in British India: Identity in a Colonial Era* (Hanover: Published for Brandeis University Press by University Press of New England, 1989), 16.

23 Although Baghdadis made: Ben-Yacov, *Perakim Be-Toldot Yehudei Babel,* 52.

24 He was quick to: Roth, *Sassoon Dynasty,* 55.

24 The two met soon: Roth, *Sassoon Dynasty,* 63. See also George Smith, *The Life of John Wilson: For Fifty Years Philanthropist and Scholar in the East* (London: John Murray, 1878).

25 Bombay Education Society: Govind Narayan, *Mumbai: An Urban Biography from 1863,* ed. and trans. Murali Ranganathan (London: Anthem Press, 2009), 5.

26 Britain imposed English: Anil Seal, *The Emergence of Indian Nationalism: Competition and Collaboration in the Later Nineteenth Century* (Cambridge: Cambridge University Press, 1971), 31.

26 He explained, with: Abraham Shalom Sassoon, "Essay on the Present War," November 27, 1855, DSA, 1543. Russia lost the Crimean War to an alliance of Britain, France, the Kingdom of Sardinia, and the Ottoman Empire.

27 Suleiman had written to: David (Bombay) to Suleiman (Hong Kong), June 2, 1856, DSA, 1551.

27 One month later, David: David (Bombay) to Suleiman (Hong Kong), July 2, 1856, DSA, 1555.

27 From another young: Solomon Ezekiel (Canton) to Solomon (Bombay), July 14, 1856, DSA, box 8, 1558.

27 It's easy to imagine: *Bombay Times and Journal of Commerce,* August 4, 1852, 501.

27 No wonder Jejeebhoy: Quoted in Stanley Jackson, *The Sassoons* (New York: E. P. Dutton, 1968), 32.

28 The final leg of: Abraham Shalom (Arthur), journal account of journey from Canton to London, 1855, DSA, box 8, 1540.

29 Aharon, the only of David's: Aaron Sassoon to Flora (wife of S.D. Sassoon), June 19, 1859, DSA, 1697.

3. WARS AND OPPORTUNITIES, 1839–1857

31 But it was outsiders: John F. Richards, "The Indian Empire and Peasant Production of Opium in the Nineteenth Century," *Modern Asian Studies* 15, no. 1 (1981): 59–82.

31 Opium was priced: Harcourt, "Black Gold," 18.

31 This practice came: Richards, "Indian Empire," 63–64.

31 The opium trade became: Richards, "Indian Empire," 66. Opium revenues were about 7 million rupees out of a total of 112 million rupees in 1839–40.

32 Opium constituted an: Weimin Zhong, "The Roles of Tea and Opium in Early Economic Globalization: A Perspective on China's Crisis in the 19th Century," *Frontiers of History in China* 5, no. 1 (March 2010): 186–205.

32 To fend off these: Peter Ward Fay, *The Opium War, 1840–1842* (Chapel Hill: University of North Carolina Press, 1975), 58–59.

32 For the farmers: Nathan Allen, *An Essay on the Opium Trade* (Boston: John Jewett, 1850), 8.

32 The number of merchants: Anthony Webster, "The Political Economy of Trade Liberalization: The East India Company Charter Act of 1813," *Economic History Review* 43, no. 3 (1990): 404–19.

33 Even the fastest clippers: Harcourt, "Black Gold," 9.

33 Crewed by "seamen": Hunt Janin, *The India-China Opium Trade in the Nineteenth Century* (Jefferson, NC: McFarland & Company, 1999), 75.

34 (One source, writing): Narayan, *Mumbai,* 354.

34 As this was beyond: Harcourt, "Black Gold," 7.

34 The same year: Harcourt, "Black Gold," 24.

35 P & O was given: Michael Pearson, *The Indian Ocean* (London: Routledge, 2003), 203.

35 The new steam carriers: Harcourt, "Black Gold," 12. Harcourt's article has the most detailed research about the P & O and opium.

35 "As long as their": Montono Eiichi, "A Study of the Legal Status of the Compradores During the 1880s with Special Reference to the Three Civil Cases Between David Sassoon Sons & Co. and Their Compradors, 1884–1887," *Acta Asiatica* 62 (1992): 45 (article 44–70).

36 It was a sign: *Bombay Times and Journal of Commerce,* November 10, 1852, 723.

36 (On the list of): Export Manifest, November 15, 1854, *Bombay Times and Journal of Commerce,* December 2, 1854, 4838; Import Manifest, *Bombay Times and Journal of Commerce,* May 13, 1853, 910.

37 Cargo traveling by: See, for instance, a letter from London, September 21, 1865, about a sunken ship, DSA, 1921, and a letter about a fire from Hong Kong, August 20, 1867, DSA, 3454.

37 Steamships were not: Reuben David Sassoon (Pune) to his brother Suleiman (Shanghai), August 12, 1866, DSA, 1986.

37 In one such instance: Abraham Shalom Sassoon (Calcutta) to Mordechai Gabbay (Shanghai), February 25, 1868, DSA, 2083. Gabbay was a relative and an employee of the firm.

37 The different Sassoon: See, for example, a letter from Shanghai to Hong

Kong, September 4, 1866, DSA, 717. It should be noted that many of these letters had on the top of the paper the information about which steamship carried the letter. In this case, it was sent with a steamship called *Genghis*.

37 One letter records: Abraham Shalom Sassoon (Hong Kong) to his brother Suleiman (Shanghai), July 24, 1865, DSA, 3553.

37 Another, from a different: Captain Vincent to S.D. Sassoon, September 19, 1861, DSA, file 9, 1833.

38 These years saw: Tom G. Kessinger, "Regional Economy (1757–1857): North India" in Dharma Kumar and Meghdad Desai, eds., *Cambridge Economic History of India*, vol. 2, *1757–2003* (Delhi: Orient Longman, 2005), 261.

38 India was gaining: Marika Vicziany, "Bombay Merchants and Structural Changes in the Export Community 1850 to 1880," in Asiya Siddiqi, ed., *Trade and Finance in Colonial India, 1750–1860* (Delhi: Oxford University Press, 1995), 345–82.

38 Joint stock enterprises: Radhe Shyam Rungta, *The Rise of Business Corporations in India, 1851–1900* (London: Cambridge University Press, 1970), 46.

38 In some parts of: P. M. Dalzell (deputy collector of customs), *Memoranda on the External Trade of Sind for 1857–58* (Karachi: Sindian Press, 1858).

38 were the prime movers: Asiya Siddiqi, "Introduction," in Siddiqi, ed., *Trade and Finance in Colonial India*, 30.

38 Powerful trade circles: Sven Beckert, *Empire of Cotton: A Global History* (New York: Alfred A. Knopf, 2014), 124–25. Beckert's book provides a comprehensive history of cotton.

39 In the 1850s: Young Sassoon David Sassoon (London) to Suleiman Sassoon (Shanghai), July 26, 1864, DSA, 1855. The son of David Sassoon who carried his name always signed as Young Sassoon David Sassoon to differentiate himself from his father. Later, he became known as S.D.

39 Prime Minister, Robert Peel: Gijsbert Oonk, "Motor or Millstone? The Managing Agency System in Bombay and Ahmedabad, 1850–1930," in *Indian Economic and Social History Review* 38, no. 4 (2001): fn. 16, 424–25 (article 419–52). Debates on this question continued over the next two decades. See House of Commons debates, June 19, 1862, *Hansard* 167: 754–93, and June 29, 1865, *Hansard* 180: 927–63.

39 By the following decade: Morris D. Morris, "The Growth of Large-Scale Industry to 1947," in *The Cambridge Economic History of India*, vol. 2, *1757–2003*, ed. Dharma Kumar (Delhi: Orient Longman, 2005), 565 (article 553–676). Morris emphasizes that Indian entrepreneurs began utilizing legal contracts for their trades.

39 The Sassoons, still: N. Benjamin, "Industrialization of Bombay: Role of the Parsis and the Jews," *Proceedings of the Indian History Congress* 61, part 1 (2000–2001): 871–87.

40 When informing one: David (Bombay) to Suleiman (Hong Kong), May 13, 1859, DSA, 1687.

41 The board of each: See minutes of the board of David Sassoon Industrial and Reformatory School, Public (Education) Dispatch to the Government of Bombay, July 22, 1857, *East India (Education) Correspondence*, 644.

41 In keeping with: Public (Education) Dispatch to the Government of Bombay, no. 10, November 4, 1858, *East India (Education) Correspondence*.

41 Jamsetjee Tata, a pioneer industrialist, was: Mircea Raianu, *Tata: The Global Corporation That Built Indian Capitalism* (Cambridge, MA: Harvard University Press, 2021).

41 The family's philanthropic: *Report of the Agri-Horticultural Society for the Year 1863*, 19 and 25.

42 As a merchant, he: John Darwin, *The Empire Project: The Rise and Fall of the British World-System, 1830–1970* (Cambridge: Cambridge University Press, 2009), 2.

42 His interests aligned: *Illustrated London News*, May 24, 1851.

42 Three years later: Ben-Yacov, *Perakim Be-Toldot Yehudei Babel*, 59.

42 The *Bombay Almanac: The Bombay Calendar and Almanac for 1855*, 244; *The Bombay Calendar and Almanac for 1855*, 375.

42 A traveler to Bombay: Ben-Yacov, *Perakim Be-Toldot Yehudei Babel*, quoting the traveler Yacov Sapir, 58.

42 One British official: Richard Temple, *Men and Events of My Time in India* (London: John Murray, 1882), 260. Sir Bartle Frere was Chief Commissioner of the Sind between 1850 and 1859. For his suppression of the 1857 Indian Rebellion he was given a knighthood. He was Governor of Bombay from 1862 to 1874.

43 When he purchased: *Allen's Indian Mail and Register for British and Foreign India, China, and All Parts of the East*, 1851, 646.

43 One newspaper, describing: *Bombay Times and Journal of Commerce*, February 25, 1852, 133.

43 Another newspaper commented: *Allen's Indian Mail*, 1852, 296.

44 Observant Jews could: See picture from the Collection of Kenneth and Joyce Robbins. The Bombay Tram Company was set up in 1873 and the first horse-drawn carriage made its debut in 1874.

45 Even as China's sovereignty: Stephen R. Halsey, *Quest for Power: European Imperialism and the Making of Chinese Statecraft* (Cambridge, MA: Harvard University Press, 2015), 81.

45 It has been argued: Julia Lovell, *The Opium War: Drugs, Dreams and the Making of China* (London: Picador, 2011), 252.

45 Whether legalization actually: Chris Feige and Jeffrey A. Miron, "The Opium Wars, Opium Legalization and Opium Consumption in China," *Applied Economic Letters* 15, no. 12 (2008): 913 (article 911–13).

45 The British Ambassador: Quoted in Martin Booth, *Opium: A History* (New York: St. Martin's Griffin, 1996), 145.

45 The opium business: Farooqi, *Opium City,* 17.

45 Whether or not opium: "The Opium Wars: Memories and Hallucinations," *Economist,* December 23, 2017, 38–41.

46 One senior British official: Samuel Laing (Financial Minister in India from 1860 and on the Council of the Governor-General), quoted in Temple, *Men and Events,* 220.

46 To quell the revolt: Metcalf and Metcalf, *A Concise History of India,* 103.

46 and between rebellion: Metcalf and Metcalf, *A Concise History of India,* 106.

47 At the apex of: Seal, *Emergence of Indian Nationalism,* 1–7.

47 According to a journalist's: *Illustrated London News,* December 5, 1863, 569.

47 The Sassoons' ascent: Frank Trentmann, *Free Trade Nation* (New York: Oxford University Press, 2008), 3.

4. BRANCHING OUT, 1858–1864

48 Frederick's palace was: Roth, *Sassoon Dynasty,* 84.

49 "It would be used": Jackson, *Sassoons,* 32.

49 "After complimenting Mr.": *Illustrated London News,* April 23, 1859, 403.

49 A rabbi from Palestine: Rabbi Jacob Sappir, translation from *Eben Sappir,* vol. 2, chapter 11. Notes of the translation are in DSA, box 35.

50 Obvious traces of the: Shaul Sapir, *Bombay: Exploring the Jewish Urban Heritage* (Mumbai: Bene Israel Heritage Museum and Genealogical Research Centre, 2013), 183.

50 When, six weeks after: Circular to chambers of commerce, March 26, 1859, *Parliamentary Papers,* 13–14.

51 He loved writing: Michael Dane, *The Sassoons of Ashley Park* (Walton-on-Thames: Michael Dane, 1999), 15.

52 The historian Sugata Bose: Sugata Bose, *A Hundred Horizons: The Indian Ocean in the Age of Global Empire* (Cambridge, MA: Harvard University Press, 2006), 28.

52 He argues that: Bose, *A Hundred Horizons,* 74.

53 The government of India: Rolf Bauer, *The Peasant Production of Opium in Nineteenth-Century India,* vol. 12, *Library of Economic History* (Bos-

ton: Brill, 2019), 64. Bauer presents details of how the opium system functioned.

53 Opium was by far: Ernest O. Hauser, *Shanghai: City for Sale* (New York: Harcourt, Brace, 1940), 72.

53 It has been argued: Carl A. Trocki, *Opium, Empire and the Global Political Economy: A Study of the Asian Opium Trade, 1750–1950* (New York: Routledge, 1999), xiii.

53 A recent empirical: Bauer, *Peasant Production of Opium*, 193.

54 "The true advantages": Richards, "Indian Empire," 79.

54 In a letter from: Abdallah (Pune) to Mordechai Nissim (Abu Shahir), 1868 (no specific date on the letter), DSA, 2159. This is a case where an employee rather than a family member was in charge of a small branch. The source of opium in Persia for the Sassoons was one of the large landowners, Agha Muhammad Ali.

54 The report indicated: *Report of the Bombay Chamber of Commerce for the Year 1868–69* (Bombay: Education Society's Press, 1870), 325.

54 The Chinese insisted: Trocki, *Opium, Empire and the Global Political Economy*, 42–43.

54 Pitfalls were everywhere: *National China Herald*, September 17, 1859, 27.

55 The judge ruled: *National China Herald*, September 17, 1859, 27.

55 Furthermore, foreign traders: Halsey, *Quest for Power*, 55.

55 In a memo to: Hannah Mordechai Gabbay (Shanghai) to Suleiman (Hong Kong), August 26, 1869, DSA, 2914.

56 Shanghai was sitting: Mordechai Gabbay (Shanghai) to Suleiman (Hong Kong), August 30, 1869, DSA, 2920.

56 as well as the prospect: Mordechai Gabbay (Shanghai) to Suleiman (Hong Kong), August 26, 1869, DSA, 2916.

56 It became increasingly: Mordechai Gabbay (Shanghai) to Suleiman (Hong Kong), September 2, 1869, DSA, 2926.

56 Despite Mordechai's misgivings: Mordechai Gabbay (Shanghai) to Suleiman (Hong Kong), September 10, 1869, DSA, 2931.

56 the strike was officially: Mordechai Gabbay (Shanghai) to Suleiman (Hong Kong), September 14, 1869, DSA, 2933.

56 When P & O arrived: Harcourt, "Black Gold," 52.

56 One method of gaining: *London and China Telegraph*, February 16, 1864, 85.

56 One was to abstain: Aharon Moshe Gabbay (Bombay) to Suleiman (Hong Kong), March 12, 1872, DSA, 635.

56 Another was to wait: Memo from A. M. Gabbay (Bombay) to Abdallah (Pune), July 7, 1872, DSA, box 12.

56 Similarly, when their: Memo from A. M. Gabbay (Bombay) to Abdallah (Pune), August 29, 1872, DSA, box 12.

57 Abdallah, David's second: As seen in a letter from Abdallah (Pune) to Suleiman (Hong Kong) about trading tactics, September 20, 1872, DSA, box 12.

57 One of his sons: *Bombay Times and Journal of Commerce,* May 22, 1858, 405; *Bombay Times and Journal of Commerce,* June 11, 1859, 375.

58 Even before entering: *London and China Telegraph,* September 27, 1865, 510. All the directors were Europeans.

58 Sassoon declared an interest: MacDonald Stephenson, *Railways in China: Report upon the Feasibility and Most Effectual Means of Introducing Railway Communication into the Empire of China* (London: J. E. Adlard, 1864), 43.

58 The average British worker: Alan Macfarlane and Iris Macfarlane, *The Empire of Tea: The Remarkable History of the Plant That Took Over the World* (New York: The Overlook Press, 2004), 179.

59 It was argued that: Zhong, "Roles of Tea and Opium in Early Economic Globalization," 89.

59 The House of London: Sassoon David Sassoon (London) to his brother Suleiman (Shanghai), August 26, 1864, DSA, 1861.

59 "Dr Juna came": Abraham Shalom Sassoon (Hong Kong) to his brother Suleiman (Shanghai), October 18, 1864, DSA, 3471.

59 It seems that Dr. Juna: Sassoon David Sassoon (London) to his brother Suleiman (Shanghai), February 10, 1865, DSA, 1884.

59 Sometimes, when tea: Sassoon David Sassoon (London) to his brother Suleiman (Shanghai), January 29, 1865, DSA, 1881.

59 A letter from Shanghai: Mordechai Gabbay (Shanghai) to Suleiman (Hong Kong), April 1, 1868, DSA, 2115.

59 A report by an: Employee [full name faded] (Shanghai) to Abraham Shalom (Bombay), September 24, 1868, DSA, box 8B, 7082.

60 Such awareness of: Young Sassoon David Sassoon (London) to his brother Suleiman (Shanghai), April 26, 1865, DSA, 1896.

60 In 1865, an English: Sassoon David Sassoon (London) to Suleiman (Shanghai), February 10, 1865, DSA, 1884.

60 It may be thanks: Sassoon David Sassoon (London) to Suleiman (Shanghai), January 29, 1865, DSA, 1881.

60 Rice followed the same: Abraham Shalom Sassoon (Arthur) from Hong Kong to Suleiman (Shanghai), October 5, 1864, DSA, 3467.

60 As with opium: Abraham Shalom Sassoon (Arthur) to Suleiman (Shanghai), December 28, 1864, DSA, 3492. For another letter documenting

clearly the arbitrage conducted between different locations, see: December 8, 1864, DSA, 3487.

60 Many years later: *Annual Report of the Department of Agriculture in Sind, 1932–33,* 4.

61 Although its focus: Abdallah (Pune) to Eli Shalom Gabbay (an employee in Calcutta), October 26, 1868, DSA, 1365.

61 Unscrupulous agents would: Abraham Shalom David Sassoon (Hong Kong) to his brother Suleiman (Shanghai), November 19, 1864, DSA, 3481.

61 When one such shipment: Young David Sassoon (London) to his brother Suleiman (Shanghai), August 18, 1865, DSA, 1867.

61 Agha Muhammad Ali: Abdallah (Pune) to Reuben (Hong Kong), September 6, 1867, DSA, 3450. For Agha Muhammad's declaration, see Reuben (Hong Kong) to Abdallah (Bombay), May 30, 1867, DSA, 3463.

61 Abdallah encouraged Reuben: Abdallah (Pune) to Reuben (Hong Kong), September 6, 1867, DSA, 3450.

61 An instruction from: Abraham Shalom Sassoon (Hong Kong) to Suleiman (Shanghai), September 25, 1864, DSA, 3464.

62 We find one of David's: Young David Sassoon (London) to his brother Suleiman (Shanghai), November 4, 1864, DSA, 1874.

62 After Suleiman purchased: David (Bombay) to Suleiman (Shanghai), September 12, 1859, DSA, 1704.

62 Only in regard to: Memorandum to Suleiman, June 28, 1859, DSA, 1699.

63 One such rift had: See, for instance, David's letter of July 29, 1861, to his son in Shanghai, DSA, 1822.

63 One wrote to him: S. Ezekiel (Bombay) to Solomon (Shanghai), September 2, 1858, DSA, file 17, 1650.

63 "Cotton shipments changed": Beckert, *Empire of Cotton,* 249.

63 The price of cotton: Beckert, *Empire of Cotton,* 255.

63 British politicians and: A. C. Brice, *Indian Cotton Supply: The Only Effectual and Permanent Measure for Relief to Lancashire* (London: Smith, Elder and Co., 1863).

64 In the 1860s: From the Bombay Administration Report of 1864–65 and the Indo-European Telegraph Department Administration Report of 1875–76, quoted in Marika Vicziany, "Bombay Merchants and Structural Changes," fn. 49, 370.

64 The telegraph was: See, for example, a complaint from the House of Bombay about two inaccurate telegraphs received from the House of Hong Kong that could have led to unprofitable trades had they not been discovered to be inaccurate, October 11, 1869, DSA, 2964.

64 In one telegram: The telegram is quoted in a letter from the brother

receiving the message in Hong Kong to his brother in Shanghai, October 26, 1864, DSA, 3472.

64 Hong Kong, relaying: October 26, 1864, DSA, 3472.

64 The House of London: See, for instance, the correspondence between Young David Sassoon (London) and his brother Suleiman (Shanghai), September 9, 1864, DSA, 1862.

64 It predicted that: Young David Sassoon (London) to his brother Suleiman (Shanghai), September 26, 1864, DSA, 1867.

65 It was essential: For a detailed analysis of the role of information in capitalism, see Steven G. Marks, *The Information Nexus: Global Capitalism from the Renaissance to the Present* (Cambridge: Cambridge University Press, 2016).

65 As Sven Beckert observes: Beckert, *Empire of Cotton,* 227.

65 The fraternal trust: See, for instance, Hong Kong House complaining to the Shanghai House that their broker did not follow Hong Kong's instructions, October 28, 1864, DSA, 3474.

65 In November 1864: Young Abraham Shalom David Sassoon (Hong Kong) to his brother Suleiman (Shanghai), November 4, 1864, DSA, 3478.

65 Yet only a week later: Abraham (Hong Kong) to Suleiman (Shanghai), November 11, 1864, DSA, 3480.

65 A few weeks later: Abraham (Hong Kong) to Suleiman (Shanghai), January 11, 1865, DSA, 3496.

66 For them, "to be": Roth, *Sassoon Dynasty,* 66.

66 "Since I no longer": Abdallah David Sassoon (Pune) to Suleiman (Hong Kong), November 13, 1867, DSA, 3440.

66 In another instance: DSA, 3474. The quotation referred to was originally in English rather than in their Arabic dialect. In the following decades, more English words written in English crept into the correspondence.

67 In one case: Many documents deal with employees' issues and transfers. See, for instance, DSA, 1910.

68 Though he did not: "Pune Today," *Imperial Gazette of India,* 1886, 214.

69 One competitor summed: Jackson, *Sassoons,* 30.

5. DEATH AND DIVISION, 1864–1867

70 This "venerable head": *The Illustrated London News,* December 10, 1864, 74.

71 The very first sentence: Last Will and Testament of David Sassoon, January 16, 1862, DSA, file 19, 1840.

71 We can say, however: Roth, *Sassoon Dynasty,* 97.

71 He bequeathed the sum: Last Will and Testament of David Sassoon.

72 Abdallah wrote to: Abdallah (Mahabaleshwar) to Suleiman (Shanghai),

November 12, 1865, DSA, box 33b. Mahabaleshwar is a hill station where the Sassoons owned a house.

72 Having settled the personal: Last Will and Testament of David Sassoon.

72 As if anticipating: Last Will and Testament of David Sassoon.

73 Another section aimed: Draft of an agreement between Abdallah and Elias, September 25, 1865, DSA, 1920.

74 Abraham Shalom attributed: Abraham Shalom (Hong Kong) to Suleiman (Shanghai), January 26, 1865, DSA, 3499.

74 Consoling Suleiman: S.D. Sassoon (London) to Suleiman (Shanghai), February 17, 1865, DSA, 1882.

74 In the same letter: Abdallah (Pune) to Suleiman (Shanghai), August 28, 1865, DSA, 3571.

75 Abraham Shalom: Abraham Shalom (Hong Kong) to Suleiman (Shanghai), March 13, 1866, DSA, 1954.

75 and a few months: Abdallah (Bombay) to Suleiman (Shanghai), June 28, 1866, DSA, 1972.

75 *The Illustrated London News*: *Illustrated London News,* July 17, 1869, 76.

75 *The London and China Telegraph*: *London and China Telegraph,* February 22, 1869, 83.

75 More down-to-earth: *Mumbai Magic,* January 14, 2014.

76 As the war in: See, for example, DSA document no. 1882, dated February 1865.

76 By the beginning: Sassoon David Sassoon (London) to his brother Suleiman (Shanghai), April 26, 1865, DSA, 1896; Sassoon to Suleiman, May 10, 1865, DSA, 1898.

76 By the end of: Abraham Shalom David Sassoon (Hong Kong) to his brother Suleiman (Shanghai), June 1865, DSA, 3537. For more details on these bankruptcies, see Stuart Muirhead, *Crisis Banking in the East: The History of Chartered Mercantile Bank of India, London, and China, 1853–93* (Aldershot: Scolar Press, 1996), 68–85.

76 A year later, it: Abdallah (Bombay) to his brother Suleiman (Shanghai), May 29, 1866, DSA, 1963.

76 Abdallah confessed to: Abdallah (Pune) to his brother Suleiman (Shanghai), July 27, 1866, DSA, 1983.

77 S.D. admitted to: Sassoon David Sassoon (London) to his brother Suleiman (Shanghai), May 25, 1865, DSA, 1902.

77 "I am worried": Arthur (Hong Kong) to Suleiman (Shanghai), June 12, 1866, DSA, 1968.

77 The firm was to: David Sassoon & Co. (Bombay) to Solomon (Suleiman) D. Sassoon (Shanghai), March 14, 1866, DSA, box 10, file 39, 3608.

77 At its nadir: Christof Dejung, "Bridges to the East: European Merchants

and Business Practices in India and China," in Robert Lee, ed., *Commerce and Culture: Nineteenth-Century Business Elites* (Farnham: Ashgate, 2011), 102 (article 93–116).

77 Even the bankrupt: Rungta, *Rise of Business Corporations in India*, 73. For a good review of the business corporations before and after the American Civil War, see 46–71, 109–35.

78 After S.D. conducted: Sassoon David Sassoon (London) to his brother Suleiman (Shanghai), August 25, 1865, DSA, 1915; S.D. to Suleiman, October 10, 1865, DSA, 1922. The first letter indicates disquiet about the state of affairs but the second one is much more reassuring.

78 A statement by: "Third Report of the Bank of Hindustan, China, and Japan," *London and China Telegraph*, May 27, 1865, 300. The report indicated that one million sterling of the total capital of four million was called up and paid. Apart from Sassoon David Sassoon, who represented his family, all the other directors were British. The bank was headquartered in London but had branches all over Asia. S.D. joined the board in early 1865. See *London and China Telegraph*, February 28, 1865, 121.

78 Fears of another: David Sassoon & Co. (Bombay) to Abraham Shalom Sassoon (Hong Kong), May 28, 1866, DSA, 1960.

78 Though the stalwarts: Abdallah (Pune) to Reuben (Hong Kong), September 6, 1867, DSA, 3450.

78 It was a serious: Abraham Shalom Sassoon (Hong Kong) to his brother Suleiman (Shanghai), January 6, 1865, DSA, 3494.

78 Abdallah Sassoon: Muirhead, *Crisis Banking in the East*, 169.

78 It was created in: Frank H. H. King, *The History of the Hongkong and Shanghai Banking Corporation*, vol. 1, *The Hongkong Bank in Late Imperial China, 1864–1902* (New York: Cambridge University Press, 1987), 19.

79 When he resigned: King, *History of the Hongkong and Shanghai Banking Corporation*, 1:166–70. The source calls him Solomon, the Anglicized name, but he never changed his name officially.

79 In return, the bank: King, *History of the Hongkong and Shanghai Banking Corporation*, 1:56.

79 As they began to: *London and China Telegraph*, November 15, 1869, 580.

79 Telling Reuben about: Abdallah (Pune) to Reuben (Hong Kong), September 6, 1867, DSA, 3450.

79 Coral was brought: Reuben Sassoon (Shanghai) to his brother Suleiman (Hong Kong), October 28, 1860, DSA, 1780.

80 when they realized: David Sassoon (Pune) to his son Suleiman (Shanghai), August 24, 1864, DSA, 1860.

80 The decline in cotton: Vicziany, "Bombay Merchants and Structural Changes," 368–69.

80 By early 1868: Abraham Shalom David Sassoon (Calcutta) to his brother Suleiman (Hong Kong), February 25, 1868, DSA, 2081. This document reflects how the Sassoons moved around: Abraham was in Hong Kong prior to being based in Calcutta, and Suleiman moved from Shanghai to Hong Kong.

80 The ledgers for opium: See, for example, the accounting ledger for the year 1872.

80 A snippet from: 1870 ledger, DSA.

81 The boundary between: Abdallah (Pune) to his brother Abraham Shalom (Bombay), June 12, 1868, DSA, 2158. Sans Souci was the Sassoons' main house in the neighborhood of Byculla, Bombay.

81 If one brother: Abraham Shalom Sassoon (Hong Kong) to Suleiman (Shanghai), September 25, 1864, DSA, 3464.

81 On a different occasion: Young Sassoon David Sassoon (London) to his brother Suleiman (Shanghai), October 17, 1865, DSA, 1923.

82 In November 1860: Joseph Chai (Hong Kong) to Suleiman (Shanghai), November 16, 1860, DSA, 1785. Joseph was the son of Abdallah and not a full partner. Born in 1843, he was then only seventeen.

82 Every member: See, for instance, credit and debit details sent to Suleiman Sassoon throughout 1874, DSA, 2686.

82 Coordinating their efforts: Solomon (Suleiman) (Shanghai) to Joseph (Hong Kong), March 18, 1866, DSA, box 10, 3606.

82 Hong Kong can be: Suleiman (Hong Kong) to Abdallah (Bombay), May 30, 1867, DSA, 3463.

82 The head office likewise: Abraham Shalom (Hong Kong) to his brother Suleiman (Shanghai), January 1866 (no specific date), DSA, 1940.

83 As Reuben, seeking to: Reuben David Sassoon (London) to his brother Suleiman (Bombay), April 24, 1868, DSA, 2126.

83 As David had written: David Sassoon (Pune) to his son Suleiman (Shanghai), July 27, 1860, DSA, 1764.

84 He reminded his son: David Sassoon (Pune) to his son Suleiman (Shanghai), July 29, 1861, DSA, 1822.

84 Born in 1841: Jackson, *Sassoons,* 41.

84 Adding insult to injury: Abraham Shalom (Arthur) traveled for a couple of months in summer 1869 in Europe. See DSA, 2904, 2930, 2939. Each letter begins with Arthur's wishes that Suleiman would travel with them next time, but he then proceeds to offer advice, criticism, and rebukes.

84 Although he was not: Abraham Shalom (Arthur) (Hong Kong) to his brother Suleiman (Shanghai), December 28, 1864, DSA, 3492.

84 but ultimately it was: All authors, such as Jackson, Roth, and Stansky, assumed that Ashley Park was purchased by S.D. Sassoon alone.

84 S.D. wrote to: S.D. Sassoon (London) to Suleiman (Shanghai), March 6, 1866, DSA, 1952.

85 Abdallah reproached Arthur: Abdallah (Bombay) to Abraham Shalom (Hong Kong), May 29, 1866, DSA, 1961.

85 Meanwhile Arthur complained: Abraham Shalom (Hong Kong) to Suleiman (Shanghai), June 12, 1866, DSA, 1968.

85 Arthur went so far as: Abraham Shalom (Hong Kong) to Suleiman (Singapore), April 2, 1866, DSA, 1956. Their brother-in-law Moshe was married to Amam, a daughter from David Sassoon's first marriage.

85 and criticized offices for: Abraham Shalom (on a trip to Hamburg) to Suleiman (Bombay), August 10, 1876, DSA, 3753.

85 One London-based employee: Suleiman Yehizkel (London) to Suleiman (Bombay), May 17, 1877, DSA, 3787.

85 Aharon Gabbay, both: Aharon Moshe Gabbay (Calcutta) to Suleiman (Hong Kong), January 8, 1870, DSA, 608.

85 Gabbay also felt that: Aharon Moshe Gabbay (Bombay) to Suleiman (Hong Kong), October 28, 1869, DSA, 2978.

85 as did his wife, Rachel: Rachel Gabbay to Suleiman, October 29, 1869, DSA, 2879.

85 Sensing criticism: Abdallah (Calcutta) to Mordechai Hayim (Abu Shahr, known as Bushir), January 15, 1869, DSA, 478.

86 The document, which bears: The document in the archives, dated January 1, 1867, was most likely an edited draft but does not contain the signature of any brother. See DSA, 3732.

6. COMPETITION WITHIN THE FAMILY, 1867–1871

88 Others followed in: Maisie Meyer, "Three Prominent Sephardi Jews," *Sino-Judaica: Occasional Papers of the Sino-Judaic Institute*, 1995: 90–91 (article 85–110).

88 Even when apart from: David Kranzler, *Japanese, Nazis & Jews: The Jewish Refugee Community of Shanghai, 1938–1945* (New York: Yeshiva University Press, 1976), 47.

88 The favored legal: Robert Bickers, *Britain in China: Community, Culture and Colonialism, 1900–1949* (Manchester: Manchester University Press, 1999), 97.

89 (Not all were quick): *Hong Kong Government Gazette*, February 5, 1876, 70.

89 In Bombay, he helped: Abraham Ben-Yacov, *Yehudei Babel be-Tfuzot* [Babylonian Jewry in Diaspora] (Jerusalem: Rubin Mass, 1985), 80.

90 The demise of this: *London and China Telegraph*, February 22, 1869, 73.

The report was filed from Shanghai on December 24, 1868. The notice was provided by E. D. Sassoon & Co. in Hong Kong.

90 The family gathered: Abraham Shalom (London) to Suleiman (Hong Kong), January 22, 1869, DSA, 2814.

90 Tellingly, however, he: Abdallah (Bombay) to Suleiman (Hong Kong), February 4, 1868, DSA, 2816.

91 According to one source: Ben-Yacov, *Yehudei Babel be-Tfuzot*, 74.

92 "Do not be negligent": Abdallah (Brighton) to Suleiman (Bombay), June 12, 1878, DSA, 3903.

92 He declared: Abdallah to Suleiman, June 12, 1878. For the request for cash, see Abdallah (Brighton) to Suleiman (Bombay), June 4, 1878, DSA, 3901.

92 Yet, barely two months: Abdallah (Brighton) to Suleiman (Bombay), August 9, 1878, DSA, 3919.

92 Sometimes Abdallah: Abdallah (Brighton) to Suleiman (Bombay), August 14, 1878, DSA, 3923.

92 In other letters: Abdallah (Brighton) to Suleiman (Bombay), July 3, 1878, DSA, 3909.

93 Complaints about the way: House of London to House of Bombay, October 11, 1878, DSA, 3935.

93 Abdallah's micromanagement: Abdallah (Bombay) to Eliya Gabbay (Calcutta), March 1, 1870, DSA, 494.

93 As he aged, he: Abdallah (Torquay) to Suleiman (Bombay), March 19, 1891, DSA, 3266.

93 Naturally, employees and: Aharon Moshe Gabbay (Bombay) to Suleiman (Hong Kong), May 11, 1870, DSA, 657.

93 One pleaded with: Suleiman Haskell to Abdallah, October 9, 1884, DSA, 4744.

93 The father of S.D.'s: Captain C. Wiseman to Mr. Sassoon (not clear to whom), February 24, 1892, DSA, 4383.

94 London did, however: H. Coke (London) to David Sassoon & Co. (Calcutta), October 18, 1894, DSA, box 34-3.

94 We can see one of: Saleh Mayer (Shanghai) to Suleiman (Hong Kong), May 10, 1871, DSA, 6363. Saleh was Suleiman's nephew.

94 He suggested that: Aharon Gabbay (Bombay) to Abdallah (Pune), August 9, 1872, DSA, box 12.

94 In a confidential memo: E. Livingstone (Manchester) to Edward Sassoon (London), January 26, 1892, DSA, 4349.

95 Writing to Abdallah: Moshe Gabbay (Bombay) to Abdallah (Pune), September 26, 1872, DSA, box 12.

95 In his letters to Abdallah: Moshe Gabbay (Bombay) to Abdallah (Pune), July 18, 1872, and July 19, 1872, DSA, box 12.

95 This was more than: Moshe Gabbay (Bombay) to Abdallah (Pune), September 23, 1872, DSA, box 12.

95 Not long after, he: Moshe Gabbay (Bombay) to Abdallah (Pune), October 10, 1872, DSA, box 12.

96 "I am so sad": Abdallah (London) to Suleiman (Hong Kong), October 24, 1873, DSA, 2681.

96 A trip from Marseilles: Kenneth Pomeranz and Steven Topik, *The World That Trade Created: Society, Culture, and the World Economy 1400 to the Present*, 2nd ed. (London: M. E. Sharpe, 2006), 64.

96 The opening of the canal: Ronald Findlay and Kevin H. O'Rourke, *Power and Plenty: Trade, War, and the World Economy in the Second Millennium* (Princeton: Princeton University Press, 2007), 380.

97 In 1874, after: *Maclean's Guide to Bombay,* 1876, 160–61.

97 The Sassoon Dock Company: *Indian Law Reports, Bombay Series.* Vol. 1 (February 1877): 513–22.

97 A glance at a manifest: *Maclean's Guide to Bombay,* 65–77; Government of India, Public Works Department Proceedings, December 1876, Indian National Archives (hereafter cited as INA), nos. 1/5.

98 Adroitly, the Sassoons: Abdallah (London) to Suleiman (Hong Kong), May 16, 1873, DSA, 2670; Harcourt, "Black Gold," 52.

98 By the early 1870s: Harcourt, "Black Gold," 53.

99 The report mentions: *Report of the Bombay Chamber of Commerce for the Year 1869–79* (Bombay: Chamber of Commerce, 1879), 325.

99 One trader, who: Aharon Moshe Gabbay (Bushir) to Abdallah (Bombay), February 14, 1877, DSA, 3768.

99 Nevertheless, trading with: See, for instance, S. Yehizkel (London) to Suleiman (Bombay), October 8, 1886, DSA, 3717.

99 Applications for navigation: See, for instance, a report by an employee from London to Abdallah, October 11, 1878, DSA, 3935.

99 It meant, for example: Aharon Moshe Gabbay (Bombay) to Abdallah (Pune), October 7, 1872, DSA, box 12.

100 On one occasion: Abdallah (Pune) to Elias Gabbay (Calcutta), October 26, 1868, DSA, 1365.

100 In another, he: Abdallah (Brighton) to Suleiman (Bombay), January 22, 1890, DSA, 3215.

100 David Sassoon & Co.: Abraham Shalom (London) to Abdallah (Bombay), January 19, 1872, DSA, box 12.

100 The company took an: Reuben (London) to Suleiman (Hong Kong), May 3, 1872, DSA, box 12.

100 He added extensions: W. S. Caine, *Picturesque India: A Handbook for European Travellers* (London: Routledge & Sons, 1890), 439–40.

101 He justified the cost: Abdallah (Pune) to Aharon Gabbay (Bombay), October 23, 1868, DSA, 1357.

101 Although sections of: My gratitude to Kayan Ghyara for her thorough investigation of the matter.

102 Abdallah, naturally: An English Club was established in Mahabaleshwar in 1881; it still functions today with very little change to its premises. Initially, it had about sixty members and allowed women to join two years later. Though the club had restrictions on "natives," it allowed those who had large estates nearby to be honorary members, including the Agha Khan. Forty years after it was set up, Indians were allowed to join as full members of the club. Though Abdallah had already left India when the club opened, other members of the family used it.

102 It was a hard: Margaret MacMillan, *Women of the Raj* (New York: Thames and Hudson, 1988), 182–83. MacMillan describes the role of women and their activities in the hill stations; Dhruti Vaidya Design Studio, *The Other Mahabaleshwar: A Template for Mindful Travel* (Pune: Mervent Technologies, 2018).

102 Visitors can take: MacMillan, *Women of the Raj*, 193. There is a Bombay Point and a Baghdad Point, and the two are different.

103 As all India was: Peter Heehs, *India's Freedom Struggle 1857–1947: A Short History* (Oxford Scholarship Online, 2012), 46.

103 He never missed an: Abdallah (Bombay) to Mordechai Hazan (Bushire), June 1868 (no specific date), DSA, 2159. Sir William Grey was the Lieutenant Governor of Bengal residing in Calcutta in 1868.

103 He could also offer: Correspondence between family members, September 26, 1867, and October 28, 1867, DSA, 3441 and 3443. The Abyssinia expedition lasted from December 1867 to May 1868 and targeted the forces of the Emperor of Ethiopia.

103 In a confidential: Abdallah (Pune) to Suleiman (Hong Kong), August 31, 1869, DSA, 2922.

104 Entertaining was key: Mary Carpenter, *Six Months in India* (London: Longmans, Green, 1868), vol. 2, 3–4.

104 One traveler to Bombay: John Henry Gray, *Journey Around the World in the Years 1875–1876–1877* (London: Harrison, 1879), 293.

104 Aharon Moshe Gabbay: A. M. Gabbay (Bombay) to Suleiman (Hong Kong), March 17, 1870, DSA, 659.

105 The effort seems to: Rutherford Alcock (London) to Abdallah (Bombay), May 20, 1870. Sir Rutherford remained an influential figure even after his retirement from the foreign service, given his knowledge of China and Japan.

105 As one commentator: *Journal of the National Indian Association* 156 (1883): 714.

105 Besides Abdallah: *Annual Report of the Sassoon Mechanics' Institute for the Year 1872–73*.

105 In short order: *Journal of the Society of Arts* (London) vol. 23 (April 23, 1875): 517.

105 as with one talk: E. A. Reade, "The Cultivation of Opium," *Annual Report of the Sassoon Mechanics' Institute for the Year 1871–72*.

105 This honor paved: Jackson, *Sassoons*, 52.

105 As early as 1864: Sir William Muir's "Minute and Correspondence Theron" in *Papers Relating to the Opium Question* (Calcutta: Government Press, 1870), 2. Sir William was a scholar and colonial administrator and served as Lieutenant Governor of the northwest provinces of India.

106 The memo warned that: Messrs. Sassoon and Co. to the Earl of Clarendon, London, March 22, 1870, in *China: A Collection of Correspondence and Papers Relating to Chinese Affairs*, 1870, no. 5, 21.

106 The same week a: *The Economist*, March 12, 1870, in *China: A Collection of Correspondence*, no. 5, 22.

107 "If you will not": Bombay to Hong Kong, September 16, 1869, DSA, 2935.

107 A month later, one: Aharon M. Gabbay (Bombay) to Suleiman (Hong Kong), October 28, 1869, DSA, 2978. Aharon was married to Abdallah's daughter Rachel, and Abdallah relied on him heavily after the split. The Gabbays were related to the Sassoons, as David Sassoon's mother was a Gabbay.

107 The new firm was: Mordechai Gabbay (employee in Shanghai) to Suleiman (Hong Kong), December 4, 1869, DSA, 2996.

108 Writing to Suleiman: Abdallah (Bombay) to Suleiman (Hong Kong), February 18, 1869, DSA, 2818.

108 Each firm watched: Marks, *Information Nexus*, 75.

108 Arthur, on a trip: Abraham Shalom (Bombay) to Suleiman (Hong Kong), April 15, 1869, DSA, 2838.

108 Even when E. D.: See, for example, House of Shanghai reporting to Hong Kong about sale of opium chests, July 18, 1869, DSA, 2873.

108 "We are losing": House of London to House of Bombay, July 22, 1869, DSA, 2878.

108 Sometimes interest gave: Calcutta to Hong Kong, January 9, 1870, DSA, 608.

109 The journal published: Letter from Messrs. David Sassoon to the editor of *The North-China Herald*, January 5, 1877, and the response of the editor, January 6, 1866, *North-China Herald*, January 11, 1877, 35.

109 In one letter: Abdallah (Bombay) to Suleiman (Hong Kong), March 4, 1869, DSA, 2820.

109 Suleiman, even-tempered: Suleiman (Hong Kong) to Abdallah (Bombay), July 29, 1867, DSA, 3456.

109 Some brothers suggested: Letter from Arthur, Aharon, and Frederick Sassoon declaring to David Sassoon & Co. their willingness to donate the building in Baghdad, October 3, 1867, DSA, 6000. The Alliance Israélite Universelle was a Paris-based international Jewish organization founded in 1860 to safeguard the rights of Jews around the world through education and professional development.

109 Whenever a trade: See, for instance, letter of Bombay office, May 15, 1877, DSA, 3787.

109 Ten years after: Abdallah (Brighton) to Suleiman (Bombay), November 26, 1878, DSA, 3949.

110 In a letter from: Suleiman Yehizkel (London) to Suleiman (Bombay), November 15, 1889, DSA, 3203.

110 One senior employee: Aharon Moshe Gabbay (Bombay) to Suleiman (Hong Kong), July 4, 1871, DSA, 644.

111 More than twenty years: Jackson, *Sassoons*, 52.

111 Even during the separation: Suleiman (Hong Kong) to Reuben (London), 1867 (no specific date), DSA, 3609. A letter sent to Reuben allowed him to do whatever he wanted with Suleiman's business and shares of the inheritance in Britain.

111 By 1867, the government: General Department, "Sassoon Hospital at Pune," May 3, 1867, no. 16, in *Abstract of Letters Received from India, 1859–1867*, 302–3.

111 The government further: Finance Department, "Contribution to the 'Sassoon Hospital' at Pune," Finance Department Proceedings, May 31, 1865, Government of India Archives, nos. 197–98.

111 In the first letter: Eliahu (Elias) from Bombay to Suleiman (Hong Kong), November 8, 1878, DSA, 3944.

112 In the second letter: Eliahu (Elias) (Bombay) to Suleiman (Hong Kong), November 10, 1878, DSA, 3945.

112 Eight months after: Amam (Bombay) to Suleiman (Hong Kong), August 4, 1869, DSA, 2891.

112 The death of Elias's: Suleiman (Hong Kong) to Abdallah (Bombay), July 29, 1867, DSA, 3456.

7. LONDON CALLING, 1872–1880

113 She graciously accepted: *Illustrated London News*, January 7, 1876, 3. £1,000 in 1865 was roughly equivalent to £112,000 today.

113 Later that year: Albert Sassoon to William Gladstone, April 5, 1865, Gladstone Papers, vol. 321, British Library, MS 44406.

114 The grounds around. *Illustrated London News,* 1872, 379.

114 Meanwhile, in England: *London and China Telegraph,* July 22, 1872, 511.

114 Albert was presented: "Presentation of the Freedom of the City of London to Sir A. D. Sassoon, CSI," at the Council Chamber Guildhall, November 6, 1873. Technically, Albert was not the first Indian-based merchant to receive this honor; Sir Jamsetjee Jejeebhoy, the Parsi philanthropist, was awarded the Freedom of the City of London in 1855 but was unable to attend to receive it.

116 London's status as: William Gervase Clarence-Smith, *Cocoa and Chocolate, 1765–1914* (London: Routledge, 2000), 93–124.

117 She had been born: Jackson, *Sassoons,* 56.

118 In 1875, for instance: "Brighton and Hove Anglo-Jewish Heritage Trail," http://www.jtrails.org.uk/trails/brighton-and-hove.

118 David Sassoon & Co.'s: Jackson, *Sassoons,* 106, 89.

119 After the Prince's: *Illustrated London News,* April 1, 1876, 318.

119 A few months after: *Illustrated London News,* July 29, 1876, 110.

119 Two years later: *Illustrated London News,* March 30, 1878, 291.

119 Officials, merchants, and residents: *Illustrated London News,* July 26, 1879, 78.

120 As the marriage: Abdallah (Brighton) to Suleiman (Bombay), November 29, 1876, DSA, 3759.

120 One letter from: Arthur (Hamburg) to Suleiman (Bombay), August 10, 1876, DSA, 3753.

121 Eight months after: David Sassoon & Co., "Announcement," October 23, 1876, DSA, 4692; note signed by the lawyers handling David Sassoon & Co.'s affairs, October 23, 1876, DSA, 4692.

121 He was described: *Hongkong Daily Press,* April 9, 1894, 2.

121 In 1878, he: Some of the information is from Ben-Yacov, *Perakim Be-Toldot Yehudei Babel,* 93–96.

122 The 1870s were years: Abdallah (Brighton) to Suleiman (Bombay), August 25, 1878, DSA, 3926.

122 Even a decade: Abdallah (Brighton) to Suleiman (Bombay), November 28, 1889, DSA, 3206.

122 From 1873 until 1897: For details about the depression, see Rendigs Fels, "The Long-Wave Depression, 1873–97," *Review of Economics and Statistics* vol. 31 (February 1949): 69–73; A. E. Musson, "The Great Depression in Britain, 1873–1896," *Journal of Economic History* 19, no. 2 (June 1959): 199–228.

122 and tariffs rose: Trentmann, *Free Trade Nation,* 142–43.

122 India's exports were: Major-General W. F. Marriott, "Indian Political Economy and Finance," *Journal of the East Indian Association* (London) 8 (1874): 188–207.

122 Only from the 1890s: John F. Richards, "The Opium Industry in British India," *Indian Economic and Social History Review* 39, nos. 2 and 3 (2002): table 2, 166–67 (article 149–180).

122 From 1862 until: Richards, "Opium Industry," table 1, 159–61.

123 Their systems had been: *Reports on Trade at the Treaty Ports in China for the Year 1874* (Shanghai: Inspector General of Customs, 1874), 20.

123 A memo reveals: David Sassoon & Co. (Hong Kong) to other branches, January 21, 1874, Collection of Kenneth and Joyce Robbins. I am indebted to Ken for allowing me to use his private archives.

123 For high-quality: David Sassoon & Co. (Hong Kong) to other branches, April 14, 1875, Ken Robbin's Archive.

123 As always, exporting: Hao, *Commercial Revolution in Nineteenth-Century China*, 310.

123 Some achieved great: China had a very complicated currency system known as bimetallism, consisting of silver and copper. For the different forms of money used, see Yen-p'ing Hao, *The Commercial Revolution in Nineteenth Century China: The Rise of Sino-Western Mercantile Capitalism* (Berkeley: University of Berkeley Press, 1986), 55–64.

123 in a single year: Trocki, *Opium, Empire and the Global Political Economy*, 119–20.

124 He also did significant: Yen-p'ing Hao, *The Comprador in Nineteenth-Century China: Bridge Between East and West* (Cambridge, MA: Harvard University Press, 1971), 114. The book has lists of compradors working for major companies such as Jardine Matheson, but unfortunately no list exists for either of the Sassoon firms.

124 Not only did his: Hao, *Comprador in Nineteenth-Century China*, 117.

125 The Resident explained: Letter from Messrs. D. Sassoon & Co. about their claims against Abdul Nabee, July 12, 1881, and comments by Lieutenant Colonel E. C. Ross, Political Resident in the Persian Gulf, October 17, 1881, Indian Archives, Foreign Department, 1882, 288/92.

125 When the shipment: "Marine Insurance," *London and China Telegraph*, February 1, 1875, 106.

125 The case dragged on: "The Principle of the Stamp Laws," *Economist*, January 1, 1876.

125 "The coexistence of": Motono, "A Study of the Legal Status of the Compradors During the 1880s," 69.

126 It took almost two: Case, DSA, box 69.

126 His son-in-law Aharon Moshe: Moshe Gabbay (Bombay) to Abdallah (Pune), September 24, 1872, DSA, box 12.

127 Only when he heard: Abdallah (London) to Rachel (Aharon Gabbay's wife), November 20, 1885, DSA, 4782.

127 He demanded compensation: S. Ezekiel to Lewis and Lewis, October 20, 1892, DSA, box 12, part 2.

127 he wrote to: S. Ezekiel to Coke of David Sassoon & Co., October 22, 1892, DSA, box 12, part 2.

127 The firm agreed: Agreement between David Sassoon & Co. and S. Ezekiel, October 27, 1892, DSA, box 12, part 2.

128 But this alliance: The Gabbays' unhappiness was manifested in numerous letters from 1870, DSA, 606.

128 "The firm acted as": Trocki, *Opium, Empire and the Global Political Economy*, 113.

128 The firm worked: Abdallah (Pune) to Abraham Shalom (Calcutta), June 11, 1868, DSA, 2157.

128 The strategy reduced: Quoted in Edward LeFevour, *Western Enterprise in Late Ch'ing China: A Selective Survey of Jardine, Matheson & Company's Operations, 1842–1895* (Cambridge, MA: Harvard University Press, 1968), fn. 80, 165. For the activities of the Sassoons, see 26–30.

128 by 1871, Jardine: Richard J. Grace, *Opium and Empire: The Lives and Careers of William Jardine and James Matheson* (Montreal: McGill–Queen's University Press, 2014), 302.

128 Thus the two Sassoon: LeFevour, *Western Enterprise in Late Ch'ing China*, 28–29.

128 In reality, the number: John M. Dalton, comp., *The Cruise of Her Majesty's Ship "Bacchante": Compiled 1879–1882, from the Private Journals, Letters, and Note-books of Prince Albert Victor and Prince George of Wales* (London: Macmillan, 1886), 172.

129 Jardine used these: LeFevour, *Western Enterprise in Late Ch'ing China*, 29.

129 In a letter dated: Abdallah (Brighton) to Suleiman (Bombay), June 12, 1878, DSA, 3903.

129 Both Sassoon companies: S. M. Rutangur, ed., *Bombay Industries: The Cotton Mills* (Bombay: Indian Textile Journal Ltd., 1927), 59.

129 As one British MP: H. Birley, MP (Manchester), *Hansard* 235 (July 10, 1877): 1085–128.

130 For instance, the first: Memorandum of Association of the Sassoon Spinning and Weaving Company Limited, 1874, DSA, box 34-2.

130 "They entered into": Amalendu Guna, "Parsi Seths as Entrepreneurs,

1750–1850," *Economic and Political Weekly* 5, no. 35 (August 29, 1870): M107 (article M107–M115).

130 Spinning generated: Abdallah (Brighton) to Suleiman (Bombay), March 1, 1887, DSA, 4807.

130 Following the early: Memorandum of Association of the Sassoon Silk Manufacturing Company, Bombay, 1875, DSA, box 34-2.

130 The company later: The Sassoon & Alliance Silk Mill Company, Directors' Report, December 31, 1941, DSA, box 23-B.

130 The sector encompassed: Seal, *Emergence of Indian Nationalism*, 32–33.

130 A previous historian: Roth, *Sassoon Dynasty*, 77.

132 (The transfer of): Accounting memo, January 31, 1874, DSA, 2698.

132 London was charging: Accounting memo, March 24, 1874, DSA, 2703.

132 Each week shipments: Accounting memo, May 1, 1874, DSA, 2708. The memo refers to deliveries made in February, March, and April 1874.

132 Even in the late: Abdallah (Brighton) to Suleiman (Bombay), November 28, 1889, DSA, 3206.

132 Whenever an office: A. M. Gabbay (Bombay) to Suleiman (Hong Kong), April 21, 1874, DSA, 2716. The memo requested that Suleiman use his influence with Shanghai to remit the opium revenues.

132 So this didn't mean: Memo re: accounting of *amanat* Hong Kong for 1873, April 29, 1874, DSA, 2719.

133 Marriages within communities: Ruth Fredman Cernea, *Almost Englishmen: Baghdadi Jews in British Burma* (Lanham, MD: Rowman & Littlefield, 2007), xxiv.

133 As in other communities: Francesca Trivellato, *The Familiarity of Strangers: The Sephardic Diaspora, Livorno, and Cross-Cultural Trade in the Early Modern Period* (New Haven: Yale University Press, 2009), 22.

133 Louise, who would: *Vanity Fair* 24 (December 18, 1880): 346.

133 The Prince was among: Jackson, *Sassoons*, 69–71.

133 Members of the aristocracy: Jane Ridley, *The Heir Apparent* (New York: Random House, 2013), 521.

133 In sharp contrast: Suleiman Yehizkel (London) to Suleiman (Bombay), June 29, 1888, DSA, 3104.

134 In a dispiritingly: Reuben (London) to Suleiman (Hong Kong), September 26, 1873, DSA, 2676.

134 "The results of the bazaar": *Vanity Fair* 21 (May 31, 1879), 317.

134 Sir Albert, meanwhile: *Vanity Fair* 21 (June 7, 1879), 355.

135 It was a house: *Vanity Fair* 22 (August 2, 1879), 65.

136 There were reportedly: Mary Eliza Haweis, *Beautiful Houses: Being a Description of Certain Well-Known Artistic Houses* (London: Sampson Low, Marston, Searle & Rivington 1882), 71–76.

8. HIGH SOCIETY, 1880–1894

139 This identification would: Peter Heehs, *India's Freedom Struggle, 1857–1947,* 46.

139 A rabbi visiting: Translation of Rabbi Sappir's notes of his travels, DSA, box 35.

139 The 1881 census: Roland, *Jews in British India,* 65–66.

139 Baghdadi Jews were: Sarah Abrevaya Stein, "Protected Persons? The Baghdadi Jewish Diaspora, the British State, and the Persistence of Empire," *American Historical Review* 116, no. 1 (February 2011): 80–108.

139 Almost fifty years later: Elizabeth E. Imber, "A Late Imperial Elite Jewish Politics: Baghdadi Jews in British India and the Political Horizons of Empire and Nation," *Jewish Social Studies: History, Culture, Society* 23, no. 2 (Winter 2018): 49.

140 (Indeed, rumor has it): Roth, *Sassoon Dynasty,* 116, fn. 1.

140 (In fact, many): Geoffrey Jones, *Merchants to Multinationals,* 227.

140 It has also been: David Cannadine, *Ornamentalism: How the British Saw Their Empire* (Oxford: Oxford University Press, 2001), 8.

140 Light-skinned Baghdadi: Cernea, *Almost Englishmen,* xxiii.

141 An examination of: Caroline Plüss, "Assimilation Versus Idiosyncrasy: Strategic Constructions of Sephardic Identities in Hong Kong," *Jewish Culture and History* 5, no. 2 (2002): 48 (article 48–69).

141 "Thus, a few elite": Jael Silliman, *Jewish Portraits, Indian Frames: Women's Narratives from a Diaspora of Hope* (Calcutta: Seagull Books, 2001), 27.

141 The changes that took: Abdallah (Mahabaleshwar) to Suleiman (Shanghai), November 10, 1865, DSA, 3595.

141 Writing to Farha: Rahamim Musa (Calcutta) to Farha (Bombay), "Memorandum," April 13, 1902, DSA, box 12.

141 At the heart of this: Silliman, *Jewish Portraits, Indian Frames,* 50.

141 When the latter suffered: Suleiman Yehizkel (London) to Suleiman (Bombay), November 15, 1889, DSA, 3203; Abdallah (Brighton) to Suleiman (Bombay), November 21, 1889, DSA, 3205.

141 with success, as Albert: Abdallah (Brighton) to Suleiman (Bombay), December 4, 1889, DSA, 3207.

142 When Jews in Jerusalem: Aharon Gabbay (Moscow) to Farha (Bombay), September 23, 1891, DSA, 3307.

142 There are three: Pramuan Bunkanwanicha, Joseph P. H. Fan, and Yupana Wiwattanakantang, "The Value of Marriage to Family Firms," *Journal of Financial and Quantitative Analysis* 48, no. 2 (April 2013): 611–36.

142 She had to be: Lorraine de Meaux, *Une grande famille russe: Les Gunzburg* (Paris: Perrin, 2018), 207.

143 The wedding itself: *Bulletin de la Société héraldique,* 1887, 622.

144 The Grand Rabbi: Roth, *Sassoon Dynasty,* 172.

144 At the reception: Peter Stansky, *Sassoon: The Worlds of Philip and Sybil* (New Haven: Yale University Press, 2003), 15. A section of the necklace was sold at auction at Sotheby's in 2016 for 665,000 CHF, roughly £530,000.

144 In the event, unlike: Edward Albert Sassoon to Mr. Hart (no details of who he is, but it seems his brother was an influential British MP), October 1887 (no specific date), DSA, 4840.

144 In a handwritten: Reuben Sassoon (London) to Sir Nathaniel de Rothschild, n.d., DSA, box 27-A.

144 The disparity had been: *North-China Herald,* February 8, 1881, 123.

146 Then he turned: Aharon Gabbay (Moscow) to Farha (Bombay), September 23, 1891, DSA, 3307.

146 Not long after: Aharon Gabbay (Moscow) to Farha (Bombay), November 6, 1891, DSA, 3315.

146 He wrote too of: Aharon Gabbay (Moscow) to Farha (Bombay), November 6, 1891, DSA, 3315; *Times,* November 8, 1912.

146 In love as in business: Chaeran Y. Freeze, *A Jewish Woman of Distinction: The Life & Diaries of Zinaida Poliakova* (Waltham, MA: Brandeis University Press, 2019), 87.

147 Zina suspected, not: Freeze, *A Jewish Woman of Distinction,* 89.

147 There were other examples: Newspaper cutting, 1893, DSA, box 21-C.

147 Albert's home in Brighton: *Vanity Fair* 26 (August 6, 1881): 82.

147 "Mr. and Mrs. Sassoon": *Vanity Fair* 25 (April 23, 1881): 234.

147 Even at embassy: *Vanity Fair* 34 (July 18, 1885): 41.

148 When a London monthly: *Lady's Realm* 6 (May–October 1899): 332.

148 The press was not: *Vanity Fair* 30 (July 28, 1883): 47.

148 Millionaires such as: *Vanity Fair* 27 (April 15, 1882): 209.

148 By then, the City: W. D. Rubinstein, *Men of Property: The Very Wealthy in Britain since the Industrial Revolution* (New Brunswick, NJ: Rutgers University Press, 1981), 106.

149 In a mode less: Diary of parties by Rachel Sassoon, DSA, box 29-2.

149 The diary carefully: Diary of parties by Rachel Sassoon, DSA, box 29-2.

149 One menu: DSA, no date.

150 It would not always: "Menu," for dinner at the Ezras' house, 3 Kyd Street, Calcutta, March 10, 1937, DSA, box 24. Sir John Anderson's name was written in its margin.

150 Upon Barnato's death: "Barnato's House," *The Sketch: A Journal of Art and Actuality,* November 1, 1899, 80.

150 *The Lady's Realm* was: *Lady's Realm* 4 (May 1898–October 1898): 608.

150 The building, lost: Haweis, *Beautiful Houses,* 76–83.

151 The fecundity of: *Evening Standard,* October 1906, Rothschild Archives (London).

152 By the mid-1880s: *Vanity Fair* 34 (December 5, 1885): 318.

152 Reuben in particular: Cecil Roth, "The Court Jews of Edwardian England," *Jewish Social Studies* 5, no. 4 (October 1943): 361 (article 355–66).

152 his "pearl-studded": Ridley, *Heir Apparent,* 342.

152 Archives indicate: George (Balmoral Castle) to Reuben, September 9, 1900. My gratitude to Joanna Sassoon in Perth, Australia, who kindly shared this and other documents and pictures.

153 One of Elias's sons: James Carter, *Champions Day: The End of Old Shanghai* (New York: W. W. Norton, 2020), 43–44.

153 Another family member: *Hongkong Telegraph,* September 24, 1881.

153 The eldest son of: Anthony Allfrey, *Edward VII and His Jewish Court* (London: Weidenfeld & Nicolson, 1991), xiv.

153 They did not always: Quoted in Allfrey, *Edward VII,* 9.

154 On another occasion: Quoted in Allfrey, *Edward VII,* 46.

154 He was seen as: Ridley, *Heir Apparent,* 342.

154 The Prince enjoyed: Alfred de Rothschild (London) to Edward Sassoon, August 17, 1892, DSA, 4571.

154 It adjoined Marlborough: Reuben (Brighton) to Abdallah (Brighton), February 19, 1890, DSA, 3217.

154 "We are not supposed": Sir W. V. Harcourt to Sir Albert, July 5, 1889, DSA, box 10, 4877/1.

154 The Prince and Princess: Arthur Ellis (Marlborough House) on behalf of the Prince of Wales to Sir Albert, July 5, 1889, DSA, box 10, 4877/2. There are more letters of thanks to Sir Albert, including some from family members.

155 Albert was well placed: For a detailed discussion of this period in Iran, see: Abbas Amanat, *Iran: A Modern History* (New Haven: Yale University Press, 2017), 247–314.

155 Informing him of: Albert (London) to Zelli Sultan [*sic*] (Isfahan), September 14, 1887, DSA, 437.

156 Albert responded by: Zelli Sultan [*sic*] (Isfahan) to Sir Albert Sassoon (London), June 12, 1896; Abdallah to Zelli Sultan [*sic*], July 17, 1896, DSA, box 36-A. The correspondence between the two was in French and English.

156 For these connections: Suleiman (Bombay) to Abdallah (London), April 24, 1885, DSA, 4762.

156 Given "the present": Assistant to Sir Albert Sassoon to His Highness Abdul Aziz bin Saeed, January 24, 1895, DSA, file 10, 981. Sir John Kirk,

a physician by training, was Consul General in Zanzibar and spent twenty years in different jobs, including as Medical Officer of Zanzibar.

156 When Shanghai celebrated: *The Jubilee of Shanghai, 1843–1893: Shanghai, Past and Present, and a Full Account of the Proceedings on the 17th and 18th November, 1893* (Shanghai: North China Daily News, 1893), 43.

156 Albert sat on the London: *China Famine Relief Fund,* 1878.

156 when floods devastated: *Shen Bao,* July 15, 1885. *Shen Bao,* known in English as *Shanghai News,* was a Chinese newspaper that appeared in Shanghai from 1872 to 1949.

156 In 1890, this school: *The Twentieth Annual Report of the Anglo-Jewish Association, in connection with the Alliance Israélite Universelle, 1890–1891* (London: Anglo-Jewish Association, 1891), 36–37.

156 Yet, the emphasis: Yaron Ben-Naeh, "Ha-Sheliach me-Hebron Mistabech Be-Bombay" [The emissary from Hebron encountered complications in Bombay], *Et-Mol,* no. 215 (February 2011): 6–9.

157 As Reuben told: Reuben (Brighton) to Abdallah (Brighton), January 30, 1890, DSA, 3216.

157 The reward for Albert: David Sassoon & Co. to Home Office obtaining the patent of the title, January 27, 1890.

157 Despite this, her: Queen Victoria's Journals, entries dated March 14, 1877, and September 11, 1889. The journals were made available publicly by the Royal Archives and the Bodleian Libraries in 2012 at http://www.queenvictoriasjournals.org.

157 when she attended: Queen Victoria's Journals, March 11, 1899.

157 Yet, *The Spectator*: *Spectator,* January 4, 1890, 3.

158 One came from a: William Murray (Drummore, Scotland) to Arthur Sassoon (London), October 31, 1887, DSA, 4844.

158 Another, from a Persian: Haji Mohamed Mehdi Malektejal (Bushir) to Sir Albert (London), May 5, 1887, DSA, 4819.

158 Their team in Hong Kong: Property Management Report, March 10, 1884, DSA, 4737.

158 Property managers were: Property Management Report, to Suleiman (Bombay), February 22, 1886, DSA, 4803.

159 The detailed twelve-page: B. Warwick & Partners (London) to David Sassoon & Co. (London), June 20, 1895, DSA, box 12, part 2.

159 There was, for instance: Yehizkel (employee, London) to Suleiman (Bombay), May 11, 1878, DSA, 3785. Interestingly London was charging 2.5 percent but argued that the costs in London were much higher than Bombay.

159 There was a notion: M. Gabbay (Bombay) to Abdallah (Pune), July 12, 1872, DSA, box 12.

159 Diversification led to: D. Sassoon & Co. (London), "Memorandum of Association of the Persian Gulf Steamship Company," 1892, DSA, 4332; note to David Sassoon & Co. (London), February 2, 1893, DSA, 3993.

159 Fluctuations in: Abdallah (Brighton) to Suleiman (Pune), August 5, 1886, DSA, 3706.

160 In 1893, David: *Proceedings of the Finance and Commerce Department,* September 1893, memos 880–929, July 4 to August 18, 1893, INA.

160 Payments in cash: *Reports on Trade at the Treaty Ports in China for the Year 1874,* 7.

161 Between 1879 and: Man-Houng Lin, "China's 'Dual-Economy' in International Trade Relations, 1842–1949," in Kaoru Sugihara, ed., *Japan, China, and the Growth of the Asian International Economy, 1850–1949,* 1:183–85 (article 179–97).

161 Chinese farmers discovered: Halsey, *Quest for Power,* 60.

161 On New Year's Day: S. Yehizkel (Hong Kong) to Edward (London), January 1, 1890, DSA, 3212.

161 Albert bombarded: Abdallah (Brighton) to Suleiman (Bombay), February 12, 1890, DSA, 3221.

161 as losses mounted: Edward Abdallah Sassoon (Norfolk) to Suleiman (Bombay), January 20, 1890, DSA, 3214.

161 By March 1890: Abdallah (Brighton) to Suleiman (Bombay), March 20, 1890, DSA, 3227.

162 But the French firm: Jules Rueff, Messageries Fluviales de Cochinchine (Paris) to A. M. Gabbay (London), October 3, 1892, DSA, 4836.

162 E. D. Sassoon regretted: Fond Gouvernement Général de l'Indochine, dossier no. 17607, Vietnam National Archives Center 1 (Hanoi). I am indebted to my colleague Diana Kim for this information.

162 Losses continued to: Abdallah (Brighton) to Suleiman (Bombay), April 1, 1890, DSA, 3230.

162 Turkish opium: "Memo re Losses on Opium" (London), June 1, 1893, DSA, 4080.

162 In a premonitory: Abdallah (Brighton) to Suleiman (Bombay), December 24, 1891, DSA, 3326.

163 The Governor-General: "Memorial from Messrs. D. Sassoon & Co. and Other Opium Merchants of Bombay Praying for a Reduction in the Pass-Duty on Malwa Opium Exported to China and Negative Orders Thereon," *Proceedings of the Finance and Commerce Department,* 1892, 494–702, INA.

163 By 1893, even: A. M. Gabbay (London) to Suleiman (Bombay), January 6, 1893, DSA, 3971.

164 A comparative statement: Report from Manchester office to Messrs. David Sassoon & Co., January 19, 1893, DSA, 3182.

164 And in spite of: House of Bombay Account with Messrs. David Sassoon & Co. (London), April 17, 1893, DSA, box 10, 4026.

165 Mr. Pease called: "The Opium Trade Resolution placed by J. W. Pease, MP," March 15, 1881, Church of England Archives (hereafter cited as LPA), Tait 286.

165 They had been encouraged: Storrs Turner (Secretary of Anglo-Oriental Society for the Suppression of the Opium Trade) to Lord Archbishop, March 18, 1881, LPA, Tait 286.

165 The news in 1881: Inspectorate General of Customs, Peking, January 29, 1881, LPA, Tait 286.

165 William Gladstone: Gregory Blue, "Opium for China: The British Connection," in Timothy Brook and Bob Tadashi Wakabayashi, eds., *Opium Regimes: China, Britain, and Japan, 1839–1952* (Berkeley: University of California Press, 2000), fn. 53, 51–52 (article 31–54).

165 The letter asserted: Letter to W. E. Gladstone, First Lord Commissioner of the Treasury, 1881 (no specific date), LPA, Tait 286.

166 In its diverse: *England and the Opium Trade with China,* pamphlet (London: Dyer Brothers, 1880).

166 In his long letter: Li Hung-Chang on the Opium Trade, Tientsin, May 24, 1881, LPA, Tait 286.

166 The anti-opium lobby: Society for the Suppression of the Opium Trade, *Who Is Responsible for the Opium Trade?,* pamphlet, n.d., LPA, Tait 286.

166 Oddly, the Archbishop: Correspondence between the Archbishop of Canterbury and the Association for the Suppression of the Opium Trade, June 1875, LPA, Tait 210.

166 In 1891, Pease: Joseph Alexander, "Open Letter," March 17, 1891, LPA, Benson 99.

166 The motion was: *Times* (London), April 14, 1891.

167 He defended the: Sir R. Temple, House of Commons Debate, April 10, 1891, *Hansard* 352: cc 330–38.

167 A flurry of correspondence: Cabinet Notes and Discussions, *CAB* 37/29, no. 19, 1891.

167 All these companies: See, for example, letter to the China Association dated December 9, 1908, signed by David Sassoon & Co. and E. D. Sassoon, *China Association Circulars* 3 (October 12, 1908–June 17, 1909).

168 He was impatient: Abdallah (Brighton) to Suleiman (Bombay), August 26, 1888, DSA, 3122.

168 He grew increasingly: Abdallah (Brighton) to Suleiman (Bombay), May 14, 1891, DSA, 3281.

169 He eventually left: Chiara Betta, *Silas Aharon Hardoon (1851–1931): Marginality and Adaptation in Shanghai,* thesis for the degree of doctor of philosophy, School of Oriental and African Studies, University of London, 1997, 296. For analysis of the battle over Hardoon's fortune, see Stein, "Protected Persons?," 81–87.

169 His death was announced: *Chemist and Druggist,* March 24, 1894, 417.

9. THE MATRIARCH, 1895–1901

170 For the vast majority: Trivellato, *Familiarity of Strangers,* 23.

170 One of the first: Dosebai Cowasjee Jessawalla, *The Story of My Life* (Bombay: Times Press, 1911), 43.

171 In spite of the: Silliman, *Jewish Portraits, Indian Frames,* 49.

172 Hannah Gabbay, whom: Hannah Gabbay (Hong Kong) to Suleiman (Shanghai), October 29, 1869, DSA, 2979.

172 In fact, Suleiman: Farha David Sassoon (London) to Suleiman (Shanghai), August 13, 1869, DSA, 2903; August 26, 1869, DSA, 2915; and September 23, 1869, DSA, 2940.

172 An altogether different: See, for example, a letter from a relative to Suleiman, August 18, 1869, DSA, 2909, confirming the arrival of a tea chest and apologizing that her husband did not update him.

172 Farha's outgoing personality: Avraham Ben-Yacov, "A Letter and Five Poems to the Honourable Suleiman David Sassoon" (in Hebrew), in Shmuel Moreh, ed., *Mihkarim be-Toldot Yehudei Iraq ve-Beterbutam* [Studies in the history of Iraqi Jews and their culture] (Or Yehuda: Centre for the Heritage of Babylonian Jews, 1981), 73–82.

172 When Reuben stayed: Reuben (Sandringham, Norfolk) to Farha (Bombay), November 11, 1891, DSA, 3316.

173 One anecdote, from after: The story is recounted in Roth, *Sassoon Dynasty,* 129–30.

173 Zinaida Poliakova: Freeze, *A Jewish Woman of Distinction,* 78.

174 By the end of 1894: David Sassoon & Co. (London), "Announcement," January 1, 1895, DSA, 1521.

174 Appropriately in the: "Epitome of Proposed Partnership," Messrs. David Sassoon & Co., January 1895, DSA, box 27-A.

175 It was a daunting: Name unclear (Pune) to Mrs. S.D. Sassoon (Bombay), January 3, 1895, DSA, 1522.

175 The firm's textile: The Sassoon Pressing Company, Directors' Report, June 30, 1894, DSA, box 23-B.

175 The pressing company: The Sassoon Pressing Company, Directors' Report, June 30, 1896, DSA, box 23-B.

175 Ezra expressed concern: Ezra (London) to Farha (Bombay), April 12, 1895, DSA, 1014.

176 In one such incident: David Sassoon & Co. (Bombay) to Faraj Haim (known as Frederick; Bombay), May 31, 1885, DSA, 4776.

176 It would be another: David Sassoon & Co. (London), "Announcement," November 29, 1895, DSA, box 12, part 2. Frederick became a partner effective January 1, 1896.

176 The rest of the board: Proceedings of the Port Canning and Land Improvement Company, August 13, 1894, DSA, 5473.

176 The firm also acted: Department of Overseas Trade to India Office, September 7, 1929, India Office, IOR/R/15/2/1241 (Qatar Digital Library).

176 The company also: Sir H. Layard, "Memorandum Respecting the Navigation of the Tigris and Euphrates," 1913, India Office Records, IOR/L/PS/18/B199 (Qatar Digital Library).

176 More successfully: Chairman of the Persian Gulf Steamship Company to David Sassoon & Co., February 2, 1893, DSA, 3992.

177 Certainly, she earned: Campbell & Newsome Architects (Bombay) to Mrs. Sassoon (Bombay), November 25, 1895, DSA.

177 Tax inspectors: Ezra (London) to Farha (Bombay), May 10, 1895, DSA, 1027.

177 At the time of his: "Statement of Investments of the Estate of S.D. Sassoon as of 1 January 1895," DSA, 1025.

177 By the end of her: Letters from these companies to Mrs. S.D. Sassoon, December 26, 27, and 29, 1895, DSA, 1504, 1505, 1506, and 1507.

178 She asked London: H. Coke (London) to Mrs. Sassoon (Bombay), November 21, 1895, DSA, 1520.

178 She sought information: Gabbay (Hong Kong) to Farha (Bombay), August 26, 1898, DSA, box 34-3.

179 It was part of: Dwijendra Tripathi, *The Oxford History of Indian Business* (New Delhi: Oxford University Press, 2004), 116–17.

179 He was suitably: Press cutting, March 26, 1895, DSA, box 21-C.

179 One note reveals: Will (Bombay) to Aunt Farha, n.d., DSA, 3959.

179 Farha arranged in: Peninsular and Oriental Steam Navigation Company to Mrs. S.D. Sassoon, October 26, 1900, DSA, box 33.

179 He wrote to his: Ruby Sassoon (Japan) to David (Farha's son), September 1, 1903, DSA, box 33.

180 In Farha's first: *First Report of the Royal Commission on Opium, with Minutes of Evidence and Appendices* (London: H. M. Stationery Office, 1894–1895), 7:1. The report is one of the most prized nineteenth-century sources on all aspects of opium.

180 "From the beginning": Owen, *British Opium Policy in China and India*, 317–18.

180 In his final statement: *First Report of the Royal Commission on Opium*, 2:145–46. Interview conducted on December 6, 1893.

180 After complimenting: *First Report of the Royal Commission on Opium*, 4:232. Interview conducted on February 13, 1894.

181 It was a sentiment: *First Report of the Royal Commission on Opium*, 4:232, 231–32.

181 Despite their professed: *First Report of the Royal Commission on Opium*, 5:145, appendix 25 of questions issued by the commission.

181 It was a colossal: *First Report of the Royal Commission on Opium*, 6:94.

182 The Commission's report: John F. Richards, "Opium and the British Indian Empire: The Royal Commission of 1895," *Modern Asian Studies* 36, no. 2 (May 2002): 378 (article 375–420).

182 Criticism from the anti-opium: Owen, *British Opium Policy*, 320.

182 Ultimately, despite the: Owen, *British Opium Policy*, 320.

182 When he died: Brighton and Hove Archives, item 46. It is not part of a cemetery but stands in the center of Kemp, a neighborhood in Brighton, and today it is partly a nightclub called the Proud Cabaret.

183 As the award of: Niall Ferguson, *The Square and the Tower: Networks and Power, from the Freemasons to Facebook* (New York: Penguin Press, 2018), 67. Ferguson is quoting John F. Padgett and Paul D. McLean, "Organizational Invention and Elite Transformation: The Birth of Partnership Systems in Renaissance Florence," *American Journal of Sociology* 111, no. 5 (March 2006): 1463–568.

183 The Chief Justice: Civil Case in the Goods of Sir Albert A. D. Sassoon (Deceased), March 20, 1897, *Indian Law Reports, Bombay Series* 21: 673–80.

183 Edward, Albert's son: Hollams, Sons, Coward & Hawksley to David Sassoon & Co., September 1, 1897, DSA, box 36-A.

184 She had reorganized: Reorganization of the Bombay Office, November 7, 1898, DSA, box 33.

184 She implemented strict: Messrs. David Sassoon (Bombay), "Note to Hong Kong, Shanghai, Calcutta," July 19, 1895, DSA, 1059.

184 Reports under her: David Sassoon & Co. (Hong Kong) to Messrs. Sassoon (Bombay), January 30, 1896, DSA, box 73.

184 When the U.S. General: Apcar & Co. (Calcutta) to Messrs. David Sassoon (Bombay), October 29, 1895, DSA, 1093.

184 that she had in 1897: *Menorah*, A Monthly Magazine of B'nai B'rith, New York, 22 (January–June 1897).

185 The partners in London: Ezra (London) to Farha (Bombay), November 3, 1899, DSA, 934.

185 Through her lawyers: See, for example, *Hong Kong Government Gazette,* May 2, 1896, 408.

185 A story circulated that: Jackson, *Sassoons,* 105.

185 A letter sent to: Messrs D. Sassoon (London) to S. Moses and S. Shellim, July 22, 1898, DSA, box 27-A.

186 She also assumed: Sophie Solomon (London) to Farha (Bombay), July 28, 1892, DSA, 4557.

186 In perusing *The: Jewish World,* 1897–98.

186 On one occasion: *North-China Herald,* September 13, 1907, 638.

186 He also contributed: *Indian Education,* 1908, 318; *Hongkong Telegraph,* November 4, 1908, 5.

187 London was looking: Ezra (London) to Farha (Bombay), May 5, 1899, DSA, 903.

187 For instance, he wrote: Ezra (London) to Farha (Bombay), July 6, 1899, DSA, 910.

187 When she complained: Ezra (London) to Farha (Bombay), November 3, 1899, DSA, 934.

188 Though he was addressing: Reuben (Sandringham) to Farha (Bombay), November 8, 1899, DSA, 935.

188 She was even: David Sassoon & Co. (London) to Farha (Bombay) re: "Administration of the Estate of the late S.D. Sassoon," December 1, 1899, DSA, 957; "Memo re Administrative Cost," December 23, 1899, DSA, 966.

188 Writing to his nephew: Frederick (London) to Edward (London but traveling), March 25, 1898, DSA, box 27-A.

188 He set about questioning: Frederick (London) to Edward (London but traveling), March 25, 1898, DSA, box 27-A.

189 Then came the real: David Sassoon & Co. (London) to David Sassoon & Co. (Bombay), March 15, 1899, DSA, box 33.

190 Its board comprised: *Financial Times,* January 1, 1902, 5.

191 The reality was less: Letter quoted in Jackson, *Sassoons,* 119.

191 She had always been: Bomayee Pestonjee (Bombay) to Mrs. S.D. Sassoon (Pune), August 1, 1899, DSA, box 33.

192 One story tells: Quoted in Jackson, *Sassoons,* 120.

10. A NEW CENTURY, 1902–1914

193 Travel grew faster: Kumar and Desai, eds., *Cambridge Economic History of India,* 2:737.

193 Hundreds of thousands: Jürgen Osterhammel, *The Transformation of the World: A Global History of the Nineteenth Century* (Princeton: Princeton University Press, 2014), 719.

194 He argued, for instance: *Spectator,* August 3, 1907, 2.

194 In a letter to: Edward Sassoon to Foreign Office, July 17, 1906, Public Record Office, UK National Archives (hereafter cited as PRO), FO371/11/273.

194 He also proposed: India Office, Koweit [*sic*] Baghdad Railway, February 25, 1903, file 53/33 II (D15).

194 After the death of: Jackson, *Sassoons,* 119.

194 Research undertaken: David Kynaston, *The City of London,* vol. 2, *Golden Years, 1890–1914* (London: Chatto & Windus, 1994), 265–66.

195 Edward was succeeded: *Financial Times,* May 28, 1912, 10.

195 He had been President: *Times* (London), May 27, 1912, 9.

195 After various bequests: *Financial Times,* July 23, 1912, 5.

196 As well as offering: *Financial Times,* July 29, 1912, 7.

197 She maintained her: See, for example, her selling a 5 percent War Loan through her brokers Seligman & Pearson, DSA, box 33.

197 She continued in: *Ardeshir H. Mama vs. Flora Sassoon,* May 21, 1928, Bombay High Court, https//:indiankanoon.org/doc/958023.

198 His wife complained: D. Bension (Calcutta) to Mrs. Sassoon (London), February 11, 1929, DSA, box 71.

198 "His wish was to": Farha (Malabar Hill) to Emma (London), April 30, 1911, DSA, box 34-3.

198 David paid attention: See, for instance, David (London) to Rachel (Calcutta), January 26, 1916, DSA, box 71.

198 He addressed most: David (London) to Rachel (Calcutta), April 22, 1915, DSA, box 71.

199 David wrote the book: David S. Sassoon, *Masa' Babel* [Babylon Journey] ed. with biography of the author, introduction and comments by Meir Benayahu (Jerusalem, 1955).

199 The Beers, originally: Eliat Negev and Yehuda Koren, *The First Lady of Fleet Street: The Life of Rachel Beer* (New York: Bantam Books, 2011), 137.

199 Frederick's father had: For more details on Rachel Beer and her marriage, see Negev and Koren, *First Lady of Fleet Street.*

199 Rachel, who strongly: Negev and Koren, *First Lady of Fleet Street,* 116.

200 Her biggest scoop: Negev and Koren, *First Lady of Fleet Street,* 217–25.

200 His energies were: *Hongkong Telegraph,* January 8, 1909, 3.

200 Jacob gave so generously: *Jewish Messenger,* March 3, 1914, 233. The newspaper was published in Calcutta.

200 From 1914, all: *Israel's Messenger,* March 6, 1935, 2.

201 He also gave: *Collegian & Progress of India* 19, no. 2 (July 1920): 57–58.

201 He was rewarded: *The Cyclopedia of India, 1907–09: Biographical, Historical, Administrative and Commercial,* vol. 1 (Calcutta: Cyclopedia Publishing Co., 1907), 280.

201 Jacob and his brother-in-law: Kynaston, *City of London,* 266.

202 a director of: *Financial Times,* December 21, 1909, 6 and 10.

202 (Through Franqui): *Financial Times,* February 14, 1917, 11.

202 The bank was: *Financial Times,* February 28, 1912, 9.

202 In fact, from the: Lin, "China's 'Dual-Economy,'" 182.

202 The impetus began: For details of the rebellion and its ramifications, see Phoebe Chow, *Britain's Imperial Retreat from China, 1900–1931* (New York: Routledge, 2017), 60–71.

202 In 1906, an imperial: Owen, *British Opium Policy,* 333.

203 It expressed doubts: J. Jordan to Edward Grey, "General Report on Opium," Trade in China, January to June 1908, *Foreign Office Correspondence* 405/185, 9443.

203 In England and India: R. K. Newman, "India and the Anglo-Chinese Opium Agreements, 1907–1914," *Modern Asian Studies* 23, no. 3 (1989): 533 (article 525–60).

203 Parliament was once: Theodore Taylor, MP (Lancashire), *Hansard* 158 (May 30, 1906): cc 494–516.

203 Predictably, among the: Letter to Colonial Secretary, Hong Kong, December 9, 1908, *China Association Circulars* (hereafter cited as *CHAS*) 3, nos. 41–60 (October 12, 1908–June 17, 1909). The China Association had its offices at 99 Cannon Street, London.

203 Although E. D. Sassoon's: Zhongli Zhang and Zengnian Chen, *Shaxun Jituan Zai Jiu Zhongguo* [The Sassoon group in old China] (Beijing: Chubanshe, 1985), 29.

203 The China Association: Jackson, in *The Sassoons,* repeatedly claimed that the rift between the two companies was permanent.

203 Others were sent: David Sassoon & Co. and E. D. Sassoon & Co. (Hong Kong) to the Secretary, Hong Kong Chamber of Commerce, April 9, 1911, *Report of the General Committee of the Hongkong Chamber of Commerce for the Year Ending 31st December 1911* (Hong Kong: South China Morning Post Ltd., 1912), 49–50.

203 By 1910, the government: Sir J. Jordan to Sir Edward Grey, Peking, December 21, 1909, *The Opium Trade, 1910–1941,* vol. 1, *1910–1911* (Lon-

don: Scholarly Resources, 1974), 6. The six volumes are a superb collection of all the British documents and correspondence related to opium during those thirty-one years.

204 A typical appeal: Messrs. E. D. Sassoon & Co. to Sir John Jordan, Shanghai, September 20, 1909, *CHAS*/MCP/13.

204 The China Association: Letters from E. D. Sassoon to the Foreign Office, July 7, 1910, and July 18, 1910, and letter from China Association to Messrs. Sassoon, July 22, 1910, China Association Circular Correspondence for the General Committee, July 22, 1910, *CHAS*/MCP/13/84, 1–3.

204 In fact, what was: Wie T. Dunn, *The Opium Traffic in Its International Aspects* (PhD diss., Colombia University, 1920), 107; Owen, *British Opium Policy,* 343.

204 The rope, however: See, for example, letters from the two Sassoons to Sir F. H. May, Colonial Secretary, November 21, 1910, and November 26, 1910, *CHAS*/MCP/14/92, 6–7.

204 In Britain, the campaign: John A. Anderson, "The Opium Question: A New Opportunity," in *The Chinese Recorder and Missionary Journal,* vol. 37, 431–34.

204 In 1908 National: Correspondence and leaflet, January 15, 1908, LPA, Davidson 147, 267–69.

204 The Archbishop of Canterbury: Letter to the Bishop of Durham, May 18, 1908, LPA, Davidson 147, 304.

204 During a period: Owen, *British Opium Policy,* 347.

205 This was an opportunity: Messrs. E. D. Sassoon and D. Sassoon and Co. to Foreign Office, May 23, 1912, in *Opium Trade, 1910–1941,* vol. 2, *1912,* part 5, no. 50, 135.

205 For all the Sassoons': China Association to Foreign Office, June 18, 1912, *CHAS*/MCP/17/130, 4.

205 One official recommended: Goffe to Jordan, Nanjing, November 25, 1909, no. 45; Jordan to Goffe, August 13, 1909, no. 28, PRO, FO 228/2427.

205 The Foreign Office: Foreign Office to Messrs. E. D. Sassoon & Co., July 15, 1912, *CHAS*/MCP/17/130, 1–2.

205 In fact, the Under-Secretary: E. S. Montagu, House of Commons debate, May 7, 1913, *Hansard* 52: 2190.

205 The memo begged: E. D. Sassoon & Co. and David Sassoon & Co. to the Under-Secretary of State, Foreign Office, May 14, 1913, *CHAS*/MCP/18.

206 Two months later: E. D. Sassoon & Co. and David Sassoon & Co. to Sir Edward Grey, Foreign Office, July 15, 1913, *Opium Trade 1910–1941,* vol. 3, *1913–1916,* no. 151, 177–78.

206 By then, however: Newman, "India and the Anglo-Chinese Opium Agreements," 545.

206 There were rumors: Owen, *British Opium Policy*, 349–50.

206 Even before the declaration: National Laymen's Missionary Movement to the Archbishop of Canterbury, Lambeth Palace, April 30, 1913, LPA, Davidson 187, 277–79.

206 Following a letter: W. Langley to Lambeth Palace, May 5, 1913, LPA, Davidson 187, 280–81.

206 The Archbishop rejected: Archbishop's Office, October 2, 1913, LPA, Davidson 187, 308.

207 While the trade waned: *Financial Times*, April 30, 1910, 7.

207 It has been estimated: Zhang and Chen, *Shaxun Jituan*, 27–28.

207 Furthermore, they claimed: *Financial Times*, December 14, 1912, 7.

207 India had become: Metcalf and Metcalf, *A Concise History of Modern India*, 125.

207 Lord George Curzon: Metcalf and Metcalf, *A Concise History of Modern India*, 155.

208 The Indian economy: Morris David Morris, "Indian Industry and Business in the Age of *Laissez Faire*," in Rajat K. Ray, ed., *Entrepreneurship and Industry in India, 1800–1947* (Delhi: Oxford University Press, 1994), 197–98 (article 197–227).

208 Mobilization of workers: Vanessa Caru, "'A Powerful Weapon for the Employers'?: Workers' Housing and Social Control in Interwar Bombay," in Prashant Kidambi, Manjiri Kamat, and Rachel Dwyer, eds., *Bombay Before Mumbai* (Gurgaon: Penguin Random House India, 2019), 217 (article 213–235).

208 The number of cotton: Sir Henry James, "The India Cotton Duties," *Hansard* 30 (February 21, 1895): 1285–361.

209 He refused to speculate: Manchester Chamber of Commerce, *Bombay and Lancashire Cotton Spinning Inquiry: Minutes of Evidence and Reports* (London: Effingham Wilson, 1888). C. J. Sassoon came before the commission on June 29, 1888.

209 In spite of the: Gregory Clark, "Why Isn't the Whole World Developed? Lessons from the Cotton Mills," *Journal of Economic History* 47, no. 1 (March 1987): 143.

209 Industrialization in India: *Financial Times*, June 1, 1909, 8.

209 Anxious to bring: S. M. Rutnagur, ed., *Electricity in India: Being a History of the Tata Hydro-Electric Project* (Bombay: The Proprietors, Indian Textile Journal, 1912), 10.

209 By the end of: Rutnagur, *Electricity in India*, 63.

209 Winston Churchill: Martin Gilbert, *Churchill and the Jews: A Lifelong Friendship* (New York: Henry Holt, 2007), 5.

210 Less than three weeks: King George (Marlborough House) to Mrs. Arthur, May 26, 1910, Rothschild Archive.

210 Louise was officially: Earl Marshal's Office (London) to Mrs. Arthur Sassoon, May 1910 (no specific date), Rothschild Archive.

210 When Arthur died: King George (Buckingham Palace) to Mrs. Arthur, March 13, 1912, Rothschild Archive.

210 When George himself: King George (Windsor Castle) to Mrs. Arthur, May 23, 1929, Rothschild Archive.

210 And when he died: Princess Mary (Buckingham Palace) to Mrs. Arthur, January 30, 1936, Rothschild Archive.

211 One book published: A Foreign Resident (anonymous), *Society in the New Reign* (London: T. Fisher Unwin, 1904), 191–92.

212 He explained how the Jews: A Foreign Resident, *Society in the New Reign*, 227.

212 Describing the Prince: A Foreign Resident, *Society in the New Reign*, 197.

212 A predictably terrible: Owen Johnson, *The Salamander* (New York: A. L. Burt, 1914). The book was serialized in *McClure's Magazine* from May 1913 to October 1914.

212 In retaliation he: Imber, *A Late Imperial Elite*, 63.

212 In a collection: Terence Pepper, *High Society Photographs 1897–1914* (London: National Portrait Gallery, 1998), 29.

212 There were plenty: See, for example, *North-China Herald*, June 22, 1906, 689.

212 The exhibition catalogs: See, for example, *The Exhibition of the Royal Academy of Arts, 1889; Catalogue of the Anglo-Jewish Historical Exhibition, 1887*.

213 They attended the openings: *Sketch,* June 6, 1900, 318.

213 One "Racing Account": Racing Account of 1928, London Metropolitan Archives (hereafter cited as LMA), CLC/8/207/ED04/03/016, 59.

213 Charities were not: Lady L. Sassoon Account, 1928, LMA, CLC/8/207/ED04/03/016, 105.

213 The ceremony took place: A diary of a family member, November 5, 1912, DSA, box 21-B.

213 A two-page spread: *Times* (London), November 8, 1912.

214 Many guests attended: *North-China Herald,* March 15, 1907, 565.

214 David advised his: David (London) to his sister Rachel (Calcutta), July 27, 1931, and September 2, 1931, DSA, box 71.

214 By the fourth: See table in Roth, *Sassoon Dynasty,* 170. See also previous chapter.

214 Their uneasiness and: Damian Collins, *Charmed Life: The Phenomenal World of Philip Sassoon* (London: Collins, 2016), 27.

214 Flora cut off all: Flora Sassoon (32 Burton Street, London) to Lady Boyle (Dudley Hotel, Sussex), September 26, 1916, DSA, box 16. Louise was born in 1873, married in 1914, and died in 1964.

215 One telegram of 1917: Foreign and Political Department, May 1917, no. 63, INA.

215 He wrote to the: Shaul Yehuda (Baghdad) to Sassoon & Co. (Bombay), September 5, 1915, DSA, box 71.

11. WAR AND UNCERTAINTY, 1914–1924

216 Siegfried Loraine Sassoon: John Stuart Roberts, *Siegfried Sassoon* (London: Metro Publishing, 1999), 1.

217 "Such were the bare": Siegfried Sassoon, *The Old Century and Seven More Years* (London: Faber & Faber, 1938), 15.

217 "Two old men": Sassoon, *The Old Century,* 39.

218 Siegfried's "attitude toward": Jean Moorcroft Wilson, *Siegfried Sassoon: The Making of a War Poet: A Biography 1886–1918* (London: Duckworth, 1998), 14.

218 He also referred: Quoted in Wilson, *Siegfried Sassoon: The Making of a War Poet,* 14.

218 The dead and wounded: Quoted in Wilson, *Siegfried Sassoon,* 293.

219 or the deceptions of: From a poem titled "The Hero."

219 "his innate self-distrust": Jean Moorcroft Wilson, *Siegfried Sassoon: The Journey from the Trenches: A Biography (1918–1967)* (London: Duckworth, 2003), 251.

219 Yet, and maybe: "A Sketch of Mr. Siegfried Sassoon," *Spectator,* March 21, 1931.

219 Siegfried was attached: Wilson, *Siegfried Sassoon: The Making of a War Poet,* 78.

220 Ironically, the day: Wilson, *Siegfried Sassoon, The Journey from the Trenches,* 184.

220 Ten years before: Jackson, *Sassoons,* 291.

220 During the war: Roth, *Sassoon Dynasty,* 211.

220 Reginald Sassoon: Jackson, *Sassoons,* 173.

220 When he died in: *Times* (London), January 18, 1933, 12.

220 Some, such as Mrs. Arthur: A. M. de Beck, ed., *Women of the Empire in War Time* (London: Dominion of Canada News, 1916), 5.

221 Although the German: Frank H. H. King, *The History of the Hongkong*

and Shanghai Banking Corporation, vol. 2, *The Hongkong Bank in the Period of Imperialism and War, 1895–1918: Wayfoong, the Focus of Wealth* (New York: Cambridge University Press, 1989), 550.

221 In one letter: David (London) to Rachel (Calcutta), January 26, 1916, DSA, box 71.

221 Even the pearl business: Ezra (London) to Suleiman (Bombay), May 21, 1891, DSA, 3284.

221 Before the war: Foreign Office, "Baghdad Railway: Navigation of the Tigris and Euphrates," India Office Records, file 2073/1913, British Library, Qatar Digital Library.

221 E. D. Sassoon was indirectly: Sir G. Lowther to Sir Edward Grey, June 23, 1913, India Office Records, FO 29510, no. 552.

222 Ten thousand pounds was seized: *Financial Times,* March 22, 1917, 4.

222 They continued to export: Persian Gulf Trade, file 1032/1914, India Office Records. Also, see Department of Commerce and Industry, 1918, file 631, INA.

222 Even before the end: Foreign and Political Department, July 1917, nos. 143–44, INA.

222 Indeed, the E. D. Sassoon: E. D. Sassoon Accounts, "Persian Gulf Commissions and Consignments Account, 1921–1925," LMA.

222 Sir Sassoon David: Roper Lethbridge, *India and the Imperial Preference* (London: Longmans, Green and Co., 1907), 6.

222 The latter had: Jackson, *Sassoons,* 200.

223 The First World War brought: Roland, *Jews in British India,* 89.

223 In April 1919: Metcalf and Metcalf, *A Concise History of Modern India,* 169.

224 According to an Indian: S. M. Rutnagur, ed., *Bombay Industries: The Cotton Mills* (Bombay: India Textile Journal Ltd., 1927), 59.

224 India offered many: Clark, "Why Isn't the Whole World Developed?," 146 and 148.

224 "Jacob had adequate": Jackson, *Sassoons,* 62–63.

224 The Sassoons and a few: David Sassoon & Co., E. D. Sassoon, and a few other mill owners to the chairman of the Hong Kong Chamber of Commerce, June 23, 1917, *Report of the General Committee of the Hong Kong General Chamber of Commerce for the Year Ended 31 December 1917* (Hong Kong: South China Morning Post, 1918), 209.

224 The cancellation of: Secretary of State to Governor of Hong Kong, August 10, 1917, *Report of the General Committee of the Hong Kong General Chamber of Commerce,* 226.

225 E. D. Sassoon was among: R. K. Sangameswaran, "Joint Stock Concerns in India," *India Review,* August 1919, 526–27.

225 The company retorted: *Speeches at the Millowners' Association,* 1920.

225 When they and other: Rajnarayan Chandavarkar, *The Origins of Industrial Capitalism in India: Business Strategies and the Working Classes in Bombay, 1900–1940* (Cambridge: Cambridge University Press, 1994), 251–60.

225 E. D. Sassoon's rationalization: See, for example, the liquidation of Empress Spinning and Weaving Co., August 21, 1916, DSA, box 34-3.

225 Yet an inquiry: Chandavarkar, *Origins of Industrial Capitalism in India,* 384–85. The inquiry referred to was known as the Stones Inquiry.

225 Raw cotton was: Letter to Sir Edward, November 13, 1923, DSA, box 27-A.

225 While the cost of: Gijsbert Oonk, "Motor or Millstone?," 419–52.

226 One newspaper wrote: *Financial Times,* March 14, 1912, 6.

226 Given the frequent: Cotton Department of E. D. Sassoon (Manchester), January 21, 1926, and January 14, 1928, E. D. Sassoon Papers and Accounts, LMA.

226 Early in 1917: A. Howard, David Sassoon & Co., Shanghai, "Memorandum Respecting Opium Stocks," January 12, 1917, in *The Opium Trade, 1910–1941,* vol. 4, *1917–1921* (London: Scholarly Resources, 1974), no. 14, 8–9.

226 The Combine was: Blue, "Opium for China: The British Connection," 42. See also Hauser, *Shanghai: City for Sale,* 118.

226 The British, who hadn't: Correspondence, October 15, 1918, and November 1, 1918, *Opium Trade, 1910–1941*, 4:3–4, part 13, no. 6 and enclosure.

226 Even though the curtain: Zhang and Chen, *Sassoon Group in Old China,* 28.

227 The firm begged: E. D. Sassoon to the Foreign Office, January 27, 1915, *Shanghai Political and Economic Reports, 1842–1943,* 134–35.

227 It seems that the: Messrs. E. D. Sassoon (Bombay) to Director-General of Posts and Telegraph (Bombay), October 25, 1918, Department of Commerce and Industry, no. 5/6, part B, INA.

227 It was not easy: Under-Secretary of the Government of India to Director-General of Posts and Telegraphs, November 13, 1918, Department of Commerce and Industry, no. 5/6, part B, INA.

228 During the first six: Finance Department (Calcutta) to the Under-Secretary (Bombay), January 15, 1924, file 20.114 SR, INA.

228 Meanwhile, the Indian: "Report on an Opium Smuggling Syndicate Discovered at a Chinese Steamship Company," August 7, 1923, Finance Department, INA

228 One report indicated: *China Mail,* March 19, 1918.

229 Opium trading during: Blue, "Opium for China: The British Connection," 45.

229 The argument that opium: Kenneth Pomeranz and Topik, *The World That Trade Created: Society, Culture, and the World Economy, 1400 to Present*, 2nd ed. (London: M. E. Sharpe, 2006), 93.

229 complicated by analysis: Lin, "China's 'Dual-Economy,'" 193–94.

230 *Israel's Messenger:* Maisie Meyer, "Baghdadi Jewish Merchants in Shanghai and the Opium Trade," *Jewish Culture and History* 2, no. 1 (1999): 68 (article 58–71).

230 S.D.'s daughter, Rachel: Quoted in Negev and Koren, *The First Lady of Fleet Street*, 43.

230 Her nephew, the poet: Siegfried Sassoon, "Ancestors," in *The Old Huntsman and Other Poems* (New York: E. P. Dutton, 1918), 61. The collection was dedicated to Thomas Hardy.

230 Jardine Matheson's: Quoted in Trocki, *Opium, Empire and the Global Political Economy*, 116.

231 The fascist Arnold Leese: Arnold Leese, *Chinese Communism? Yes, but It Was Jewish When It Started*, pamphlet (Surrey: Arnold Leese, 1949).

231 One-third of China's: Hauser, *Shanghai: City for Sale*, 119.

231 Economically, laissez-faire: Madeleine Zelin, "Chinese Business Practice in the Late Imperial Period," *Enterprise & Society* 14, no. 4 (December 2013): 769–93.

231 As a consequence: King, *History of the Hongkong and Shanghai Banking Company*, 2:40–42.

232 This was a case: C. A. Bayly, *The Birth of the Modern World, 1780–1914: Global Connections and Comparisons* (Oxford: Blackwell, 2004), 170 and 184.

232 The Shanghai Municipal: Zhang and Chen, *Sassoon Company in Old China*, 37–38.

233 In one case, they: *The Municipal Gazette*, March 28, 1911, 94.

233 It became one: Wang Jian, *Shanghai Jewish Cultural Map*, trans. Fang Shengquan (Shanghai: Shanghai Brilliant Publishing House, 2013), 66.

233 The amalgamation was warmly: Vaudine England, *Arnholds: China Trader* (Hong Kong: Arnhold & Co., 2017), 94.

234 In 1915 a law: Jacob Sassoon Baronetcy, Act no. 2 of 1915, South Asia Archive.

235 He paid one visit: *Times of India*, December 5, 1924, 9.

235 In a manner typical: Jackson, *Sassoons*, 206.

235 She had a strong: Victor to Yvonne, January 23, 1926, Sir Ellice Victor Elias Sassoon Papers and Photographs, Southern Methodist University (hereafter cited as Victor's Papers, SMU).

236 He would use: Maisie Meyer, *Shanghai's Baghdadi Jews: A Collection of Biographical Reflections* (Hong Kong: Blacksmith Books, 2015), 267.

236 His sensitivity about: Jackson, *Sassoons*, 203.

236 Sybil was mostly: Stansky, *Sassoon*, 15.

237 Furthermore, there was: Collins, *Charmed Life*, 22.

238 He also became: James Knox, "Sir Philip Sassoon, BT: Aesthete, Connoisseur, Patron," in Christie's, *Works of Art from Collections of the Cholmondeley Family and the Late Sir Philip Sassoon, Bt.* (London: Christie's, 1994), xxv.

239 A patron of John Singer Sargent: Stansky, *Sassoon*, 144.

239 Kenneth Clark, the famous: James Stourton, *Kenneth Clark: Life, Art and Civilisation* (New York: Alfred A. Knopf, 2016), 92.

239 Chaim Weizmann: Chaim Weizmann, *Trial and Error* (New York: Schocken, 1966), 261.

239 In spite of being a member of: Knox, "Sir Philip Sassoon, Bt," xxiv.

239 Sybil likewise kept: Stansky, *Sassoon*, 29.

240 Some derided his role: Quoted in Stansky, *Sassoon*, 101–2.

240 Mosley's anti-Semitism: Quoted from *Blackwood's Edinburgh Magazine*, February 1921, in Collins, *Charmed Life*, 118.

240 C. K. Scott-Moncrieff: Quoted in Stansky, *Sassoon*, 110.

241 "The Prince of Wales": Quoted in Collins, *Charmed Life*, 170. See also Stansky, *Sassoon*, 116.

241 "Iraq was the first": Philip Sassoon, *The Third Route* (New York: Doubleday & Co., 1929), 106.

241 While there, Philip: Sassoon, *Third Route*, 112.

242 He was there on: Sassoon, *Third Route*, 113.

243 He came as an Englishman: Collins, *Charmed Life*, 187.

243 Despite his father's: Collins, *Charmed Life*; Stansky, *Sassoon*.

243 Most of his friends: Collins, *Charmed Life*, 29.

243 In a brochure about: Michael Dane, *The Sassoons of Ashley Park* (Surrey: Ian Allan Printing, 1999), 8.

243 Whenever a relative: Roth, *Sassoon Dynasty*, 136.

244 It was an allusion: Address delivered on Speech Day of Jews' College, London, April 13, 1924 (Oxford: Private Circulation, 1924). Farha's quote from the Bible is Judges 4:8, DSA, box 33.

244 Jews are generally buried: Selina (Jerusalem) to parents (London), December 25, 1924, DSA, box 33.

245 A couple of years: Indenture, 1927 (no specific date), DSA.

245 A journalist, who: *Do'ar Ha-Yom*, June 17, 1927. Name of journalist is given only by his initials, Y.H.

245 He was willing: David Solomon Sassoon, *Masa' Babel*. Details about David and his collection were provided in a preface by Meir Benayahu.

245 In 1914, one of the: Sotheby's Catalogue, *Sassoon: A Golden Legacy*, auc-

tion catalog (New York: Sotheby's, December 17, 2020). The catalog quotes Elkan Nathan Adler (1861–1946).

245 "Between tea and dinner": Rachel Ezra, "From Damascus to Baghdad: A Trip Across the Syrian Desert," DSA, box 69.

12. FROM BOMBAY TO SHANGHAI, 1925–1949

247 Victor was known: *Times of India,* October 11, 1926, 11.

248 Recounting his experiences: *Times of India,* September 13, 1928, 13.

248 In reality, the final: Metcalf and Metcalf, *A Concise History of Modern India,* 185, 188.

248 The mill owners in: *Times of India,* March 10, 1925, 4.

248 He told a journalist: *Times of India,* December 8, 1925, 6.

249 His letter bristled: Victor Sassoon to Yvonne Fitzroy, July 22, 1923, British Library, Mss.Eur.E 312.

250 He disagreed with: Victor Sassoon to Yvonne Fitzroy, January 23, 1926, British Library, Mss.Eur.E 312.

250 The letter mocked: Letter to *Times of India,* January 8, 1927, 7.

250 The same newspaper: *Times of India,* August 30, 1927, 7.

250 He was convinced: Victor Sassoon's speech in the Legislative Assembly, Delhi, February 5, 1929, *Times of India,* February 6, 1929, 11.

250 Unlike David Sassoon: Rutnagur, ed. *Bombay Industries: The Cotton Mills,* 364.

251 One Indian shareholder: *Times of India,* January 18, 1927, 4.

251 He compared the industry: *China Mail,* September 8, 1927, 1.

251 Unfortunately, there is: Samuel, Samuel & Co. to E. D. Sassoon, July 31, 1924, Lloyds Banking Group Archive, Samuel Papers, S/1/1/b/262, f. 229. I am indebted to Professor William Clarence-Smith for bringing this document and other information about Samuel, Samuel & Co. to my attention.

252 At a time when: *Times of India,* July 24, 1925, 8.

252 The grand prize, however: Quoted in Jackson, *Sassoons,* 210.

252 As with his predecessors: Deputy Secretary to the government of India, Home Department, December 22, 1925, INA, DO, no. 1514.

252 Without fail, he: Diary 1927, Victor's Papers, SMU. At the time, he took a cruise on the *Naldera,* owned by P & O, which sailed from London to Marseilles at the end of July 1927.

253 In a talk: Press cutting from July 1927, Victor's Papers, SMU.

253 From his diaries we: See notes on August 30, 1927, Victor's Papers, SMU.

253 For another, in December: "Instruction Card No. 1," for dinner party on December 19, 1929, Victor's Papers, SMU.

253 He was visiting: Extract from a speech by Sir Victor Sassoon in the Legislative Assembly, March 5, 1929, INA, no. 436-I.T./29.

253 His value to the: Central Board of Revenue (Simla) to Khan Vachha, Commissioner of Income Tax, Bombay, June 21, 1929, INA, no. 436-I.T./29.

253 In his final speech: Memo by Central Board of Revenue, May 29, 1929, INA, no. 436-I.T./29.

254 He admonished the: *Times of India,* March 13, 1929, 13.

254 As a result, by: See reports on company meetings of three E. D. Sassoon mills, *Times of India,* June 17, 1930, 4.

254 Labor relations in Bombay: *Times of India,* March 17, 1931, 7.

254 He believed that: *Times of India,* October 10, 1930, 10.

254 He foresaw considerable: Metcalf and Metcalf, *A Concise History of Modern India*, 123.

255 Apart from the mills: *Financial Times,* July 18, 1931, 6; *Times of India,* July 18, 1931, 12.

255 The announcement was: *Irish Times,* July 18, 1931, 10; *China Mail,* July 18, 1931, 7.

255 It was a tone: *Times of India,* October 6, 1931, 3.

255 Not all were affluent: Meyer, *Shanghai's Baghdadi Jews*, 27.

256 Victor, a late entrant: Jackson, *Sassoons*, 98.

256 He still participated: Diary entry, October 4, 1938, Victor's Papers, SMU.

256 it is plausible that: Meyer, *Shanghai's Baghdadi Jews*, 279.

256 A letter of 1931: Mozelle Solomon (Shanghai) to Lady Ezra (London), February 17, 1931, DSA, box 72-1.

256 After a rare meeting: Meyer, *Shanghai's Baghdadi Jews*, 280.

257 The taipans (heads of): Hauser, *Shanghai: City for Sale*, 278.

257 When a woman: Harriet Sergeant, *Shanghai* (London: Jonathan Cape, 1991), 134.

257 One estimate put: "The Shanghai Boom," *Fortune,* January 1935. Currencies in the article were quoted in Mexican dollars. As mentioned, the Chinese currency, the yuan, was a silver dollar and sometimes loosely called the Mexican. At the time one Mexican dollar was worth 34 cents.

257 The upper part: *North-China Herald,* May 5, 1928, 189.

258 The building was designed: Peter Hibbard, *The Bund Shanghai: China Faces West* (New York: W. W. Norton, 2008), 75.

258 The building was opened: Wang Xuyuan, *The Bund and Architecture of One Century* (Shanghai: China Architecture & Building Press, 2008), 220.

258 From the air, passengers: Taras Grescoe, *Shanghai Grand: Forbidden Love and International Intrigue in a Doomed World* (New York: St. Martin's Press, 2016), 24.

259 However, navigating: Meyer, *Shanghai's Baghdadi Jews,* 271.

259 By the mid-1930s: "Shanghai Boom."

259 According to the company's: "Comparative Statement of Land Values in Shanghai, 1929–1933," LMA, CLC/B/207/ED08/01/001.

259 One recent Chinese: Zhang and Chen, *Sassoon Company in Old China,* table 6, 41.

260 Victor did, in fact: Jackson, *Sassoons,* 234.

260 In spite of this: Shanghai Municipal Archives, File Q6-6-1146, 32, July 22, 1938.

260 Ovadia joined his cousin: *Financial Times,* December 24, 1934, 7.

261 The firm began: *Financial Times,* January 17, 1935, 5.

261 Even where the bank: Frank H. H. King, *The History of the Hong Kong and Shanghai Banking Company,* vol. 3, *The Hongkong Bank Between the Wars and the Bank Interned, 1919–1945: Return from Grandeur* (New York: Cambridge University Press, 1988), 367.

261 A perusal of E. D.: E. D. Sassoon Banking Archives, 1931, LMA, CLC/B /207/ED04/03/021.

261 There were some notable: *Financial Times,* January 25, 1936, 4.

261 According to a Chinese: Zhang and Chen, *Sassoon Company in Old China,* table 30, 146.

261 The study's authors: Zhang and Chen, *Sassoon Company in Old China,* 147.

261 Victor's "palliative solution": *Hongkong Daily Press,* November 30, 1935, 6; *Hongkong Telegraph,* March 28, 1935, 1, and March 30, 1935, 1.

262 He continued to: *Financial Times,* March 28, 1935, 7.

262 The U.S. Silver: Niv Horesh, *Shanghai, Past and Present: A Concise Socio-Economic History* (Brighton: Sussex Academic Press, 2014), 59.

262 He proposed that: *Times of India,* April 12, 1934, 11.

262 In 1930: Private diaries of 1930, 1931, 1932, 1933, and 1934, Victor's Papers, SMU.

263 The house was designed: *Israel's Messenger,* January 1, 1934, 4.

263 In his private: Diary entry, January 23, 1935, Victor's Papers, SMU. He commented that the model he photographed was an American dancer with a good figure who dined with him afterward.

263 One socialite who: Stella Dong, *Shanghai: The Rise and Fall of a Decadent City* (New York: Perennial, 2000), 221.

263 To those with whom: Dong, *Shanghai,* 221.

263 After some redrafting: Emily Hahn, *China to Me: A Partial Autobiography* (New York: Doubleday, 1944).

263 Victor faithfully cut: Press cutting, in diary, December 11, 1945, Victor's Papers, SMU.

263 In one letter: See, for example, Sunday, September 14, 1930, Victor's Papers, SMU.

264 he wrote: "I tried": Victor to Giulia, June 18, 1933, Victor's Papers, SMU.

264 Enclosing a nude: Victor to Giulia, February 20, 1934, Victor's Papers, SMU.

264 On one of the trips: Diary entry, October 26, 1931, with the newspaper cutting of September 30, 1931, titled "Europe Day by Day," Victor's Papers, SMU.

264 Flicking back a few: Diary entries, January 1, 1935, and Christmas 1934, Victor's Papers, SMU.

264 His banking expenditure: Victor Sassoon accounts, 1934, E. D. Sassoon Banking Archives, LMA, CLC/B/207/ED04/03/018.

265 He told one journalist: Meyer, *Shanghai's Baghdadi Jews,* 274. She quotes the *Miami Herald* of October 22, 1960.

265 In spite of his: Diary entry, June 10, 1933, Victor's Papers, SMU.

265 Shanghai in the early: Quoted in Paul French, *Destination Shanghai* (Hong Kong: Blacksmith Books, 2019), 115.

265 He threw a large: Diary entry, August 21, 1935, Victor's Papers, SMU.

265 Later, after he left: *Times Literary Supplement,* May 25, 1951.

265 According to the preface: S. E. Lucas, comp., *The Catalogue of Sassoon Chinese Ivories* (London: Country Life, 1950).

265 Some are kept: Meyer, *Shanghai's Baghdadi Jews,* 275. Today's values are calculated from MeasuringWorth.com.

266 At the same time: Meyer, *Shanghai's Baghdadi Jews,* 275.

266 He contributed a large: Diary entry, October 11, 1935, Victor's Papers, SMU; Meyer, *Shanghai's Baghdadi Jews,* 277.

267 To her son, David: Farha Sassoon's will, November 1, 1935, DSA, box 68.

267 In her obituary: *Hongkong Telegraph,* February 17, 1936, 3.

267 The Chief Rabbi: Jennifer Breger, "Three Women of the Book: Judith Montefiore, Rachel Morpurgo, and Flora Sassoon," *AB Bookman's Weekly,* no. 101 (March 30, 1998): 861–63 (article 853–864).

267 It was said that: Roth, *Sassoon Dynasty,* 139.

267 "Her greatest joy": Roth, *Sassoon Dynasty,* 139.

267 "Silver-haired, imposing": Jackson, *Sassoons,* 208.

268 In a piece titled: "Women and Their Emancipation," *Westminster Review* 161 (1904): 417.

268 Later it managed: Sergeant, *Shanghai,* 296.

268 A boycott of Japanese: Dong, *Shanghai,* 213.

269 While foreigners in: Peter Harmsen, *Shanghai 1937: Stalingrad on the Yangtze* (Havertown, PA: Casemate Publishers, 2015).

269 The Japanese erroneously: Carter, *Champions Day,* 152.

269 The world's fifth-largest: Paul French, *Bloody Saturday* (Australia: Penguin, 2017), 3. French paints a vivid picture of the city during the attack.

269 One landed at: French, *Bloody Saturday,* 41.

270 The Shanghai branch: *Financial Times,* August 20, 1937, 7.

270 By October, the effect: *Financial Times,* October 11, 1937, 7.

270 Early in 1938: Victor to Derek Barrington Fitzgerald, January 7, 1938, Victor's Papers, SMU.

270 he expressed his fears: Victor to Derek Barrington Fitzgerald, January 11, 1938, Victor's Papers, SMU.

270 Although daily hostilities: *Financial Times,* August 18, 1938, 7.

270 One of the two: Gao Bei, *Shanghai Sanctuary: Chinese and Japanese Policy Toward European Jewish Refugees During World War II* (Oxford: Oxford University Press, 2013), 59.

271 They demanded guarantees: *Minutes of the Shanghai Municipal Council* 27 (May 5, 1938): 256.

271 The number of Jews: Gao, *Shanghai Sanctuary,* 5.

271 The Brazilian government: *Israel's Messenger,* August 12, 1938, 13.

272 They asked the Japanese: Kranzler, *Japanese, Nazis & Jews,* 268.

272 Representatives on the: *Minutes of the Shanghai Municipal Council* 27 (May 5, 1938): 356.

272 Though he was anxious: Meyer, *Shanghai's Baghdadi Jews,* 275.

272 He calculated how: *China Records of the Intergovernmental Committee of Refugees, 1938–1947,* November 13, 1939, U.S. National Archives.

272 At the beginning: *Times of India,* October 20, 1939, 8.

272 The chasm between: *Hongkong Telegraph,* February 27, 1940, 1.

272 Even Ellis Hayim: *Israel's Messenger,* March 20, 1940, 16.

273 For the Japanese: Gao, *Shanghai Sanctuary,* 105.

273 In the years following: Heehs, *India's Freedom,* vol.2.

273 He resumed his criticism: *Times of India,* October 9, 1940, 1.

273 When Victor argued: *Times of India,* January 21, 1942, 7.

273 At that time, he: Letter from Victor to Lord Reading (former Viceroy of India, and in 1931, briefly, leader of the House of Lords, and in 1931 Secretary of State for Foreign Affairs), September 23, 1930, British Library, Mss.Eur.E 238/105.

274 His record was: Press cutting, August 25, 1941, Victor's Papers, SMU.

274 He spent five of: *Hongkong Daily Press,* July 7, 1941, 5.

274 In a speech he gave: Speech given to the Boston Chamber of Commerce, April 24, 1942, Victor's Papers, SMU.

274 In an interview: Press cutting, April 8, 1941, Victor's Papers, SMU.

275 On a visit to Hollywood: Rathbone Party, Hollywood, February 4, 1940, box 7:2, 1940–1957, Victor's Papers, Parties, SMU.

275 The tone of the minutes: *Minutes of the Shanghai Municipal Council* 28 (1940 and 1941).

275 It marked the final chapter: Nicholas R. Clifford, *Retreat from China: British Policy in the Far East, 1937–1941* (London: Longmans, 1967), 158.

275 The Japanese occupied: Kranzler, *Japanese, Nazis and Jews,* 453–54.

275 They were aware that: Note translated from Russian signed by an E. Kerganeff, August 20, 1940, Shanghai Police Files, 1894–1945, U.S. National Archives.

276 Life in the camps: "The Kadoorie Memoir," letter from Lord Lawrence Kadoorie of Hong Kong to a friend, February 6, 1979, British Library.

276 Presiding over an: *Financial Times,* May 30, 1944, 4.

276 He also advocated: Unedited stenographic transcript of a luncheon conversation between Sir Victor Sassoon and Henry B. Sell, February 1943, Victor's Papers, SMU.

277 He believed that by: *Times of India,* December 24, 1945, 1.

277 He advised that this: *Times of India,* May 16, 1945, 9, and November 24, 1945, 4.

277 As a result of: Press cutting, Victor's diary, May 7, 1945, Victor's Papers, SMU.

277 From a press cutting: Press cutting, Victor's diary, September 19, 1943, Victor's Papers, SMU.

277 He proposed that: Press cutting, Victor's diary, November 23, 1945, Victor's Papers, SMU.

278 The cost of living: Key money is money paid to a landlord as an inducement by a person wishing to rent a property.

278 Furthermore, ambiguous: *Financial Times,* July 10, 1946, 2.

278 He even talked: *Times of India,* December 19, 1947, 8; *China Mail,* December 18, 1947, 1.

278 That same week: Horace Kadoorie (Hong Kong) to Victor Sassoon (Shanghai), December 19, 1947, Kadoorie Archives (Hong Kong).

278 One piece of good: *Financial Times,* January 1, 1947, 1.

279 Rumors circulated: *Washington Post,* August 13, 1947, 4B.

279 Victor returned to: Meyer, *Shanghai's Baghdadi Jews,* 295.

279 Newly independent: A. Vaidyanathan, "The Indian Economy Since Independence (1947–70)," in *The Cambridge Economic History of India,* vol. 2, *1757–2003,* Kumar and Desai, eds., 947–94.

279 Asked about it, he: *Honolulu Star-Bulletin,* June 25, 1948, 4.

279 He told the *Los Angeles*: *Los Angeles Times,* September 21, 1948, 5.

280 He had visited Nassau: Press cutting, Victor's diary, May 14, 1947, Victor's Papers, SMU.

280 For many, abandoning: Bickers, *Britain in China*, 236.

280 Although he recognized: *Los Angeles Times*, November 29, 1948, 5.

280 Victor was, however: *Los Angeles Times*, November 29, 1948, 5.

281 "He closed his eyes": Jackson, *Sassoons*, 268.

13. THE FINAL COUNTDOWN, 1949–1982

282 He left behind: Stansky, *Sassoon*, 246.

282 His estate was valued: *Hongkong Telegraph*, August 18, 1939, 13.

283 Longcroft's time in: Jackson, *Sassoons*, 218–19.

283 Longcroft came from: James Phillips-Evans, *The Longcrofts: 500 Years of a British Family* (London: CreateSpace Independent Publishing, 2012), 131–32.

283 Although the company: *Hongkong Telegraph*, October 1, 1928, 2.

284 Philip's collection opened: *Spectator*, April 12, 1930, 47.

284 Similarly, his house: Dennis Farr, *English Art 1870–1940* (Oxford: Clarendon Press, 1978), 336.

284 Clark thought that: Stourton, *Kenneth Clark*, 107.

284 Indeed, it isn't even: David Sassoon & Co. (Karachi) to Eastern Bank (Bahrain), November 9, 1934, India Office Records, British Library, IOR/R/15/2/346.

285 He concluded by the late: Wilson, *Siegfried Sassoon: The Journey from the Trenches*, 365.

285 One reviewer stated: M. Gaster, ["Review of] Ohel David, Descriptive Catalogue of the Hebrew and Samaritan MSS. in the Sassoon Library, by David Sassoon," in *Journal of the Royal Asiatic Society of Great Britain and Ireland*, no. 3 (July 1935): 542–43.

285 It relates to: Correspondence between S.D. Sassoon (Letchworth, Herts) and David Sassoon & Co. (St. Swithin's House, London), March 3, March 14, 1969, DSA, box 64-A.

285 The family's investments: R. Sassoon (London) to Rabbi Solomon (Jerusalem), May 6, 1975, DSA, box 64-A.

286 African Mercantile operated: *Financial Times* (London), August 13, 1952, 4.

286 Interestingly, the company's: Frank H. H. King, *The History of the Hong Kong and Shanghai Banking Corporation*, vol. 4, *The Hongkong Bank in the Period of Development and Nationalism, 1941–1984: From Regional Bank to Multinational Group* (New York: Cambridge University Press, 1991), 252–55.

286 David Sassoon & Co.: *Financial Times,* April 6, 1981, 9.

286 In 1982 Gerald Panchaud: *Observer,* August 29, 1982, 12.

286 However, in August: *Times* (London), August 30, 1983, 15.

286 The company initially: *Times* (London), September 6, 1983, 15.

286 In 1988, the: *Financial Times,* August 5, 1988, 16.

287 An American newspaper: *Daily News* (New York), February 14, 1950, 198.

287 His diary of that: Diary entry, February 4, 1950, Victor's Papers, SMU.

287 The relationship with: Press cutting, March 27, 1951, Victor's Papers, SMU.

287 He was still taking: Diary entries, January 1, 1951, and February 10, 1951, Victor's Papers, SMU.

287 Horse racing continued: *Washington Post,* September 9, 1953, 16.

287 A report in: Press cutting, March 11, 1950, Victor's Papers, SMU.

287 "Racing was more": Jackson, *Sassoons,* 276.

288 Even his powers of: *Green Bay Press-Gazette,* September 30, 1952, 13.

288 While receiving treatment: Jackson, *Sassoons,* 275.

289 The following April: Diary entry, February 13, 1955, Victor's Papers, SMU.

289 The gossip pages: Press cuttings, May 20, 1955, Victor's Papers, SMU.

289 Victor was growing: *Daily Telegraph,* September 9, 1957, 8.

289 He was spending several: Diary entry, September 30, 1959, Victor's Papers, SMU.

289 Its main sponsors: *Financial Times,* January 22, 1957, 1.

289 There was no income: *Financial Times,* March 2, 1959, 1.

289 Victor was a typical: *Miami Herald,* February 5, 1958, 2-B.

290 It was announced: *New York Times,* March 9, 1958, 8.

290 He bought land: *Nassau Guardian,* April 3, 1960, 7.

290 British assets lost: *Baltimore Sun,* May 20, 1952, 2.

290 As Victor told: *China Association Circulars,* December 22, 1958, *CHAS/MCP/556.*

290 The glorious days: *Manchester Guardian,* August 27, 1954, 1.

291 To his credit, he: *Guardian,* April 13, 1960, 10.

291 Asked why he chose: Jackson, *Sassoons,* 283.

291 His diary that day: Diary entries of April 1, 2, 3, and 4, 1959, Victor's Papers, SMU.

291 A year later: *Daily Mail,* June 1, 1960, 16.

291 He was hoping: *Nassau Guardian,* June 2, 1960, 5.

291 A few months later: *Nassau Guardian,* September 16, 1960, 8.

291 His condition stabilized: *Nassau Guardian,* January 8, 1961, 15.

291 He did improve: *Nassau Guardian,* February 9, 1961, 4.

292 "When the time came": Jackson, *Sassoons,* 287.

292 *The New York Times: New York Times,* August 13, 1961, 88.

292 *The Times* of London: *Times* (London), August 18, 1961, 12.

292 He did not allow: Press cutting, March 11, 1960, Victor's Papers, SMU.

293 The E. D. Sassoon bank's capital: *Daily Telegraph,* May 24, 1967, 2.

293 The plan was that: *Financial Times,* September 15, 1967, 26.

293 By the autumn: *Wall Street Journal,* September 15, 1967, 12.

293 Fitzgerald had married: A draft of a brochure for the bank, "A Century of Service to Finance and Trade," 1967, LMA, CLC/B.207/ED09/01 /001-002.

293 The bank also invested: *Financial Times,* June 6, 1969, 26.

293 The investment of the: *Daily Telegraph,* February 18, 1969, 3.

293 In the late 1960s: *Guardian,* August 5, 1971, 13.

294 By summer 1972: *Financial Times,* December 1, 1972, 22; *Economist,* December 9, 1972, 100.

294 Even at home in: *Financial Times,* February 13, 1978, 22.

294 It was renamed: *Financial Times,* September 25, 1978, 33.

AFTERWORD

295 In a world that: A Swiss trading family, the Volkarts, realized, like the Sassoons, the importance of culture, reputation, and local languages. See Dejung, "Bridges to the East," 96.

295 They had to choose: For a general discussion of the importance of information in global capitalism, see Marks, *The Information Nexus.*

296 A long analysis: Faraj Haim (Frederick) (London) to Suleiman (Bombay), August 11, 1887, DSA, 3050.

296 Frederick concluded by: Faraj Haim (London) to Suleiman (Bombay), August 11, 1887, DSA, 3050.

297 In this they were: Martin J. Wiener, *English Culture and the Decline of the Industrial Spirit 1850–1980,* 2nd ed. (Cambridge: Cambridge University Press, 2004), xvi, 97.

297 By 1870, however: Quoted in Wiener, *English Culture,* 12.

297 Industry was pushed: Wiener, *English Culture,* 130.

297 One letter from Arthur: Quoted in Kynaston, *City of London,* 2:34.

298 As one commentator: Knox, "Sir Philip Sassoon, Bt," xiii.

298 For Albert, "Society": Roth, *Sassoon Dynasty,* 117.

298 Over the course of: Wiener, *English Culture,* 146–47; Robert Henriques, *Bearsted: A Biography of Marcus Samuel* (New York: Augustus M. Kelley, 1970).

298 One key difference: For an exhaustive and in-depth study of the Rothschilds, see Niall Ferguson's two-volume history of the family: *The House of Rothschild: Money's Prophets, 1798–1848* (New York: Penguin Books,

1998); *The House of Rothschild: The World's Banker, 1849–1999* (New York: Penguin Books, 1999).

298 David instituted: See: Interview with David Rothschild, "Lunch with the FT," *Financial Times*, September 22, 2018.

298 "acting in unison": Ferguson, *The House of Rothschild: The World's Banker,* 78.

299 By 1917, Tata Sons: Chikayoshi Nomura, "The Origin of the Controlling Power of Managing Agents over Modern Business Enterprise in Colonial India," *Indian Economic and Social History Review* 51, no. 1 (2014): 108 (article 95–132).

299 At the time when: Jackson, *Sassoons,* 101.

299 As one historian: Robert Bickers, *China Bound: John Swire & Sons and Its World, 1816–1980* (London: Bloomsbury, 2020), 430.

300 One observer called: Roth, *The Sassoon Dynasty,* 206–9.

300 In 1940, the Colonial: Colonial Office, Economic/West Indies, "Business activities of Mr. Steiner of Arnhold and Company," memorandum, January and February 1940, PRO, CO 852/310/11.

300 A penetrating and: England, *Arnholds,* 139.

301 One Baghdadi Jew: J.F.R. Jacob, *An Odyssey in War and Peace: An Autobiography* (New Delhi: Lotus, 2011).

301 Another more recent: Interview by the author with Sir Michael Kadoorie, Hong Kong, November 23, 2018.

302 In England, his estate: Jackson, *Sassoons,* 44.

302 An heir to two: O. W. Holmes, *The Autocrat of the* Breakfast-Table (New York: Sagamore Press, 1961 [original in 1860]), quoted in Peter Dobkin Hall, "A Historical Overview of Family Firms in the United States," *Family Business Review* 1, no. 1 (Spring 1988): 51 (article 51–68).

302 Here, the adage: Harry Levinson, "Conflicts That Plague Family Businesses," *Harvard Business Review* 49, no. 2 (March 1971): 90 (article 90–98).

302 (She left £300,000): *Daily Telegraph,* February 27, 1968, 15.

302 Flora and Suleiman's: Lady Ezra's will, DSA, box 71.

302 Arthur held assets: "The Estate of the Late Mr. Arthur Sassoon," correspondence, Rothschild Archive.

303 Other estates took: "Case Between the Executors of Louise Sassoon (Deceased in August 1943) and the Commissioner of Inland Revenue in the High Court of Justice," Rothschild Archive.

303 *The Daily Telegraph*: *Daily Telegraph,* November 20, 1961, 17.

303 According to one source: Jackson, *Sassoons,* 259.

304 As early as 1917: Bryan Ellis, *Walton Past* (West Sussex: Phillimore & Co., 2002), 41.

304 At some point he: Press cutting from *Daily Mail,* May 9, 1950, Victor's diary, May 31, 1950, Victor's Papers, SMU.

304 So many minor royals: "Houghton Revisited," *Vanity Fair,* October 1994.

304 She lived in Houghton Hall: "Houghton Revisited," *Vanity Fair,* October 1994.

305 *The Times* reported: *Times* (London), December 9, 1994, 10.

305 Some of the religious: Meir Ronnen, "Collectibles of the Fabulous Sassoons," *Jerusalem Post,* March 28, 1999, 7.

305 At the 2020 auction: Sotheby's Catalogue, *Sassoon: A Golden Legacy.* See also *Guardian,* October 29, 2020.

305 The interconnection between: For a comprehensive review of globalization in general and for globalization during the Industrial Age of the nineteenth and twentieth centuries, see Jeffrey Sachs, *The Ages of Globalization: Geography, Technology, and Institutions* (New York: Columbia University Press, 2020), chapter 7.

306 His conclusion was: Roth, *Sassoon Dynasty,* 5.

306 "No, things are not": Mann, *Buddenbrooks,* 426.

307 One astute observer: Roth, *Sassoon Dynasty,* 210.

BIBLIOGRAPHY

ARCHIVES

Babylonia Jewry Archives (Tel Aviv)

Brighton and Hove Archives

British National Archives (London)

China Association Papers, School of Oriental and African Studies, London University

Church of England Archives (Lambeth Palace, London)

David Sassoon Archives (National Library, Jerusalem)

Indian National Archives (Delhi)

India Office (British Library, London)

Kadoorie Archives (Hong Kong)

Collection of Kenneth and Joyce Robbins

London Metropolitan Archives (London)

Ottoman Archives (Istanbul)

Queen Victoria's Journals, Bodleian Libraries, Oxford University

Rothschild Archive, The (London)

Shanghai Municipal Archives

Sir Ellice Victor Elias Sassoon Papers and Photographs (Southern Methodist University, Dallas)

South Asia Archive (Qatar Digital Archives)

REPORTS, CATALOGUES, PROCEEDINGS, ETC.

Annual Report of the Department of Agriculture in Sind, 1932–33.

Annual Report of the Sassoon Mechanics' Institute.

Ardeshir H. Mama vs. Farha Sassoon. Bombay High Court, May 21, 1928.

Bombay Administration Report of 1864–65.

Bombay and Lancashire Cotton Spinning Inquiry: Minutes of Evidence and Reports. London: Manchester Chamber of Commerce, 1888.

British Parliamentary Debates. *Hansard.*

Catalogue of the Anglo-Jewish Historical Exhibition 1887.

Christie's catalogue, *Works of Art from Collections of the Cholmondeley Family and the Late Sir Philip Sassoon, Bt.* London: Christie's, 1994.

England and the Opium Trade with China, pamphlet, London: Dyer Brothers, 1880.

Fifty-First Annual Report. London: Board of Guardians for the Relief of the Jewish Poor, 1909.

Foreign Office (Great Britain). *China: A Collection of Correspondence and Papers Relating to Chinese Affairs,* 1870.

The Indian Law Reports, Bombay Series.

Indo-European Telegraph Department Administration Report, 1875–76.

"Presentation of the Freedom of the City of London to Sir A. D. Sassoon, CSI." Council Chamber Guildhall, November 6, 1873.

Proceedings of the Legislative Council of the Governor of Bombay, 1919.

Public Education Reports, Government of Bombay.

Report of the Agri-Horticultural Society for the Year 1863.

Reports of the Bombay Chamber of Commerce.

Reports of the General Committee of the Hong Kong Chamber of Commerce.

Reports of the Royal Commission on Opium, 1894, 1895.

Reports on Trade at the Treaty Ports in China.

Shanghai Political and Economic Reports, 1842–1943.

Sir William Muir's correspondence, Papers Relating to the Opium Question. Calcutta: Government Press, 1870.

Sotheby's Catalogue, Sassoon: *A Golden Legacy.* New York: Sotheby's, 2020.

Speeches at the Millowners' Association, 1920.

The Twentieth Annual Report of the Anglo-Jewish Association, in Connection with the Alliance Israelite Universelle, 1890–1891.

NEWSPAPERS, JOURNALS, ETC.

Allen's Indian Mail and Register for British and Foreign India, China, and All Parts of the East

The Baltimore Sun

The Bombay Calendar and Almanac

The Bombay Times and Journal of Commerce

Bulletin de la Société Héraldique

Chemist and Druggist

The China Mail

The Collegian & Progress of India

Daily Mail

Daily News

The Daily Telegraph

Do'ar ha-yom

The Economist
Financial Times
Fortune
Green Bay Press-Gazette
The Guardian
Hongkong Daily Press
The Hong Kong Government
    Gazette
Hongkong Telegraph
Honolulu Star-Bulletin
The Illustrated London News
Imperial Gazette of India
Indian Education
India Review
The Irish Times
Israel's Messenger
The Jerusalem Post
The Jewish Messenger
The Jewish World
Journal of the National Indian
    Association
Journal of the Royal Asiatic Society
    of Great Britain and Ireland
Journal of the Society of Arts
The Lady's Realm
The London and China Telegraph

Los Angeles Times
The Manchester Guardian
The Manchester Times
McClure's Magazine
The Menorah
Miami Herald
Mumbai Magic
The Municipal Gazette
The Nassau Guardian
National China Herald
The New York Times
North China Daily News
The North-China Herald
The Observer
The Scribe
Shen Bao
The Sketch
The Spectator
The Times (London)
The Times Literary Supplement
The Times of India
Vanity Fair
The Wall Street Journal
The Washington Post
The Westminster Review

BOOKS AND ARTICLES

Allen, Nathan. *An Essay on the Opium Trade.* Boston: John Jewett, 1850.

Allfrey, Anthony. *Edward VII and His Jewish Court.* London: Weidenfeld & Nicolson, 1991.

Amanat, Abbas. *Iran: A Modern History.* New Haven: Yale University Press, 2017.

Anderson, John A. "The Opium Question: A New Opportunity." In *Chinese Recorder and Missionary Journal* 37 (Shanghai: Presbyterian Mission Press, 1906), 431–34.

Bauer, Rolf. *The Peasant Production of Opium in Nineteenth-Century India.* Boston: Brill, 2019.

Bayly, C. A. *The Birth of the Modern World, 1780–1914: Global Connections and Comparisons.* Oxford: Blackwell, 2004.

———. *Indian Society and the Making of British Empire*. Cambridge: Cambridge University Press, 1990.

Beck, A. M. de, ed. *Women of the Empire in War Time*. London: Dominion of Canada News, 1916.

Beckert, Sven. *Empire of Cotton: A Global History*. New York: Alfred A. Knopf, 2014.

Benjamin, N. "Industrialization of Bombay: Role of the Parsis and the Jews." *Proceedings of the Indian History Congress* 61, no. 1 (January 2000): 871–87.

Ben-Naeh, Yaron. "Ha-Sheliach Me-Hebron Mistabech Be-Bombay" [The emissary from Hebron encountered complications in Bombay]. *Et-Mol*, no. 215 (2011): 6–9.

Ben-Yacov, Avraham. "A Letter and Five Poems to the Honorable Suleiman David Sassoon." (in Hebrew) In *Mihkarim be-Toldot Yehudei Iraq ve-Beterbutam* [Studies in the history of Iraqi Jews and their culture], edited by Shmuel Moreh. Or Yehuda: Center for the Heritage of Babylonian Jews, 1981.

———. *Perakim Be-Toldot Yehudei Babel* [Treatise in the history of Babylonian Jewry]. Vol. 1. Jerusalem: Olam Ha-Sefer, 1989.

———. *Yehudei Babel be-Tfuzot* [Babylonian Jewry in diaspora]. Jerusalem: Rubin Mass, 1985.

Betta, Chiara. "Silas Aaron Hardoon (1851–1931): Marginality and Adaptation in Shanghai." PhD thesis, School of Oriental and African Studies, University of London, 1997.

Bickers, Robert. *Britain in China: Community, Culture and Colonialism, 1900–1949*. Manchester: Manchester University Press, 1999.

———. *China Bound: John Swire & Sons and Its World, 1816–1980*. London: Bloomsbury, 2020.

Blue, Gregory. "Opium for China: The British Connection." In *Opium Regimes: China, Britain, and Japan, 1839–1952*, edited by Timothy Brook and Bob Tadashi Wakabayashi, 31–54. Berkeley: University of California Press, 2000.

Booth, Martin. *Opium: A History*. New York: St. Martin's Griffin, 1996.

Bose, Sugata. *A Hundred Horizons: The Indian Ocean in the Age of Global Empire*. Cambridge, MA: Harvard University Press, 2006.

Breger, Jennifer. "Three Women of the Book: Judith Montefiore, Rachel Morpurgo, and Flora Sassoon." *AB Bookman's Weekly*, no. 101 (March 30, 1998): 853–64.

Brice, A. C. *Indian Cotton Supply: The Only Effectual and Permanent Measure for Relief to Lancashire*. London: Smith, Elder and Co., 1863.

Bunkanwanicha, Pramuan, Joseph P. H. Fan, and Yupana Wiwattanakantang. "The Value of Marriage to Family Firms." *Journal of Finance and Quantitative Analysis* 48 (2013): 611–36.

Bustani, Mehdi Jawad Habib al-. "Bağdad'daki Kölemen Hâkimiyetinin Te'sisi ve Kaldırılması İle Ali Rıza Paşa'nın Vâliliği (1749–1842)" [The Establishment and Decline of the Mamluk Rule in Baghdad and the Governorship of Ali Rıza Pasha (1749–1842)]. PhD dissertation, Istanbul University Faculty of Literature, 1979.

Caine, William Sprotson. *Picturesque India: A Handbook for European Travellers.* London: Routledge & Sons, 1890.

Cannadine, David. *Ornamentalism: How the British Saw Their Empire.* Oxford: Oxford University Press, 2001.

Caro, Robert. *Working: Researching, Interviewing, Writing.* New York: Alfred A. Knopf, 2019.

Carpenter, Mary. *Six Months in India.* Vol. 2. London: Longmans, Green, 1868.

Carter, James. *Champions Day: The End of Old Shanghai.* New York: W. W. Norton, 2020.

Caru, Vanessa. "'A Powerful Weapon for the Employers'?: Workers' Housing and Social Control in Interwar Bombay." In *Bombay Before Mumbai,* edited by Prashant Kidambi, Manjiri Kamat, and Rachel Dwyer, 213–35. Gurgaon: Penguin Random House India, 2019.

Cernea, Ruth Fredman. *Almost Englishmen: Baghdadi Jews in British Burma.* Lanham, MD: Rowman & Littlefield, 2007.

Chandavarkar, Rajnarayan. *The Origins of Industrial Capitalism in India: Business Strategies and the Working Classes in Bombay, 1900–1940.* Cambridge: Cambridge University Press, 1994.

Chow, Phoebe. *Britain's Imperial Retreat from China, 1900–1931.* New York: Routledge, 2017.

Clarence-Smith, William Gervase. *Cocoa and Chocolate, 1765–1914.* London: Routledge, 2000.

Clark, Gregory. "Why Isn't the Whole World Developed? Lessons from the Cotton Mills." *Journal of Economic History* 47, no. 1 (1987): 141–73.

Clifford, Nicholas R. *Retreat from China: British Policy in the Far East, 1937–1941.* London: Longmans, 1967.

Collins, Damian. *Charmed Life: The Phenomenal World of Philip Sassoon.* London: Collins, 2016.

The Cyclopedia of India, 1907–09: Biographical, Historical, Administrative and Commercial. Vol. 1. Calcutta: The Cyclopedia Publishing Co., 1907.

Dalrymple, William. *The Anarchy: The Relentless Rise of the East India Company.* New York: Bloomsbury Publishing, 2019.

Dalton, John N., comp. *The Cruise of Her Majesty's Ship "Bacchante," 1879–1882: Compiled from the Private Journals, Letters, and Notebooks of Prince Albert Victor and Prince George of Wales.* London: Macmillan, 1886.

Dalzell, P. M. *Memoranda on the External Trade of Sind for 1857–58*. Karachi: Sindian Press, 1858.

Dane, Michael. *The Sassoons of Ashley Park*. Walton-on-Thames: Michael Dane, 1999.

Darwin, John. *The Empire Project: The Rise and Fall of the British World-System, 1830–1970*. Cambridge: Cambridge University Press, 2009.

Dejung, Christof. "Bridges to the East: European Merchants and Business Practices in India and China." In *Commerce and Culture: Nineteenth-Century Business Elites*, edited by Robert Lee, 93–116. Farnham: Ashgate, 2011.

Dhruti Vaidya Design Studio. *The Other Mahabaleshwar: A Template for Mindful Travel*. Pune: Mervent Technologies, 2018.

Dong, Stella. *Shanghai: The Rise and Fall of a Decadent City*. New York: Perennial, 2000.

Dossal, Mariam. *Imperial Designs and India Realities: The Planning of Bombay City, 1845–1875*. Bombay: Oxford University Press, 1991.

Dunn, Wie T. *The Opium Traffic in Its International Aspects* (PhD diss., Columbia University, 1920).

Dwivedi, Sharada, and Rahul Mehotra. *Bombay: The Cities Within*. Mumbai: India Book House, 1995.

Eich, Stefan. "The Problem of the Rupee." In *The Cambridge Companion to Ambedkar*, edited by Anupama Rao and Shailaja Paik. Cambridge: Cambridge University Press, forthcoming.

Ellis, Bryan. *Walton Past*. West Sussex: Phillimore & Co., 2002.

England and the Opium Trade with China. London: Dyer Brothers, 1880.

England, Vaudine. *Arnholds: China Trader*. Hong Kong: Arnholds & Co., 2017.

Farooqi, Amar. *Opium City: The Making of Early Victorian Bombay*. New Delhi: Three Essays Collective, 2006.

Farr, Dennis. *English Art, 1870–1940*. Oxford: Clarendon Press, 1978.

Fay, Peter Ward. *The Opium War, 1840–1842*. Chapel Hill: University of North Carolina Press, 1975.

Feige, Chris, and Jeffrey A. Miron. "The Opium Wars, Opium Legalization and Opium Consumption in China." *Applied Economic Letters* 15, no. 12 (2008): 911–13.

Fels, Rendigs. "The Long Wave Depression, 1873–97." *Review of Economics and Statistics* 31 (1949): 69–73.

Ferguson, Niall. *The House of Rothschild: Money's Prophets, 1798–1848*. New York: Penguin Books, 1998.

———. *The House of Rothschild: The World's Banker, 1849–1999*. New York: Penguin Books, 1999.

———. *The Square and the Tower: Networks and Power, from the Freemasons to Facebook*. New York: Penguin Press, 2018.

Findlay, Ronald, and Kevin H. O'Rourke. *Power and Plenty: Trade, War, and the World Economy in the Second Millennium*. Princeton: Princeton University Press, 2007.

Fischel, Walter J. "Bombay in Jewish History in the Light of New Documents from the Indian Archives." *Proceedings of the American Academy for Jewish Research* 38/39 (1970–1971): 119–44.

———, ed. *Unknown Jews in Unknown Lands: The Travels of Rabbi David D'Beth Hillel, 1824–1832*. New York: Kent Publishing, 1973.

A Foreign Resident (anonymous). *Society in the New Reign*. London: T. F. Unwin, 1904.

Freeze, Chaeran Y. *A Jewish Woman of Distinction: The Life & Diaries of Zinaida Poliakova*. Waltham, MA: Brandeis University Press, 2019.

French, Paul. *Bloody Saturday*. Melbourne: Penguin Books, 2017.

———. *Destination Shanghai*. Hong Kong: Blacksmith Books, 2019.

Gao, Bei. *Shanghai Sanctuary: Chinese and Japanese Policy Toward European Jewish Refugees During World War II*. Oxford: Oxford University Press, 2013.

Gaster, M. ["Review of] Ohel David, Descriptive Catalogue of the Hebrew and Samaritan MSS. in the Sassoon Library." *Journal of the Royal Asiatic Society of Great Britain and Ireland*, no. 3 (July 1935): 542–43.

Gilbert, Martin. *Churchill and the Jews: A Lifelong Friendship*. New York: Henry Holt, 2007.

Grace, Richard J. *Opium and Empire: The Lives and Careers of William Jardine and James Matheson*. Montreal: McGill–Queen's University Press, 2014.

Gray, John. *Journey Around the World in the Years 1875–1876–1877*. London: Harrison, 1879.

Grescoe, Taras. *Shanghai Grand: Forbidden Love and International Intrigue in a Doomed World*. New York: St. Martin's Press, 2016.

Groves, Anthony N. *Journal of a Residence at Baghdad During the Years 1830 and 1831*. London: James Nisbet, 1832.

Guha, Amalendu. "The Comprador Role of the Parsi Seths, 1750–1850." *Economic and Political Weekly* 5, no. 48 (1970): 1933–36.

Hahn, Emily. *China to Me: A Partial Autobiography*. New York: Doubleday, 1944.

Hall, Peter Dobkin. "A Historical Overview of Family Firms in the United States." *Family Business Review* 1, no. 1 (Spring 1988): 51–68.

Halsey, Stephen R. *Quest for Power: European Imperialism and the Making of Chinese Statecraft*. Cambridge, MA: Harvard University Press, 2015.

A Handbook for Travelers in India, Burma, and Ceylon. London: J. Murray, 1909.

Hao, Yen-p'ing. *The Commercial Revolution in Nineteenth-Century China: The*

Rise of Sino-Western Mercantile Capitalism. Berkeley: University of California Press, 1986.

———. *The Comprador in Nineteenth Century China: Bridge Between East and West.* Cambridge, MA: East Asian Research Center, Harvard University, 1971.

Harcourt, Freda. "Black Gold: P & O and the Opium Trade, 1847–1914." *International Journal of Maritime History* 6, no. 1 (1994): 1–83.

Harmsen, Peter. *Shanghai 1937: Stalingrad on the Yangtze.* Havertown, PA: Casemate Publishers, 2015.

Hauser, Ernest O. *Shanghai: City for Sale.* New York: Harcourt, Brace, 1940.

Haweis, Mary Eliza. *Beautiful Houses: Being a Description of Certain Well-Known Artistic Houses.* London: Sampson Low, Marston, Searle & Rivington, 1882.

Heehs, Peter. *India's Freedom Struggle, 1857–1947: A Short History.* Oxford Scholarship Online, 2012.

Henriques, Robert. *Bearsted: A Biography of Marcus Samuel.* New York: Augustus M. Kelley, 1970.

Hibbard, Peter. *The Bund Shanghai: China Faces West.* New York: W. W. Norton, 2008.

Horesh, Niv. *Shanghai, Past and Present: A Concise Socio-Economic History.* Brighton: Sussex Academic Press, 2014.

Hunt, Tristram. *Ten Cities That Made an Empire.* London: Penguin Books, 2015.

Imber, Elizabeth E. "A Late Imperial Elite Jewish Politics: Baghdadi Jews in British India and the Political Horizons of Empire and Nation." *Jewish Social Studies: History, Culture, Society* 23, no. 2 (Winter 2018): 48–85.

Issawi, Charles. *The Fertile Crescent, 1800–1914: A Documentary Economic History.* Oxford: Oxford University Press, 1988.

Jackson, Stanley. *The Sassoons.* New York: E. P. Dutton, 1968.

Jacob, J. F. R. *An Odyssey in War and Peace: An Autobiography.* New Delhi: Lotus, 2011.

Janin, Hunt. *The India-China Opium Trade in the Nineteenth Century.* Jefferson, NC: McFarland & Company, 1999.

Jessawalla, Dosebai Cowasjee. *The Story of My Life.* Bombay: Times Press, 1911.

Johnson, Owen. *The Salamander.* New York: A. L. Burt, 1914.

Jones, Geoffrey. *Merchants to Multinationals: British Trading Companies in the Nineteenth and Twentieth Centuries.* New York: Oxford University Press, 2000.

The Jubilee of Shanghai, 1843–1893; Shanghai, Past and Present, and a Full Account of the Proceedings on the 17th and 18th November, 1893. Shanghai: North China Daily News, 1893.

Kessinger, Tom G. "Regional Economy (1757–1857)." In *The Cambridge Economic History of India*. Vol. 2, 1757–2003, edited by Dharma Kumar, 242–70. Delhi: Orient Longman, 2005.

King, Frank H. H. *The History of the Hongkong and Shanghai Banking Corporation*. Vol. 1, *The Hongkong Bank in Late Imperial China, 1864–1902: On an Even Keel*. New York: Cambridge University Press, 1987.

———. *The History of the Hongkong and Shanghai Banking Corporation*. Vol. 2, *The Hongkong Bank in the Period of Imperialism and War, 1895–1918: Wayfoong, the Focus of Wealth*. New York: Cambridge University Press, 1988.

———. *The History of the Hongkong and Shanghai Banking Corporation*. Vol. 3, *The Hongkong Bank Between the Wars and the Bank Interned, 1919–1945: Return from Grandeur*. New York: Cambridge University Press, 1988.

———. *The History of the Hongkong and Shanghai Banking Corporation*. Vol. 4, *The Hongkong Bank in the Period of Development and Nationalism, 1941–1984: From Regional Bank to Multinational Group*. New York: Cambridge University Press, 1991.

Kranzler, David. *Japanese, Nazis & Jews: The Jewish Refugee Community of Shanghai, 1938–1945*. New York: Yeshiva University Press, 1976.

Kumar, Dharma. *Cambridge Economic History of India*. Vol. 2, 1757–2003. Delhi: Orient Longman, 2005.

Kynaston, David. *The City of London*. Vol. 2, *Golden Years, 1890–1914*. London: Chatto & Windus, 1994.

Leese, Arnold. *Chinese Communism? Yes, but It Was Jewish When It Started*. Surrey: Arnold Leese, 1949.

LeFevour, Edward. *Western Enterprise in Late Ch'ing China: A Selective Survey of Jardine Matheson and Company's Operations, 1842–1895*. Cambridge, MA: Harvard University Press, 1968.

Lethbridge, Roper. *India and the Imperial Preference*. London: Longmans, Green and Co., 1907.

Levinson, Harry. "Conflicts That Plague Family Businesses." *Harvard Business Review* 49, no. 2 (1971): 90–98.

Lin, Man-Houng. "China's 'Dual-Economy' in International Trade Relations, 1842–1949." In *Japan, China, and the Growth of the Asian International Economy, 1850–1949*, vol. 1, edited by Kaoru Sugihara, 183–85. Oxford: Oxford University Press, 2005.

Longrigg, Stephen Hemsley. *Four Centuries of Modern Iraq*. Oxford: Clarendon Press, 1925.

Lovell, Julia. *The Opium War: Drugs, Dreams and the Making of China*. London: Picador, 2011.

Lucas, S. E., ed. *The Catalogue of Sassoon Chinese Ivories*. London: Country Life, 1950.

Macfarlane, Alan, and Iris Macfarlane. *The Empire of Tea: The Remarkable History of the Plant That Took Over the World*. New York: The Overlook Press, 2004.

Maclean, James Mackenzie. *Maclean's Guide to Bombay*. Bombay: The Bombay Gazette Stream Press, 1875.

MacMillan, Margaret. *Women of the Raj*. New York: Thames and Hudson, 1988.

Mann, Thomas. *Buddenbrooks: The Decline of a Family*. Translated by John E. Woods. New York: Vintage, 1994.

Marks, Steven G. *The Information Nexus: Global Capitalism from the Renaissance to the Present*. Cambridge: Cambridge University Press, 2016.

Marozzi, Justin. *Baghdad: City of Peace, City of Blood—A History in Thirteen Centuries*. London: Da Capo Press, 2014.

Marriott, W. F. "Indian Political Economy and Finance." *Journal of the East Indian Association* (London) 8 (1874): 188–207.

Masters, Bruce. *The Arabs of the Ottoman Empire, 1516–1918: A Social and Cultural History*. New York: Cambridge University Press, 2013.

———. *Christians and Jews in the Ottoman Arab World: The Roots of Sectarianism*. Cambridge: Cambridge University Press, 2001.

Meaux, Lorraine de. *Une grande famille russe: Les Gunzburg*. Paris: Perrin, 2018.

Metcalf, Barbara D., and Thomas R. Metcalf. *A Concise History of Modern India*. 3rd ed. New York: Cambridge University Press, 2013.

Meyer, Maisie. "Baghdadi Jewish Merchants in Shanghai and the Opium Trade." *Jewish Culture and History* 2, no. 1 (1999): 58–71.

———. *Shanghai's Baghdadi Jews: A Collection of Biographical Reflections*. Hong Kong: Blacksmith Books, 2015.

———. "Three Prominent Sephardi Jews." *Sino-Judaica: Occasional Papers of the Sino-Judaic Institute* 2 (1995): 85–110.

Moreh, Shmuel, ed. *Mihkarim be-Toldot Yehudei Iraq ve-Beterbutam* [Studies in the History of Iraqi Jews and Their Culture]. Or Yehuda: Center for the Heritage of Babylonian Jews, 1981.

Morris, Morris D. "The Growth of Large-Scale Industry to 1947." In *The Cambridge Economic History of India*, vol. 2, *1757–2003*, edited by Dharma Kumar, 553–676. Delhi: Orient Longman, 2005.

Motono, Eiichi. "A Study of the Legal Status of the Compradors During the 1880s with Special Reference to the Three Civil Cases Between David Sassoon Sons & Co and Their Compradors, 1884–1887." *Acta Asiatica* 62 (1992): 44–70.

Muirhead, Stuart. *Crisis Banking in the East: The History of Chartered Mercantile Bank of India, London, and China, 1853–93*. Aldershot: Scolar Press, 1996.

Musson, A. E. "The Great Depression in Britain, 1873–1896." *Journal of Economic History* 19, no. 2 (1959): 199–228.

Narayan, Govind. *Mumbai: An Urban Biography from 1863*. Translated by Murali Ranganathan. London: Anthem Press, 2009.

Nawwar, Abdul Aziz. *Dawud Pasha: Wali Baghdad* [Dawud Pasha: Governor of Baghdad]. Cairo: Dar al-Katib, 1967.

Negev, Eilat, and Yehuda Koren. *The First Lady of Fleet Street: The Life of Rachel Beer*. New York: Bantam Books, 2011.

Newman, R. K. "India and the Anglo-Chinese Opium Agreements, 1907–1914." *Modern Asian Studies* 23, no. 3 (1989): 525–60.

Nieuwenhuis, Tom. *Politics and Society in Early Modern Iraq: Mamlūk Pashas, Tribal Shayks, and Local Rule Between 1802 and 1831*. The Hague: Martinus Nijhoff, 1981.

Nomura, Chikayoshi. "The Origin of the Controlling Power of Managing Agents over Modern Business Enterprise in Colonial India." *Indian Economic and Social History Review* 51, no. 1 (2014): 95–132.

Oonk, Gijsbert. "Motor or Millstone? The Managing Agency System in Bombay and Ahmedabad, 1850–1930." *Indian Economic and Social History Review* 38, no. 4 (2001): 419–52.

Opium Trade, The, 1910–1941. Four volumes. London: Scholarly Resources, 1974.

Osterhammel, Jürgen. *The Transformation of the World: A Global History of the Nineteenth Century*. Princeton: Princeton University Press, 2014.

Owen, David E. *British Opium Policy in China and India*. New Haven: Yale University Press, 1934.

Palsetia, Jesse S. *Jamsetjee Jejeebhoy of Bombay: Partnership and Public Culture in Empire*. New Delhi: Oxford University Press, 2015.

Pearson, Michael. *The Indian Ocean*. London: Routledge, 2003.

Pepper, Terence. *High Society Photographs, 1897–1914*. London: National Portrait Gallery, 1998.

Phillips-Evans, James. *The Longcrofts: 500 Years of a British Family*. London: CreateSpace Independent Publishing, 2012.

Plüss, Caroline. "Assimilation Versus Idiosyncrasy: Strategic Constructions of Sephardic Identities in Hong Kong." *Jewish Culture and History* 5, no. 2 (2002): 48–69.

Pomeranz, Kenneth, and Steven Topik. *The World That Trade Created: Society, Culture, and the World Economy, 1400 to the Present*. London: M. E. Sharpe, 2006.

Raianu, Mircea. *Tata: The Global Corporation That Built Indian Capitalism*. Cambridge, MA: Harvard University Press, 2021.

Ray, Rajat K. "Asian Capital in the Age of European Domination: The Rise of the Bazaar, 1800–1914." *Modern Asian Studies* 29, no. 3 (1995): 449–554.

———, ed. *Entrepreneurship and Industry in India, 1800–1947.* Delhi: Oxford University Press, 1994.

Richards, John F. "The Indian Empire and Peasant Production of Opium in the Nineteenth Century." *Modern Asian Studies* 15, no. 1 (1981): 59–82.

———. "Opium and the British Indian Empire: The Royal Commission of 1895." *Modern Asian Studies* 36, no. 2 (2002): 375–420.

———. "The Opium Industry in British India." *Indian Economic and Social History Review* 39, nos. 2 and 3 (2002): 149–80.

Ridley, Jane. *The Heir Apparent.* New York: Random House, 2013.

Roberts, John Stuart. *Siegfried Sassoon.* London: Metro Publishing, 1999.

Roland, Joan G. *Jews in British India: Identity in a Colonial Era.* Hanover: Published for Brandeis University Press by University Press of New England, 1989.

Roth, Cecil. "The Court Jews of Edwardian England." *Jewish Social Studies* 5, no. 4 (1943): 355–66.

———. *The Sassoon Dynasty.* Reprint of the 1941 edition. New York: Arno Press, 1977.

Rubai'i, Nabil al-. *Tarikh Yehud al-Iraq* [The history of Iraq's Jews]. Beirut: Al-Rafidain, 2017.

Rubinstein, W. D. *Men of Property: The Very Wealthy in Britain Since the Industrial Revolution.* New Brunswick, NJ: Rutgers University Press, 1981.

Rungta, Radhe Shyam. *The Rise of Business Corporations in India, 1851–1900.* London: Cambridge University Press, 1970.

Rutnagur, S. M., ed. *Bombay Industries: The Cotton Mills.* Bombay: Indian Textile Journal Ltd., 1927.

———. *Electricity in India: Being a History of the Tata Hydro-Electric Project.* Bombay: Proprietors Indian Textile Journal, 1912.

Sachs, Jeffrey. *The Ages of Globalization: Geography, Technology, and Institutions.* New York: Columbia University Press, 2020.

Sapir, Shaul. *Bombay: Exploring the Jewish Urban Heritage.* Mumbai: Bene Israel Heritage Museum and Genealogical Research Centre, 2013.

Sassoon, David Solomon. *A History of the Jews in Baghdad.* First ed. 1949. London: Simon Wallenberg Press, 2007.

———. *Masa' Babel* [Babylon Journey]: ed. with biography of the author, introduction and comments by Meir Benayahu. Jerusalem, 1955.

Sassoon, Philip. *The Third Route.* New York: Doubleday & Co., 1929.

Sassoon, Siegfried. *The Old Century and Seven More Years.* London: Faber & Faber, 1938.

———. *The Old Huntsman and Other Poems*. New York: E. P. Dutton, 1918.

Seal, Anil. *The Emergence of Indian Nationalism: Competition and Collaboration in the Later Nineteenth Century*. Cambridge: Cambridge University Press, 1971.

Sergeant, Harriet. *Shanghai*. London: Jonathan Cape, 1991.

Siddiqi, Asiya, ed. *Trade and Finance in Colonial India, 1750–1860*. Delhi: Oxford University Press, 1995.

Silliman, Jael. *Jewish Portraits, Indian Frames: Women's Narratives from a Diaspora of Hope*. Calcutta: Seagull Books, 2001.

Smith, George. *The Life of John Wilson: For Fifty Years Philanthropist and Scholar in the East*. London: John Murray, 1878.

Stansky, Peter. *Sassoon: The Worlds of Philip and Sybil*. New Haven: Yale University Press, 2003.

Stein, Sarah Abrevaya. "Protected Persons? The Baghdadi Jewish Diaspora, the British State, and the Persistence of Empire." *American Historical Review* 116, no. 1 (February 2011): 80–108.

Stephenson, MacDonald. *Railways in China*. London: J. E. Adlard, 1864.

Stourton, James. *Kenneth Clark: Life, Art and Civilisation*. New York: Alfred A. Knopf, 2016.

Temple, Richard. *Men and Events of My Time in India*. London: John Murray, 1882.

Trentmann, Frank. *Free Trade Nation*. New York: Oxford University Press, 2008.

Tripathi, Dwijendra. *The Oxford History of Indian Business*. New Delhi: Oxford University Press, 2004.

Trivellato, Francesca. *The Familiarity of Strangers: The Sephardic Diaspora, Livorno, and Cross-Cultural Trade in the Early Modern Period*. New Haven: Yale University Press, 2012.

Trocki, Carl A. *Opium, Empire and the Global Political Economy: A Study of the Asian Opium Trade, 1750–1950*. New York: Routledge, 1999.

Vaidyanathan, A. "The Indian Economy Since Independence (1947–1970)." In *The Cambridge Economic History of India*, vol. 2, *1757–2003*, edited by Dharma Kumar, 947–94. Delhi: Orient Longman.

Vicziany, Marika. "Bombay Merchants and Structural Changes in the Export Community, 1850–1880." In *Trade and Finance in Colonial India, 1750–1860*, edited by Asiya Siddiqi, 345–82. Delhi: Oxford University Press, 1995.

Wang, Jian. *Shanghai Jewish Cultural Map*. Translated by Fang Shengquan. Shanghai: Brilliant Publishing House, 2013.

Wang, Xuyuan. *Shanghai China: The Bund and Architecture of One Century.* Shanghai: China Architecture & Building Press, 2008.

Webster, Anthony. "The Political Economy of Trade Liberalization: The East India Company Charter of 1813." *Economic History Review* 43, no. 3 (1990): 404–19.

Weizmann, Chaim. *Trial and Error.* New York: Schocken, 1966.

Wellsted, J. R. *Travels to the City of the Caliphs Along the Shores of the Persian Gulf and the Mediterranean.* Philadelphia: Lea & Blanchard, 1841.

Wiener, Martin J. *English Culture and the Decline of the Industrial Spirit, 1850–1980.* 2nd ed. Cambridge: Cambridge University Press, 2004.

Wilson, Jean Moorcroft. *Siegfried Sassoon: The Journey from the Trenches: A Biography (1918–1967).* London: Duckworth, 2003.

———. *Siegfried Sassoon: The Making of a War Poet: A Biography (1886–1918).* London: Duckworth, 1998.

Woolfson, Marion. *Prophets in Babylon: Jews in the Arab World.* London: Faber & Faber, 1980.

Yehuda, Zvi. *The New Babylonian Diaspora: The Rise and Fall of the Jewish Community in Iraq, 16th–20th Centuries C.E.* Leiden: Brill, 2017.

Zelin, Madeleine. "Chinese Business Practice in the Late Imperial Period." *Enterprise and Society* 14, no. 4 (2013): 769–93.

Zhang, Zhongli, and Zengnian Chen. *Shaxun Jituan Zai Jiu Zhongguo* [The Sassoon group in old China]. Beijing: Chubanshe, 1985.

Zhong, Weimin. "The Roles of Tea and Opium in Early Economic Globalization: A Perspective on China's Crisis in the 19th Century." *Frontiers of History in China* 5, no. 1 (2010): 86–105.

ILLUSTRATION CREDITS

55 Record registering "nil" exports of opium, 1911. Photo: Collection of Kenneth and Joyce Robbins.

67 View of Pune from the Tower of the Ohel David Synagogue looking North-West. Photograph, c. 1870. Photo: Royal Collection Trust / © Her Majesty Queen Elizabeth II 2021.

68 The Sassoon Hospital at Pune. Engraving from *The Illustrated London News,* 1868. Photo: Courtesy of Edwina Sassoon.

76 Statue of David Sassoon, 1865, by Thomas Woolner, in the David Sassoon Library, Mumbai. Photo: Helen Jackson.

95 Shipping at Port Said on the Suez Canal. Photograph, late nineteenth century. Photo: Pump Park Vintage / Alamy.

97 Visit of the Viceroy of India to the Sassoon Dock at Bombay. Engraving from *The Illustrated London News,* 1875. Photo: Collection of Kenneth and Joyce Robbins.

98 Sassoon & Company house, Fuzhou, photograph, c. 1870s. Photo: Bath Royal Literary and Scientific Institute.

101 Garden Reach, Pune. Photograph, c. 1870. Photo: Courtesy of Edwina Sassoon.

102 Abdallah Sassoon's bungalow, Mahabaleshwar, Western Ghats. Photo: Agoda.com.

115 Presentation of the Freedom of the City to Albert Sassoon at the Guild-hall, London. Engraving from *The Graphic,* 1873. Photo: Shutterstock.

116 Gold casket presented to Sir Albert David Sassoon by the City of London. Engraving from *The Illustrated London News,* 1873. Photo: the author.

117 Albert Sassoon. Photograph, late nineteenth century. Reproduced with permission from the Sassoon Family Album, *Ashley Park.*

118 Unveiling of the statue of the Prince of Wales presented to the City of Bombay by Sir Albert Sassoon. Engraving from *The Graphic,* 1879. Photo: Artokoloro / Alamy.

119 Visit of the Prince of Wales to Sans Souci, Bombay. Engraving from *The Illustrated London News,* 1876. Photo: Dinodia / Alamy.

131 Communiqué from the Hong Kong branch of David Sassoon & Co., January 1874. Photo: Collection of Kenneth and Joyce Robbins.

133 Eugenie Louise Sassoon (née Perugia). Photograph by Cyril Flower, 1st Baron Battersea, 1890s. Photo: © National Portrait Gallery, London.

135 Reuben Sassoon's house, Brighton. Photograph, 1896. Photo: Royal Collection Trust / © Her Majesty Queen Elizabeth II 2021.

143 Joseph, S.D.'s son, at Ashley Park. Photograph, late nineteenth century. Reproduced with permission from the Sassoon Family Album, *Ashley Park.*

145 The Sassoon family coat of arms.

148 Arthur Sassoon (*left*) and Reuben Sassoon (*right*) in costume for a fancy-dress ball. Photographs by Lafayette, 1897. Photos: © National Portrait Gallery, London.

151 Group photograph of Edward and Aline Sassoon at their Scottish estate with members of the Marlborough Set. Photograph, c. 1895. Photo: Reproduced with the permission of The Trustees of The Rothschild Archive London.

152 Letter from the Duke of York to Reuben Sassoon, September 9, 1900. Photos: Courtesy of Joanna Sassoon.

155 The Shah and international royalty at the Empire Theatre, London, for Albert Sassoon's Ballet Entertainment. Engraving from *The Illustrated London News,* 1889. Photo: Look and Learn / Bridgeman Images.

178 Farha Sassoon and her daughter Rachel. Photograph by Major Stanley Smith, 1902. Photo: Archive of Mordecai Wolff Haffkine, The National Library of Israel, Jerusalem. Reproduced by permission.

195 The Sassoon Family Mausoleum, Brighton. Photograph, 1953. Photo: Shutterstock.

206 *A National Anti-Opium Sunday: Some "Pros." and "Cons."* Pamphlet issued by the Anti-Opium Lobby, January 1908. Photo: Church of England Archives, Lambeth Palace Library.

208 Share certificate for one of E. D. Sassoon's mills in Bombay, issued 1921. Photo: Collection of Kenneth and Joyce Robbins.

211 Louise Sassoon's invitation to the funeral of Edward VII, May 1910. Photo: Reproduced with the permission of The Trustees of The Rothschild Archive.

229 Rachel Beer (née Sassoon). Photograph by H. Walter Barnett, 1900–1903. Photo: © National Portrait Gallery, London.

234 The Japanese Morning Room in Edward and Leontine Sassoon's house, 46 Grosvenor Place, London, 1896. Photo: The Bedford Lemere Collection / Historic England.

237 Philip Sassoon's house, 25 Park Lane, London, 1918. Photo: TopFoto.

238 Interior at 25 Park Lane, 1922. Photo: Mary Evans Picture Library.

240 *Sir Philip Sassoon in Strange Company.* Cartoon by Max Beerbohm from *A Survey,* pub. Heinemann, 1921. Photo: Collection of Kenneth and Joyce Robbins.

242 Philip Sassoon on tour as Under-Secretary of State for Air, 1928. Photo: Collection of Kenneth and Joyce Robbins.

252 Seating plan for a dinner pasted into Victor Sassoon's diary, September 13,

1927. Photo: Sassoon Papers and Photographs, DeGolyer Library, Southern Methodist University (SMU), Dallas, Texas.

258 Sassoon House under construction, Shanghai. Photograph, 1920s. Photo: British Steel Collection, #2328. Reproduced with the permission of Teesside Archives.

259 Business card for Victor Sassoon's nightclub, Ciro's, Shanghai, c. 1945. Photo: Private collection.

264 News clipping from *The Boston Globe* pasted into Victor Sassoon's diary, April 22, 1942. Photo: Sassoon Papers and Photographs, DeGolyer Library, SMU.

266 Victor Sassoon with one of his horses at a race meeting, 1953. Photo: Sassoon Papers and Photographs, DeGolyer Library, SMU.

269 Chinese civilians with Japanese soldiers at checkpoint. Photograph by Victor Sassoon, 1937. Photo: Sassoon Papers and Photographs, DeGolyer Library, SMU.

First Color Plate

1 Reproduced with permission from the Sassoon Family Album, *Ashley Park*.

2 (*top left*) Reproduced with permission from the Sassoon Family Album, *Ashley Park;* (*top right*) Collection of Kenneth and Joyce Robbins; (*bottom*) Bonham's.

3 Collection of Kenneth and Joyce Robbins.

4 (*top*) Courtesy of Edwina Sassoon; (*bottom left*) Boaz Rottem / Alamy; (*bottom right*) Joseph Sassoon.

5 (*top left*) ephotocorp / Alamy; (*top right*) Dinodia / Alamy; (*bottom*) Boaz Rottem / Stockimo / Alamy.

6 (*top*) © Arun Bhargava / Dreamstime; (*bottom*) Collection of Kenneth and Joyce Robbins.

7 (*top left*) Bridgeman Images; (*top right*) Peter Jackson / Bridgeman Images; (*bottom*) Collection of Kenneth and Joyce Robbins.

8 Jeffrey Isaac Greenberg / Alamy.

Second Color Plate

1 Library of Congress.

2 (*top*) Chronicle / Alamy; (*bottom left*) Arnold Wright, *Twentieth-Century Impressions of Hong-Kong, Shanghai, and Other Treaty Ports of China*, pub. 1908; (*bottom right*) Artokoloro / Alamy.

3 (*top left*) © Tate, London; (*top right*) TopFoto. © Churchill Heritage Limited; (*bottom*) © National Portrait Gallery, London.

4 (*top left*) Courtesy of Sotheby's, Inc., © 2020; (*top right*) Stanley Jackson, *The Sassoons*, pub. Heinemann, 1968; (*bottom*) Courtesy of Sotheby's, Inc., © 2020.

Third Color Plate

1 (*top*) Reproduced with permission from the Sassoon Family Album, *Ashley Park;* (*bottom left*) Library of Congress; (*bottom right*) AF Fotografie / Alamy.

2 Sassoon Papers and Photographs, DeGolyer Library, Southern Methodist University (SMU), Dallas, Texas.

3 (*top*) Sassoon Papers and Photographs, DeGolyer Library, SMU; (*bottom*) Siwabud Veerapaisarn / Dreamstime.

4 (*top*) Helen Jackson; (*bottom left*) Author collection; (*bottom middle and right*) Courtesy of Joanna Sassoon.

INDEX

Page numbers in *italics* refer to illustrations.

DSC = David Sassoon & Company; ESC = E.D. Sassoon & Company

Oslo

St. Petersburg

Moscow

Liverpool
Manchester
London
Brighton
Paris
Seine

Trieste

Marseilles

Naples

Constantinople

Malta

Aleppo

Tigris

Mashh

Port Said
Beirut
Alexandria
Cairo
Shoubra
Suez

Euphrates

Baghdad

Isfahan

Basra
Bushir

Suez Canal

*Per.
Gu*

Bahrain

Nile

Red Sea

Oma

Aden

*ATLANTIC
OCEAN*

Zanzibar

0	1500 miles
0	2000 km